Kezia
Xmas 2018

One Maestro's Journey

Still Life Enterprises
One Maestro's Journey: A Celebrated Life of Music & Ingenuity
Heinrich Hammer (deceased)

All aspects of this book's development, interior/cover design & copyediting:
S.A. Jernigan, Renaissance Consultations, (www.MarketingAndPR.com); cover violin photo: Johanna Vogt

If you would like to do any of the above or purchase individual or bulk copies, please contact:

Still Life Enterprises
906 Washburn Drive
Leander, TX 78641
www.StillLifeEnterprises.com

Published by Still Life Enterprises in the United States, printed in the U.S.A.
ISBN 978-0-692-05150-4
First edition

The publisher believes, and we acknowledge others strongly disagree, that memoir allows the writer to work from memory instead of from a strict journalistic or historical standard. The firsthand recollections herein are being published in the fall of 2018 (2019 pub. date) and were authored by an individual who died in 1954.

All photos herein are in the public domain or the property of the publisher unless otherwise noted.

One Maestro's Journey

A Celebrated Life ^{of} Music & Ingenuity

[the late] Heinrich Hammer

1862 – 1954

Still Life Enterprises

Leander, Texas

Dedication

For my children and grandchildren, that they might know those who went before them.

His journey

Introduction

All my life I've heard stories about my grandfather, and I've always been proud of him. I was only about 18 months old when he died. I first read his autobiography in my late twenties or early thirties, and at that time I was more interested in his life here in America (e.g. my mom's history), so I skipped through his European years and didn't pay as much attention to that early period of his life. But when my own kids reached their teens, my mom gave me his typed manuscript (it was on that filmy onionskin paper and shoved into a three-ring binder) and asked me to re-type it and put it on disc so my kids and grandkids would have it when the original finally disintegrated.

As I carefully typed page after page, I really became aware—for the first time—of what an extraordinary life he made for himself. My grandfather was one of the lucky, lucky people who knew from an early age what they wanted to be and had a keen focus throughout his life; he also had the passion and the perseverance to spend his entire life in pursuit of his dream.

The thing that most impressed me though was Fahta's sense of joy and adventure. He loved nature (Mom said any view of hills, mountains, trees, flowers, whatever, would cause him to take a deep breath, throw out his arms, and exclaim, "Isn't it GLORIOUS?!"). He was also physically active until the very end of his life: walking, hunting, farming…and mentally active and productive as well. He seemed to me to have a boundless sense of appreciation, optimism, and not least of all, determination.

My grandmother, Munna (Fahta's second wife), would occasionally tell stories of his early life in Europe, the composers he knew, the many languages he spoke, as well as memories of the music he composed. She taught me to play piano, and since she lived closest to us out of her six sons and daughters, my brothers and I spent a lot of time with her as children growing up. I wish now I had paid more attention to her colorful stories of the Old Country.

My mother had stories of her own about growing up with him along with her five brothers and sisters. She lived with Munna and Fahta during the war when my dad was in the Navy and stationed abroad on a minesweeper. Fahta used to read to her in the evenings while she sewed; he loved Zane Grey westerns, and Mom said it was hard not to laugh as he tried to imitate the "cowboy" language with his oh-so-proper German accent ("You guys!" was one of her favorites of his). We tried to get her to write these recollections of hers down, my brother even got her a tape recorder one time, thinking that might be easier—but like most of us, she just never got around to it. And, sadly, she recently passed at 90 years of age, just a little younger than Fahta's 92-year lifespan.

I think Fahta lived in a golden age of music. As I read about his European years, I found myself actually yearning for what always seems to have been a slower, more graceful, and culture-rich age replete with Sunday symphonies in the parks and families gathering on the grass with their picnics to enjoy these outdoor concerts together.

I truly love music and, to me, there must be no greater thrill than being able to express your interior life through an instrument you love to play. I believe music is the voice of beauty, a human bridge across cultural divides. My Fahta could play every instrument in an orchestra. According to my grandmother, the only instrument he didn't really care for was the guitar.

I've always wished I could hear the music he wrote performed. You can tell so much about people by the kind of art, music, and literature they're drawn to, don't you think? My Uncle Randy told me one time he remembered Fahta sitting at the piano, his fingers dancing over the keys, with the most beautiful melodies just flowing out of his head. It almost seems like, for some people, that may be the first language they learn. *What a gift!*

I do feel a great loss in thinking all of his grandchildren and great-grandchildren may never be able to hear the music he composed throughout his life. In fact, it's long been a dream of mine to find some way to produce it.

While I don't want to give away the end of his story, it's been the impetus for me in wanting to share his rich and varied journey beyond just our family—especially in hopes his personal memoir would be entertaining but also hopefully inspire us to see that we all have a dream for our lives, and a life lived in pursuit of your dream *is* a worthwhile life, no matter what. I believe that will be a fitting legacy indeed for him to have left behind…

P.S. The chapter headings were created by yours truly.

Melinda Monaghan

Acknowledgements

First of all, to the grandfather I never knew, who led such an inspiring existence and lived to tell the tale; to his second wife—my grandmother—who brought him to life in the stories she told about him, and finally to my mother whose memories of him were filled with love and laughter. But most of all to S.A. "Sam" Jernigan, Renaissance Consultations, creative publishing consultant and marketer extraordinaire, whose vision for this book far exceeded my own and who was an absolute pleasure to work with. Cheers, Sam!

PART I

Chapter 1   Childhood

Dear reader, will it be possible to arouse and hold your interest, inviting you to follow me through a 90-year-long life—a life of heights and depths, full of dramatic episodes, joys and sorrows, contacts with peoples from many nations, incidents of unusual variety: catastrophes, shipwrecks, railroad accidents, being shot at, tragic family disasters and multiple extraordinary happenings? If so, let us start this narrative on October 27, 1862, the day I was born in Effurt, the 2000-year-old capital of Thuringia, the beautiful flower-city of the province of Saxony.

My father, a distant cousin of my mother and one of numerous members of the Hammer clan, was a captain of the artillery. He died two months before my birth, his death being the result of an unhappy jump by his horse, killing both horse and rider. This tragedy endangered both my young 19-year-old mother's and my own evolving life in her womb. By the time of my birth she was near insanity—she left her parents' home afterward, moved to Berlin and entered a sanatorium. I never saw her before my ninth year.

My grandparents took care of me until the awakening of my conscious life which started when I was about three years old. I remember clearly my grandmother's sweet face and erect figure, also when I fell down the stairs from the second story, breaking my nose but, thankfully, no bones. I must have been a wild youngster. I recall when I was found in the horses' stable, crawling cheerfully around, over, and under the horses, causing Granny great dismay.

In the spring of 1866, that abominable scourge, cholera, took a terrible toll on human lives. One of the victims was my beloved grandmother. Alas, I remember less the great grief occasioned by her death than the nice black velvet suit and black gloves I wore to her funeral, an event attended by my Uncle Ritter who arrived with his many shining, tinkling decorations covering his breast as he was a former regimental comrade of my dead father from the Austria-Prussian War.

After Grandma's death, Grandfather sold the house and moved nearer his place of occupational activity, the great national arms factory, where he worked as an inspector. Grandfather's family consisted of three sons and three daughters. All but the two youngest had left home before the death of Grandma. The youngest daughter, then about 17, kept house. The youngest son, 16, was still at high school, a wild and true oppositionist.

I was then a freelancer and did as I liked, until one day another little boy, about a year older than me, took up a big stone and said, "Shall I throw it at your head?"

"Yes, I dare you to."

He did, and I fled, bleeding and shrieking, across the street to our house. My young aunt—Marie was her name—nearly fainted, but was game enough to bandage my head and make me comfortable. The mark the stone made is still adorning my forehead to this day.

From then on, however, my freelancing was at an end and I was, following Grandfather's command, put under strict orders. I had to learn to read and write, which later turned out not to be to my advantage, and discipline was now the rule, to my great dismay.

Soon, the task to continually watch over me seemed too strenuous for my young aunt and as Aunt Henrietta (the second oldest daughter of my grandfather) was married to Uncle Ritter and childless, both she and Uncle proposed to take me into their home to continue my education. I was then five years old and the most unfortunate years of my young life began there.

A quaint custom followed in Thuringia at that time which made the entrance into school life a real festival. Children were taken to school by their parents or guardians who brought, unknown to their new little students, a horn-of-plenty, approximately two feet long and filled with all kinds of goodies—little cookies, candies wrapped in silky paper, and a variety of delightful treats. Each horn, bearing the name of a pupil, was handed to the teacher who started the school year by distributing these precious gifts to the future scholars. I remember clearly the joy I felt at this exciting spectacle. We, the heroes of this wonderful day, heartily exchanged gifts and entered with unanimous gaiety our careers as soon-to-be-educated citizens.

However, the following day brought with it an unexpected occurrence.

First real school day! Teacher at the blackboard writes the very familiar [to me] letter "A." I holler, "Oh! That is 'A'!" All faces turned toward me following my outburst. Teacher, ignoring my interruption, says, "Class, repeat: This is the letter A." The lesson continued until letter "D," including three interruptions on my part, followed by a sharp reprimand from the teacher. Thus ended my first school session.

After such a beginning my interest in school life faded. Why should I listen to a teacher repeating information I already knew? I recovered my long-lost liberty by not going to school and instead "ditched" my school material: a slate, pencils, and a book. I enjoyed resuming my freelance life again, roaming, roaming, roaming. Consequences? What does a five year old care for such? The few days of my Odyssey found an abrupt end by the appearance of the Schuldiener (a uniformed truant officer) at my home, inquiring after my absence. Result: a thorough whacking and a daily escort to school. Shortly afterward though, we moved to another part of the city and in consequence I entered another school which I liked much better and thus made satisfactory progress.

My Aunt and Uncle were high-strung people and ill-matched—she, exceedingly quarrelsome; he, a soldier through and through, with both good and bad attributes, a strict disciplinarian. I remember vividly when walking with him once, we met a soldier who did not render Uncle the salute due him. Uncle called him back, slapped his face hard and roared at him, "This will serve you better than the brig! I am sure you will never forget in the future to render honor to whom honor is due."

Uncle liked his beer and Schnapps. Often when he would come home in a good mood Aunt would demonstrate her bad temper and a long drawn-out quarrel would start. Reproaches flew back and forth and I, the poor witness of these atrocious scenes, would take flight. One of these occasions remains indelible in my memory. Repeated clashes between two strong characters are bound to lead to an unavoidable climax in time. This climax duly played out one bright spring afternoon in my presence.

Uncle came home in high spirits. My aunt received him with a scathing dressing down. Invectives flew hither and thither, voices rising to screaming proportions. An insulting accusation thrown in a high-pitched voice at Uncle Ritter infuriated him to such a degree that he lost mastery over his actions. He drew his sword and, grabbing Aunt roughly, threw her to the floor, uttering in a wild outburst, "I'll kill you!" Aunt shrieked, "Kill me, kill me, why don't you?" He lifted his sword, ready to strike. My desperate scream broke his stance. His sword clattered to the floor and I, utterly frightened, fled to a safe hiding place. All these scenes made a deep impression upon my young mind.

In contrast to these outbursts, Uncle always spoke to people about the love he felt for me. However, Aunt never expressed a sentiment akin to this. I had an abiding respect for Uncle but none at all for her, only constant fear for her tattle-telling to him about unimportant details of my daily life. Aunt was a decidedly scolding type; Uncle, a commander and outspoken disciplinarian—so he would listen to her complaints about me and then decide upon the proper punishment. My daily time schedule had to be strictly adhered to. For example, five minutes' play lasted five minutes, not seven minutes. Upon coming home and hearing of a time infraction (always gleefully reported by Aunt), Uncle would take up a hazel switch, which he would harvest during one of our excursions to the shooting range where hazel bushes grew profusely. My punishment was always cruelly the same. He took my head between his knees, closed my mouth with his big hand to stifle my howling and applied the switch to my behind. To sit down after this round treatment was more painful than the switching itself.

There was never the slightest tendency on the part of my guardians to satisfy my intellectual curiosity. Never any help with my schoolwork, which by now aroused my liveliest interest, as it was the only activity in which I could freely indulge. From my seventh year onward I was, and still am today, an ardent pupil.

In 1870, the Franco-Prussian War began. My uncle's regiment was one of the first to leave for the front. The atrocious scenes between Uncle and Aunt now belonged happily to the past. But my hours at home with Aunt certainly were no improvement upon my formerly dreary years. The slightest infringements of the iron rules laid down for me were followed by corporal punishment she administered in his absence. There simply was no love between Aunt and her unfortunate sister's child. She seemed to feel an active resentment and hostility toward me, and this sentiment was reciprocated. As a result, I became stubbornly resistant. Subsequently, more severe punishments were meted out to me, including being forced to perform the most menial tasks.

This period of my early youth reached its breaking point one day when I was sent to take a message to a lady who was an acquaintance of my Aunt. Unbeknownst to me, this kind lady had a son my own age who was also a pupil in the school I attended. She showed great interest in my schoolwork and asked me to stay awhile. She served her son and me a cup of chocolate each and some delicious cookies. I forgot time and Aunt, enjoying my stay in the friendly lady's home.

But, oh, what a welcome awaited me upon returning home! Aunt was sweeping when I came in. Broom in hand, she worked herself into a frenzy concerning my delayed return. This caustic disapproval aroused my childish anger as I felt deeply that this time I had not trespassed and I answered, defending my guiltlessness. She screamed, "You dare to contradict me?" and, in her overpowering anger, she turned the broom upside down and with a resounding whack, broke its handle upon my shoulder. I fled out of the house and made the firm resolution never to return there again.

The trying times I lived through under Aunt Henrietta's regime were instrumental in planting the idea of running away in me, one I thought about frequently. Now, this latest severe punishment had broken the donkey's back and I felt the time had come to execute my long-cherished plan. My childish mind thought it a small matter to walk to Magdeburg—which was hundreds of miles away—and find my Uncle Karl, grandfather's oldest son, who occupied the position of Weinkellermeister of the Rathouse (City Hall), a world-famous institution, housing the finest wines available in a mile-long underground cellar. Through Uncle Karl, I surmised I could then find my mother, who was remarried to a friend of his, Gustaf Neuman, a successful businessman and owner of an apartment house in Friedrichstadt, a nearby suburb—in spite of the fact I'd forgotten the address.

I was clad in a new, fine, white summer suit, and roamed through town, carefully avoiding policemen, choosing nice, friendly-looking people to ask where the road to Magdeburg was. They looked at me incredulously and passed by without responding. Evening approached, and, with it, a terrible thunderstorm. Crackling lightning and rolling thunder frightened me. A gnawing hunger reminded me of a few pennies in my pocket and I entered a bakery where I bought some buns. I devoured them, walking in the streaming rain. Upon a side street stood an unoccupied tea-wagon. I crept into it and happily curled up under the covering, with "donner und blitzen" making a raucous din above me.

When I awoke, the thunderstorm was over and a new day's sunshine bathed the now-cleansed city in golden light. I hurriedly left my safe asylum and began my wandering anew. I was exceedingly hungry and spent my last pennies for bread. Lustily chewing my precious food, I walked and walked, scanning every street sign until I at last found one reading "Magdeburger Strasse." What great joy!

At this point I would like to devote a few lines to exploring the intuitional processes of an eight-year-old boy's mind. Sitting down and thinking about the unraveling of a complicated problem does not belong in the realm of a boy this age, even if he is the possessor of a high I.Q. If he's a high-spirited lad, he is apt to intuitively choose the right path, and that was true in my case. The moment I left my home it seems as if a spiritual awakening had taken hold of me. The sense of the long-wished-for and now actualized liberty being experienced dominated my entire being. Jubilantly, I walked intently toward my goal: Magdeburg and my mother. The thought of school did not disturb me as it was summer vacation time.

I knocked decisively at strange doors, asking for a "stulle" (sandwich). Kind ladies never disappointed me (and this is still true today). Following a cross-country road, still on the Magdeburger Strasse, I kept an eye out for haystacks as evening drew near and crept gratefully into one, enjoying a restful night's sleep. By and by, my nice white summer suit took on a grayish aspect. Sometimes, not finding a haystack, I would sneak into a barn and sleep almost as well. All the people I met were exceedingly hospitable. Hardly a day would pass without me receiving a nourishing, warm meal from yet another kind stranger.

One day, many miles away from my dreadful home, I arrived at a railroad station. There, I saw a train which appeared destined to follow the direction of the Magdeburger Strasse. All was quiet and deserted. I sneaked into a third-class car and crept under one of the benches. Soon passengers began to arrive and several men entered my compartment. When the train had covered some distance, one of the men discovered my presence. I crawled out from my hiding place and was quizzed extensively, but thankfully in a non-hostile manner. The answers I gave, I am sorry to say, were far from straight, but in my plight I was so terribly afraid of being sent back to Aunt Henrietta that I invented more or less credible answers, apparently to the satisfaction of my inquisitors. They even collected some money for me.

Presently, the conductor came into the compartment. Although he was in a friendly mood, I nevertheless had to leave the train at the next station. Today, thinking about all these events, I am astonished that none of the individuals I accosted for help even made a report to authorities about a young boy who seemed to be a lost sheep, for grandfather told me after my return that there were numerous newspaper articles concerning my disappearance. It was even surmised the young boy had perished in the big thunderstorm which occurred on the day of his flight. Be that as it may, the boy in question, after departing his abruptly-ended train ride, was now endowed with the means of buying food and simply continued to follow his strong intuition—still marching courageously in the direction of Magdeburg.

Two full days of joyful progression passed. Both nights I slept peacefully in handily situated haystacks. The third day, after sunup, I reached the suburbs of a large city, the first I had seen since leaving Erfurt. As my monetary sustenance was exhausted and my poor stomach empty, I had to choose a house where I could ask for something to eat. This task was lightened when I saw a neatly dressed housewife with a little boy about my own age on the front steps of an inviting-looking residence. I stoutly asked if she would be so kind as to give me a piece of bread. She arose and entered the house with her boy, asking me to follow her inside. Gratefully, I complied and entered a friendly, well-furnished living room where she made me sit down with her son, leaving the two of us to attend to my request. When she came back with a tray on which was heaped a wonderful pyramid of delectable things, she said, "this is our second breakfast and I invite you to keep us company." I stood up, bowed deeply, and thanked her for her kindness. After such a friendly invitation, the cravings of my empty stomach and the sight of the tempting food, consisting of some appetizing sandwiches, an assortment of small cakes, plums, peaches, and glasses of milk, made me nearly forget my pleasant company as I selfishly dove into the culinary riches set before me.

My joy, however, was not of long duration, for the lady quickly began to question me. I reluctantly gave her my name, but when she extended her probing, being strenuously preoccupied by first things first—namely filling my stomach—I short-shrifted my fantasy answers used in my former interviews. Soon she looked doubtful about my story and her manner toward me became more restrained. I felt a little uneasy about this development, but still the duty towards my stomach took the upper hand and I continued to plow through everything edible that had been placed in front of me.

So it was I was just emptying my second glass of milk when a policeman entered the room.

I got frightfully scared and sat there, purple from ear to ear. The officer was the husband of the good lady. He greeted me in a friendly way and then looked inquiringly at his wife who related my story to him. When she mentioned my name, he looked sharply at me. "I know you, Heinrich Hammer," he said. "Now, don't you tell me fibs like you told my wife. You ran away from your Uncle Ritter in Erfurt. The newspapers have told all about your disappearance. We have to tell your uncle that we have found you and need to send you back to him."

I started crying, pleading with him not to send me back to Uncle, but instead to my grandfather. He did not actually respond to my plea, but asked grandfather's address, which I gladly gave him. He told me I had to stay at his home until things were straightened out.

The few days of my stay in this friendly, happy home where I was given the same treatment as the son of the house were the happiest episode of my odyssey. The city where I was so hospitably received was Halle, the birthplace of the great Handel, composer of The Messiah. I later learned that upon arriving there, I had covered more than half the distance to Magdeburg (nearly 70 miles)!

The policeman soon informed me of the arrival of a letter from grandfather and subsequently the official order for my departure back to Erfurt. The next morning he took me, accompanied by his son, my newly-won friend, to the railroad station, bought a ticket for my return to Erfurt, guided me to a compartment, and gave me a big bag of food and some money. Here, I bade a tearful farewell to them and, as the whistle blew, they departed—leaving me alone, and overwhelmed by grief. These few golden days during which I had lived amidst this benevolent, happy family brought home to me the difference between their life and mine at my uncle's home. It strengthened the longing I felt for my own home with my own mother. Erfurt-bound, these thoughts consumed my young mind.

When I arrived at my destination, Grandpa was there to greet me. Scrutinizing his face, I wondered…what will it be—punishment or gladness at my return? But he was very calm in his demeanor. When we entered his home, now empty, as Aunt Marie and Uncle Robert had left, we were met by his old housekeeper who had prepared a fine meal for the now-recovered escapee. Happy to again be with Grandfather, I needed no urging to make me sit down and, with a sound appetite, devour everything set before me. Upon Grandfather's request, I freely told of my adventures and the pleasant days I had spent in the home of the Halle family, asking Grandfather to write them a letter to thank them for the royal treatment they had provided me. After the meal, I followed him to the parlor where he asked me to sit down while he, pacing back and forth, told me that I could not stay with him as there would be no one to take care of me. He said, "I want you to live with your Aunt Henrietta whom I have admonished to treat you better."

"No-o, Grandfather!" I cried out, "if you send me there, I'll run away again."

"Wait, son, don't interrupt me. I have written a letter to your mother and asked her to take you into her new home. There is a boy, two years younger than you, the son of her new husband, who will be a playmate for you. It will be a fine home. You will only have to stay at your uncle's house a little while."

This distasteful thought of resuming life with Aunt again did not find my easy agreement; but as the time could not be of long duration, I reluctantly consented.

After a day's stay with Grandfather, I was given a new outfit of clothing and he took me back to the old dreaded place. My aunt, utterly destitute of the mental qualities and serene position of an effective housefrau and mother to a lonely child, received me with a make-believe friendly attitude—one which naturally aroused my suspicion. She had sown the wind and was now reaping the whirlwind. I scorned versus liked her. She invited Grandfather and me to a second breakfast—a meal eaten about 10 a.m. by every German family—which, as a hearty eater, assuaged my recalcitrant spirit somewhat…momentarily at least. Grandpa told her of his decision to send me to my mother and reminded her not to repeat her harsh treatment of me again.

"The sooner he leaves for good, the better," she muttered.

Grandfather left and right after his departure, Aunt, put me straight to work.

The Franco-Prussian War ended in May 1871, and a letter from Uncle Ritter arrived shortly thereafter informing Aunt of his early return. This occurred about a week after my re-entrance into my old, now more-detested-than-ever home. As the glorious army returning to Erfurt was of considerable number, the decision was made by the General's staff not to discharge it there, but some distance from the city, at a suburban station. Aunt and I went there and were fortunate to find Uncle quickly. He, hearty and hale, bubbling with lively spirit, was happy to be home again. All in all, it was a joyful reunion. The arrival of his army corps impressed me greatly, and these hundreds of thousands of people loaded with flowers and presents were a gay attestation to their joy in welcoming their conquering heroes home again. This jubilant mood also prevailed under our roof … for the day.

Early the next morning, Uncle had to report to duty again and we did not see him until the following day—when the misery I'd fled began again. Aunt unfolded her old habits when she told Uncle of my flight and its accompanying circumstances, Grandfather's visit, and so forth. I saw Uncle's countenance morph into his familiar thunderstorm which typically preceded a downpour of chastisement. I sneaked out and ran, frightened, straight to Grandfather's home. I burst out crying, "I want to go to my mother!" He calmed me and said, "You stay here with me until your mother's letter comes." Filled with gratitude and relief, I embraced him and promised I would be a good boy.

This stay at Grandfather's, enjoying unbounded liberty, was also of very limited duration. Grandfather received Mother's response to his letter very soon. She informed him of the train schedules and asked him to write her about the day and hour of my arrival there. The joyous expectancy of finally seeing my own mother face to face overwhelmed me to such a degree that no other thoughts were powerful enough to displace this longing. I plagued Grandfather with my unceasing question, "When do we go to the railroad station?" This grand event was to take place two days later. That morning, Grandfather found me awake early.

"Today you will see your mother!" he said, beaming. I jumped out of my bed and hugged him. Half-crying, I then dressed and was ready for breakfast in no time and finished it in a hurry while Grandfather made preparations for our departure. When we arrived, Grandpa gave me a train schedule, equipped me with the necessary supplies of food for the long journey, and admonished me to "Be a good boy." We walked side by side to the waiting train where we bade an emotional farewell to one another. Shortly afterward, the train started chugging me toward my new home.

Chapter 2   My Mother's Home

That evening, approaching Magdeburg, a beautiful sunset glowed with splendid purple hues which seemed to me a good omen. As the train entered the station, my mother looked for the boy with a red bandana around his neck—the way which had been designated by my grandfather for her to recognize her own young son, Heinrich, and she easily found me amongst the multitude of passengers. Weeping, she held me in her embrace…and I suddenly felt a new sense of absolute security. I clutched her hand violently and could not take my eyes off this beautiful lady—my mother! She had brought me some sweets too. Then, with animated conversation, we strode together to the station's exit where we found our waiting wagon.

North of Magdeburg, the river Elbe divides into three branches. The navigable part of the Elbe is called the Stromelbe and extends from Hamburg to the boundary of Czechoslovakia. It flows so swiftly past Magdeburg that only chain steamships can navigate it—a process which entails running along a grounded, hundreds-of-miles-long chain. The bow of the ship lifts out of the water, the chain is then run the length of the boat, and subsequently dropped back into the river again. A truly ingenious invention and the only means of going upstream on this particularly turbulent waterway.

The middle branch of the Elbe is only about three miles long, commencing at the east end of Magdeburg, and running westward to form a kind of lagoon. It is called the Zoll Elbe (toll Elbe) as all the ships have to pass Customs inspection there.

The third branch of the river is called the Alte Elbe (old Elbe), the original single riverbed. Between the Zoll Elbe and the Alte Elbe is situated the small suburb of Magdeburg called Werder. On the west side of the Alte Elbe lies the suburb, Friedrichstadt, a little town founded by Frederic the Great in 1621. This was my mother's home. After crossing three beautiful bridges and passing the famous prison which housed military and political culprits, we arrived at last. The wagon halted in front of a fine, white, three-story brick apartment house located near the church and marketplace.

The exuberance which had possessed me up to this point ceased and an anxious feeling, accompanied by a quickening heartbeat, took its place. A red-haired boy approached the wagon. Mother said, "This is your brother,

Gustaf." We shook hands and looked each other over suspiciously, awkwardly exchanging a few words.

As we entered the living room of the house, my new father, rising from an easy chair, kissed my mother, then took both my hands and welcomed me to my new home. This heavy-set, serious, like-his-son red-haired man made a rather favorable first impression upon me. However his dialect was strange to me, as I was from the sing-song country of Thuringia while he was from the northern part of the province of Saxony—the industrial capital, with its soberly-inclined citizens.

The exhaustion of our conversation was the signal to move into the dining room where a bedecked table awaited us, inviting us to share a substantial meal to which we did full justice.

The discussion took a livelier course and, by and by, my serenity returned. What a difference between the treatment meted out in Aunt Henrietta's home versus here at my mother's! Although it seemed to me my mother was more attentive to Gustaf's needs than to mine. However, the happy milieu in which I was now to dwell left no room for petty jealousy.

The next day, Gustaf and I went outside where he showed me the outbuildings and his animal possessions. To me, the most precious of these was a friendly poodle who greeted me as if I were an old comrade; I promised him I would not disappoint him in showing me such favor. There were rabbits, guinea pigs, a goat buck, a little wagon, an old crow, two fine horses (the ones which had guided us so gently home from the station), and a great choice of playthings.

What a wonderful paradise I had entered!

Gustaf then took me on a guided tour of the street, the marketplace, and the small church. Friedrichstadt seemed to be a neatly tidy little town. I then asked to see the school. It was a few blocks from our house: a fine building with a high, fancy iron grill doorway and some large fruit trees in the front yard.

When we arrived home again after our refreshing walk, Gustaf showed me his school books and other miscellaneous items. He was only two years younger than me but was three grades below me in school. In talking about studies, I inferred he was not very clever and he complained about having to go to school. When I expressed my liking for it, he appeared to react with displeasure at my attitude.

After our conversation, we busied ourselves attending to the animal's needs. The poodle, Hector, gave me an occasional sniff, and by vividly wagging his stump-tail, showed his satisfaction with my presence. In reliving my past five years in retrospection, it was hard for me to look at present happenings as actual realities. This was the fulfillment of my dreams: my mother and a home. At long last.

I was busy with Hector and the animals from morning to night. Father Newman told us boys to look upon the whole animal complex as now belonging to both of us.

It was on a Wednesday afternoon when a new experience was crowded into my already overloaded schedule (Wednesday and Saturday afternoons were the free half-days of the school week in Germany). After dinner, which was always served precisely at 12:30 p.m., a cabinetmaker came to give us boys lessons in carpentry in a room atop the horse stable where there was a long working table and all the tools a carpenter needs. Gustaf was already an advanced pupil in this work for which he showed much interest. I was the awkward beginner, but an ardent zealot. In the progressive weekly stages of my learning, I earned the praise of our teacher. (You will see how this acquired experience was taken advantage of in later years.)

After a few weeks of these lessons, I tried my skill by building a pigeon loft in a corner under the roof of our workshop, with Gustaf's help. Our father approved of our work and added two pairs of pouting-pigeons to our existing menagerie. The successive weeks saw the number of pigeons grow to nearly a hundred pairs. The daily flights of this mass of birds was a joy to behold. Our possession of such a flock engendered the growth of another enterprise: Gustaf and I began the sale and exchange of our newly-obtained riches and, through this process, received a nice amount of pocket money for ourselves.

These hectic days left no time for calm reflections. Summer vacation was over. The day for my registration for school arrived and, a few days later, I had to pass my entrance test. I was examined by the rector of the school, a fine, tall, friendly gentleman, who decided to place me in a class which was a grade higher than the one I had left in Erfurt. School hours were from 8:00 a.m. to noon and from 2:00 p.m. to 4:00 p.m. As a newcomer, I naturally had to suffer the hazing period; but as I was a well-developed, strong youth, I could withstand a good fight. However, I had to endure additional torment, consisting of annoying remarks concerning my Thuringian dialect. Children quickly adjust themselves though, so I soon learned to express myself in the idiom of my co-scholars. From this time onward, I diligently attended to my school duties and was rewarded by good treatment from all of my teachers.

The instructor of music was my favorite one. I had a good soprano voice and an accurate ear, both of which earned Mr. Steindorf's satisfaction with my vocal presentations.

My home life, as it unfolded, was not as I hoped it would be. But even if I was not entirely happy—the reason for this will follow later—the difference between this life and my former existence was SO immense that I accepted my new situation gratefully and made the best of it.

It was at this point in time that becoming a musician became an unalterable necessity of mine. I remember that from my earliest consciousness, whenever I was asked what I wanted to be, 'a musician' was my answer. Now, in the midst of such an understanding music teacher, I was more determined than ever to choose that career. When I spoke to Mother about my desire to take music lessons she gave her consent, promising to speak to her husband about it. Meanwhile, I had acquired—through some pigeon exchange—a harmonica, the forerunner of the accordion. Every free minute I would try to play some familiar tunes on this primitive instrument, and, after a short while, I was able to handle it with some skill. One day, when I was joyfully trying out new stunts on my harmonica, Father Neuman entered the room, violently yanked the instrument from my grasp, broke it, and threw it in the fireplace, paying no attention to my weeping. Mother came in remonstrating. He said angrily, "I want no fiddler in my house!"

I was entering my eleventh year when I was appointed "Ordeniggsschuler" (orderly) of my classroom. As such, I had to take care of the library and a number of old cupboards which contained all kinds of articles of more or less ancient vintage—among them an old unstrung violin and a bow. My music teacher's violin always having been the object of my admiration, one day I compared his and the foundling violin and discovered to my great astonishment that both were alike. Inside the old violin cases I found some gut strings. I chose some which looked like the ones strung on my teacher's instrument. After carefully studying the system of stringing, I was successful in imitating—though with some difficulty—the same appearance. Aided by the inborn keenness of my ear, I succeeded in tuning my new friend as best I could after similarly studying the example of the other instrument. How happy I was to see my task completed! It was late by now and I had to hurry home, but I could not resist the temptation to reach for the bow, hold it as the teacher did, and draw it over the strings—which produced an ugly, scratchy tone. I quickly put everything away and hastened homeward, with great difficulty keeping my sweet secret to myself.

As soon as possible after school the next day, I rushed to my new treasure and tried to make some progress in creating a better tone. I tried to play a simple school song, but found to my great dismay that to play the violin was not as easy as I had imagined it would be. However, after some time, I was able to do it, although not exactly in an artistic fashion. My rather strenuous efforts combined with my eagerness to improve my playing induced me to make my mother a participant in my secret as I begged her to ask my stepfather to help me as I surely needed a teacher. However, her repeated efforts on my behalf resulted in the same strong opposition as before. Here I was with the great ambition to learn to play an instrument yet thwarted in my desire. Nevertheless, his decision, hurtful as it was, did not keep me from stubbornly continuing my abominable self-directed fiddling.

My stepfather and a friend of his had rented extensive hunting grounds which were situated several miles from our home. Located on this property was a lodge where they occasionally spent a few days together. I often heard their conversations about hunting and camping and took great interest in these discussions, begging them to take me along some time.

Often on Sunday mornings it had been the custom for my stepfather, Gustaf, and I to take long walks to the woods and outlying small hamlets. A cherished avocation of Father was woodland lore, and we boys were ardent listeners to his fascinating stories. These walks and talks awakened in me a strong love for the outdoor life which has stayed with me to this day. This enthusiasm found vigorous expression one Saturday afternoon when my stepfather made preparations for a hunting trip with his partner.

When they drove off, I followed their wagon as it wended its way through our small town. My stepfather made signs for me to turn back but I stubbornly pursued them, even when a faster tempo of the vehicle forced me to run to keep up. He angrily continued to wave me back, but his friend, laughing, seemed to ask him to relent and bring me along. The wagon stopped and I finally reached it, out of breath, and was reluctantly invited to climb in, accompanied by a few cordial words from his friend concerning my spunk and fine running.

Toward evening, we arrived at the rustic hunting lodge. The horses were led to the stable, rubbed down and fed, and the two gentlemen prepared a tasty supper which was greatly enjoyed by yours truly. After the meal, I was bedded on a comfortable cot where I fell asleep immediately.

Before the break of day, I awakened. A hearty breakfast was quickly dispatched and, at sunup, we stepped outside, entering the woods—and so commenced one of the most beautiful days of my life. From the woods, we crossed large fields where we saw a rabbit rise here and there, only to make off in lightning-like haste upon spotting us. Very soon thereafter a covey of quail arose in the morning sky. Each gentleman had shot a doublet (two quail) and put them in his rucksack, when nearby, a rabbit jumped up, ending its sprint when downed by my stepfather. We continued our hunting for several hours, gathering enough game for the necessary meals.

After our dinner, both men took a nap and I occupied myself with the horses outside and explored the surroundings. The afternoon was occupied with target practice, and my father's friend taught me the proper handling of a gun. What a holiday for me! Some neighbor-friends came for a little hunting with us and we shot a few quail and rabbits with the help of two excellently trained Irish setters. Toward evening, we departed for the journey home, arriving back about midnight, happy but very tired. The next day, it took a great deal of effort for me to stay awake in school.

After this trip to the hunting grounds, my stepfather took me with him several times. He taught me how to shoot and I was, after some time, fortunate enough to bag a few rabbits and squirrels myself. On my twelfth birthday, Neuman gave me a fine 16-gauge double-barrel shotgun, a wonderful present I highly valued, although I would have liked a violin even better. He was always good to me; never made me conscious of the fact I was not his child. I even came to feel he loved me more than his own son, Gustaf.

As stated before, the latter did not like school. Even with the help of private teachers, it was uphill work for him to make his grades. We never entered into a close relationship as the difference in our backgrounds was too great: he having lived a sheltered existence while I had been tossed about like a small vessel adrift and battered upon a stormy sea.

Now, however, this little boat had reached a safe harbor, and the wings of my soul unfolded. Circumstances had changed sufficiently and my sense of security seemed firmly anchored.

School duties accomplished, I was free to spend the rest of my time leisurely. Not far from home was the "glacis," hundreds of acres of densely wooded territory. Here and there ditches lay amongst decaying walls, remnants of the old fortress of Magdeburg. This entire area became my beloved playground. Every free hour I would roam there, looking for bird's nests, a great number of them existing in this quasi-sanctuary. When I found a nest with eggs, I returned to it often, eagerly awaiting the emergence of the baby birds.

As soon as I saw the parents feed their little fledglings, I watched to learn what kind of nutriment they received. I would then do some searching, and if I could not find that type of food, I used crumbs of bread, worms, or flies which I always had on hand to fill the eager, wide-open beaks of the tiny winged creatures. When I started this practice, the parent birds, alarmed, would fly around me, screeching angrily. However, after a few visits, they became accustomed to my presence, and, sitting upon nearby branches, uttered their sweet-voiced contentment.

I never made any real friends at school. Nevertheless, I found myself the leader of a gang consisting, comically enough, of boys whom I had helped with their homework. When a small drum corps was established in our school, I was also selected by our music teacher to be its leader and I enjoyed this activity immensely. We used to parade through the town, arousing great glee among the citizens. However, this delightful new enterprise was interrupted shortly by an ugly accident.

One Sunday my mother told me we were to go on an excursion, a drive to a nearby village to visit some friends, the trip to take place in the afternoon. Gustaf and I asked permission to pass the morning at the "Anger," a very large field not far from our home, used by the soldiers for their exercises and war games. Some artificial sand-fortresses were built there, inside one of which we found two boys, one an acquaintance, a few years older than us, who were busily inspecting a small cannon-like plaything. Gustaf and I watched the manipulations of these two boys with great interest.

They placed the cannon on the ground. Gustaf and I stood close by as one of the boys lighted a match and put it to the powder hole. A tremendous explosion followed. I looked up, stunned, and couldn't see the cannon. It had vanished. "Where's the cannon?" I asked, and felt a peculiar rushing in my right leg. Still searching about for the cannon, I found myself standing in a pool of blood augmented by a stream flowing through my right trouser leg from a large hole in my calf.

"I am going to die! I am going to die!" I screamed. However, thankfully, I had enough sense to take my handkerchief (luckily, one of my stepfather's large ones), and wind it around my leg, yelling to Gustaf, "Get the wagon! Get the wagon!" Upon seeing the unexpected calamity, one of the boys ran away, but the remaining ones carried me upon their shoulders homeward. When we came to the outskirts of the city, Mother and Father met us in the wagon. Mother wept profusely but I tried to console her. At home, I was put to bed and the "feldscheer" (a former chief medical corpsman) was summoned. He bandaged my leg with pure arnica which hurt outrageously.

A few hours later our house doctor came. He was the chief surgeon of a Magdeburg regiment. He probed into the wound, looking for pieces of iron from the exploded pseudo-cannon. The so-called Listerine[1] bandage was used, a medicinal innovation at the time and

[1] English doctor **Joseph Lister** demonstrated in 1865 that use of carbolic acid on surgical dressings would significantly reduce rates of post-surgical infection. Lister's work in turn inspired American Joseph Lawrence to develop an alcohol-based formula for a surgical antiseptic which included eucalyptol, menthol, methyl salicylate, and thymol. (Its exact composition was a trade secret.) Joseph Lawrence named his antiseptic "Listerine" in honor of Joseph Lister. (Hicks, Jesse. "A Fresh Breath." Thanks to Chemistry. Chemical Heritage Foundation)

a very complicated, expensive process. It was changed every day for about three weeks and cost three marks per day. I was told to hold the sole of my right foot horizontally, but could not do it. The pain was too excruciating. This neglect on my part caused the shortening of my leg by an inch. My means of propulsion after the completed healing process was a cane. Fortunately, after six months, my limping ended and I had full use of my leg once more.

All these happenings occurred during summer vacation, and my confinement period enabled me to read and contemplate my aims in life. I still kept stubbornly to my decision to be a musician. How to attain this goal without help and in the face of resistance by my stepfather—who wanted me to study law, medicine, or be a businessman like him—was an ever-present problem in my mind. I had stopped my fiddling on the school violin as the quasi-progress I made in this endeavor did not satisfy me.

My stepfather, Neuman, was a man of peculiar habits: firm in his decisions but at times entirely losing control of his actions, a situation typically caused by over-indulging in spirits. Uncle Ritter's behavior traveled in another direction. Whereas Uncle Ritter was rarely the instigator of a quarrel, my stepfather always was.

One day, upon arriving home after a long absence, my mother served him a bowl of soup. He took a spoonful, apparently extremely hot, then seized the plate and smashed it violently on the floor, an action accompanied by ugly swear words and reproaches to my mother. Gustaf and I fearfully watched him. He then stormed out, slammed the door, and left—only to return the next day, behaving in a natural manner as if nothing had happened. After this outburst, several months of normal life followed until another of his violent displays erupted. Throughout all these changing-mood periods he never struck us boys. But I suffered in seeing my poor mother victimized by this tyrannical aspect of her husband's demeanor.

The climax of his viciousness came one night when we all were sound asleep. We were suddenly awakened by a big crash caused by a breaking window. My mother screamed as a large brick dropped perilously close to her head. Gustaf and I jumped out of bed and ran into her room. Through the broken windowpane my stepfather unfastened the catch and climbed in. My mother got up, exclaiming sharply, "Is this the way you want to kill me?" The realization of what he had done seemed to have a sobering influence upon him. "I forgot my key," he then uttered meekly. These continual scenes of upheaval in our home shattered my peace of mind and again awakened in me a spirit of revolt—and I concluded the only solution to this problem would be for me to run away once more.

I was now nearing my fourteenth year. The natural growth of my body and spiritual capacities had brought with it sounder judgment concerning my life at this point. Therefore, after yet another dreadful episode, one day

I told my stepfather, "Father, if these terrible fights do not end, I'll run away." He looked at me in great astonishment and said nothing.

Several months of peace ensued. My schoolwork, continual visits to my beloved birds, reading, and our Sunday tramps filled happy days, occasionally interrupted by a hunting trip.

One of our family trips to the country brought us to a little pond, with the poodle Hector in the rear of the wagon. It was completely overgrown with graceful water-lilies, a beautifully tranquil spot. Leaving the wagon, we took our picnic paraphernalia to the shore of the pond and spread a blanket on the grass where we lounged together, consuming sandwiches, potato salad, cookies, and fruit with relish.

After the meal, Hector came bounding toward us, bringing a long twig in his mouth to Father Neuman, who threw it in the pond for him to retrieve. Excitedly, he jumped into the water and swam toward the twig. In the center of the pond he got so entangled in the dense growth that it was impossible for him to move about. Anxiously we watched him struggle, encouraging him to come back. All his efforts to free himself were futile. After a short while, he was near complete exhaustion. Hector was the spoiled favorite of my stepfather who ran around the pond using endearing phrases to hearten the dog, but all in vain. As I looked at Neuman, I saw tears running down his cheeks. He frantically searched the area, found a long heavy plank, carried it to the water and shoved it toward Hector. With all his remaining strength, Hector succeeded finally in putting his front paws upon it and was pulled to the safety of the shore. The poor dog was completely spent, but our caresses soon revived him and restored his cheerful spirit.

A few days after this event, Father Neuman came home in his cantankerous drink-induced mood once again. He flung insulting words at Mother in the presence of Gustaf and me and brought a spirit of distress to the household

On the upper floor of our house lived a distant cousin of Stepfather's. His son, Herman, was of my same age and one of my gang. That night, I asked him if he would run away with me and was encouraged when he said he was very willing.

It was Saturday, a free afternoon, when we decided to leave. Each of us owned a few saved pennies. We left after the noon meal and started our trip in high spirits, pledging at the outset to each other never to return. After several miles of fast walking and having already passed two villages, we stopped at the outskirts of the last one to rest in an inviting little group of trees, emptying our knapsacks of the food we had gathered before our departure.

Herman did not seem to enjoy our adventure as much as I did. He started talking about his mother and home and wanted to turn back. I tried to persuade him, portraying for him the alluring features of a free roaming life, telling him of the experiences I had on my Erfurt to Halle adventure. His courage revived somewhat, he joined my side after the conclusion of our meal as we set back upon the road. The ensuing darkness found us very tired and happily in front of a nice, big barn. I inspected the place and discovered it was filled with straw and hay. We entered, completely worn out, and crawled into the sheltering straw pile, falling immediately asleep. With sunup we arose, found a pump, washed, and dispatched the rest of our food. Herman's spirit was at a low ebb though. He announced his unwillingness to proceed any further away from home. All my entreaties led to nothing. So he took his own course back. Convinced my repeated remonstrations against his intentions were without avail, I then began thinking about my mother's grief resulting from our departure and reluctantly followed him. Crestfallen and utterly exhausted, we arrived at Friedrichstadt by dusk. The reception we received upon returning home was not a joyful one. I was put to bed immediately with dire predictions by Mother concerning what would befall me tomorrow—judgment day loomed! In a great crescendo, my usually-docile mother worked herself into a frenzy of wrath, giving me such a whipping that my stepfather had to forcibly stop her. He told me of the anxiety they had endured in searching everywhere for us boys. This disclosure, which ended by administering a few telling whacks, pained me more than Mother's more vehement beating.

Shortly after this ill-conceived journey a new member joined our family. Mother gave birth to a healthy baby boy who was christened with Grandfather's name: Ernst. We two boys took very little notice of this disturbing new addition to our household. Father Neuman was elated at the introduction of another male into the family, another who would carry on his name. His demeanor became entirely different thereafter. He stopped indulging in strong drink. He was considerate to everyone and also more communicative to us boys. My mother dared to take advantage of his improved state of mind, asking him again to agree to my longed-for music lessons. He still declined to change his mind on this score though.

Chapter 3   Youthful Decisions

Another year went by, and it was now 1877. Nearing 15, my insatiable thirst for knowledge was nurtured by the study of foreign languages, mathematics, and other academic subjects in addition to my continuing orderly duties, gymnastics, leadership of the drum corps, carpentry lessons, plus the educational visits to my bird friends including caring for the pigeons and animals. As you might imagine, all these activities filled my days. As a result, little time was left for quiet musings concerning the lifework destiny had mapped out for me.

From my earliest youth I was a real Wasserratte (water rat) as Uncle Ritter had taught me to swim when I was five years old. All these years I lived with my mother, I was an ardent admirer of the Alte Elbe river, only ten minutes' walk from home, and a number of my school friends and I would take daily swims, enjoying all kinds of water sports during the summertime. Hector, a water rat like me, was my constant companion for these trips to the river. His performance of various droll tricks advanced him to the position of our crowd's mascot.

During a two-week furlough of his, a sailor friend of mine was an entertaining visitor at our frequent swims. Vivid accounts of his exciting life at the Naval Academy and his humorous quips found eager young listeners grouped around him while we lounged together in the sun upon the warm sand. The days following his departure, our continuous discussions about him kept the picture of the happy, life-savoring sailor vividly in my mind.

My father still absolutely refused to let me be a musician. What choice of vocation would find his consent? One day I asked him—hesitatingly—if he would agree to me becoming a sailor.

"Yes, why not?" he said. "Do you think you can pass the examination?"

"Yes, I think I can" was my reply.

My mother was not very enthusiastic about my intention.

When I entered high school, I chose the studies necessary for the entrance examination. Always having been an ardent pupil, it was not difficult for me to make progress in my scholastic endeavors. After six months of diligent preparation, I was ready.

I passed the examination successfully. For the physical tests though, I found I could not clearly read the lines pointed out by the doctor on the eye chart. There were 13 applicants. I waited until the last, having meanwhile learned the designated letters by heart—and using this ploy, I slipped through and just passed.

My confirmation was near when I received the summons to be at the Naval Academy for another physical examination. At the confirmation in church the following Sunday, every communicant had to answer questions posed by the pastor. Afterwards in his sermon he included some touching remarks concerning my leaving the community for a career at sea. Ours was a very small church and congregation where everyone knew everyone, and it was only fitting that he would do so.

I quit school and prepared for my departure for Kiel, home of the Academy. My family escorted me to the station where I met up with the other 12 aspirants. After a tearful farewell from our relatives, we were finally on our way.

Evening was near when we entered Kiel, and we followed a guide to the place of our destination. We had been shown to our rooms and were busy unpacking our paraphernalia when older cadets arrived and gave us a good taste of conventional hazing. These hazings, an ugly remnant from prehistoric times, were kept up incessantly.

The second day after we arrived, the physical examinations started. These were much more severe than those of the civilian doctors. I passed the body examination well, being a strong and healthy individual. At the eye test, I used the same tactics as before, succeeding for some time—until the doctor pointed to a line that I had not had a chance to memorize. I started guessing. The doctor uttered an astonished, "Uh-oh," guided me through some more strange territory, and relayed his judgment to an assistant, "Unfit for naval service." This sudden pronouncement terminated my hoped-for sailor's career. Crestfallen, I returned home. Father Neuman was disappointed, but Mother behaved with joyful relief at my homecoming.

A very disturbing period followed. I took a job in a prominent lawyer's office, but was disgusted and quit after just a little while. A businessman friend of my stepfather then offered me an apprenticeship in his office. After a few months with him I was so incensed by what was to me undesirable work that I said to my parents frankly, "I like music so much that I cannot concentrate on anything else. Please let me take a few lessons with Professor Pott, the famous violinist, and let him be the judge about my fitness for a career as a musician." After an earnest discussion between my parents, my stepfather finally acceded to my plea.

The next day, I went to the violin class at the Music Conservatory in Magdeburg where Professor Pott was an instructor. With my enthusiasm at its highest pitch, I entered with zest into my new studies. After two weeks of lessons daily, he informed my parents of my rapid progress, counseling them to let me continue my study with him. For a whole year thereafter I had the privilege of being his pupil. I also took lessons in organ, harmony, and composition. My teacher in these subjects was the famous organist at the cathedral of Magdeburg, August Gottfried Ritter[2]. After the year's work I played first violin in the Conservatory's orchestra.

Upon my leaving the Conservatory, my parents placed me in a music boarding school, a quite modern institution at that time. There, the pupils had to learn to take care of themselves by doing household chores, making their beds, sweeping the rooms, cultivating the garden, and so forth. Every morning, stripped to our waists, we washed under a pump in the yard. This was a joyful experience in summertime, but oh, in the winter! There was also no heat in our dormitories. Walking two stories downstairs, half-naked, through a long hall and out into the yard, traversing across four to six inches of snow in icy cold weather before sunup was quite a task. Reflecting back, I wonder that all of us did not get terrible colds…or worse.

Our meals were served by the youngest pupils of the institution in a large mess hall and under the surveillance of the middle-aged son of the school director. The food was never abundant. In fact, it was so scarce that every one of us had to rely upon weekly supplements of food from home arriving in parcels.

[2] **August Gottfried Ritter,** co-creator, together with **Felix Mendelssohn Bartholdy,** of the first example of Romantic Organ Sonata (the first one was composed in 1845); he moved in 1847 from being organist in Merseburg cathedral to become organist in Magdeburg cathedral. In his critical writings, Ritter condemned the Renaissance organ composers referred to as the "Colorists" for overindulging in ornamentation. (www.MusOpen.org)

In our younger group, one of the boys was the son of a farmer. His parents once sent him a whole side of bacon. It looked so beautiful, we all asked him if he would give us a little taste of it. The owner of this precious gift, known by all as a very stingy chap, angrily closed his trunk containing the bacon, screaming, "Nobody can have any!" So we worked out a plot aimed at appropriating this culinary treasure. Our plan succeeded. Every time he was occupied with his private lesson, under the leadership of the oldest amongst us, our "rotte cora" would equally divide pieces of the delicious meat for us hungry scoundrels. Furiously angry, the farmer's son would accuse every one of us as the culprits upon discovering the theft. He was, however, absolutely powerless to carry his complaint to the head of the school as it was strictly forbidden to receive food from home. To circumvent that rule, each week we would receive packages hidden in the laundry bag returning to us from home including the provision of butter and other useful edibles.

On my frequent visits home, I noticed a remarkable change in my stepfather's behavior. His ebullient, forceful spirit, often climaxing in an irresistible dominance, had apparently morphed into an I-don't-care, morose attitude. Questioning Mother about my observation, she explained that her husband's conduct was as much a riddle to her as it was to me. She told me that lately she had found a revolver in his pocket several times, removing it—only to always find it again in the same pocket. Before my next visit home, I received a letter from Mother. In it she wrote that my stepfather had ended his life at the grave of his first wife with a shot through his heart. This tragic end of Father Neuman left my mother with the care of three children upon her shoulders, luckily in favorable financial circumstances at least.

Another year elapsed and other happenings of great importance occurred. My mother, still young and accustomed to married life, soon wed a ship owner of about her own age. As I was attending boarding school, I had no occasion to become well-acquainted with him. That said, I simply did not like him, though my mother seemed very happy with my second stepfather whose name was Mr. Gabel. At this point, my visits home became much more infrequent.

My life at school was certainly not what it could have been. The strict discipline employed destroyed the already limited cooperative spirit necessary to creating a smooth working order, instead generating a general undercurrent of dissatisfaction among the students.

Only one thing made my school life at all bearable. I was studying violin with the vice-principal, the son of the director, a well-known violin virtuoso. My lessons with him were very fruitful, to such an extent in fact that he placed me next to him at our Symphony Orchestra concerts —in the Concertmaster's seat. He encouraged me to play several violin solos with him accompanying me, and when he established a string quartet for pupils, I played first violin. A love for ensemble chamber music was spawned in me which has remained throughout my life.

To diligent pupils in our institution was given the unique opportunity to acquaint themselves with the different orchestra instruments. I was especially interested in acquiring knowledge in this branch, given my desire to be a symphony orchestra conductor someday. In fact, this idea had grown to the proportion of being an obsession with me. I begged my teacher to make it possible for me to conduct an orchestra rehearsal sometime. When this favor was finally granted me, I enjoyed the experience so much that it utterly affirmed my decision to make this field of music my life's work.

The director of our school was an irascible gentleman and a bad conductor, although a shrewd businessman and strict to excess. His absolute lack of integrity made us despise him. I became increasingly displeased with conditions at school and finally decided to leave. Another boy from Magdeburg, a year my senior and one of the many other malcontents, proposed to go with me, returning home together to our parents. Our school was a large, well-enclosed building, which none could leave without permission. To exit, one had to pass through the main hall and entrance, on each side of which were the living quarters of the director and his family. This made the transportation of our trunks in that direction impossible. Therefore, we had to scale the high side-port gate. This was a very laborious task. I climbed over first. Then, being on opposites of the gateway, we hauled the trunks up and over by means of ropes we had discovered in the barn, and my friend climbed up afterward. All this occurred after midnight so that we disturbed no one. Our wagon arrived at our respective destinations in the early morning hours. My parents were anything but elated; however previous letters of mine had prepared them, more or less, regarding an eventual break of relations with the institution.

I stayed at home a week and addressed a letter to the principal of a competing music school located in the same town as the one I had left, soliciting for a position as teacher. Soon, I received notice that my proposition would be accepted with certain modifications. The next day, I departed to enter into my new station in life. I was then 17, an ambitious and somewhat conceited fellow, though eager to satisfy my new employer and proud to earn my first salary, however small.

My pride was quickly squelched.

After a few days' engagement as music teacher, a policeman arrived at the school, displaying a warrant for my arrest to the principal, signed by my former school's director! I had to go with the officer to City Hall where I was placed in a single cell. I asked him to send a telegram to my mother, notifying her of my incarceration and the reason for it. But a very peculiar bit of serendipity came to my aid. I had previously been acquainted with the policeman as he was a good trombone player who used to help out sometimes in our symphony orchestra. He sympathetically advised me, supplied me with good food, and expressed his regret concerning my awkward position. I passed an awful day followed by a sleepless night, raging, condemning this foul deed by my old, detested, and musically-incompetent principal.

Early the next morning, my mother arrived, asking for my release and stated her willingness to take me back to the boarding school. Very reluctantly I went with her. The principal seemed greatly surprised upon seeing us. In scathing terms, my mother reproached him for his cruel action. He used mollifying phrases in response, attempting to justify himself. He spoke of the preference which he alleged had always been accorded me, never surmising the possibility of my running away. My mother's manner grew more calm and I could see I was going to be made to stay there. After a warm farewell to me and a conventional one to the director, Mother left.

Immediately the principal advanced threateningly towards me.

"I'll make you pay for this! I'll beat you 'til the dogs lick your blood!" he screamed.

Violently, the door was thrown open. My mother, who had lingered in the hall, entered. She grabbed my hand, shouting at him angrily, "I would rather see my son apprenticing in a butcher shop than with you! Come, Heinrich!"

Dumbfounded, he watched our exit. We departed, unmolested, and another episode of my turbulent young life was closed.

Chapter 4   Military Music

At home, Mr. Gabel could not disguise his ill-feeling toward me; and I felt likewise, so I made up my mind not to stay at home any longer. I solicited for a position as violin teacher in the province of Pomerania. A few days later I received the confirmation of my acceptance. I quickly departed for my new destination, a small town in beautifully wooded area. The principal of the academy was a well-mannered and congenial gentleman who did everything to make my life as agreeable as possible. I liked the atmosphere of the small private school and was encouraged by the zeal of my pupils.

On a radiant free day, the principal invited me on an outing, introducing me to the old town of Colberg, a unique bathing resort and the only one on earth combining sea and salt baths. We attended a concert by the resort's orchestra, a group of fine musicians who executed a semi-classical program. I was informed that this orchestra was composed of band members of the infantry regiment No. 54, stationed in Colberg. My companion explained to me about the orchestra as he also knew many of its members. He told me these musicians of his acquaintance had been with the regiment for 20-25 years each and were receiving from 10-50 marks a month extra outside of their army pay, an arrangement which required each officer of the regiment to pay monthly dues. All the members of the band had to be proficient on both a wind and a string instrument. In light of their contribution, none of them were ever subjected to common military duties. In fact, he described them as the spoiled babies of the regiment.

This interesting story gave birth to a new direction in my thoughts, the result of which was the eager question I asked my guide: "If I would apply for a position in this band, do you suppose my application would be accepted?"

"Why not?" he answered.

The recounting of my past has shown that I always took the shortest road to my goals.

Being strong and healthy, I would have to serve time in the military services. This could be done in one of two ways. I could serve as volunteer from my seventeenth 'til my twentieth year, or be drafted at 21. Now age 17 and having the opportunity to choose the former course, I decided if I could find a place in a first-class band I was ready to volunteer.

After my return to the school, I wrote a letter to the conductor of the band I had heard in Colberg, asking him to admit me as first violinist and flugelhorn player. In a few days I received a friendly letter agreeing to my request. Shortly thereafter, I left my position and departed for Colberg where I reported to the conductor. He sent me, with his orderly as my guide, to their headquarters, where, after passing the doctor's examination, I was led to the quartermaster's building to receive my soldier's uniform. Civilian quarters had been provided for me so I was taken there. Proudly, I exchanged my civilian suit for my fine new military-issued attire and entered a new way of life with many surprises ahead.

The name for a military band man in Germany is hoboist—not in any way connected with the word "hobo." The service of the hoboist in the 54th Regiment was a great deal more of a musical than a military one. For instance, I never had to attend drills and never handled a gun during my enlistment in Colberg. Instead, my duties were comprised solely of rehearsals and concerts. We rarely had parade exercises but sometimes the band went to the outskirts of the town to wait for the regiment to return from a field maneuver. Then, amidst colors and music and marching at the head of the regiment, we crossed the city heading towards the barracks. Outside of my meager pay which consisted of 20 pfenige (5 cents!) a day, I earned enough money to lead a comfortable existence. There probably was not one military band in Germany which was equal in earning power to the 54th.

I was placed on the last stand of the first violin section. There were 12 first violins. After playing in six consecutive concerts I acquired enough knowledge of the capacity of my section that, without conceit, I knew that many of the violinists ahead of me did not play as well as I did. Therefore, one day I approached the conductor and asked him to assign me to another stand, also telling him I would greatly appreciate it if sometime I were allowed to play a solo. He turned me down roughly, saying, "This is your place and will be so until I am ready to change it." I regretted my forwardness and, to my great dismay, discovered his deportment towards me had changed from a certain amiability to a stricter military attitude.

On one occasion, he even tried to humiliate me in front of my comrades. At a band rehearsal, our first cornet player was absent. I had to take over the solo part, consisting primarily of a cadenza. I did my best to perform it "comme il faut" (properly) and thought I had executed it as prescribed. After concluding, the conductor made me repeat it. I had the great satisfaction when, after the close of the rehearsal, my older colleagues told me that my first performance had been right. I only cite this experience to show that I was "persona non grata" in the opinion of the bandmaster!

The summer season in Colberg was nevertheless one of continuous enjoyment for me as we gave two concerts a day. Between them, we tumbled around in the Baltic Sea and did some fishing, taking full advantage of our proximity to the water and fine weather. Once that beautiful summer concluded we began strenuous rehearsals for the winter season's symphony concerts. My place was still the same—the last of the 12 first violins.

No solo playing either.

About the month of January, the government announced the formation of a dozen new infantry regiments. On the first of February at our daily assembly, our bandmaster notified us that volunteers were needed for the completion of the band of the new 129th Regiment.

"Who will volunteer for this purpose?" he asked.

Only two of us answered by stepping out in front: the first French horn player and me. Sneeringly, the bandmaster addressed me, "You do not like it here, eh?"

"I would like to advance and do not see any chance to do so here," I answered.

After the assembly, a number of my comrades told me of their desire to also volunteer, but they feared if they had done so and were unsuccessful in their endeavor, their stay in the 54th would not have been an agreeable one. Neither was the remainder of mine. I had to pass through some quite unpleasant months thereafter.

A certain degree of psychic sense has been one of my assets since my early youth. One of these manifestations of this peculiar faculty took place after my decision to leave the 54th for the 129th Regiment. A short while later, at one of our rehearsals, it was reported that the 3rd Battalion of our regiment, which was stationed in Cöslin, had received orders to depart in three weeks for Bromberg, the home for the new 129th Regiment. After the rehearsal, the first French horn player and I were surrounded by our colleagues who were teasing us two about not having been called. Strange as it may seem, I had the firm conviction that I would go to Bromberg.

The following night, a vivid dream disturbed me. I saw a railroad station. A strange regiment gathered, formed ranks, and marched down the main street, headed by a band of mediocre caliber, though they were received enthusiastically by a densely massed population of onlookers. After this dream a real obsession took hold of me as I was now absolutely sure I was going to Bromberg. During the ensuing weeks I tried to bear with equanimity the remarks of my associates as I would calmly state, "I am going to Bromberg" which would always be followed by rousing laughter. Our third battalion's departure was set for the next day.

"Now, Hammer, you are going tomorrow too, huh?" was voiced by the French horn player.

My friends continued to tease me, but, oddly enough, I still stuck to my guns. A fraternal atmosphere prevailed amongst us 12 comrades. Some of them expressed their gladness that I was staying in their midst; others spoke of their regret about my thwarted ambitions. The hour of 10 struck, the signal for our return to quarters. At the moment of our leaving, an orderly arrived. He called my name and gave me a command from headquarters. Then he said, "Hammer, come with me to receive further orders for joining the 3rd Battalion at the crossing station for the journey to Bromberg. The train starts at five o'clock tomorrow morning."

I leave it to you to picture the consternation of my comrades. After a hasty farewell, I left them. With the exception of one, I never saw any of them again.

I received orders to be at a certain railroad crossing to meet the 3rd Battalion and to report to the major who was commander of the unit. When I did so, the major, seeing me clad in the uniform of the 54th was nonplussed given his soldiers were wearing that of the newly-formed 129th Regiment. I handed him my order and explained its late arrival. After this short interview, the battalion boarded the train for Bromberg which we reached by nightfall.

The assembly of the 129th Regiment was ordered for 7 a.m. the next morning. At the muster I looked rather out of place—one lone man in red and white; 1,199 in red and blue. No wonder the colonel spotted this monkey at once. He came galloping up to me on horseback, screaming furiously, "What are you doing here?"

"Herr Obrist, I only received my marching order last night at ten o'clock."

Red-faced, he turned his steed and rode away. The regiment dismissed, I was led to the quartermaster's equipment rooms and received my new uniform. I then arranged to rent a room near our regimental quarters (the members of a military band were allowed this privilege). The next morning the band was commanded to its first rehearsal. The bandmaster was a middle-aged gentleman, just graduated from the Imperial Conservatory's course for military bandmasters. He was an outstanding trombonist and excellent pianist. The band was the only unit of our newly-organized regiment which was still incomplete. I was placed, as before, as flugelhorn player. The day after, a symphony orchestra rehearsal was ordered and I was put at the Concertmaster's stand.

Busy days followed and I soon found out that, soldierly speaking, I amounted to nothing, having never even been taught to handle an army gun. However, my experiences at Father Neuman's hunting grounds had given me some knowledge of a gun's mechanism, enabling me to take apart and reassemble our military weapons quite easily. When it came to shooting exercises at the rifle range, I felt more at home; in fact, I finished the first three classes in rifle shooting in one session. My superiors seemed to be satisfied with my efforts to be a good soldier, as, shortly after, I was promoted to the grade of corporal.

The officers of the regiment and the hoboists were the only ones allowed to wear civilian clothes after service hours. This privilege made it easy for me to indulge in my cherished sports: horseback riding, skating, gymnastics, swimming, and so forth. The service was easy enough; I was enjoying it.

Several beautiful intermissions also came my way. It happened that a major, a captain, and a lieutenant, intending to form a string quartet, were unable to find the necessary viola player. They asked our bandmaster for help and he sent me to the quartet session to fill the spot. The major was a cellist, the captain (en passant, the most detested drillmaster of the regiment, but luckily not my company commander) was a very good violinist, and the lieutenant an acceptable second violin. I looked forward with enthusiasm to the days when we played quartets. All of them were friendly to me, but kept their distance.

I was also asked by the captain of the 12th Company, a very humane, music-loving gentleman, to organize a male chorus from the men under his command and was pleased upon discovering some exceptionally fine voices amongst the aspirants. Even the noncommissioned sergeants, the master sergeant included, were valuable assets under the direction of me, the humble corporal. The chorus serenaded the higher officers' families and, by and by, advanced to be a social mainstay for our recreational meetings.

Besides the rehearsals under the sensitive direction of our conductor, whose name was Luther, I enjoyed giving a number of civilian pupils music lessons. Given my combined additional income from concerts and lessons, it was possible for me to live in comfort.

Nevertheless, even with all these duties, I did not neglect my studies as I was intent upon advancing in my expertise. An "Institute of Musical Art" directed by Professor Steinberg, a renowned instructor, was the foremost institution of its kind in Bromberg. I was asked by Professor Steinberg to play two Beethoven sonatas with his best piano pupil there. It was a successful concert and, afterwards, I made a proposition to the professor. I offered him my services for playing violin-piano sonatas with his advanced students in exchange for lessons in counterpoint and composition. He gladly accepted my proposal. Our contract was loyally adhered to and resulted in fruitful ensemble work.

Our bandmaster was a rather frail person, of insufficient physical stamina to withstand his often tiring obligations. For instance, after a strenuous morning rehearsal, he would show such a degree of fatigue at an afternoon rehearsal with us youngsters that he had to hold his conducting right arm up with his left hand. He and I would occasionally play violin and piano sonatas together and, when I was slated to play a solo, he would rehearse it with me. He seemed to like me and I was very fond of him in return. It was a natural evolution that when weariness came upon him at the afternoon sessions, he would hand his baton to me and ask me to lead the men. This task I always fulfilled with great zeal and apparently to the satisfaction of our Kapellmeister (leader). As I made further progress in my conducting, now and then the chief would even entrust me with leading the entire band. Thus was laid the foundation for my future career.

These were pleasant days. Military drilling lessened and, as the number of my private pupils grew, our director would dispense with my attendance at afternoon rehearsals every time I asked him. My sport activities diminished greatly as I had little spare time at this point. I had to find some means of counterbalancing the nerve-shattering, strenuous music activities with vigorous body exercise.

At a convenient distance, I found a place to rent horses. A friend of mine, an agriculturist who served in my regiment, would join me in spending our Sundays horseback riding, both of us clad in civilian clothes. One Sunday afternoon, after a long ride, we came to our parade grounds which was a large, sandy plain, recently sown with clover to solidify its soil. As it was late, we decided to take a shortcut to our destination across the field, disregarding the sign: No Trespassing. On the other side of the tract was a pine forest in which was located a powder magazine, guarded by two soldiers. We were nearing the railroad crossing which marked the end of the field when one of the guards stepped out of the woods, commanding, "Halt!" and grabbing the reins of my friend's horse which was in front of mine. On hearing him bark, I turned my horse swiftly and went off head-long in the opposite direction to the main road at a full gallop. There, as if nailed to the ground, stood the master sergeant of my company, grinning at my foolhardiness.

"Now, Hammer, what are you up to this time?" he queried.

I couldn't answer. Turning, I rode homeward. The next day my friend and I were called to parole and con-demned by the colonel to three days in the brig for trespassing on the clover-sown parade grounds. This was a hard blow for yours truly, the proud Heinrich Hammer! After this risky ride we were also unable to quell our comrades' joking remarks. Nevertheless, the succeeding Sundays found us once again on horseback. This sport has been one of continuous enjoyment for me until very late in my life.

The course in counterpoint and composition taken with Steinberg brought forth fruit when two young Jew-ish friends who had written a little operetta libretto asked me to write the music for it, the opus to be performed at the wedding of one of their sisters. I gladly accepted the challenge. The operetta was successfully performed and the compensation for my composition was six fine linen dress shirts and some handkerchiefs.

At one of our concerts in the officers' casino, Brigadier General von Kamoke, a nephew of the former Kriegsminister (Secretary of Defense) was the honored guest. He had been Colonel of the regiment during my period of service in the 54th. Having noticed me in my Concertmaster's seat, he came over and asked me how I liked the service, and I gave him a satisfactory answer. He then asked me if I would not like to remain in the service and be sent to the Imperial Music Conservatory to prepare for a band-mastership, and I told him in reply of my ambition to go to Italy and France to continue my musical studies.

Some days later, an order was issued concerning new gun-drill exercises for band men. On a field sown with small rocks we proceeded with our task the next day, when the command "Down!" was called. This order had to be executed with lightening-like speed. In hitting the ground, I landed with my shin on a rock, opening my old shot wound. As there didn't seem enough hours to fill my pressing obligations, I neglected the injury. Consequently, a serious inflammation occurred which should have necessitated my seeking medical care. I, however, followed my crowded work schedule. The inflammation took its malignant course until some of my colleagues who knew about my wound admonished me to go to the doctor after seeing it in its advanced state—threatening they would report me if I did not comply.

The time for the field maneuvers was near, but my injury was serious and the outlook of a well-deserved rest period in the hospital was an enticing one. The next day I reported for examination at the doctor's office. Command: "Report at the hospital tomorrow." With a clean, refreshing bandage on my leg, I went home and informed my friends and pupils of my entrance into the hospital. After a week spent there, the field maneuvers started and a change of doctors occurred. A great surprise to me was the appearance of the new chief medic, as he was the father of one of my pupils, although he acted as if he did not know me. Over the next few days I wondered at the change in my menus as I suddenly began receiving an abundance of the tastiest dishes! I was kept longer than necessary in the hospital, although perfectly cured and in excellent physical condition. I was released a day before the arrival of the regiment back from maneuvers. In civilian clothes, I was waiting at the station to greet my jealous comrades.

The routine circle of military life took its regular course again. To my extra-curricular activities was added an exultant awakening; the development of my first love. The object of this new, overwhelming sentiment was the niece of a well-known German composer and conductor. She was six months my senior, a very beautiful girl, who was already through her first year of college. Her mother looked with disfavor upon my all-too-frequent visits, an attitude which forced us to resort to secret meetings. How little command parents have over their children if the latter decide to go their own way! Selma would accompany her little sister to visit a girlfriend, leave her there, and rendezvous with me at our trysting place.

Selma's mother, suspicious of her daughter's surreptitious absences, determined to sever our association and concluded to send her to the country where her uncle owned a large estate. At our next very short meeting, Selma informed me that her departure would take place the afternoon of the following Wednesday, by post-wagon. We then decided to make this farewell trip together.

I met her at the first stop station. To my great disappointment, I had to take the only place left, located outside, seated next to the driver. What a calamity! At the next station I asked Selma to come sit outside with me. She and I squeezed onto the narrow seat with the driver, dismally whispering about our approaching parting, and arrived at our destination near sunset. There, Selma's uncle received her warmly, guided her to his coupe and ordered the driver to start homeward. We two poor souls had been unable even to shake hands at this fateful parting. This was the last time I ever saw her. It would not be amiss to state that continuous thoughts about this pure, fine girl were for years to come my incentive in leading a sound moral existence.

Chapter 5   Wanderlust

In 1883, the three years of my military service came to an end. I had long had a fervent desire to study the music of foreign countries so I decided to begin in Italy, and consequently proceeded leisurely southward to Dresden following my discharge. There an uncle of mine, married to my Aunt Marie, lived in a comfortable home. I took full advantage of my stay there by exploring the rich assets which this lovely city possessed: the residence of the art-loving King of Saxony, the renowned "Zwinger," one of the finest art galleries on earth containing Titians and other examples of the world's celebrated masterworks in abundance, as well as the famous court orchestra composed of the finest artists available—Weber and Richard Wagner were former conductors of this marvelous body of musicians.

The King's palace and the Schlosskirche were connected by an elevated bridge along which the monarch and court attendants would enter to hear the renowned Friday morning masses with chorus and orchestra. These were always inspiring performances. After a visit to the Schlosskirche, I would wander over to the nearby Elbe River where hilly terraces on both shores formed an unforgettable panorama including expansive vineyards and exquisite homes, some of monumental proportions. My two weeks' sojourn with Uncle and Aunt was spent primarily in seeing Dresden's wonders and, on occasion, enjoying refreshments and good music at the attractive tea gardens situated on the outskirts of the city. With great regret but filled with soul-stirring memories, I then left Dresden. Accompanying me now was a valuable leather shoulder-strap satchel for traveling which had been added to my possessions, a gift from my uncle.

My next stop was Bayreuth, where I, a fervent Richard Wagner disciple, visited the Festsepielhaus where yearly performances of his dramas were held. To my deep sorrow, the soul of my beloved ideal composer had left its earthly abode two weeks before my arrival.

The large reception hall located on the second floor of the edifice was filled with funeral tributes to the great master. There were large gold wreaths from the Czar of Russia, the old Emperor Wilhelm of Germany, King Ludwig of Bavaria and others, ringed with countless gifts from all over the world. What a lamentable fact that this great genius was 62 before he was released from his long exile. King Ludwig of Bavaria, a great admirer and friend of the master, was the motivating force in bringing about his release. He asked him to come to Munich to perform his dramas, promising to put all the necessary resources at the command of the composer. After having paid my silent "pace internus," I left the room to explore the theater itself which has and continues to host the brightest stars of our globe.

I inspected the stage with its intricate mechanisms and, last but not least, the elliptic sunken orchestra pit which is constructed in such a way that the musicians are invisible to the audience as they are concealed by an oval hood. One long narrow opening enables the conductor to follow every phase of the actions upon the stage. I could not withstand the desire to sit awhile in the concertmaster's and conductor's chairs and let my thoughts wander to far distant possibilities.

After my thorough investigation of the Festspielhaus and the tasteful landscapes of the hill upon which it stands, I went to the city proper to see "Wahnfried," the home in which Richard Wagner spent his final years. His handsome and massive St. Bernard voiced a ferocious bark of greeting and signs posted on the iron grill, "Entrance Closed," notified the visitor that to enter the master's home was impossible. Leaving Bayreuth, I again traveled southward towards my destination: Italia.

At the little town of Stockach, near the Bodensee, I was fascinated by the lovely nature scene consisting of a small wooded hill, sparkling in the smiling light of the sun. I was immediately eager to scale the height. I started the climb with gusto, enthusiastically proclaiming my joyful mood in an appropriate, lusty marching song, a reminder of my past soldier life. Arriving at my destination, the top plateau, I then burst out in a loud Swiss yodel, enjoying the majestic view of the lake, peaceful little villages, animals grazing in green meadows, the town of Stockach at my feet, and a vista of unlimited blue horizon. After a while, I realized my extended stay at this superb "point de culmination" had made it impossible for me to arrive on time for a meeting in Stockach with a gentleman pianist which I had arranged the day before. Then, an idea. I said to myself, "This little mountain has an easy slope. Why not go straight down and avoid the long snake turns?" So, beginning as determined, I started in a firm gait straight down towards Stockach. By and by, my pace accelerated uncontrollably. I began running faster and faster. I came to a somewhat steeper spot, lost my balance, and started in a quick tempo, sliding, sliding downward. A short tree stump caught my trousers and, with a tearing sound, my whole trouser leg was ripped from cuff to seat. Uh-oh! How to go through town with only one whole trouser leg? But I managed, holding it together the best I could, sneaking through alleys and side streets back to my hotel where I bathed, dressed, and proceeded to the dining room to keep my appointment with Mr. Furtwängler, the tumble having ultimately expedited my journey nicely. In sharing our experiences the evening before, I had told him of my plans. He was so interested that he had asked me to see him again.

At our meeting this day I was surprised to hear him express his desire to go with me to Italy for more extensive study. This pleased me immensely and I told him of my elation at having his companionship on my sojourn.

We also discussed the feasibility of arranging to give concerts together on our journey. As the idea sounded plausible, we agreed to it. He was free and a bachelor like myself, though several years my senior, so nothing prevented him from making quick arrangements to join me.

Before taking our departure we gave a concert in this, his hometown, which brought in its wake a slight addition to our traveling funds. We then crossed the Bodensee and landed on its south shore in Switzerland. We performed occasional evening programs en route through that country and wherever we went we were received hospitably. At some places we were even asked to give a second performance. Our traveling continued in this manner, stopping at Locarno, Lugano, and reaching the Italian frontier at Como and the beautiful blue Lago di Como—from there, Milano was only a short distance. The historic traditions attached to this modern fountainhead with its indescribably glorious cathedral, fine galleries, and wide boulevards made such an impression upon both of us that we lengthened our stay beyond our earlier plans. We left this jewel-city reluctantly and proceeded to Lodi where we found the carnival season in full swing.

For the first time in our journey, both of us decided to stop our tourist's way of traveling and spend some time in earnest study. The next day each of us sincerely gave several hours to fulfilling yesterday's resolution. The following day found us two weak souls back in the streets, partaking in the vivacious carnival spirit.

A very peculiar aspect of this ebullient festival impressed us. The Italian houses, like many in France, are adorned with small iron balconies at each story. As one is allowed to kiss any girl going unprotected through a street at carnival time, the feminine members of the population generally stay safely at home. Standing upon these balconies, the young ladies will throw some oranges when spying a male to their liking. The object of the bombardment must be prepared by having his pockets filled with oranges to be able to throw more back than were thrown at him. It seemed we two were in a very unfavorable position!

At the time of our stay in Italy, the Germans were looked upon as genuine friends, so as soon as we passed a balcony manned by lady bombardiers they would scream "Tedeschi!" (German) and throw a barrage of oranges at us. This vigorous play kept up for some time. The street urchins took an extremely lively part in all these proceedings. Every fruit missing its goal was quickly pounced upon and devoured, skin and all. I wore an olive-green summer overcoat, made for me as payment by a tailor for music lessons I'd given to his little daughter. When we were through with our gallantries my overcoat was a striped one, dripping in orange juice from top to bottom.

Back at the hotel, I took up my neglected violin and practiced seriously for a while until a knock at the door interrupted me. My "Entrez!" was followed by the appearance of a stranger. After a friendly "Bon jour," in fluent French—a language I spoke better than Italian—he told me he was the director of the opera playing in Lodi at present. He said that he had heard me play and asked if I would be willing to perform a solo in the Entr'acte of the opera the following night, and offered me the small sum of 100 lire. I was very eager to accept his proposition. Having composed "Saluti al Italia," a little piece for violin with piano accompaniment following our entrance into Milano, I thought this an appropriate time to give it its first public performance, along with a part of Wieniawski's Violin Concerto.

At this point in time, I had changed my name to its Italian counterpart, Enrico Martelle.

The next day during my customary early morning walk, I saw a number of men busily pasting onto walls and windows big sheets advertising "The famous violin virtuoso, Enrico Martelle" as soloist in the Entr'acte at the opera. Poor Heinrich, the "famous violin virtuoso!" The calf had fallen into the pit; let it extricate itself.

That evening, after a restless day interrupted by intermittently hectic attempts to study, Furtwängler and I entered the opera house. Our program followed the conclusion of the second act. Two nervous young fellows entered timidly, were greeted by a thunderous clapping of hands, and performed their task, progressively mastering their stage fright; at the end of their presentation, rousing "Brava's" accompanied welcome applause. Even the musicians in the orchestra pit joined the crowd in lauding our work. After the curtain fell, a number of Lodi citizens complimented us. We returned to our hotel and spent the evening in a festive mood indeed.

The next morning we went to the opera director's apartment—he lived in the same hotel—to receive our 100 lira. The floor was filled with an unruly crowd consisting of the singers and musicians of last night's opera. Murmurs and loud outcries of "That scoundrel!—thief!—swindler!—sneak!" and other more forceful adjectives were swelling in volume, all in expressive Italian, and the corridor was filled with this fortissimo. Out of this wealth of outcry, we drew the unhappy conclusion that the nice director had absconded with a full purse, the result of last night's sold-out house. We had already recklessly spent some of our lean resources, induced by our promised gain of 100 lira, making a dire breach upon our capital. There was just enough left to pay our fare to Spezia where I had asked my mother to send her next check.

Arriving there, my first errand was to ask at the post office if my letter had come. It was there, but I had to plead fervently while the clerk scrutinized my papers closely till he was satisfied that the translation of my name from German to Italian was correct, finally handing it into my eager grasp. Overjoyed, I took my merciful deliverer, the check, straight to the bank. The cashier looked from the check to my identification, and shook his head, saying, "I see you are Heinrich Hammer, not Enrico Martelle." My explanation of the situation was of no avail this time—he said he could not cash the check, and instructed me to see the German consul. If anyone could help me, he said he could. Distressed, I went to the consul. Same result. "I cannot cash the check for Heinrich Hammer as it clearly belongs to Enrico Martelle."

A happy bit of inspiration then flashed upon my mind. It was the date of the old Emperor Wilhelm's birthday. I said to the consul, "Today is our Emperor's birthday; if my friend and I received the check we would be able to empty a bottle of wine to toast the great father of our country." These words seemed to move the heart of our patriotic consul. He cashed my check, and, just as I had promised, we boisterously executed a fine toast to the Emperor.

Spezia, the largest harbor of Italy, is a lovely city with an artistically conceived park, its main attraction consisting of a great number of fine orange trees. The next morning on my daily walk I wandered through the park and sat down on a large bench which happened to be occupied by a lady of seemingly Teutonic descent. Seeing my blonde hair, the lady addressed me and inquired if I was German. When I said I was, she replied that she also was from my country. A lively chat ensued during which I learned she was governess to the Countess Chissetti di Consano. She also told me her mistress had often expressed a desire to take piano lessons from a German teacher as she herself spoke the language perfectly and loved the German classics.

I was greatly surprised to meet the German lady again at the same place the following day. More surprising still, she told me she had spoken to the countess about me and her mistress had told her to ask me to come and see her. I of course replied I would be pleased to accept her invitation.

The next day, I received a letter apprising me of the wish of the countess to see me in her home at a stipulated hour. At the appointed time, I found myself entering an elegant salon where the countess received me very courteously. She was a frail, aristocratic person and expressed herself in fluent German, asking me if and when I could give her piano lessons. After settling upon the time for the first lesson I was then treated to a glass of fine old port after which I left in high spirits. That afternoon, Furtwängler and I visited the wide, impressive harbor where numerous ships of all classes rested upon their moorings.

At her first lesson, I appreciated the countess's eagerness and previously-acquired technical ability punctuated by the possession of a strong rhythmic sense and innate talent for music. She was one of the best pupils I have ever had the pleasure of teaching.

At this point, I enjoyed an experience of an extraordinary nature in witnessing a pyrotechnical show given in celebration of the King of Italy's birthday. In the sky above a large plain in Spezia was displayed—entirely in fireworks—the history of the Italian kingdom. I have seen many remarkable fireworks over the course of my life but never any of this magnitude and artistry.

The lessons at the palatial residence of the countess extended into the second month and then, "nolens volens" (whether someone likes it or not), I let her know I must leave for Florence to begin violin lessons with Mr. Fisher, a violinist with a renowned reputation. She regretted losing her teacher as much as I my pupil, especially as she had made such remarkable progress in such a short period of time. We left our hospitable hotel where we had been treated like members of the proprietor's family and went on our way.

Stopping at Pisa, we admired that beautiful monument, the famous leaning tower, and the city's monstrous stores, all containing not only miniature likenesses of the tower but a wealth of sculptures in general. It seemed as if every inhabitant of this quaint town was a professional artist.

We departed Pisa and arrived shortly in princely Florence where I soon paid a visit to my future teacher, Mr. Fisher, who occupied a cozy, artfully furnished home with his family near the Arno river. There I was received cordially and, after some practical counsel, was asked to come for my first lesson the next morning. I would actually have liked to postpone it as my playing was a little rusty after all the pleasant times I had rather too greedily enjoyed recently. Nevertheless, I went at the appointed hour, unpacked my beloved instrument and played—although not as well as I could have when I was in good trim and certainly not at the level Mr. Fisher had expected. He pronounced my technique shaky and requested I "brush up" and come back soon. The next lesson, following said brush up, I did better.

Meanwhile, I had made the acquaintance of a group of artists from various countries. It was a joyous aggregation of painters, sculptors, writers, and several music students—all members of a newly-formed artist's club. I was asked to join and enthusiastically agreed. The following events will illustrate this was not a wise move!

My lessons were progressively less and less fruitful as the activities of the artist's club occupied more and more of my time. A substantial number of hours were spent at club meetings in and out of town, on endless group visits to the city's magnificent palaces, each a museum filled with its abundance of masterworks, and also at the Arno bridge with its wealth of the finest jewelry stores in the world. After months of more or less unprogressive work with my serious, well-meaning teacher, he admonished me to quit my gallivanting and membership in the artist's club and give more or, preferably, all my time to serious study.

Admittedly, the sweltering summertime conditions in Florence were not very conducive to my artistic endeavors either, and after another two months with Mr. Fisher, I decided to my great regret that remaining in the city's scorching heat was a detriment in boosting my budding career.

Furtwängler had not joined the club but occasionally he had followed us to the museums as he was an ardent admirer of the great masters of art, being himself a good designer and creator of some quite artistic watercolor paintings. His art teacher was elated with his progress, a man my friends had highly praised for his teaching capacity and serene spirit. Therefore, when I told my friend of my decision to leave Florence, I had great difficulty persuading him to go back home with me. I did eventually prevail and, after a year's stay in this pearl of cities, we departed for Germany, hiking part of the time and traveling the rest of the way by train.

We stayed a little while here and there en route and arrived refreshed in the northeast part of Italy where Lake La Garda lies, surrounded by large 200-year-old chestnut trees. In Triente, we gave our first recital in what was then Austria; after our concert spending an enjoyable evening at the officer's club, having been invited by the colonel of the infantry regiment. From Triente to Botzen we were engaged for a soiree in a prominent lawyer's home and treated royally by our hosts. We also gave a concert in Franzensfeste, a fortress secured within a mountain's tunnel at Brenner Pass. There we again passed a nice evening with the officers and their families.

Two more recitals followed: one in Meran, another of the quaint towns of Innsbruck, the old boundary between Tirol and Germany. We were so enthralled by the beauty of the nearby "bayerische Hochgebirg" (Bavarian High Mountain) that we lingered here and there to admire the grandiose mountain buttresses and enjoy friendly interactions with the local inhabitants. Finally we came to Munich, arriving at the time of its famous bock bier (beer) festival.

We went to the Hofbräuhaus, not only to join the overcrowded mass of frolicking humans, but to pass an enjoyable last hour together as Furtwängler had decided to part company with me and go see his parents in the Schwarzwald, having not seen them for four years. These large Bavarian beer castles are the only ones, to my knowledge, where you serve yourself cafeteria-style. You find an empty stein in the courtyard or inside the hall, clean it under a running faucet and advance, pressing forward through the dense crowd to the primitive bar where several men are busily tapping the famous "bock" out of enormous barrels. There is hardly ever any sitting room available in the large hall where local women with baskets cry out "Rettich! Rettich!" offering a radish-like vegetable which helps digest your beer.

Being deprived of a sitting place inside, we went out to the courtyard and sat upon a big empty barrel, perching the large quart steins in our laps and indulging in our precious last drink amongst a jumble of people who had come from everywhere to ensure the hospitable Bavarians had a successful Bockbierfest. As we sat there, someone tapped me on the shoulder. I turned around and there stood a master-sergeant hoboist from the Bavarian guard regiment, a former comrade of mine from the 129th who had sat next to me at the first stand of the violins! He had left the 129th before me and, unbeknownst to me, had entered this guard regiment under very favorable conditions. We conversed awhile about old times and he departed after we made plans to get together the next day.

At the time of our exit from Germany a year earlier, Furtwängler had suffered from a serious heart condition. Sometimes on our walks, this resulted in him experiencing frequent attacks which forced him to enter the front hall of the nearest house and lay stretched out on the floor until the episode receded. By and by, these seizures became less and less severe, occurred more rarely, and then ceased entirely. Now an examination in Munich disclosed that the healing process was accomplished. Relieved at this prognosis, I accompanied my companion to the railroad station where he promised to pay me a visit in Magdeburg in the near future and we said our goodbyes.

I spent a few more days in Munich, seeing everything worth seeing, and passed a few hours with my old army colleague—visiting the unique lakes, on the shores of which were some of the magnificent castles of the King of Bavaria, and paying our respects to the city of Ulm where I had the opportunity to compare its leaning cathedral with the leaning tower of Pisa. I then took the direct route home to Magdeburg.

Chapter 6   The First Rung of My Ladder

Circumstances at home had taken an unforeseen turn after my leave-taking a year earlier. My stepfather had done his best to squander not only his but also a great part of my mother's fortune by high living and drinking to excess. His irresponsible behavior caused great grief to my mother and made my stay there absolutely impossible. Responding to my appeal, my mother subsequently rented a small but comfortable apartment for me in Magdeburg where I could make contact with the city's musical life.

It so happened I made the acquaintance of a small group of earnest young musicians who had formed a string orchestra and could not find a capable conductor. As a freelancer, I asked them to let me conduct one of their rehearsals, leaving them to judge my ability. The rehearsal took place and, by unanimous consent, I was chosen as the orchestra's leader.

Thus I stepped onto the first rung of the ladder leading to my lifework—conducting. This was an insignificant start, but thanks to it, I was given the chance to develop, and step by step I was subsequently lifted to the heights I so fervently strove to attain, ripening through experience and study.

Our small orchestra gave two concerts weekly in a popular tea garden. An occasional engagement outside our garden concerts augmented our meager income somewhat and kept us from starving. We made ardent attempts to broaden our circle of musical activity, although our efforts were in vain. The orchestra was composed of very young, earnestly striving musicians who, by continuous study, had made remarkable strides in improving their techniques. Some of my fellow performers wanted to look for more well-paying positions but felt constrained in light of our fine esprit de corps, so they remained on in hopefulness. All of us became keen advertisement scanners of every issue of the Deutsche Musikerzeitung (German musican's newspaper).

One day we found a posting from a circus director wanting an established orchestra. As we were one and all adventurous souls eager to gain a financially secure footing, we decided to apply for the position. I wrote the necessary letter and was greatly surprised when I received an affirmative answer from Baden-Baden, the famous bathing resort in the Black Forest. As there was very little time given us to put our affairs in order, we arranged our trip hastily, all of us eager to enter our new field of endeavor. A 24 hours' railroad journey brought us to our place of destination, and while it was not easy for us to find suitable quarters in the overcrowded tourist town, I found lodging at the home of the first double-bass player of the resort's symphony orchestra. With motherly affection, Mrs. Schneider duly spoiled me like her own son.

Our service to the well-established circus, Blumenfeld[3] consisted of two daily sessions. No wild animals belonged to our organization, only a great number of well-trained horses, a mule, and a donkey. The finest horse of all was a beautiful power-engine stallion, trained and masterfully ridden by Mr. Blumenfeld's oldest son. The Blumenfeld family consisted of father, mother, and nine children, every one of whom contributed his/her talents and efforts to make the father's enterprise a lucrative one. The oldest daughter was what one might call a circus genius as well as a proud example of feminine beauty. She shone in high-wire artistry, trapeze stunts, formidable gymnastic tricks, double-horse exercises, and was a circus dictionary for every member of the troupe. Sometimes she would even replace her brother and lead the unruly stallion through his performances.

A wealthy young Adonis who was deeply in love with her attached himself to the circus, buying from young Blumenfeld a dandy dapple-gray mare which had been blinded in one eye by an unhappy whiplash applied by the owner in a training exercise. The new owner of this fine little horse took lessons in horsemanship from Miss Blumenfeld, explaining to her father his desire to join the crew of the circus.

He asked me to compose a score for Diana's paces. Each of these trained horses knows the music played for his own routine. He will display an unwillingness to perform if the right piece is not played, which is a fine illustration of the intelligence of equines. I composed the numbers to be used for Diana's act and the work I did was amply rewarded by her owner. This man stayed with the circus, constantly courting his ideal, Miss Blumenfeld, although seemingly without success as she was friendly to him but no more. By the end of my stay with Blumenfeld's the young man's prospects seemed to brighten and, about a year later, I heard of their betrothal after I had long left the circus.

A circus in Europe is entirely different in its institutional makeup than an establishment of its same type in the United States. A more refined atmosphere dominates the European organization. Only in one large circus in Germany, circus Renz, are wild animals—lions, tigers, leopards, bears, etc.—displayed in dressage, but never large animals like elephants, giraffes, or apes. The music is performed by a good orchestra, not by a band. The European accompaniment consists of classical or semi-classical pieces, not jazz or contemporary material. These orchestras are of large, symphonic proportions. I mention these differences only to avoid a false judgment in the reader's mind about my position as conductor of a circus orchestra! The skills of the members of my orchestra were as desirable as could be wished for.

Our clientele was comprised of a great number of aristocratic guests of the resort. Two performances a day fulfilled our obligations, leaving us with ample time to join the morning promenades to the spring, accompanied by the strains of music by the resort orchestra. There, we would drink a glass of its beneficial water, or make excursions through the Schwarzwald (Black Forest) with its innumerable ruins of ancient feudal castles. Our two

[3] The founder of the official **CIRCUS BLUMENFELD** was Maurice Levi Cerf (1783-1867), who also went by Moritz Hirsch Levy. He was from a French-Alsatian family and owned a menagerie featuring birds and apes. When he married a Blumenfeld daughter in Beuel (near Bonn), Germany, he applied for (and was granted) official permission by the city to take her last name. Beginning in 1811, the family went on tour as "Circus Blumenfeld" with four horses, two bears, and a mix of performers, and quickly became the foremost of the Jewish circuses.

Many circuses created their own dialects; the Blumenfelds created Blumenfeldsprache, a mixture of French, Yiddish, Romance (Gypsy dialect), and technical circus jargon, reflecting their ethnic and religious background.

Maurice/Moritz Blumenfeld and his wife had nine children: Moritz, Meyer, Emanuel, Sophia, Nathan, Leopold, Herman, Mina, David, and Simon. Most of these children performed with the Circus Blumenfeld, and many started their own circuses. In 1874, the Circus Blumenfeld bought a permanent headquarters in Guhrau, Germany (now Góra in Poland). When Emanuel died in 1885, his widow continued to run the circus until 1896, during which time they featured 80 horses and imaginative trained animals including a "Wonder Pig." In one seven-month season, the circus visited 120 locations; in 1897, the Circus started using rail to move locations, which meant they had longer stays in fewer locations. At this time, the Circus usually featured six tents, 130 horses, and its own string orchestra, and averaged about 4,000 visitors. (blennow-genealogy.files.wordpress.com)

months' stay in this temperate, healthful climate with its lush pinewoods (meticulously cared for by well-trained foresters) was richly invigorating to our minds as well as our bodies.

From Baden-Baden, the circus proceeded to Heilbronn. The famous castle Weibertreu was only a few miles further and we musicians were eager to visit this remarkable place as had the hundreds of thousands who had paid their respects before us. The historic facts narrated herein will explain its renown.

During the Thirty Years' War, this castle of Weibertreu, well-supplied with dried grains, had withstood a bloody siege by the Austrian army for a long period, but finally the last remnants of their sustenance vanished. Those in the castle held counsel, the outcome of which was the decision to send some delegates to the besieging commander to inform him of their eventual surrender. They made only one request; that the women be freed and that he allow each to carry her most precious possessions with her. The commander consented, eagerly anticipating the rich loot which would soon be his.

He was to be badly disenchanted.

Behold! As the building's heavy iron gate opened, out marched hundreds of women, each carrying her husband or lover upon her shoulders. This event gave birth to the name Weibertreu —a woman's unwavering attachment to her loved one. The commander, dumbfounded but honest, left the crowd unharmed but then laid the castle in ruins, leaving only the four indestructible surrounding walls standing—and these have since been inscribed with thousands of visitors' names.

After vainly combating the desire to pick some of the nearby vineyard's lusciously plump purple grapes, frankly we gave into our desire and stole a few, refreshing in their tender sweetness.

As sojourn for our circus, Heilbronn did not offer as much attraction as Baden-Baden. When it had been announced that we would move to Heilbronn at the conclusion of our engagement in Baden-Baden, I had a serious thinking session and decided this routine life did not add one iota to my further professional advancement.

One day not long after while scrutinizing the Deutsche-Musikerzeitung—German Musicians' Journal—I found an advertisement offering a conductor position leading a cooperative orchestra in Oldenburg. I solicited for the post and, after arriving in Heilbronn, received a letter from Oldenburg telling me I had been chosen to fill the vacancy.

Following our return from Weibertreu, I informed Mr. Blumenfeld of my decision to leave his employ. He was not happy to lose me and I had great difficulty getting my final salary from him. My colleagues also grumbled, saying they did not like to see our harmonious ensemble dismembered. I told them the concertmaster would, as a capable successor, keep the ensemble in its present state. Still, our last days together were not very joyful as the members of the orchestra and I had formed a tightly-knit group of serious musicians, but it was also understood we each needed to attain the best compensation we could in pursuing our careers in music.

The orchestra which I was now engaged to conduct consisted primarily of musicians who had served Philomela[4] for a good many years and were now in a predictable routine, capable men who seemingly liked this placid duty. Here then was the task of the young Kapellmeister: to awaken ambition in them and lead the group to higher musical achievement.

The first clarinetist, a man past middle age, was the president of the cooperative. He was a well-educated, solid fellow of executive ability with whom I had a serious talk concerning my goals and he earnestly promised his full support of my endeavors. The Concertmaster was an outstanding violinist and excellent symphonic player, however I lament to share he was somewhat given to over-imbibing.

Hard work lay ahead of me, but I plunged into it with confidence and incisiveness, aided by the goodwill and cooperative spirit of the agreeable musicians. The performances improved markedly within a short period of time and were praised by a friendly public and press. We gave weekly symphony concerts and made an increasing number of appearances in nearby regions.

A main source of the unit's income came from the widely known Oldenburg horse auction which was held twice a year, lasting several days each time. Here, the orchestra gave daily concerts and played lively ball music every evening under the clarinetist-president's leadership. The returns from each of these festivals ran into thousands of marks and became avenues to the smiles of fortune. The income derived was divided in equal parts, each member receiving one part, and the conductor two parts. This not only would not withstand comparison with the salary a conductor receives today, but was below the standard of that time as well. Nevertheless, I rejoiced even at its meagerness, having learned to live by the principle "he is happiest who needs least." I saved a nice amount of my income though I lived "comme il faut" (properly).

A steady if not rapid progress had been made by us both in our artistic striving and in terms of our financial gain when another symphony orchestra arrived in town under the direction of Max Julius Loewengard. It was soon apparent that an attempt was being made to wrest our hard-earned laurels from us. The new conductor was a good musician, a pupil of Raff in Frankfurt, and he had begun as an opera conductor and then founded this

---

[4] Philomela was a female character in Greek mythology who, as a result of a violent attack, had her tongue cut out. The gods turned her into a nightingale and she is often used as a symbol for literary, artistic, and musical works. (www.greekmythology.com)

group. However, his trial period only lasted a few months as he was unsuccessful in damaging our enterprise. Before leaving, he asked me if I wished to buy his repertoire of orchestra music from him, which I did, thereby giving him a better chance of extracting himself from the resulting financial difficulties. I met him again in later years when I conducted my first concert with the Berlin Philharmonic Orchestra and he was music critic for the Börsen-Zeitung. He wrote a very favorable review of my work.

In the nearby city of Jever was an association called Die Getreuen von Jever—The Loyal Ones of Jever. Their purpose was to send to Bismarck, the long-time Chancellor of Germany, 100 plover eggs as a present on his birthday each year, as these were a fine delicacy. In a like spirit, on his 70th birthday, I composed a short work called Auf nach Jever (On Jever) and dedicated it to him. I was greatly astonished when I receive this letter from Bismarck soon after I had sent the piece to him. It had been written with a quill pen in gothic letters:

> Sehr geehrter Herr!
>
> Die mir ubersante festgabe und die sie begleitenden Gl ckwunshe haben mich sehr erfreut und bitte ich Sie, für diesen Beweis Ihres Wohlwellens meinen berbindlichsten Dank entgegen zu nehmen.
>
> von Bismark

(Very honorable gentleman! The birthday gift and the accompanying congratulations have given me great joy. I beg you to accept for this testimonial of your well-wishing my sincerest thanks. von Bismark)

Among my new acquaintances were an organist for the Lutheran church who was also a fine pianist, a jeweler who had formerly played viola in an amateur string ensemble, and a professor at the college who was a well-trained amateur violinist. At our intermittent social gatherings, these three repeatedly expressed the wish to form a piano quartet but regretted they were unable to find a violoncellist. Still as bold as ever, I declared at one of our get-togethers, "Alright, I would love to be a part of your quartet, so, if you want me to, I will try to fill the vacancy." They said they would be glad to have me.

At the time of my stay at the music school I had often attempted to study the various string instruments and the cello had always been a favorite one of mine. I have not mentioned my continuing endeavors to keep my violin repertoire at par. As a result of my efforts, at intervals I played solos with the orchestra or at social events. Now I had taken on an additional obligation! This meant sitting down and relearning the cello which I undertook with mounting eagerness.

The four of us assembled once a week in the jeweler's spacious living room to dwell, if only for a short time, in the glorious melodies of the masters. Later you will see how this experience of playing the cello brought unforeseen consequences.

I did not find entire satisfaction in this prosaic bourgeois milieu. So when an old companion philosopher joined my orchestra, a talented double-bass player from the music school and the orchestra's sole cellist, he and I formed a unit which performed successfully in concerts. I was the piano accompanist for their solos. Those of the double-bass always produced a unique effect.

It seemed as if each of us young chaps cherished the same adventurous spirit. So it was not surprising when, one day, Oelze, the bass player, brought up the theme of an eventual world tournament. The cellist and I listened eagerly to him and gave the proposal serious thought. My eternal ad astra ("to the stars") ambition awakened again. After we weighed the pros and cons for some time, the pioneer-adventure devil was duly conquered. I composed a plan, marking down the time of our departure and other details. The most important item on our agenda was financing the project. The cellist was unable to add anything to the pool while Oelze could draw on his small inheritance—so we concluded that with his money and what I had saved, we could finance the trip. After the next day's rehearsal we discussed more of the fine points of the matter, adopted my plan, and consented to Oelze's leaving for his home to straighten out his financial status. We chose a date on which to meet in Hamburg where we then intended to embark for New York. In the meantime, I informed the orchestra of my resignation. On the specified day, the cellist and I arrived at the hotel designated as our meeting place. Our double-bass player was not there. We waited two long weeks. At last he came, notifying us that he had been unable to untangle his monetary affairs.

The enchanting dreams of our trio were cruelly brought to naught. The realization of our present position—a two weeks' hotel bill for two and no further means of sustenance—made a sauve qui peut (rush to escape) a necessity for each of us. The cellist and Oelze decided to go home. My reluctance to see Mr. Gabel again amidst regretting being unable to see my mother made it impossible for me to follow the same course.

At the dining room in our Hamburg hotel one day, a very interesting lady had been seated nearby. She had spoken to me in glowing terms of the city of Hanover, its excellent opera and its outstanding symphony concerts. After I accompanied my two colleagues to the railroad station I turned back to the hotel, contemplating my next move. I remembered the woman's account of Hanover and decided to go there to look for possible employment. No use staying any longer in Hamburg! Again the victim of quick decisions, I packed my trunk, my double violin case and umbrella, and took the train to Hanover.

I found a decent inexpensive apartment to rent in a well-situated home, meals included. Notwithstanding its reasonable price, the bill for the first month's rent and food was to create a vacuum in my now depleted capital. Dauntless though, youth's stamina never seems to falter, hope is always the guiding star. Here, however, my dear Heinrich, you will find the realization of your hopes unattainable.

The next day found me on the road inquiring about jobs. No encouragement anywhere. Two weeks were spent in useless search for occupation. Not enough money left for the next month's sustenance; my efforts to at least earn some means in whatever form of work must lead somewhere. Scanning the advertisements in a newspaper, I found one by a restaurateur, asking for a pianist to do evening entertainment in his establishment. I immediately applied and was installed in this new employment the same evening. What a change! From a world concert tour to piano entertainer in a restaurant! But, I tried to be true to my core principle—whatever you do, do your very best to do it right. My piano improvisations seemed to please my listeners, although the atmosphere there was torture for me.

In some instances, two months are a relatively short time interval. In this case, they seemed like an eternity. The money I earned was not enough to take care of my necessities, a dire reality which forced me to search for other fields of activity. To give myself time for speculation on this subject, I decided to go to Erfurt to visit Aunt Henrietta. To make the journey possible I had to hock my less-costly violin for traveling expenses. Light of heart, I quit Hanover and exchanged it for Erfurt.

The position as conductor of the philharmonic orchestra in Erfurt was vacant and guest conductors had since been engaged in lieu of a permanent hire. Arriving in Erfurt, I learned of this fortuitous situation and proffered my services. Happily, I was invested with the conductorship and was pleased indeed to further my music career in the place of my birth. I went zestfully into the fulfillment of my new obligations—two concerts weekly and daily rehearsals.

Uncle Ritter had died by this time and, at his deathbed, had exacted the promise of his dearest friend, Ernest Sillig, to marry my Aunt Henrietta. The marriage was consummated a year after his death. What a surprise my aunt's behavior was to me! The irascible, always-ready-for-a-fight individual had now toned down to a calm, contemplative, rather sociable lady. Heinrich, her sister's formerly maltreated child and ward, had now been elevated to the position of favorite nephew, having attained some small success in the world. She did everything possible to demonstrate her goodwill and helpfulness toward me and was a supportive fan.

The environment of my hometown was a pleasant one, socially and musically, and fairly satisfying. But still that discontent of ambition was simmering within me. My income was rather a moderate one and my capital was decidedly at low ebb. How to remedy this condition was often an object of my cogitation. While I continually strove to bring the status of the orchestra into ascent, I experienced more and more reluctance on the part of the orchestra committee to fulfill my demands. And this musical stagnation bothered me.

One day my friend, Oelze, who had joined our group, told me he had been accepted for a place in a newly-formed Swedish orchestra and showed me his letter from the conductor. Reading it, I came upon the following statement, "I would be very grateful to you if you could bring a cellist with you. His contract would be akin to yours." These sentences pricked into motion my constant irrepressible companion, the spirit of adventure. Quickly and loudly I pronounced my intention: "Why, that's wonderful. I'll go with you as cellist!"

He laughed boisterously, replying, "You're crazy! If you wanted to go as violinist, I would be very proud to recommend you, but as cellist?! That would be a little too risky."

"You don't know that I have played my part as cellist in a piano quartet," I then informed him. "And I'm sure that with some additional study I could do this."

"You have no instrument at present plus no time for decent preparation."

"When are you leaving?"

"A week from today."

"Alright, I'll buy a cello and practice as much as I can until then. Will you send a telegram to the conductor and tell him you're bringing the cellist with you?"

"Yes, I will. You know I am always glad to have your companionship. But the risk is yours."

He was right; it was a risk. I had no instrument, but my beautiful Steiner violin was worth several ordinary cellos. So, with youthful recklessness, which I would soon bitterly regret, I sold my beloved fiddle and bought a decent violoncello, leaving myself enough money to reasonably weather most eventualities. I informed my orchestra committee of my immediate resignation, and with the Hammer energy, devoted every free minute to my new instrument, the full-voiced violoncello.

Chapter 7   Northern Lights

We left Erfurt, eagerly looking forward to our new traveling experience. We arrived in Lübeck, the point of embarkation, the evening before the ship was to raise its anchor. The steward guided us to our cabins where we disposed of our luggage, bathed, and changed into fresh clothes. We were told our supper awaited us in the dining room where a great surprise materialized. At the dining table we'd been assigned sat the former solo-cellist of Loewengard's competitive Oldenburg orchestra, an old acquaintance of ours. We inquired about his destination whereupon he answered, "Sweden. I am to be cellist of the orchestra in Herköping."

What a shock! Who was really engaged, he or I? But, confident as ever, I decided not to worry about the outcome of this now-complicated affair.

We arose early the next morning to watch the preparations for our departure from Lübeck. It was a glorious day. The golden sunlight translated into a silver glitter on the deep blue waters and was a picture of sublime beauty. Soon a hearty breakfast consisting of a rich variety of excellent food was tendered us. We were surely embarking upon our journey in style.

Our ship was a freighter, accommodating only a few passengers, a fine vessel with a convivial captain and well-mannered crew. We spent the whole day on deck, interrupted only by a sumptuous dinner and a similar supper. A new experience to us was the smorgasbord offered. It is actually meant to be an introduction to the main meal but is composed of such a number of delicious little tidbits—small fishes, miniature meat patties, salmon, radishes, and countless other fine delicacies—that you would probably take for granted, as we did, that this generous sustenance constituted the entire meal, and be greatly astonished when the main course arrived afterward!

This short sea voyage was an entirely new experience for the three of us. We enjoyed it immensely and arrived in Sweden refreshed and excitedly awaiting the commencement of our work in this new musical arena. We were greeted by a sunny morning and immediately went to see the conductor of the newly-organized orchestra.

He was a native German, about 30, unmistakably an artistic type. He received us cordially and then embarrassment was obvious on his face when he was notified of his error—having engaged two cellists instead of only one. I, trying to clear the atmosphere, explained the probable source of his mistake.

"I needed a first violinist, not another cellist," he said.

"That can easily be corrected," I replied. "I am a much better violinist than cellist, and I will gladly accept the violinist's post."

This solution of the ticklish situation pleased him greatly and our first orchestral rehearsal began in perfect accord.

The demotion from a conductor's to an orchestra player's stand was entirely to my liking, as I was rid of a leader's responsibilities for a time. My place was next to the Concertmaster, at the first stand. My desk mate was a young man, three years my senior, and my better as a violinist, as I gladly acknowledge. A fine, modest artist, manly, and mannerly ex perfecto.

The orchestra was engaged for a five months' summer season with one concert daily which was held in a tastefully arranged and cozy tea garden. It was a small group, composed of first-class musicians—all well-behaved, dependable gentlemen. Another reason, a slight one of course, for my contentment was the fact I was being paid more than twice as much as I had received at my last engagement as the musician's salaries in Sweden were, at that time, the highest in Europe.

The Swedish people are truly a music-loving nation. No prominent restaurant in that country was without a small yet choice orchestra. The music they played was never of a trashy type, as, regretfully, was too often the case in our country. The repertoire ranged from the classics, even symphonies, arranged for small groups and avidly listened to by the patrons. An absolute silence would reign at performances and the musicians occupied a higher social standing than any of their colleagues in other countries. The cordial treatment accorded us everywhere spurred each one of us to keep the standard of our performances high and also live like gentlemen, faithfully executing our duties, and most were of German origin.

These were wonderful summer days and the northern nights were enchanting. The sun worked overtime all through the months of June, July, and August. It is usually light enough in the northern countries to read by sunlight till nearly midnight.

The night of the Midsommardagen, a renowned summer celebration in Sweden, found all the members of our orchestra co-feasting with the entire country. No one went home before the next morning, as was the annual custom, not even the King. This festival was later re-created in a musical film entitled Midsommervaka by my dear friend Hugo Alfvén [5]. It is one of the many compositions of great beauty carrying his name, all of which enjoy a well-merited importance in musical centers.

Very eager to learn the language of this new country, I studied it earnestly and, within a few months, wrote and spoke it quite understandably. One day as I was faithfully reading my daily newspaper—my past experience had shown this to be the shortest route towards acquiring a foreign language—I found an article describing the founding of an orchestra in Stockholm, the country's capital. As my engagement in Norrköping was nearing its end, I solicited for the Concertmaster position in the new organization. A few days afterward I received a contract which was to take effect October 1st. My friend Oelze also received a contract and, on the day we departed Norrköping, we were both animated by joy at our new prospects and departed together on a very short but pleasant cruise to Stockholm. The entrance to the unique harbor there is of such surpassing loveliness that it needs a better pen than mine to describe it adequately. The steamer passes at least a thousand small idyllic, wooded islands, each surmounting another in its picturesqueness. All of these are inhabited although some are so tiny, there hardly seems enough room to build a house; nevertheless, there is usually a stately villa situated on the shore.

After this romantic journey, still other imposing sights awaited us when we entered the city's harbor. Our ship moored in front of the Grand Hotel, the majestic and ancient castle of the Swedish kings located to our left. After a grateful expression of our appreciation to the captain and the ship's personnel, we left the good vessel and searched for and found lodging in pleasant quarters with friendly, hospitable folk straightaway.

Before assuming our new duties, we spent our two

[5] **Hugo Alfvén** is one of Sweden's most performed composers. Although his works clearly derive from the national-romantic era, most of them have never lost their popularity. Moreover, Alfvén composed what have become repertory works in different genres. Alfvén started as a violinist, but soon developed his musical interest into both composing and conducting. Beside a successful career as composer, he was very much appreciated as both orchestral and choral conductor. For many years he conducted the famous male choir Orphei Drängar, also writing several compositions for this ensemble. Alfvén wrote his key works for orchestra rather early in his career, continued later to compose mostly for choir (both male and mixed choir) and for voice and piano. (Gunnar Ternhag)

days of liberty exploring this "Northern Vienna," a gay, musical city. Behind the castle was located the famous hundreds-of-years-old Ridderkyrka, a church of Lutheran denomination, with its simple, impressive interior, which served as the burying place of the nation's rulers. A turbulent stream, the Nordstrom, rushed by the castle and found its outlet in the harbor. Upon a small peninsula on one side of the stream was erected a beautiful restaurant. On a rotunda, outside, the Royal Opera Orchestra, a large, well-balanced ensemble played the overture of the opera Vignon under the leadership of a capable conductor. We felt a sense of pride in being members of a new symphony orchestra which would have the obligation of upholding the fine tradition created by the body we had just heard perform so artistically.

Our concert hall had been an architectural gem: square, well-conceived, and with a 2,500 seat capacity. In this hall which was known throughout the land, an orchestra of about 40 members had been giving performances. The crowds attending its daily concerts had grown to such proportions that the building could not possibly hold them all and the owner decided to enlarge the establishment. The architect designed an adjoining rectangular hall with the same seating capacity as the original. A favorable consequence of this now double hall—double orchestra—was that the engagement of a considerable number of additional artists was required. The newly-expanded symphony orchestra set out to establish the necessary balance for this unorthodox hall in its first rehearsal, a task any conductor might well look upon as an important test of his ability. Our old conductor—he was then 65 and had always conducted the lighter genre of music—was not able to accomplish this task alone. Very soon we found we had to teach him to attain decent performances of the large symphonic literature vs. him teaching us.

We performed two concerts daily, one from 3–5 o'clock in the afternoon and another from 8-10 o'clock in the evening. Both the concerts and daily rehearsals were really nerve-racking sessions as they were extremely prolonged affairs. Our conductor made wrong conceptions numerous times which was highly annoying and contrary to our traditional experience. Oelze and I frequently had lengthy talks concerning these working conditions and I told him that already, after only one month of the exhausting near-torture, I was so worn out I couldn't stand it much longer, having always been one who gives his all to the playing of worthwhile music. He laughed at me and said, "You restless fellow! You want to see new shores again, hmm?"

A few days afterward, I received a letter from my old desk mate in Norrköping who had taken an engagement with a conductor he had been with before his sojourn there. He asked me to help him find a pianist for their small but fine little orchestra in Sundsvall, located in North Sweden. With one bold stroke I marked Stockholm off my list and again decided to embark upon new roads. My reply to him you might easily guess;

I wrote him that it would be a great pleasure for me to agree to his request—I would be their pianist. He soon sent a telegram, informing me of my acceptance. I then asked for a discharge from my present position which I was granted.

Refreshed after my languorous steamship voyage to Sundsvall, the center of Sweden's wood-pulp industry, and breathing deeply its vigorous northern air, I went to the hotel where my friend had his lodging. He took me to the conductor's room which was located in the same building. We were cordially received and I signed a contract binding me to the remainder of the orchestra's engagement in Sundsvall; it was subject to renewal in Finland where the orchestra was scheduled to play after the expiration of the Sundsvall contract.

Our so-called orchestra here was actually a miniature of the real thing. The conductor, a fine Jewish musician, played his first violin part, standing, facing the public. He was a man of about 60, a well-bred gentleman, popular and well-known in those northern countries—Sweden, Norway, and Finland. The rest of the orchestra consisted of my friend, the Concertmaster, an excellent flutist, a double-bass player and me. We were a very small group, but musically quite effective and we played in a tastefully-designed dining room in the hotel where I had first gone, the city's largest.

We also all lived therein. As part of our lodging arrangement, we had the free use of the dining room's facilities, could eat and drink what we wanted as a part of our salary, which was large enough to satisfy every want and also enabled each of us to save a nice amount besides. In fact, we all felt we were living like kings, (especially in light of these generous culinary privileges!)

Our leader discovered my ability as cellist and he often put a number on our program in which I played the cello. The Concertmaster, who in later years became director of a Dresden conservatory, occasionally played a violin concerto or other concert pieces to which I always performed the necessary accompaniment with great pleasure.

Life was pleasantly enriched by invitations now and then to the homes of music lovers. Through these acquaintances, some of which led to real friendships, I was fortunate to be recommended to persons who wished to take music lessons. These pupils, who apparently enjoyed their studies, subsequently brought others. As a result, inside of two months, every free moment of my time was filled with teaching both piano and violin; even harmony and composition students asked for time which I could not grant them.

The end of the orchestra's engagement neared and the conductor offered me the renewal of my contract for the Finnish season. By now I had so many pupils I had easily earned enough to make my way in Sundsvall without outside income, especially as their number was still increasing. Therefore, I told the conductor of my reluctance to leave this field of useful activity. I thanked him for his kind offer but said I had decided to stay where I was.

Now I was once more sole master of my destiny.

I made a strict schedule for my daily work (a procedure which I still employ fruitfully today) and settled down to the life of an instructor.

The mode of living in a city of the northern latitude like Sundsvall is, in wintertime, more complicated in nature than in a temperate zone. Artificial light is necessary till about noon and again after approximately 3:00 p.m. Nights are luminous to such a degree that skating is an exquisite pleasure. Skiing is also possible then, but does not flourish to the same extent as during early to mid-afternoon. The surrounding terrain of Sundsvall being quite hilly, an excellent opportunity is offered for pursuing this exhilarating sport.

As there were only a few bathrooms in town at the time of which I speak, bathing was enjoyed at the ocean in summertime and in winter in the steam-bathhouse. This was a building containing a number of cell-like rooms. It was situated at the shore with a large fence enclosing it and included a sizable portion of the ocean. It was equipped with large wooden benches built against the walls. A person would enter one of these heated rooms in Adam's costume. A man would come in with big pails of steaming hot water, and dump them on one of the slightly-inclined benches. A cloud of steam would arise and fill the entire room. You lay down upon the bench and a thoroughly hot steam-bath was your reward, accompanied by a lot of perspiration (of course). Then you carried your limp body, still as naked as before, outside to the ice-covered sea water and took a quick dip, followed, if you could accomplish it, by a few swimming strokes, whereupon you left your luxurious bath in a hurry, red-hued as a well-cooked lobster. All this was a glorious experience for those who could physically stand it.

Anyone who did not take advantage of this lauded manner of bathing had the opportunity to use the well-established, privately-owned bathhouses instead. These were richly furnished with large, sunken bathtubs, tile steps descending down into them. In each of these establishments were typically found several middle-aged matrons who brushed and massaged every customer thoroughly. I took full advantage of all these facilities in order to keep my body in good physical condition.

As I became more well-known as a teacher, I made a number of influential acquaintances who, when they learned I had been a conductor, began to call me "Musikdirectören Hammer." After one month of residence in my new little house, I was asked by the owner of the hotel's restaurant (where our orchestra had played before) to engage and then conduct a similar ensemble for his establishment. I was willing and eager to accept his offer with the stipulation that I be allowed to enlarge the orchestra slightly to augment its tonal quality. He consented and I retained a very well-recommended pianist, a former school teacher from Dresden, an excellent cellist from Berlin, pupil of Klengel, professor at the Leipzig Conservatory, two good violinists, a violist, a double-bass player, a flutist, a Swedish trumpet player, and a 75 year-old trombonist who was the finest I had ever heard. All of these musicians arrived in Sundsvall on schedule and, in the first rehearsal, each of them readily proved I had chosen well.

The fine, reserved gentleman who was our pianist—a philosopher, meritorious musician, and highly gifted improviser—was a great asset to our ensemble. Twice or thrice a week I set aside a special spot on our program for him alone. I would ask the audience to give me a theme for the pianist to improvise upon. He accomplished this task with ease and rich modulation. One evening, one of the guests suggested the beautiful Värmlands-visa, one of the most exquisite folksongs on earth [6]. It is harmonically quite complicated, however this pianist handled it masterfully; I wish I could have recorded it, but of course at that time recording was not yet born. One old music teacher who was almost a permanent fixture there, somewhat exhilarated by the famously treacherous Swedish punch, evidently could not believe a human brain could conceive such an inspiring piece of music, and cried aloud, "That's a lie!" to the embarrassment of the whole audience, who applauded the talented pianist vociferously.

Towards the end of our engagement, I received a letter from a city north of Sundsvall, Hernösand, inviting us to give a series of concerts there. It was springtime and to travel there was judged to be rather hazardous at that time of year so it was not easy to find two sled owners who were willing to carry us. The day we departed, it was sunny but, luckily, still cold. We had to cross several streams, amongst them the broad Indalselven. Sometimes our sleds would have to travel through several feet of water on the streams; though the top ice had melted, the lower part was still thick enough to carry our weight. Some of the passengers, especially the cellist, uttered their complaints loudly about these perilous maneuvers. Nevertheless, still in one piece, we arrived in Hernösand where we were welcomed by our friendly host.

Our performances seemed to be very much appreciated and the audiences were more vehement in their applause than any I had hitherto met in Sweden. Our return to Sundsvall was accomplished via a ferryboat which was swift in comparison with our earlier method of travel. A renewed engagement of short duration followed in the same hotel in which we had played before.

A guide had told me of a Laplanders' camp a few miles from Sundsvall. I happened to mention it to the

---

[6] There is a particularly beautiful version of this song on You Tube, performed by Monica Zetterlund.

orchestra and they became eager to visit the camp. You, dear reader, are perhaps aware of some of the reindeer's habits. This animal, like our buffalo, constantly searches for virgin feeding grounds. Summer pastures are abundant in Lapland, but with the onset of winter he must move southward. He is forced to dig under the snow to find the scarce moss which is his only food at that time of year. And the nomad Laplander must subsequently follow these animals, his only source of nourishment. It is rare to see a herd of reindeer as far south as Sundsvall. We knew that and decided to take advantage of this unique occasion and the guide told us he would be glad to help.

A period of sharp spring frost following a bout of strong north winds had once more solidified the upper crust of ice, but it was broken into such rugged contours that our skating was exhausting. We all carried shotguns so we could notify the rest of the group by shooting three times in case of a mishap. Proceeding towards the camp upon this treacherous ocean of ice was difficult to say the least, and the distance to the camp was much farther than the guide had assumed. After three hours of this extremely laborious and fatiguing skating, we finally reached the camp where we were received kindly by the herders. Both men and women were dressed alike, the difference in the sexes discernible only by their headgear, with the men wearing red while the women wore blue, high pyramid-shaped head covers. Both women and men smoked pipes and spoke distorted Swedish. From their camp they came once a week to Sundsvall to sell reindeer meat.

While exploring the camp, I entered a small tent and was stormed by a snarling dog flashing his dangerous teeth, and I would undoubtedly have been left with a bleeding leg if his master had not bent and grabbed his neck with lightning-like swiftness within inches of him making a successful attack. A few forcefully uttered words in the Lapland tongue sent the somewhat subdued but still snarling dog back to his lair. Returning to the center of the encampment, tin cups of scalding coffee mellowed by reindeer milk were offered us, accompanied by a dark bread spread with a fine-tasting cheese made from reindeer milk. Our thanks for this friendly hospitality were expressed through the presentation of our own sandwiches which were happily accepted by our hosts in return. As we had to perform back in Sundsvall that same evening, our stay with the sympathetic Laplanders had to be of shorter duration than we had anticipated. After a hearty "på återseende" ("till we meet again"), we started homeward.

The trip back, however, offered greater difficulties than the way thither. It was 3 o'clock in the afternoon when we left and three hours of tiring skating awaited us. As noted earlier, the condition of the ice was abominable. The occasional snowfalls with attendant winds piling the snow in uneven heaps, followed by thawing and then a frost, had not left any free surfaces for decent skating. After the three hours' travel that morning, it was a hard task for all of us to make our trek home in good time—although everyone was an accomplished skater—and you will comprehend how easy it was for our little company to be broken up as a result.

After two hours of this laborious skating, one of the straps on my right skate broke. I was forced to remove my gloves; my fingers became icy cold and I had great difficulty repairing the damage. When I finished that task I saw that all my companions had passed me and discovered I had been left behind, solo. It was difficult for me to see through the gathering dusky semi-darkness, but even with the growing dimness surrounding me, the flickering of the multitude of luminous stars lent me sufficient light to spy a large island to my left. At the west end of this five-mile long island, an approximately 200' wide branch of the Baltic Sea separates it from another smaller island. This is called Devil's Island because of the treacherous arms of the sea enfolding it. I was not too disturbed when I saw the larger island, but suddenly, just as I found myself skating straight towards it, I heard three shots ring out, the signal of distress. With one more vigorous stroke forward I halted and looked around me. There, directly in front of me at a distance of about four feet, was the open sea.

For the second time in my life I had miraculously escaped death. The explanation of this near-disaster was obvious. Instead of traveling straight towards Sundsvall I had deviated, however slightly, to the left, whereupon I was soon at the edge of the sinister ocean. After this shocking experience it seemed as though new energy flooded my body and I struck out vigorously back in the right direction and soon came to the stopping place of my comrades, who, upon nearing town, had missed me and fired three shots to inform me of their whereabouts. Happily, once again joined "in toto," we arrived in town half an hour before the obligatory performance. We did our best to make it a good one, but in our estimation, we only partially succeeded in our goal that night.

That was to be our last expedition together as our winter engagement soon ended. As the owner of our concert hall was also the proprietor of an exclusive summer resort lying on the far side of a small creek outside Sundsvall, he asked me to engage a larger orchestra for the summer at his resort, which I gladly agreed to do.

I had long nurtured the desire to study in Paris with a great teacher; to my delight this possibility was now approaching nearer and nearer. When I had begun my short teaching career in Sundsvall (it had been necessary when I became the conductor of the hotel orchestra to give up my pupils), I had rented a small house, also suitable as a musical studio. I purchased the essential furniture and then began to accumulate capital with which I could someday make my Paris dream a reality. The summer engagement I had just contracted would augment my savings sufficiently for me to finally execute my scheme. Joyfully, I planned for it ahead of time, taking up my French language lessons again in earnest. My two years of life in Sundsvall, despite their daily quantities of professional obligations, skiing, skating, and social life (reduced to a minimum), nevertheless did not lack daily workouts on my fiddle, which was of course the key motive for my plan. I still adhered to a strict schedule such as I had begun to use during my teaching period. I not only had enough extra time to learn French but even started a diary in which each day's events were carefully noted. This diary, which eventually was to fill two large volumes, was faithfully filled with details of my daily life for 15 years. Somewhere along the road of my extensive travels, it was lost though. If it were still at hand, it might not only stretch this narrative's dimensions but also, dear reader, probably challenge your patience!

During the interlude between the winter and summer seasons, Tivadar Nachéz [7] came to Sundsvall accompanied by his impresario, and the appearance of this great Hungarian violinist created such a furor that he was spurred to perform five consecutive, sold-out concerts. I became acquainted with him at one of these concerts. He was actually three years my elder, but 10 years my senior in savoir-faire and witty repartee. We enjoyed many fine hours spent together. His valuable suggestions and counsel concerning my violin playing and musical pursuits in general were a great help to my ongoing studies. Nachéz continued his exceedingly successful worldwide concert tours and composed numerous estimable works. When I last heard of him he had made his home in beautiful Santa Barbara, California.

The days lengthened into a promising summer and soon the newly-engaged members of the orchestra arrived and I changed my domicile to a place nearer the resort. The orchestra was again made up of well-trained, capable artists, and once more they were mostly of German descent (as not many good Swedish musicians were available at that time.) We were all well-satisfied with prevailing conditions, and this group of individuals was transformed into a fine ensemble in short order. On the first of June we gave our first concert, gaining fine moral support from an attentive, appreciative audience. The manifestations of the public's approval of the orchestra's performances served to encourage us in our efforts to continue to justify their sentiments.

Oh! If only we had known that this enchanting period would be followed by such a disastrous event.

Midsommardagen was drawing near. This festival is held on the longest day of the sun, June 21st—almost 24 hours. But it might actually be said this day is the shortest in the year for almost every citizen of this merriment-loving country for festivity is everywhere that day, in the smallest hamlet as well as the largest cities. Everyone, rich and poor, partakes in the general mood of exhilaration. No one goes to bed that night as I mentioned before, and all high school and university alumni wear their white graduation caps for these 24 hours, regardless of their ages.

I was very eager to make it possible for the orchestra personnel to also have a part in this unique feast day so I asked an acquaintance who owned several good-sized row boats if he could lend me two of them for an outing to a charming little lake which lay a few miles above the resort where the narrow canal was bounded between Sundsvall proper and the summer resort. He magnanimously complied. Substantial food supplies were stored in the boats and, directly after that evening's concert, we began our Midsommardagen celebration. The metamorphosis from musicians to sailors was enthusiastically accomplished and it was about 3 a.m. when we arrived at the picturesque scene. We then spent several idyllic hours on the carpet of moss under the glossy green foliage of the birches, reveling in the sight of the glorious spring wildflowers which surrounded us along with the water lilies crowding the lake. Orpheus wooed us into blissful contentment as if to give us enough beauty to compensate a little for the ugly tragedy which would soon touch us all. After some exploration of the surroundings, we prepared our boats and hurriedly navigated homeward, mindful of our impending afternoon concert.

The next morning, after a productive rehearsal, I asked the tympani player to go with me to the seashore to take a refreshing dip as he was a good swimmer. We had hardly gone a few hundred steps when a fire alarm reached our ears. It seemed to come from behind us. The next moment fire engines and ladder wagons rushed by.

[7] **Tivadar Nachéz** (1 May 1859 – 29 May 1930) was a Hungarian violinist and composer for violin who had an international career, and made his home in London. He was born in Budapest, where he studied under Sabathiel, the leader of the Budapest Opera's orchestra. Franz Liszt heard one of these performances and gave his approval. Then he studied under Joseph Joachim in Berlin, and afterwards with Léonard in Paris. He performed at the foundation of the Bayreuth Festspielhaus and made a debut in Hamburg in 1881. His first appearance in England was at the Crystal Palace on 9 April 1881, and after that he gave continuous concerts and made tours in England and elsewhere. (A. Eaglefield-Hull [Ed] A Dictionary of Modern Music and Musicians; G.B. Shaw Music in London 1890-1894)

Both of us turned back and followed them. Great was our surprise when we saw the reason for the excitement: a house spewing flames which would soon destroy it, and this was the property of our boat lender [8]. Some barrels of oil occupying a large space in the backyard near the house also erupted in fire, augmenting the infernal blaze. Fearing further expansion of the flames due to the strong windstorm afoot, the firemen spread heavy canvas sheets over the walls of the house next to the one burning and sprayed them. But while the firemen employed untiring energy in striving to confine the conflagration, the sparks from the burning building were carried by the high winds to the roof of a church situated upon a nearby hill, and it ignited with a brilliant flash, creating a more threatening problem yet. It must be mentioned here that all of the town's buildings were all wooden structures except the city hall, post office, one bank building, and some of the warehouses along the shore. A messenger then came running to inform the fire chief that the sparks from the burning church upon the hill had ignited a lumberyard at the other side of the town. As the efforts of the fire brigade to save the houses next to the already ruined property of my friend seemed in vain, they left hurriedly to try to arrest the fire at the lumberyard. But by now nothing could possibly be done to hold the ever-increasing ravaging flames in check.

My companion and I ran to the center of the town where everything seemed to be ablaze. The fire had just attacked the home of the city's foremost newspaper, Sundsvall Tidning. I knew the old gentleman editor who occupied the upper floor with his unmarried daughter. At the moment we were entering the building to help save what we could, he and his daughter came rushing out. He shouted crazily, "Let it burn! Let it burn!" Nevertheless, we hastened upstairs into a bedroom, tore a big sheet off the bed and filled it with precious volumes from the editor's library. The heat mounted steadily and the roof, burning fiercely, was threatening to collapse. Quickly, we grabbed the sheet with its heavy cargo and made our hurried retreat, hauling it to the shore of the canal where people were piling their belongings. Turning back, we saw a number of individuals hurrying out of a jewelry store, carrying watches, precious stones, and other valuables. I halted as many as I could and took their loot forcibly from them by necessity. I asked my friend to deposit it on the shore next to the other rescued articles and watch over it all. Then I entered the jewelry store and remained there as self-appointed guard. After a while, breathless from running, the jeweler entered. When he saw me on duty he dropped onto a chair, relieved, and gratefully exclaimed, "Thank you! Thank you! When you marry, I will present the rings to you." (You will see how he later fulfilled this promise.)

I left the jewelers and told my companion he could also leave his post now. I asked him to come with me to my city house to see if any damage had been done. Neither of us had any idea what enormous dimensions this tragic holocaust had assumed. Arriving at the center of the city, we saw the city hall and its wooden sections being consumed by flames two blocks away (the substantial brick walls remained unharmed). I ran to the building and into the lodge hall where I had been initiated as a member some time ago, cut down the costly brocade curtains with my pocketknife and, opening the window, threw them into the street below. Sadly, I lost my cherished pocketknife on that occasion by leaving it on the windowsill. After this, I turned toward my residence—what did I find? Just a heap of ashes! My furniture, clothes, library of books and music—everything lost. And thoughtlessly, I had never carried any insurance. Only now was I aware of the immensity of the fire. Not only my house, but the entire town was one enormous heap of ashes, and the 12' lampposts lay strewn in the streets, looking like twisted ropes.

I neared the harbor where I beheld crowds of citizens rushing from several large ravaged warehouses on the shore, loaded down with sacks of flour, cheeses, and boxes containing goods of all kinds. I came upon one man rolling a huge four-foot wheel of cheese through the street. Bakeries, still burning, were looted, windows smashed with fists and the contents divided among the hungry bystanders. There was no other food left in the town. A continuous stream of frantic, panic-stricken people came running to the shore, boarded the anchored ships and placed their salvaged possessions on the decks without even caring that these ships would soon be bound for new ports.

Panic, panic and more panic abounded. Everything was in complete turmoil.

Sundsvall after the fire

[8] In 1888 on June 25th, strong wind and dry conditions contributed to two city fires in Sweden on the same day. In Sundsvall, 9,000 people became homeless in just 9 hours. In the wake of the fire the city was looted on what was left. When evening came on 25 June, the city of Sundsvall was a smoking ruin. (Kenneth Fahlberg, Sundsvall Fire – The News That ST Missed, Sundsvall Tidning [In Swedish])

As all the city's authorities were also victims of the disaster, there was no one to restore even a semblance of order. Sauve qui peux (French: "save yourself if you can") was the prevailing theme. I became deeply depressed witnessing this terrible human helplessness in the face of the most devastating of circumstances and pitied the thousands of sufferers who had lost most of their earthly possessions and must start their lives anew—including me.

Soon hundreds of large tents and loads of provisions began to arrive from the Swedish government and the Red Cross. They also took steps to prevent more stealing by self-serving evildoers. Miraculously, in this calamity of such tremendous proportions, only four lives were lost of the city's 25,000 inhabitants.

I finally went to my summer abode which was situated upon the other side of the canal along with only a few widely disbursed houses and the resort. They had been located upwind from the fire so these were consequently the only buildings spared. I found my living room cluttered with unfamiliar articles—money boxes, clothes, trunks, etc. The room looked like the salesroom of a second-hand store or pawnshop. Where all these goods had come from was a question only the following days could disclose.

The tympanist, whom I had lost in the city, found me at my house and asked me to come and meet with the members of the orchestra who had assembled in the rehearsal hall to discuss the problem of our immediate future. There I found a greatly agitated group of musicians awaiting me. The double-bass player, the oldest of them, advocated their return to Germany. My suggestion for them to stay in Sweden and tour the country as the orchestra from the stricken city of Sundsvall fell on deaf ears. My fine, sympathetic artists who only two days ago had enjoyed the loveliness of a midsummer night's celebration together now chose to disband—and all of us were forced to find new means of subsistence.

I returned home and took stock of my situation. Paris had now completely receded from view, although my decision to someday study there did not waver. However, now I must find lucrative employment…as soon as possible.

I wrote to a resort proprietor I had met in Örebro where I had spent a few days before entering my Stockholm position, following my engagement in Norrköping. He offered me a two weeks' contract as conductor of his orchestra. At the same time I had written to Malmö, the southernmost city in Sweden, where a Mr. Christian I had heard of, a Copenhagen theater director, planned to begin a tour with his group's production of Sullivan's Mikado. As his enterprise was to start two days after the termination of my engagement in Örebro, I was very happy to receive notice of my appointment as conductor of the Mikado.

Chapter 8   Örebro & Goodbyes

During my short stay in Örebro, I made the acquaintance of a refined, elderly gentleman, the head cashier of the town bank. His name was Carl Årman and our friendship was destined to last until his death. He was a former civil engineer who had built several Swedish railroads and was the finest amateur pianist I was ever to meet—he could play any piece of music set before him and played Chopin as Chopin should be played.

Örebro Castle

He had learned the bassoon at the age of 58, enabling him to fill a place in the orchestra of which he was the founder. Chamber music was his special love. One of the professors at the college in Örebro, a capable cellist as well as a good flute player, accompanied me in spending many pleasure-filled hours with him, playing piano trios without regard to time—all three of us dwelling in an enraptured state in the enchanting realm of music.

Carl asked me to come back to Örebro after my engagement with the Mikado troupe and I promised to give his suggestion serious consideration. I liked this nice, clean town—its wide streets, the beautiful old city hall, built during the Gothic period, the large Lutheran church, the fine opera house, the ancient castle, home of the governor and provincial offices, and the excellent bathhouse on the shore of the small river next to the town.

Leaving my two new friends and many interesting acquaintances behind, I started for Malmö to enter a new field—opera conducting. There I was greeted by Mr. Christian and his wife, cultured people and seemingly a well-matched couple. This first favorable impression became one of permanence and to my satisfaction led us into an abiding friendship.

Mr. and Mrs. Christian played the two main parts in the opera. They were both gifted, seasoned artists, meriting the aesthetic and financial rewards their enterprise deserved. My labors in conducting a good orchestra, well-trained soloists and chorus, was a continuous source of gratification to me. Our successful performances in Sweden and Norway (often twice a day) kept us all in good spirits and we were committed to holding our standard to a continuously high level. But the constant traveling with its frequent annoyances—new quarters every day, rehearsals to get acquainted with, the acoustic properties of each concert hall, etc.—took up so much time that it was impossible for me to follow my strong inclination to explore the towns and cities where we made our appearances.

My acquaintance with Mr. and Mrs. Christian had ripened into a beautiful friendship (I have always drawn a strict line between the connotations of the words acquaintance and friendship), and they soon bade me come to their home in Copenhagen to enjoy a short vacation when our strenuous schedule was over—an enticing invitation to be sure! I gladly accepted their generous offer and, after our last performance in Malmö, we embarked from its fine harbor for Denmark. An hour's pleasant crossing brought us to that country's capital just at the opening of a huge World's Fair[9]. We drove through the venerable old city of the Danish kings to its pleasant outskirts where the Christian's charming home was located, his parents having been its faithful guardians during their absence. Mr. Christian, Sr. and his wife were the same sort of lovable people as their son and daughter-in-law, receiving us warmly, with everything

[9] **The Nordic Exhibition of Industry, Agriculture, and Art of 1888** was an exhibition that aimed to feature the best of art, industry, and agriculture from the five Nordic countries. It was a joint-venture between 29 organizations and institutions, with the weight on the private side, represented foremost by the Association of Copenhagen Industrialists. The exhibition was located in Copenhagen, Denmark and was visited by 1.3 million people. (Revolvy.com)

prepared for a hearty homecoming feast.

For two weeks, I remained in these congenial surroundings, my hosts doing everything to make each of these days full and interesting for me. Several times we visited the vast World Exposition where I saw, among other new inventions, a piano equipped with a complicated mechanism making it possible for a composer's improvisations to be reproduced on paper as they were created. Another innovation was a piano with a threefold, slanted keyboard something like that of a large organ. You could draw one finger down this keyboard and produce a half-tone scale, a feat impossible on a common piano. We also went to the Thorvaldsen Museum—an immense edifice erected by the people to glorify the name of this giant of sculpture, painting, and science—a noble Danish tribute to a great man as this block-long building contains almost all of his works. We also enjoyed some fruitful visits to the Royal Opera House with its excellent orchestra, conductor, and singers, and to the Tivoli, where a splendid concert orchestra under capable conductorship gave free, well-patronized concerts daily, and these outings completed the remainder of my, alas, all-too-short stay. The desire to tell you more of Copenhagen is great, but would swell this account unnecessarily. You can find in any library all the information you might be eager to acquire about this gay city and the fine little self-sustaining country of Denmark. On with my story!

Several letters from my friend Carl Årman had urged me to come to Örebro after the conclusion of the tour to take over the leadership of the symphony orchestra and the chorus of the Philomela Society. He also told me he had the names of a number of individuals who wished to take lessons with me and it appeared to be a sound prospect. Reluctantly leaving the hospitable Christian home, I again crossed the narrow channel to Malmö and departed to Örebro by train.

My friend Carl met me at the station and took me to a well-situated home-like apartment which had an atmosphere I immediately appreciated. In the studio was a huge "Kachelofen," a stove about eight feet high and four feet wide, built of white square tiles. The common practice was to start a big fire in it at daybreak. When the entire stove was hot, you closed the damper and the tiles kept the heat for 12-15 hours. The room was made cozy by an agreeably even temperature and I loved to stand in front of this massive stove and warm my backside.

In the next few days the pupils Carl had gathered for me began to arrive, and a very busy chapter was initiated. Within a week thereafter the first orchestra rehearsal took place.

There were a few adjustments necessary, but the spirit of the players was of the highest order and, according to an appropriate adage: "Where there is a will, there is a way," the first chorus rehearsal of the Philomela Society was held just a few days later. Here was assembled a wonderful assortment of typically Swedish voices, strangely unique given their certain Northern metallic quality. Such a lively eagerness and perfect discipline reigned among the members that I anticipated a gratifying season ahead for us all.

My work schedule was a crowded one and to balance it with some recreation was not an easy task. I looked for a long stay in Örebro, especially as I expected to use it as a springboard to Paris. Therefore, I spent hours devising a working system. I had to lengthen my days' waking hours to make the schedule doable. I was anxious to indulge in my beloved sports—horseback riding, hunting, swimming, and skating. I had to steal two early morning hours and one noon hour to accomplish this. My agenda was subsequently: horseback riding 5:00–7:00 a.m. (a horse stable was nearby), breakfast and lessons 8:00–11:00 a.m., swimming or skating 11:00–12:00, lunch, lessons 1:00–6:00 p.m., supper, and orchestra, choral rehearsals, or ensemble playing with my friends in the evenings. At free moments, I grabbed some study time for violin and theory and, on Sundays, enjoyed group riding or hunting. My hunting companion was always a young forester whose sister was organist for our large Lutheran church.

The chorus rehearsals for which Carl was our excellent accompanist always ended with a social gathering, tea and some "doppa" (the Swedish name for delicious little cakes which are always dunked). I remember well the tall, gracious daughter of the Governor who was the hostess for the tea. Sometimes my friend would, with his fascinating rhythm, play a waltz or a polka, to which everyone would whip onto his feet and into an impromptu dance. The work of the chorus improved immensely and their performances in several of our opera productions, including Faust, Carmen, and Martha, elevated them to a high peak by music lovers. The Stockholm Royal Opera singers who often lent us soloists praised their work, even claiming they were better than the Royal Opera chorus.

One ardent member of our Philomela chorus, Mrs. Borch, the possessor of a ringing, well-trained soprano voice, asked me to give her son, Gaston[10], cello lessons. He was by no means a diligent student, although certainly talented. Later, they moved back to their original Parisian home, where I learned he studied with Delsart and Masseret. The tale goes that Masseret became engaged to Mrs. Borch (thus providing Gaston's opportunity to study with the master). Liszt, however, persuaded Massenet to break his engagement to this poor, albeit good-looking singer and find himself a wealthy woman instead, which Massenet finally did. Most of Gaston's life was spent in the United States where he became well-known as a composer of "shorts" used in movie theaters during the silent picture era.

A rather frustrating circumstance took place about this time.

I was asked to arrange a concert in Örebro's largest church for Sweden's crown prince (and later King), who was then Colonel-Commander of the Nerike hussar regiment. To mark this occasion, I programmed a very seldom-performed quartet for four trombones by Beethoven in addition to some violin and organ soli. The programs were already printed when I learned that not one music store was able to furnish the music as it appeared it was out of circulation. What to do? Use ingenuity! I composed a work for four trombones in the style of Ludwig van Beethoven. What presumptuousness! But who knew? My effort at imitating the great composer I hope finds your forgiveness, dear reader, as it served its purpose satisfactorily—though you may say that makes my impertinence all the worse. Nevertheless, at the time, I seemed to have found this fraudulence quite necessary.

The summer months were passed in a very agreeable manner. I was again engaged to conduct the resort orchestra. All my pupils were on vacation and I took prompt advantage of this liberation to enjoy more swimming and hunting. On Sundays, I would go with a group of young ladies and gentlemen for horseback excursions through the countryside. We would start early in the morning and, after hours of invigorating riding, eat lunch at one of the nearby cozy inns.

Though a few had their own horses, most of us used cavalry horses. You will wonder, why cavalry horses? Here is the answer. The Swedish soldier at that time served only about six weeks a year. The rest of the time the horses were kept on farms, but the farmers were not allowed to employ the animals for heavy duties. They could use them only for pulling light wagons carrying not more than 150 pounds of freight. A farmer keeping

[10] **Gaston Borch** played the cello. He studied for three years with Massenet in France, with Jules Delsart and also at the Valand School of Fine Arts in Sweden. His mother, Emma Hennequin, a pianist and soprano, was a friend and pupil of Jules Massenet. (Who's Who is Music and Drama 1914, H. P. Hannaford and Hines; The Art of Music, Mason, Daniel G.; Axel Törneman, 1880-1925 Vid pianot, Signerad.)

a horse or horses was credited with the cost involved in lieu of taxes paid to the state. Some of the farmers, not deriving any actual profit from taking care of the horses, began to lend them to responsible people for care and food, with the stipulation that the animals only be used for riding. A number of us young people took advantage of these circumstances and I always kept one of the horses stabled for my recreational use.

Sunday evenings were always spent either in Dr. Wallstrom's (the cellist and flutist I mentioned earlier) or Carl Årmand's home, where we enthusiastically played chamber music together. These sittings would usually last till midnight or later.

With all this activity, I still did not forget my studies—the promise of the future was my ever-present guiding light. As I never pleasured in carousing, drinking and living with the in-crowd, I confined most of my social life to the company of older people, carefully choosing those whose intelligence and wisdom would help satisfy my educational needs.

The pleasant summer with its light-hearted days neared its conclusion and I began to make plans for an interesting winter season. I decided on three operas: Faust, Carmen, and Der Freischütz. As Philomela's 50th year jubilee was at hand, I composed a Marcia Triumphale and a chorus for this festivity, with lyrics provided by one of the members of the Society. The orchestra rehearsals started in October and progressed successfully. So did the chorus rehearsals for Haydn's Creation.

My studio occupied the second story of a corner building facing the canal. Across the water lived a dear friend of mine, Lieutenant Nettelblad and his family consisting of his Danish wife and two children. He owned a large home with a fine tennis court. He also had a small boat in which he would often cross the narrow canal, whistling in a familiar way which I always recognized as it floated up to my studio. He would row me across for an afternoon of tennis and dinner in the evening. I came to love this fine, hospitable family and I corresponded with them for many years after I left Örebro.

The time I passed in this pleasant community, surrounded by a supportive public and understanding, genial friends—among them the mayor who was become like a father to me—left with me with a dear and abiding memory, and it was there that I made my application for Swedish citizenship. The Governor of Närke, Mr. Bergstrom, through whom it was granted, was elevated to the position of Minister of State by the King a few years later. He became widely renowned as the Bismarck of Sweden.

November brought with it freezing temperatures with consequent ice forming atop the river and the canal which extended from the river. Every morning at 11 o'clock I would step down to the well-groomed canal ice to enjoy some invigorating skating. After a few days, some young lady members of the chorus joined me. Their number was augmented by some of the feminine participants in our horseback outings. I was the only representative of my sex; what other man had time to skate in the mornings? And this lone bachelor seemed to be the attraction. Soon the envious young men of the town began to call the young ladies "the Hammer girls." The girls, upon hearing this characterization, suddenly ceased skating, and I saw them no more—I was once again nearly the only person on the ice in the mornings. But after a week, all the "Hammer girls" were back again, although we were never free of the teasing.

The 50th anniversary jubilee of Philomela, a festival enthusiastically supported by the music-loving population of Örebro and surrounding territory, was the "point de culmination" of my career in Sweden. My Marcia Triumphale and the chorus composed for the occasion were performed at the first concert with Haydn's Creation and Gounod's opera, Faust, performed the second day. Two sold-out houses and milestone profits were the just rewards for our careful preparation and resulting artistic performances. Everyone seemed to feel that music in Örebro had reached a height previously unattained.

Our regular piano trio get-togethers knitted the friendship of us three musicians closer and closer. Sometimes we played other compositions with additional people, one of whom, a mill owner, was a versatile performer—a violinist, double-bass player, cornetist, and flutist, all in one. In expanding our skills, we once played the septet of Beethoven in which I played the French horn part!

My violin work was never neglected though, and sometimes, in a few rare moments of leisure, I would ponder over my present, more-than-satisfactory position alongside my still-strong longing to round out my music studies in Paris. I must once more mention the fact that the well-trained musician in Sweden occupies a fine social standing.

My 26th birthday was near and the Latin tempus fugit ("time flies") assumed a really threatening meaning for me at that point as I was acquainted with a number of wealthy girls and was convinced I could have married one of them and settled down to a peaceful domestic life. But every time I considered the possibility, the "up and on" internal prodding to further myself in the music field retained its upper hand in my mind—I wanted to study French music. I assumed two or three years in Paris should enable me to complete my education and give me the right to aspire to higher positions yet, as a first-class conductorship was still my foremost aim. So I decided to stay where I was through the coming summer in order to increase my store of capital.

Winter again morphed into the verdant spring and then summer. The second season of summer concerts under my direction began and nearly all the members of the previous year's orchestra occupied their old posts. One of them, a youthful violinist named Kaempfert, had made astounding progress during the year, so I changed him from the second violin section to a place in the first violins. In free moments, using some music paper he always carried in his violin case, he would scribble down string quartets with amazing speed—not masterworks, but good, light compositions. More about him later.

That summer's engagement augmented my savings enough to make my Paris plan a reality. You, dear reader, who have followed the recital of my two year's stay in Örebro's congenial milieu, might at this point have a reproach in the form of a few harsh sentences for me. It might be along the lines of, "Why didn't you have enough business sense to stay where you found such a fruitful field for your work?" Or, "How could you ever have decided to leave your splendid friends?" Some of you, however, might judge differently, and be that as it may, my explanation is this: Though I was near my 27th birthday, my philosophy of life at that time was still very youthful. In fact, until I was at least 50, I was a boy, living from day to day without much intense thinking except in reflecting upon the goal from my earliest childhood—that I wanted to be a musician. It was a most specific desire now, and outweighed any of the more vague ones—vague primarily because my days were too crowded to allow for any deep assessment of their importance. Thus my decision was made: on to Paris!

My friends and acquaintances made my 27th birthday an unforgettable event. My dear forester-hunting friend, ending his 27th year on the same day as I, was one of the participants in these festivities. Many expressions of disappointment concerning my leaving were uttered by all, somewhat dampening the gay spirit. In the coming two weeks I was to dedicate myself to recreation before my much-lauded departure, having promised several families I'd befriended who owned country estates that I would pay them a visit before leaving Sweden. So I packed everything I was to take on to Paris in order to leave as soon as I returned to Örebro from these visits to my friends' homes. The evening before my departure for the country, an intimate circle of my friends gathered for a farewell supper. Our hearts were heavy. It was an evening of many sincere wishes for my artistic and physical welfare. Downcast, I returned home to spend my last night, nearly sleepless, in my beloved studio.

Early the next morning, seated on the cavalry horse that one of my riding companions had so generously lent me, I was on my way. It was the dawn of one of those crystal-clear, indescribably colorful autumn days of Sweden's which lifts one's soul in praise and gratitude. The pure air filled my lungs, and, notwithstanding my previous sorrowful evening, I felt like bursting into a jubilant song as I rode along in the gentle sunshine. The family of one of my younger pupils was number one on my list and the distance to their estate was a four hours' ride.

Those four hours gave me ample opportunity to get acquainted with my new traveling companion. A cavalry horse is, according to my experience, a queer fellow. He will be dutiful only in company he likes. This one was chestnut and a lively, almost neurotic example of horsiness. The simplest disturbance of his equanimity, which happened often, made him jump and fret. Coming to a bridge, he absolutely refused to cross it. Talking softly and patting him availed nothing. Despairing, I turned him around and barked "Back out!" Over the bridge he went, backwards. Surprisingly enough, my steed, no less dripping wet than his mount, arrived at our destination without broken leg or neck.

Hospitality is a prominent characteristic of that sparsely settled country's population and a cordial welcome was tendered me upon my arrival. I was advised to quickly change my clothes and partake of the lunch which was in preparation, an invitation that was sweet music. With dispatch, I showered and dressed, entering the quiet, elegantly-arranged dining room where, upon a large table, a sumptuous lunch awaited me. An exquisite selection of smörges dainties and platters filled with diverse meats adorned the immaculate white tablecloth. No need to urge the starved horseman to satisfy his healthy appetite!

My hosts were Mr. and Mrs. Nylander—aristocrats like almost all owners of large estates in Sweden. Their only child was my pupil, a handsome boy of eight, the image of his beautiful mother. A lively conversation lasted throughout our lunch, interspersed with questions concerning my riding adventures and my future plans. Soon, Mr. Nylander said there were a number of tasks waiting for him to do before dinnertime. We rose and I said my "tack för mat och dryck," ("thank you for the food and drink"), shaking hands with my host and hostess, a formality one must never forget to perform after being a guest at a meal in Sweden.

Mr. Nylander escorted me to the courtyard and proudly gave me a tour of his stables, barns, the smokehouse, and a building in which hundreds of foot-wide discs of knäckebrö, or what Americans call rye crisp, with holes in the centers, were hung on long horizontal poles like pearls are strung on a thread. Knåckebrö is the bread primarily eaten by country people in Sweden. It is baked only twice a year as it keeps its good quality ad infinitum. As we turned back to the house, my little pupil met us and told his father he wished to take me crawfishing. Mr. Nylander said, "Certainly, if our guest would like to." I said I would and the boy guided me to an outbuilding which was filled with farming implements, taking from a big box approximately 30 small nets about 10" across with long strings attached at their centers.

We carried them to a nearby creek where a manservant awaited us. He had a box containing many tiny pieces of sparrow meat. The boy took one of the pieces and tied it to the middle of the net. With a long stick he pushed the baited net to the bottom of the creek. I helped him, and every few feet we dropped a net until all 30 were deposited. We went back along the creek to the first net, lifted it out with the stick and there was a crawfish, busily munching the bait, our unwitting prisoner. Many times we went up and down our trap-trail and had just counted 62 crawfish in our big basket when a messenger came calling us to dinner. We were received at the house with a clammer of congratulations for our afternoon's work.

At dinner we conversed animatedly as the pros and cons of country life were being discussed. There was a tall crystal bowl in the center of the table filled with cherry compote, completing the ornamental design of the tabletop's arrangement. As it was a little bit in my way, I attempted to move it, but instead of lifting it, I inadvertently pushed it due to its unexpected weight. The table was an extended one and I hit the slightly raised place where the leaves came together. The elegant vessel tumbled, spreading its contents all over the snowy white tablecloth. Quel horreur! In response, my hostess conducted herself like the perfect lady she was. Seeing my wordless embarrassment, she said, "It was my fault. I should not have placed the bowl so insecurely."

"Madame, my clumsiness is inexcusable," I said, mortified. They tried to console me, but I felt like a social pariah at this point and decided I had to leave the next morning. Entreaties for me to stay longer were in vain. At dawn of the following day, I regretfully but necessarily carried out my resolve and departed.

Passing through peaceful meadows and timberland, I was soon to see a dear old friend again. He was an enthusiastic music apostle who did not mind driving 20 miles in any wintry weather to attend the Örebro Symphony Orchestra rehearsals where he performed in the violoncello section, despite being 75 years of age. Certain beautiful passages in compositions would affect him so deeply that tears would run down his cheeks. He was very grieved by my decision to leave Örebro and immediately invited me to his country home for a visit and a moose-hunt before my departure. At sunup this morning when I had left my pupil's family, my amiable host had been on horseback at my side, guiding me to the boundary of his extensive property consisting of large, well-cultivated fields and majestic pinewoods. At the end of our ride he gave me directions for the course to my friend's home, expressing once more his regret about my hasty leave-taking. I bid farewell and set out alone again, horse and rider in tune and enjoying comradeship, hastening to meet my beloved friend.

His was a somewhat smaller estate, a cozy, tranquil dwelling. He and his wife were the exemplification of a truly happy marriage—two bodies with one soul; lovely people they were. He and I went on a moose-hunting trip, found lots and lots of tracks, but no moose. Three days were passed in their idyllic surroundings followed by a sad goodbye to my dear friend and his sweet, charming little wife, closing this never-to-be-forgotten interval in the chapters of my life.

The next morning found me on the road to my last promised visit. This was the most lengthy ride of my vacation. This friend, of Norwegian descent, was the owner of one of the largest estates in the province. He had about 40,000 acres which were also known as the best moose-hunting territory. Axel Borg, the renowned moose painter, one of my intimate Örebro friends, had invited me a year ago to an outing at the Norwegian's estate. There, we had been entertained royally for a week. When we left I was urged to repeat my visit again and, when the landowner learned I was soon to go to Paris (a metropolis he knew well), he asked if the days before my departure could not be the time to fulfill this invitation.

Embarking toward this destination, my horse was extremely frisky on the long trip, cavorting, bucking, and champing at his bit. I gave him the reins and let him run to his heart's content, enjoying it as much as he did. Though we had to cover a considerable distance, my desire to relish the multicolored fall season's splendor caused me to slow him down to a comfortable trot. My thoughtful hosts of the past days had supplied me with an abundant lunch and my horse, Rosinante, with his oats ration. We ate at noon by the waters of a sweetly murmuring brook, then resumed our ride for another three hours.

Finally we arrived, both of us tired and bespattered, and were greeted by a group of excited dogs. We entered the courtyard in a decidedly less than brisk tempo. My friend appeared, calling the yelping dogs to order in a loud voice, and shouted a hearty salutation to me. Horse and rider were shown to their respective quarters and, in a short time, I looked presentable again and went down to the imposing, gracefully-furnished salon.

The two ladies of the house were there—the beautiful, doll-like wife of my friend and her lady-in-attendance. They offered me a refreshing drink and we chatted amiably until the butler announced, "Dinner est servie!"—and what a dinner! The main dish was young moose steak, a little strong-fibered but tasty, which directed our conversation to Axel Borg, who passed the moose-hunting season here every year, giftedly capturing this majestic animal on his canvases. I learned that one year the King of Italy hunted and shot a moose on this estate and bought one of Axel's marvelous paintings of this other royal individual, the King of the Nordland woods.

After our repast, my interest was aroused by a little fig tree, heavy with fruit, growing in a container in the living room. Sweden's climate was too severe for this tree so no one had figs there, but these people had let their house shelter one. Inquiring about it, I was told nobody liked the fruit.

"When I was in Italy," I said, "I visited the fig country where I ate great quantities of the delicious fruit, preferring it above any other."

"Are ours ripe?" my hostess asked me.

"They are ripe as soon as they are soft," I replied, then picking one and tasting it. "Yes, they are fully ripe."

"It is always a great pleasure to us to make our guests feel our home is their home," my hostess said, "so do as if this were your own fig tree and eat all you like. The memory of having picked ripe figs in the high north might be a means of directing your thoughts back to our home in time to come."

And so it is. Every time I eat figs in sunny California, my thoughts fly back to my hospitable Norwegian friends in Sweden.

The next day my friend took me on a tour of his grounds. I was impressed by it all, especially a large greenhouse, taken care of by an expert gardener. A variety of ripe grapes, several rare fruit trees, and many kinds of lovely flowers filled it to capacity. In the wagon houses were several pleasure vehicles, both open and closed ones. One of these, a dandy light four-wheeled Wagonette, drew my special attention. I thought how nice it would be to put it behind my horse and sit upon a wagon seat instead of a saddle for a change, the horse in front of me versus under me. With this thought in mind I asked my host for the privilege of using this Wagonette for a little tryout. He said he would be pleased to grant my wish.

My now well-rested horse was a little skittish when the groom put the fine, shining harness on him, but he soon calmed down and seemed eager to proceed. A little cluck of my tongue and off we went in a light trot. What joy! Driving along, high atop my comfortable seat through stately pinewoods. My delight was to be short lived. For some reason, the unruly spirit of my horse suddenly exploded. Wildly, he ran off the road and down an embankment. The quick lurch of the wagon threw me off the seat, but luckily I glided straight down. I was imprisoned in the narrow space between the horse's hind hooves and the wagon tongue. Trying to keep my senses as his heavy hooves barely missed me, I spoke as calmly as I could to the horse. It was utterly difficult for me to trot along at this pace. Fortunately, I kept the reins in my hands and tightened my hold on them and finally brought my runaway to a stop. Whew! What an adventure! Laboriously, I managed to mount the embankment back to the road, a still-nervous horse in front of me. Coming to a large, open, and luckily flat field, my steed then made another attempt at running away, once more leaving the road in a violent dash over the field. But this time I was prepared and able to check him. Incensed by his ornery behavior, I drove homeward, keeping him at a strict, well-controlled trot. Not one more of these adventures for me!

The next few days we spent hunting successfully, shooting partridge, orre, and tjäder (all three birds belong to the species of the Gallinaceous. Some have been transplanted to this country where they seem to prosper.)

The tocsin (bell) sounded and the vacation's enchantment suddenly belonged to the past as my fretting horse and I departed, the kindest wishes and a cheerful "på återseende" ('see you later") ringing in our ears. My horse was not different from the rest of his kind—they all seem to be aware of their traveling homeward. He was apparently so eager to go, go, go, hastily shortening time and distance, that I had to restrain him, being the one of our pair who possessed enough savoir faire to successfully assert control.

I arrived in Örebro late at night, left the horse at his stable, and asked the owner to take care of transporting my luggage to the canal boat I was to board early the next morning for Stockholm. I had no inclination to take a second farewell of anyone except dear old Carl Årman whom I had advised of the time of my departure. I thought I noticed the glistening of a tear in Carl's eye when we shook hands, and mine were no drier. We thanked each other once more for the harmonious hours we had passed together, expressing the hope that the future would prove gracious enough to allow us to see each other again.

The steamer for Stockholm took the unique route over the Mälaren Lake, a fascinating excursion toward the country's capital, the 24 hours' travel taking us through scenic canals. At the many locks, where the boat had to be lowered or lifted into the caissons, the passengers had time to leave the boat before it entered these chambers and take a leisurely walk through an attractive countryside and on to the next lock. No traveler in Sweden should forget to put the trip to the Mälaren on their agenda. The entrance to this, Sweden's largest lake, is altogether captivating. It is somewhat like the Baltic Sea entrance to Stockholm, where, as I mentioned before, a thousand small islands form a thrilling vista, and this lake is also dotted with islets. The exit from the lake into Stockholm is very picturesque with Mariahissen in the background. This is a 200' high elevator, probably the oldest on earth. During my engagement in Stockholm I often used this easy means of climbing the densely populated hill Maria.

Once in Stockholm I spent a pleasant day, full of reminiscences, and enjoyed a splendid performance of La Boheme at the Royal Opera House. After a night's refreshing sleep at the Grand Hotel, I boarded a boat moored nearby and made the trip to Lübeck. From there, I departed by rail to Paris, eager to hasten to the city of which I had long dreamt.

Chapter 9   City of My Dreams: Paris, 1890

Friends in Sweden had given me the address of a pensione (what one might call a refined boarding house) on the Rue Vaneau so there I went when I arrived. I was soon to be exceedingly grateful to my friends for suggesting this pensione which was owned by an elderly couple who were aided in its upkeep by their married son and a bevy of accommodating servants, for after a short period I came to feel completely at home in its congenial atmosphere of friendly, well-educated people of various nationalities.

One constant inhabitant was a count, a former officer of the French fleet, who was a welcome guest of Napoleon the Third at court. The food we were served was above reproach and at dinner every male guest was given "une caraffe du vin" (a quart of wine); the ladies "une demi-carafon" (a half-quart). Here then, a new life in a strange country began its course onward…

Though my eagerness to start work immediately was strong, it was conquered by the wish to see something of this grandiose city first. So I set out to explore, following the method I had successfully used in other capital cities. This was my system. I would pounce (literally pounce) onto any bus that happened along. They were cumbersome two-story vehicles with two big Percheron (draft) horses delivering the motive power, except on steep streets like Rue Montmartre where three horses were usually employed. These buses were generally extremely full and would hardly stop for additional passengers. The driver was in front on the second story and, whenever possible, I tried to sit behind him so I could ask questions about the sights along our route. After that I was more at ease in the city's labyrinth-like streets.

When I was through playing sightseer, I carefully considered my next move. It was my firm decision to choose the best teachers available so I did some inquiring. I learned the foremost violin teacher of that epoch was M.P.J. Marsick [11], the teacher of Henri Marteau, Thibaud, and Kreisler, as well as the most outstanding teacher of the singer Mme. Viardot-Garcia [12].

As I also wanted to study philosophy, I chose Anatole France [13].

The first visit I paid to the famous violin teacher and professor was at the Conservatoire de Paris (founded in 1795). He was a lively little gentleman of cordial manner and I duly played for him. Of course, beforehand, I made sure he knew about my last few study-less days and assured him of my eagerness to follow his seasoned counsel. His price for lessons was steep. However, hours were arranged and, filled with a mixture of hope and doubt about continuing the necessary expenses for very long, I returned home.

[11] **Martin Pierre Joseph Marsick** (9 March 1847 in Jupille-sur-Meuse – 21 October 1924 in Paris), was a Belgian violin player, composer and teacher. (Weir, Albert Ernest, Macmillan Encyclopedia of Music and Musicians, Vol. 2.) His violin was made by Antonio Stradivari in 1705 and has since become known as the Ex Marsick Stradivarius. In 1854, seven-year old Marsick was admitted to the Royal Conservatory of Music in Liege (in other words, the Liege Conservatory.) He studied violin with a very obscure teacher named Desire Heynberg and graduated in 1864. Brahms was about 31 years old at the time. Marsick then continued his studies in Brussels with Hubert Leonard. Later still (1868) he went to Paris – which he made his home from that time forward - to study with Joseph Lambert Massart at the Paris Conservatory. He was 21 years old. Sponsored by the Belgian government, he went to Berlin in 1870 to study privately with Joseph Joachim. In 1871, he founded a string quartet – not an unusual thing to do for recently-graduated violinists. His debut took place in Paris in 1873. He then concertized in Europe and the United States for about 20 years. He was by then playing a Nicolo Amati violin from 1652, given to him by a member of the French nobility. In 1892, Marsick was appointed professor of violin at the Paris conservatory. He was 45 years old. He stayed until 1900. In that year, he left his job, his students, and his wife and did not return until 1903. The woman he lived with during this brief time was married and the situation, which was widely known, created a scandal. It has been said that this incident ruined his career. (www.pronetoviolins.blogspot.com)

[12] **Paulina García Sitches**, also known as **Michelle Pauline Viardot Garcia** (Paris , 18 July 1821 -18 May 1910) was a singer of opera (mezzosoprano) and composer. She was the daughter of the tenor and master of bel canto Manuel Garcia and soprano Joaquina Briones , and sister of diva Maria Malibran and influential baritone and teacher of singing Manuel Vicente García. (Eric Blom ed., Grove's Dictionary of Music and Musicians, 5th Ed. 1954)

[13] **Anatole France**. French novelist and critic. His works have a penetrating irony, reflecting a pervading cynicism in politics and religion. (New Webster's Dictionary and Thesaurus 1972)

The next day, after a few hours of earnest study, I decided to pay a visit to a distant relative, Uncle Richard Hammer, a well-known violinist who lived on Rue Blanche. He was then about 60 and two years before had married a singer with a fine alto voice. She had one daughter, a talented pianist and gifted writer, about 24. Uncle Richard and his family were surprised to see me but received me very graciously. After an enjoyable tea hour and an invitation to repeat my visit, my uncle promised his help in getting some engagements for me in chamber music work for which I expressed my profound gratitude.

The following morning I went to see Mme. Viardot-Garcia, asking her if she would enroll me as one of her pupils. Be it said here that I was the possessor of a passable voice of tenor quality, but my object in taking vocal lessons was not to be a professional singer, but to be qualified to teach, to the musicians who would be members of the orchestras I expected to conduct in the future, especially in terms of better phrasing and making the orchestra sing.

My first lesson at Mme. Viardot-Garcia's studio was something entirely different from what I had expected. Within the first few minutes after my arrival I discovered that Mme. was a woman of explosive temperament. I had just spoken a couple of sentences in French when she gave me an impulsive, vigorous punch in the ribs, exclaiming angrily, "Vous ne parlez pas bien!" ("You do not speak well.") You can imagine my astonishment.

"Before you sing, you must learn to speak right," she explained firmly. In consequence, the following two months I was taught speaking, not singing. After that period the renowned artist's remarkable revelations enabled me to gather that knowledge which, in the coming years, was to contribute greatly to my success.

Uncle Richard meanwhile opened a new source of income to me. The high cost of my lessons added to the necessary living expenses, made a deeper inroad on my capital than I had calculated, therefore his endeavor was highly valued. One day I received a letter from him telling me to come that evening to Count Osmont's home to play viola in a piano quartet. The Count loved music and wished to have us play for him and his sister. A well-known pianist, Mme. Moller, was to play, along with Uncle Richard, Mr. Marx, the former solo-cellist of the Grand Opera (and father of the famous Berth Marx, the accompanist of Sarasate), and me. Arriving in haste at Count Osmont's mansion, I suddenly found that my nose was bleeding. When the butler opened the door I was standing there with my face buried in a handkerchief. I mumbled embarrassedly that I had a nosebleed and the compassionate valet immediately hurried me into another room where we put some cold compresses on my misbehaving breather. Then the Count came in, having evidently heard the commotion, and comfortingly helped to restore my equanimity. We spent a musically and socially rewarding evening together (not to mention the welcome financial aspect). After playing, we sat down to a delicious supper, joined by the Count, a bachelor, and our hostess, his unmarried sister.

This was our first session in the home of two people deeply interested in the finest chamber music. Once a week we played in the Count's home and were always treated like friends of the house. Through these sessions, my funds were increased amply. Soon I was engaged for similar soirees at a young banker's home. He was a talented violinist and played string trios with Liégeois, one of the finest cellists in Paris, and me. To these two sources of substantial income I was happy to begin to add money by giving lessons, acquiring several pupils, among them an apt young Russian from Odessa whose grandmother lived in my pensione.

The lessons with Marsick, one a week, took their natural course, but that course was not to my satisfaction. I worked diligently at my tasks—instead of the one etude stipulated for my next lesson, I always prepared two. After I had played them, Marsick would simply say, "Go on to the next." That was all. This kind of work brought me to near desperation and I had come to the conclusion I must stop my lessons with him when I conceived an idea which might remedy the awkward situation. At the succeeding lesson I asked the maestro to play the prescribed lesson for me. He did with a certain pride and I, watching him carefully, earned my reward in him demonstrating his "know-how" to me as he was certainly not offering the needed guidance verbally. Each time after that, I did the same thing and those demonstrations of his masterful skill were of the greatest fruitfulness for my career-minded purposes.

Being encouraged by progress and the sympathetic attitudes of my teachers and Uncle Richard, I finished my first season's work in Paris, somewhat weary of my strict adherences to the tasking schedule I had set up for myself. A summer sojourn at some small seaside resort seemed to be a good place to relax and gather new strength for another season's work. There I hoped I could once again indulge in some swimming and other water sports, so I told Uncle Richard of my plans. He then told me about a little village, Les Petit Dalles—a picturesque place, a painter's paradise, where hotel accommodations could be obtained for a moderate sum. This sounded like the right place for me so after cheerful "au revoir's" to friends, acquaintances, and the winsome pensione-owners, I lightheartedly climbed aboard a train for northern France.

Les Petit Dalles is located a few miles north of Fècamp, a small city near the point of our famous D-Day invasion, also the home of the monastery in which the renowned and highly praised Benedictine liqueur is crafted. On arriving in Les Petit Dalles, I went directly to its one large hotel which was situated on a narrow street with a four-foot stone wall between it and the Atlantic Ocean. The shoreline was one large jumble of fist-sized stones for its entire length and these were the bane of the bathers at low tide. However, at high tide they were covered entirely and a person could dive into the water from quite near one of the four-by-four dressing rooms located several feet above the ocean. When the water was at low ebb, the section of the beach closest to the ocean was a marvelous solid sand plain which almost compensated for the treacherous rocks above.

Les Petit Dalles is a lucrative fishing territory where the highly-praised and delicate langouste (rock lobsters) breeds, the defenseless cousin of the lobster (he has no shears). The arrival of the fishing boats with their precious cargo was always an event of interest. Discovering the impossibility of an individual buying one of these delicious langoustes—the fishermen were bound by contract to deliver their catch immediately to Parisian firms—was a deeply regretted fact of life locally.

The guests at the hotel were fine convivial people of various nationalities. At mealtime an aristocratic family of four: parents, a little four-year old girl and a boy of six, sat "vis a vis" (face to face) from me. The boy, a handsome, well-behaved little gentleman, was a violin student. His parents apparently heard my daily practicing and asked me to take their son under my musical wing. Next to me at the table sat the Vice-Governor of the province and his wife. He was a man of athletic proportions (a rarity among French gentlemen), she, a buxom lady, able to perform a singular feat in the water which none of us could match: with her fists clenched on the surface near her chin, she would hang completely motionless in deep water, taunting us to imitate her if we could. All the young crowded around her—she was very good-looking—trying to emulate her, but always with the same result; an unavoidable descent into the deeper watery regions. We would reappear, laughing, but disappointed, on the surface, greeted by gleeful re-

Note from Melinda...

[14] Upon trying to find information on this painter, I ran across a website which features this painting signed "J. Poulin" which is listed as "Original Vintage French Impressionist Oil Painting of Cottage on River in Winter." The owner of the website (candlestickinthelibrary.com) estimates it was painted "around the turn of the century (likely a trifle earlier)." I like to think maybe this is the same painter.

marks from the others.

The proprietors of the hotel kept a fine medium-sized donkey and a beautiful little wagon for the guests' use. One day a painter from Paris, Mr. Poulin [14], came to the hotel. I made his acquaintance and guided him on a tour of inspection. He did not find the situation "À son gout" (to his taste) and desired to go to the next village north of Les Petit Dalles, where an aggregation of painters resided every summer. The landlord, knowing of my fondness for the horse tribe, asked me to drive Mr. Poulin to the town.

This artist was a typical taciturn Parisian, an old bachelor with all the adherent peculiarities generally displayed by this genre of the human species. When we caught sight of the little village in question and began to descend a moderately inclined hill, I gave my strong little donkey free rein. He broke into a light trot and the wagon went easily along. Mr. Poulin, in a fit of nervous agitation, screamed at me to modify the tempo. I did so, disgusted with his scarecrow attitude. I mention this little episode only to acquaint you, my reader, with Mr. Poulin, of whom you will hear much more later on.

You might think that most of my time was filled with recreation at this stage. No, it only took—according to my schedule—at the utmost three hours of each day. My work went its usual course with the aid of some strong self-discipline. My progress was not as rapid as before, but of a more thorough nature as I now worked at theory and composition and added something new as I also made a serious study of Abbé Michon's graphology, which was later the source of many a disquieting moment as, at social functions, I was often requested to examine the handwritings of persons present. They thought of it as a novelty but soon discovered they were hearing the truth about themselves, which was not always welcome! I otherwise derived great pleasure from the science.

A gentleman of about 60, a talented miniature painter, took possession of a small room in an annex, installing his studio there. After mentioning in a casual conversation the extreme heat in my upstairs room which was making my violin study more difficult, he suggested I come to his studio and practice while he painted. I expressed my anxiety about disturbing him and he said in reply, "Oh, no, Mr. Hammer, I would love to have you here." So the painter and I formed an industrious pair as each of us was occupied with the careful execution of his own task. Intermittently, he assured me he did better work with my musical accompaniment. In these peaceful hours, I had ample opportunity to prepare a recital program which I intended to give in the hotel's salon.

I had been in Les Petit Dalles for approximately two months when a young Russian gentleman, about my age, arrived at the hotel. At one of our evening gatherings he sat down at the grand piano and played a Chopin nocturne, not only technically correct, but in an exquisitely tasteful style. After his performance, I engaged him in conversation and he expressed the wish to join me in playing chamber music. I was delighted with the prospect, and the next day we played Beethoven's Kreutzer Sonata together. I chose this difficult composition to assure myself of his capacity. He played Beethoven as well as Chopin and his technique was flawless. A natural process led from the acquaintance of two concordant souls to a sympathetic friendship which, I am sorry to say, did not go beyond this vacation period. Alexis was a well-educated, fine example of Russian patrician youth, a nephew of the great Russian poet, Pushkin. However, he was a spoiled young man, having lost his parents to death in his tender years, and finishing his education in the home of indulgent relatives. He studied music with master teachers and was sent to Paris to prepare for a virtuoso career. Unfortunately, he joined a crowd of irresponsible, high-living young French men and women, several of them dope-addicts. The enervating society life of Paris takes a high toll on unsuspecting youth, and many a budding artist is among its victims. Alexis was prone to sink into periods of moroseness—a price almost every serious music student has to pay. He was always urged by his dope-addicted friends to take a dose to combat these recurring attacks.

A new member had joined this bohemian circle of theirs. She was a young lady singer of Alexis's age who had been thwarted in her ambition to attain a high reputation in the world of song. She was a typical French beauty and sarcastic to the extreme. Alexis, who occasionally accompanied her singing, was not only deeply impressed by her reproachless interpretations, but also enraptured by her beauty, and he fell deeply in love with her. His proposals were met with only acid replies as she cruelly taunted him by accusing him of flabbiness—not having the courage to drown his frequent "blues" in the higher regions, as she put it, of a fuller life. These explosive outbursts convinced him of her addiction to the dope habit. After several conversations with her, sadly he also fell prey. All this he explained to me in a moment of mutual confidence.

Alexis's musical ability and his willingness to be my accompanist furthered my plans for the recital and we set its date for the following month. We designated several hours daily for practicing together and faithfully kept to this schedule, arranging an attractive program.

The day of the recital arrived and we were in a small room behind the stage. It was shortly before the time of our entrance into the concert hall when Alexis experienced the approach of one of those faltering, devitalized moments, now so lamentably familiar to him. From his coat pocket he took a small silver case, opened it and removed a surgeon's syringe. From a tiny vial he pumped fluid into the syringe. He opened his sleeve and, with a quick jerk, stuck the needle into his arm. After putting his illicit case back in his pocket again, he whispered, "In a few minutes I'll be ready." Seeing poor, exhausted Alexis stretched out on the settee, my heart was filled with deep compassion. I anxiously waited for the passing of the "few minutes." Not 10 of them had elapsed when he sat up, clear-eyed and brisk, and said, "Let us go!" My astonishment was boundless in witnessing such a rapid change in my friend. He rose and strode energetically out of the wings and onto the stage. The concert was a successful venture, but after its close, Alexis was again the same helpless being. Poor boy! I am glad I did not know before the concert what a short time his vigor would last. A few days later Alexis left Les Petit Dalles, giving me his Paris address, and I gave him mine. We promised to keep in close contact, but we never saw each other again.

The summer season neared its conclusion and I returned to Paris, refreshed and with increased capital. Back in the pensione, my routine followed the old schedule. Uncle Richard's kindly work in promoting me was still enlarging the scope of my professional activity. New pupils demanded my attention, one of them the eight-year old daughter of a famous coutourière of whom I shall speak later. My own lessons with the maestro, who had also just returned from a summer vacation, resumed where we had left off.

My correspondence with Mother had always been very lively, but lately her attitude had become more downbeat. She complained of failing health and other troubles caused by her husband's irresponsible financial manipulations. She told me he was instrumental in getting her to sell their home to a neighbor for only a fraction of its real value. My impotence to help her in her distress weighed upon me. How easily such a knowledge of utter helplessness depresses one! Commiseration is no solace in such moments although I answered

[15] **Carl August Nielsen** (9 June 1865 – 3 October 1931) was a Danish musician, conductor and violinist. Nielsen's songs retain an important place in Danish culture and education. . . while outside Denmark Nielsen is largely thought of as the composer of orchestral music and the opera Maskarade, in his own country he is more of a national symbol. (Niels Krabbe (2012, the Carl Nielsen Edition – Brought to Completion.)

[16] **Edvard Hagerup Grieg** (15 June 1843 – 4 September 1907) was a Norwegian composer and pianist. He is widely considered one of the leading Romantic era composers, and his music is part of the standard classical repertoire worldwide. His use and development of Norwegian folk music in his own compositions put the music of Norway in the international spectrum, as well as helping to develop a national identity, much as Jean Sibelius and Antonín Dvořák did in Finland and Bohemia, respectively. (Daniel M. Grimley, Grieg: Music, Landscape and Norwegian Identity, 2006.)

her message in a consoling tone and expressed my heartfelt wishes—not only for her recovery, but also for better behavior from Gabel. To this letter I received no reply. The sorrowful reason was soon to appear.

One day Carl Nielsen [15] and I became acquainted over lunch in one of Paris's so-called student restaurants—he was later to become conductor of the Royal Opera in Copenhagen, Director of the Royal Conservatory of Music, and a prominent Danish composer. Drinking "une tasse de café au lait," Carl, who was studying violin and composition in Paris on a stipend from the Danish government, said, "I am going to visit Grieg [16], why don't you come along? He likes to have serious young music students around him."

Note from Melinda...

My grandmother, Munna, began giving me piano lessons when I was probably six or seven years old. I remember her telling me the story of Fahta having tea with Edvard Grieg, composer of the music for Henrik Ibsen's play Peer Gynt and I was always fascinated by the title: In the Hall of the Mountain King. Of course, when the British rock group, The Animals, did a take-off of it later, it lost a lot of its thrill.

We went and found the maestro busily at his work, trying out a new song he had just finished, with Mrs. Grieg nearby. He gave us a friendly greeting and then said, "Sit down and keep still!"

We did and witnessed a unique scene. The little composer, with a slight hunchback, sat at the piano and the delicate figure of Mrs. Grieg stood at his side. In a voice of pleasing quality and with an intense interpretation of her beloved husband's eloquent lore, she sang his new song with spirit and feeling. We were fascinated. At the end of the song the master rose and crossed the room.

"Did you like it?" he asked, looking at us intently with his piercing blue eyes.

Our enthusiasm knew no bounds. We expressed our admiration in typical youthful over-abundance. The well-known Norwegian hospitality found expression in Mrs. Grieg then inviting us for some refreshments. The maestro inquired about the progress of our studies and so began a pleasant conversation. We left greatly inspired and we visited the Griegs twice more, listening to other songs sung so warmly by Nina Grieg and accompanied on the piano by her famous husband. These occasions were a subject of our conversation when, after many years,

I visited Carl in Copenhagen where he was then conductor of the Royal Opera and I was on my way to Göteborg (Gothenburg) to conduct that orchestra.

If you live in a world-famous capital like Paris, it will happen that, from time to time, friends or acquaintances from home, who are indulging themselves in a visit to the city, will come to you for counsel and guidance. Here is what happened to me on such an occasion. One day a Swedish couple, acquaintances of mine, arrived at my pensione and rented an apartment there. As I had been a guest at their home several times I was glad to return their hospitality by showing them Paris, taking them to the various places they wished to see and obligingly playing tour guide. One day, after a long morning's sightseeing, we stopped at the popular and excellent Café de l'Opera. The husband was anxious to test the treacherous absinthe as he had heard so much about Parisians drinking it. He asked me to order it for us and I did as requested. Leaving the restaurant, I felt a little wobbly.

Back at the pensione, I excused myself, went to my room and then to bed, nursing a ghastly headache. After missing several meals in the dining room, I was visited by the proprietor of the pensione who asked about the source of my suffering. Being unable to give a truthful answer, I assured my visitor my confinement would not be of long duration. My statement was not justified, however, as I continued to be listless and entirely bereft of energy. I could eat none of the food brought me, only water, which slid sickeningly down into my stomach. After two more days of this steady decline there came a rap at my door. At my "entrez!" a young woman appeared to whom I had spoken casually at the dinner table a few times. She was a physician from Amsterdam.

"What a mess!" she exclaimed as she appraised the disorderly condition of my room in one keen glance. It struck me vividly that she should focus on the cleanliness of the room before the examination of the patient. After she had finished her quick tidying up she felt my pulse and noted a high fever. She prescribed a soothing remedy and promised she would come again the next morning with another doctor. So it happened. As my sickness was an internal one and this Dr. du Saar was an eye specialist, she did not want to take the responsibility for the diagnosis, and thus brought with her the next day Dr. Delbet, the medicus of the Interior Department of France and a famous pathologist (a street in Paris, Rue Delbet, is named for him). Dr. Delbet, a fine, learned old gentleman with a distinguished white beard, examined me thoroughly. Diagnosis: jaundice and flu combined. He explained to me that the absinthe had caused the former and the second was due to a prevailing epidemic. After this, the kind gentleman came every day with the lady doctor for two full weeks. He was a compassionate man and seemed to take a great interest in me.

He then proposed that I join the orchestra in Vichy to be near the source of the healing waters there. He was like a father to me and I came to love him. Even when I was completely cured, he asked me to come daily to him. I did for a while, but felt embarrassed to take up his valuable consultation time, the antechamber always being crowded with patients. When I once met him in the street, he took my arm and we walked together for several blocks. He gently asked me about my studies and freely dispensed philosophical principles about life in this wicked city. His generosity was infinite. He never sent me a bill, and after my insistence that he do so, he answered, "A good doctor should practice two maxims. Those for whom a medical bill would be a burden too heavy to bear should be served without charge; the wealthy patients should be charged insofar as to balance the budget." After this memorable meeting, I never saw the dear Dr. Delbet again; but the other doctor continued my treatment, though in another direction.

I was still very weak and, because Dr. du Saar felt I should have some healthy sunshine and fresh air, she kindly passed her free hours with me in the green beauty of a nearby park. The recuperative period through which I passed was accelerated greatly by the interesting conversations we shared together. She spoke German and French fluently and was a highly intelligent woman. Sitting with me upon a bench in the park, Place des Invalides, she told me about her difficulties in entering the Amsterdam University [17].

"Since my early youth I cherished the thought of

[17] **Marie Du Saar** [was] in 1890 the first female doctoral student in Amsterdam." (Professors Of The City - The Athenaeum Illustre and the University of Amsterdam, 1632-1960 by Peter Jan Knegtmans, page 262). 'What a spectacle such a Herr Fraulein' "After all, not Groningen, but Amsterdam has the honor in 1888-1889, the first assistant in the person of Marie C. du Saar have appointed . . . Marie du Saar was assistant to the device for Ooglijders of the Amsterdam University." (Nieuwe deelgenoten in de wetenschap by Inge de Wilde)

[18] **Louis de Wecker** (Wecker in German Ludwig and Ludwig von Wecker) Louis de Wecker (1832-1906) was a famous French ophthalmologist and was considered one of the greatest ophthalmologists of his time with worldwide reputation. He introduced many innovative surgical techniques such as his method for iridotomy, "anterior sclerotomy," and the so-called "de Wecker's capsular advancement" for the treatment of strabismus. (Hirschberg J. Die Augenheilkunde in der Neuaeit. Band I-II. Leipzig, Germany: Engelmann; 1915-1918)

being a physician. I liked school and study. After passing a teacher's examination, I was eager to enter the University to study medicine. However, I soon learned this path was closed to me as only men were admitted. But it happened that the school offered a stipend to an outstanding student who wished to study medicine and it was to be given to the person having the highest rating in an examination. I decided to try for it. Thirty-seven aspirants competed but I was the happy victor. When I appeared before the judges, their president said 'Don't you know, Miss du Saar, that this is a men's university? No ladies are admitted.'

"I opened my application and said, 'Mr. President, gentlemen: in this paper it says nothing of only men applying for this stipend. It says it will be given to 'a Hollander.' Am I not a Hollander?' After a discussion of many pros and cons, I was duly admitted, the first woman student at the Amsterdam University."

Permit me to give an explanatory sidelight. Dr. du Saar was born in the capital of Friesland, Leeuwarden. Friesland is the only part of Holland which was not conquered by Spain in the Eighty Years' War. The people of Friesland are rightly proud of this fact and she was a true adherent to this pride. Therefore, her confident question, "Am I not a Hollander?"

Several days in succession she took my arm and guided me on short walks to put the sustaining power back in my legs. The conversations we engaged in during these walks gave me a deep insight into her character. She was completing a tour of Europe, having visited the clinics of the eminent oculists of that period. Now in Paris, she attended and observed the famous Baron de Wecker's [18] clinic. Her earnest endeavor to learn the newest methods of her profession and to increase her knowledge aroused my admiration. She was now in the process of the selection of paraphernalia necessary to fully equip her office in Amsterdam, and would soon be ready to leave for her home.

In her manner toward me I had begun to detect more than the ordinary concern of a doctor for her patient. I saw as we became better friends that she was falling in love with me. Though I did not feel the same for her, I began to think of asking her to marry me. Her character was one of superior integrity, practicality, intellect, and rare sensibility, and I highly esteemed these qualities. We got on well together so, after much thoughtful, careful weighing of the merits of my life here in Paris with its good financial prospects versus those of a home with the companionship of a fine woman, I chose the latter. My proposal was very matter-of-fact and so was her acceptance. We discussed everything in very practical, unemotional tones. I had to continue my present work in Paris so she left, both of us promising we would keep up a constant correspondence. (In Europe at that time it was customary for a couple to be engaged for at least a year before marrying.)

Chapter 10   Armand's Rat

After the departure of my fiancée, I plunged earnestly back into my strenuous tasks. About this time, I entered a class in philosophy at the Sorbonne led by Anatole France. Through that master's wise teachings my life became richer; I looked about me with more curiosity than ever before and my views were significantly broadened. Uncle Richard, ever my patient mentor, encouraged me in my work and continued to find new sources of income for me. He advised me to give a recital in putting my name before the public so as to possibly attract more pupils. I decided to follow his counsel and informed my teacher of this idea. He gave my plan warm approval and I commenced preparing my program.

Two friends of mine were President and Secretary of the École Laïque, a forerunner of the schools later established following the legal separation of school and church. They offered me the position of Professor de Musique at the institution. I gladly accepted this offer, but on a trial basis.

My department consisted of several branches and my duties were manifold. In addition to instructing classes in string, woodwind, and brass instruments as well as voice and piano, I taught a course in the theory of music and also conducted the chorus. Quite a quota! I took great pride in the fact the weekly inspection of this small "conservatoire de musique"-was always satisfactory. The pupils were all just out of elementary school and not easy to handle, but most of them were eager to acquire knowledge and succeed. After a few weeks of serious effort to mold my sections into some homogeneity, my struggle was rewarded with success—but the work was so taxing and took up so much of my time that I felt my own studies had lost momentum as a result. As I had assured my friends that I would take over the position only on a trial basis, I told them I now saw the difficulties involved in serving two masters at once and therefore asked them to look for another professor to fill my place.

Another bit of synchronicity occurred a few days after my release from this professorship, just as I was beginning to resume my intense daily studies. During one of my visits to his home, Uncle Richard told me his stepdaughter intended to give a piano recital at the Pleyel Hall (Salle Pleyel). He asked me if I would lend a helping hand in playing the double-bass part in the small orchestra for the Saint Saëns Piano Concerto in G minor as Uncle Richard knew I was capable of handling all the string instruments. As I was in the midst of practicing diligently for my own debut in Paris, I did not relish the idea of abusing my left hand on the giant strings of the bass. But, grateful for his continuing kind assistance, I nevertheless agreed.

The recital was crowned with success; but oh, my poor left hand! And here comes Maestro Ravina (at that time a well-known composer of semi-popular music) to ask me if I would like to play the double-bass in a concert he was going to give soon! I gave him a quiet but firmly negative reply. Now back to serious study for my own recital!

At least three months in advance I rented La Salle d'Agriculture for the program. Many times in my long life important events have almost overlapped, one threatening the potentiality of the other—and this was one of those times. A few days before the planned recital, I received a letter from Uncle Karl informing me of my dear mother's death and burial. Deep grief and regret at not having been at her bedside overwhelmed me and my first thought was to postpone my plans. But calmer thinking after the initial shock subdued this vacillating inclination and I recovered at least a degree of mental composure, deciding it would be best not to change the performance date after all. I sent a letter to Gabel expressing my astonishment that I was not told earlier of my mother's grave illness and then I tried to put balm on my torn nerves by practicing harder than ever.

At last the day of the recital arrived. Before the beginning of the concert, Les Agents des Pevres at the cashier's desk asked their donation for the poor of Paris. But even with all the expenses involved, the recital was artistically and financially a satisfying affair. Maestro Marsick, Uncle Richard, his family and friends, almost all the residents of the pensione, as well as my own friends, pupils and their families were all there plus many other music lovers resulting in a large, attentive audience.

One day, I was surprised to receive a letter from Mr. Poulin, the irascible painter who was introduced to you in Les Petite Dalles. He invited me to his studio on Rue Montmartre, so as soon as I had time, I went to see him. Arriving there, I found him vigorously putting the last brush dabs on a large and luminous landscape painting. When he had finished with his brushes, he took down one of the costly mandolins which hung on the walls of his studio and stood strumming it before his canvas. He told me of a peculiar habit of his; after finishing a painting he liked to salute his work with music. He knew of my métier and therefore I was not astonished when he asked me to take another mandolin and play a duet with him. As the stringing of the mandolin is the same as the violin, it was not difficult for me—so together we tinkered away, paying homage to his latest creation. That done, he asked me to dine with him in the Restaurant Swedeis on Boulevard Montmartre close to his home. On becoming better acquainted, I found him a real gentleman, very well-mannered. He also seemed to wish for a closer friendship with me and invited me to dinner once a week thereafter. We enjoyed one another's company, engaging in philosophical skirmishes, mandolin tinkering, and always-sumptuous French fare.

My fiancée and I had exchanged numerous letters by this time, each full of the latest happenings and reports on our respective progress. We discussed plans for the future, she always expressing her sentiments so adequately that my interest in my own undertakings became less avid. With spring approaching, she asked me in one of her letters to come to Amsterdam at the close of the winter season to get acquainted with her friends and her work, proposing I stay at the home of two elderly lady friends of hers. One of them was a well-known painter of flowers [19] and an intimate friend of the fine painter of Holland interiors, Betsy Repelius [20], in whose house my fiancée lived plus also had her offices. I gladly accepted her offer and made plans accordingly.

One evening, while visiting a friend's home, I was given an invitation from the Swedish Embassy in Paris to attend the "Ball des Officiers de la Garison de Paris." This was to be an elaborate affair held in the Grand Opera House. The seats in the main hall were removed and the floor waxed to a sparkling sheen for dancing. The chairs in the foyer were also removed and it was prepared to accommodate more dancers yet. The music in the main hall was directed by the composer Waldteufel with a 200-man orchestra at his command. In the foyer, guests danced to the music of the famous band of the Gardes Républicains. The reception committee consisted of about twenty richly-dressed and brilliantly decorated generals of the French army. They stood on

[19] Quite probably **Marie Heineken**, niece of the famous brewer Gerard Adriaan Heineken.

[20] **Johanna Elisabeth Repelius**, known as Betsy (born Amsterdam 31-1-1848 - gest. Amsterdam 23-1-1921), paintings and watercolors. Betsy  Repelius dedicated herself to painting and watercolor genre performances and made interiors with figures in particular. During her academic period, Repelius became a member of Arti et Amicitiae in 1875. From 1878 she exhibited her work, including at the annual exhibitions of Living Masters. In addition, Repelius exhibited abroad, such as Paris, Munich and St. Petersburg. Her work received some good reviews and was distinguished several times. Up to four times, the artist even received a gold medal. (Hanna Klarenbeek, Repelius, Johanna Elisabeth, in Digitale Vrouwenlexicon van Nederland.)

Grand Opera House, Paris

both sides of the imposing white marble staircase, greeting every visitor. What a splendid array! The opulent setting was filled to capacity by an aristocratic, bejeweled mass of humanity the whole of which formed a fascinating, glittering fete indeed. I tried to dance several times but it was impossible. The crowd was so dense that you could not execute a single ordinary dance step, instead all was one gigantic congested shuffle.

The real excitement came at midnight when the Bataille des Fleurs—Battle of the Flowers—began. This was opened by the ladies in the several tiers of boxes above the main floor who threw thousands of small violet bouquets down upon the large crowd below who then responded by bombarding the attacking ladies with their own flowers, and the atmosphere quickly became oversaturated with the sweet scent of the "viola odorata."—a unique spectacle, this semi-annual "battle" with flowers.

In 1892, after nearly two years of residence at the Pensione Rue Vaneau, I moved to the Quartier de l'Élysées near the Arc de Triomphe. The reason for this was I had recently met a baroness who told me her sister's son was a "high I.Q.'r" but seemingly an incurable introvert, and she thought I might be a suitable teacher for him. I said I would be happy to give him lessons so she recommended me to his mother and I was soon engaged. The baroness's sister and her boy, Armand, 17 and just graduated from high school, lived in Avenue de Courcelles Parc Monceau. It was much too far from the pensione, so I moved. My new employer's home was only a few minutes' walk from my new address.

I was to be the young man's mentor and music teacher for three weekly lessons. On these three days I was always their dinner guest as well. The most extraordinary happening occurred on these days. Armand was an undisciplined, absolutely disobedient boy. His mother was a very tender-hearted, easily discouraged, wealthy widow of middle-age who was never able to control her unruly son's outbursts of temper.

He was the owner of a big white rat. This animal's domain was the entire luxuriously furnished apartment. It was an exceedingly tame and rather beautiful creature—white as snow with bright pink eyes. Armand used to put it in his sleeve from where it scrambled up and came out of his shirt and onto his shoulder. He would then bring it to the dinner table and let it run free, feeding it tidbits.

One day the butler brought in a big beef roast. After carving it, he left the room, and we then served ourselves while Armand put the rat upon the table. The animal, attracted by the delicious aroma of the meat, went at it, attacked it and flung pieces of the roast over the immaculate tablecloth! Needless to say, Madame and I refrained from finishing our dinner. Armand just laughed. His mother simply sighed and said, "Oh, Armann-n-d."

After a month of serious work with him, he changed his attitude somewhat. He not only was a good scholar, he seemed to have some respect for me in due course and appeared to listen to my counsel—the rat ever-present. Thankfully, he did not put it on the table again at dinnertime but still insisted on keeping it with him otherwise. When it came time for my departure to Holland, I had to accede to Madame Gerard's request to continue my mentorship with Armand when I returned to Paris.

Light of heart with my expectations at high tide, I took to the road again towards a strange new land. It is a pleasant sojourn from Paris to Amsterdam—from gay Paris through the sober, peaceful countryside, passing from Normandy to the densely-populated country of Belgium, and through its two prominent cities, Brussels and Antwerp—then from Antwerp to Holland and on to its capital, The Hague (called s-Gravenhage in Holland). After traversing miles and miles of multicolored fields of flowers, I finally arrived at the railroad station of Amsterdam which was built by Pierre Cuypers, the renowned architect of the Rijks Museum which contains Rembrandt's priceless painting, The Nightwatch.

Marie, my betrothed, was waiting at the station to greet me. We drove in a taxi to the home in which she stayed through this, the only city in the world built below sea level. I was introduced to Miss Repelius, the owner of the large, richly and artistically furnished house, although she received me rather coolly. Her attitude is easily understood given her anticipation that my fiancée would always live with her as she showed without reserve a deep gratitude to the doctor who had saved her life at one time.

After a light lunch, Marie took me to the home of the two elderly sisters who were kind enough to grant me hospitality during my vacation. Their home was situated at the edge of the beautiful, well-planned Vondel Park. However, I was with them very little as my fiancée took pains to make my time in Amsterdam agreeable and instructive. During my visit, the serious problems of life, its material and philosophical aspects, our occupations and social positions were broadly discussed. To my profound regret I discovered how little earnest thought I had hitherto given to most of these weighty subjects. My nearly 30 years on earth still found me just a big boy. My interests were sparked through these discussions though, and my respect for this sincerely loving lady, my future wife, deepened.

Tempus fugit ("time flies")! It did now to a greater degree than I had ever experienced before; and now the time had come for me to leave. We had decided to marry in the coming fall, a few months hence. To the two ladies who had taken such fine care of me I expressed my sincere thanks and the hope that I would see them again upon my return. Marie, who had made this two-week vacation a real pleasure, accompanied me to the railroad station. We parted, promising each other to correspond regularly as I waved adieu and entered my wagon du lit bound for Paris.

Entrée triumphale a Paris! How familiar yet how fresh everything looked to me upon my return. But as it was the beginning of the summer season, I came home to discover an unfortunate shrinking of the number of my pupils plus the cessation of the lucrative chamber music performances with Uncle Richard, both of which upset my financial calculations.

On my visit to Armand Gerard's home shortly after my arrival back in Paris, Madame Gerard told me of her decision to pass the summer in her family home in Sweden and asked me to take care of Armand, making the Gerard home my own during her absence. Gladly accepting her invitation, this timely proposition would change my financial status very favorably. A week later, Madame Gerard departed for Sweden and I transported myself and my paraphernalia to Avenue de Courcelles.

Madame Gerard, a wealthy lady, had left a large sum at my disposal to cover all necessities, but life with Armand was nevertheless a complicated affair. He and I were the only two occupants of the spacious home. An elderly man attended to the apartment but did not live there, so we two had to take care of our meals. Armand liked his new liberty, but oh! what a complex situation to live within close proximity to him continually.

His music studies interested him greatly and reading philosophy and studying mathematics were his intellectual food. This new existence though, changing his mode of living entirely, carried with it some complications which proved very difficult for this extremely stubborn boy to overcome. He was so extraordinarily shy with strangers that he had never gone to a restaurant, even with his mother. The most laborious of my educational duties then was to accustom this unruly creature to eating in such public places. Among other challenges, no food was of satisfactory quality for him. I could never understand the boy. Stoicism in its extreme form dominated all his actions. Often if I would ask him to do something he decided he did not like he would just grunt under his breath—and then do precisely what he wanted instead.

The white rat, which still reigned supreme in its comfortable nest in the underpart of a costly settee, made the environs of his home a shambles. He gnawed the precious heavy damask draperies to tatters and put everything topsy-turvy like a puppy might. The damage he did amounted to thousands of francs. I loathed this beautiful yet demonic creature. One day as I was walking near the Gare Saint-Lazare, I noticed a shoemaker's establishment in a basement (shoemakers in Paris are generally located in basements, and through a window you can clearly see them busily working away). It was then an idea struck me. I went into the shop and asked the shoemaker if he would like to adopt a white rat to put into his window as an attraction. I knew most of them liked to have some kind of animal in their showcases. He said he would. One day while Armand was out I caught the little white hellion and took it to the man who promised to take good care of it. Can you imagine

Armand's wrath when he came home and vainly searched for his four-footed friend? I weathered the ensuing storm and told him frankly of the comfortable relocation of the culprit (although naturally not the precise location). A long sulking period followed, but thankfully he did not procure another rat!

At about this time a notable event occurred: the 1,000th performance of the opera Faust, with its aging composer present, Gounod. A real affair of "pomp and circumstance." It is a peculiar habit of the Grand Opera's management to continue to bill a work almost ad infinitum. Sometimes I saw operas reach their 150th or 200th consecutive performances. Thanks to Armand's perseverance we obtained two tickets to Faust and were happily able to attend this truly national festival.

The proverbial Parisian heat made its unpleasant appearance about this time and I wrote to Madame Gerard suggesting a short stay in Baden-Baden for Armand and me. She gave her consent.

A surprise awaited me one day as I was seriously occupied with repairing my sinking violin technique. A timid knock sounded at my door. When I called "entrez!" Max Kaemfert entered. You will remember him as the young man who advanced so quickly in artistic efficiency in my orchestra in Sweden and who dashed off quartets by the dozens. Knowing his usual financial circumstances, I could not help but voice my surprise to discover him in Paris. He, carefree, as youth has a habit of being, said, "I knew you were here and would be able to help me."

"My dear Max," I said. "Paris is not as easily conquered as Örebro."

I gave him a few "carta de interés" and sent him to Dancla, professor of violin at the Paris Conservatoire. After his visit to Dancla he returned telling me jubilantly of his cordial reception at the master's studio and of his unusual and generous offer of free instruction. Knowing Max's musical ability and fine character I gladly helped him in his efforts to earn some money and was overjoyed when, at a later visit, he told me his teacher had sent him some pupils. My preparations for the planned visit to Baden-Baden being completed, I turned some of my pupils over to Max for the period of my absence.

I ordered a new summer suit for Armand, and, well-supplied financially, we left the grandiose capital city and took passage for Baden-Baden. Knowing the town well from having lived there previously, it was not too difficult to find us suitable quarters. Here, however, the real trouble with Armand commenced. He suffered from an unconquerable bug phobia and would not sleep in one of the spotlessly clean beds—every night he lay on the hard, bare floor instead, fully dressed in his new clothes. My reprimands concerning this senseless behavior were without effect. After one month, his tramp-like appearance was so embarrassing to me that I told him I would cease to accompany him to the waters and the symphony concerts by the excellent resort orchestra (of which

Mr. Schneider, the double-bass player and my former landlord, was still a member). He only shrugged and said, "Alright, buy me a new suit." Nolens volens (willy-nilly), that's just what I did.

At this time, Germany was at the height of an unusual political upheaval. The young Kaiser Wilhelm, dissatisfied with the policies of the over-powerful Prince Bismarck, dismissed him as Chancellor, eager to take the reins into his own hands. Bismarck was at the peak of his fruitful career and the object of high admiration, beloved by every German non-socialist even though he was called "the iron Kanzler" ("iron chancellor"). A wealth of indignation caused by the Emperor's action stirred the whole country and Bismarck retired to his beloved Kissingen where he typically summered, although now his health was failing. To this place came an unceasing stream of adherents to his political creed. A great number of the inhabitants of the grand duchy of Baden decided to also make an opposition trip to Kissingen and I wanted to have Armand, a French citizen, witness the event.

Five trains, containing about 5,000 passengers, moved toward Kissingen, with the two of us occupying seats in one of them. Real German "Gemüthlichkeit" (geniality) prevailed throughout the journey. The country through which we passed was brilliant, golden with summer luminosity embellishing woods and fields; we passed through friendly villages and past isolated prosperous-looking farmhouses, a harmonious landscape overall.

Arriving at Kissingen, it was not an easy task for officials to arrange those patriotic thousands into some form of a well-organized group. But when it was done, we marched in fairly orderly formation to Bismarck's retreat, situated in the main building of a former salt mine, the source of benevolent waters. An unforgettable scene spread out before us, an expressive picture of humanity. As the crowd moved toward the building, their enthusiasm became audible as they fervently cried, "Hoch! Hoch! Hoch!" (a traditional shout). The uniquely German "Es braust ein Ruf wie Donnerhall" (a mighty call like thunder burst) was then sung. As Armand and I marched, we saw the Chancellor standing on a balcony overlooking the scene. He was apparently overwhelmed by this thundering ovation of the 5,000 as tears rolled down his cheeks and deep emotion shook his entire, mighty body. The exaltation of the dense crowd knew no bounds. Behind Bismarck, holding him by the shoulders, stood his faithful physician Professor Schwenninger. The multitude marched around the building and into the large court, waving their hats in the air and continuing their enthusiastic shouts: "Hoch! Hoch! Hoch!"

When we had all gathered in a neat circular formation, Dr. Schwenninger appeared at the second balcony and announced that, as the Chancellor was not well, his son Herbert would speak to us. What a disappointment! A very ordinary speech uttered with all the mannerisms of a real Prussian lieutenant was, to say the least, a poor substitute, relieved only by the presence upon the balcony of the tall, spiritual, and much-idolized Princess Bismarck. The Chancellor must have divined the cold impact his son's speech had created and the crowd was duly roused by seeing her. A few minutes after the lieutenant's unsuccessful address, the object of our admiration, Bismarck himself, then appeared in our midst. A 45-minute-long oratorical masterpiece delivered in Bismarck's inimitable Brandenburg dialect (he pronounced all g's like y's) aroused our heartiest acclamations. A fine twinkle shone in his light blue eyes which, from time to time, seemed to issue lightning-like flashes. With his big Danish dog, Tyras, always by his side, after his speech Bismarck passed through the throng, addressing individuals here and there. He then went back inside the building, thundering applause following him. The crowd continued to mill about the immense courtyard, fraternizing, looking for old acquaintances and making new ones, when the Chancellor appeared once more and spent another half-hour with us, even making a second speech.

I would like to interject one remark here about his speaking voice. This tall, powerful personality who had an unusually large head was paradoxically the possessor of a high tenor voice, and, at times, seeking for an expressive word in the middle of a phrase, he would take a strongly audible breath and then with a loud forzando (a musical reference to using emphasis), the intended word would burst out like the bark of a dog. With this speech and another tour of the crowd, he then went back into his home, escorted by the inspiring bars of the beloved German folk song, "Deutschland, Deutschland über alles." What a powerful witness to pride and love of country! History attests to the truth that any nation whose populace loses its patriotic feeling is doomed to downfall.

Armand, the proud young Frenchman, was not an enthusiastic spectator of these purely German proceedings and followed me grumblingly back to Kissingen. However, he was not unwilling to partake of a substantial German dinner.

After a short period in Baden-Baden enjoying its splendid music, we returned to Paris where we found everything in the same state of disorder in which we had left it. Lessons taken and lessons given along with preparations for my approaching marriage filled the greater part of my days.

Two more important events took place meanwhile. One was the appearance of Peter Tchaikovsky at a Cologne concert at the Théâtre du Châtelet in which he conducted his Symphony No. 6. He was a shy, beautifully bearded and very elegant gentleman, hesitatingly presenting himself time and again on stage to accept the audience's hearty applause. The second event was the first recital in Paris by Ignacy Paderewski [21] which was a sensation! France is the only country in the world where such public manifestations of emotion are possible. At the conclusion of Paderewski's performance, pandemonium broke out among the crowd. The ladies jumped to their feet and threw their handkerchiefs and bouquets at him with raucous cries; I even saw one of them swoon. This concert was followed by four more of the same sensational quality, the forerunners of many future such performances. (In later years I would have the pleasure of knowing this musical hero-heartbreaker more intimately.)

The following month was spent primarily with farewell visits and preparations for my upcoming departure for Holland. The last concert I attended was one of the numerous highly artistic Gilman organ concerts with a soloist and symphony orchestra which was held in the Trocadere, an auditorium seating 11,000. The soloist at this concert was Pablo de Sarasate.

In the meantime, Madame Gerard had returned from Sweden to find Armand the same unmanageable individual. While I was still there, a scheming female pianist gained entrance into the small circle of friends of the Gerard family and aroused Armand's interest. I later heard of her success in snaring the young rich boy into marriage.

I paid a last visit to Uncle Richard during which he told me, "Heinrich, after my death, my Stradivarius violin will be your property." Alas! A dream denied.

[21] **Ignacy Jan Paderewski, GBE** (18 November [O.S. 6 November] 1860 – 29 June 1941) was a Polish pianist and composer, politician, and spokesman for Polish independence. He was a favorite of concert audiences around the globe. His musical fame opened access to diplomacy and the media. (Carol R. Ember Melvin Ember; Ian Skoggard, Encyclopedia of Diasporas: Immigrant and Refugee Cultures Around the World). Paderewski played an important role in meeting with President Woodrow Wilson and obtaining the explicit inclusion of independent Poland as point 13 in Wilson's peace terms in 1918, called the Fourteen Points. (Hanna Marczewska-Zagdanska, and Janina Dorosz, Acta Poloniae Historica (1996), Issue 73, pp 55-69.) He was the Prime Minister of Poland and also Poland's foreign minister in 1919, and represented Poland at the Paris Peace Conference in 1919. (Hartman, Carl, AP via *The Daily News* (26 June 1992).

My friend Poulin and others had not yet returned from their vacations, so I could not bid them goodbye. Adieu, beautiful Paris unique!

Note from Melinda...

It was a matter of great discussion in the family whether one of Fahta's two violins was indeed a Stradivarius. (Doesn't everyone think their family violin just might be a Strad?) The one with the lion's head scroll had a Strad label inside, which was really exciting. My Uncle Mark took them to have them appraised, and the verdict was they weren't worth anything, but the appraiser offered to buy them, so a suspicious Uncle Mark brought them home again. When my daughter, Libby, was old enough to play a full-sized violin she played the lion's head one (which I mistakenly thought was Fahta's main violin). Her teacher, Leonard Rachoff, an accomplished violinist had, at one time, owned a Guarneri violin until it was stolen by another violinist in the well-known orchestra he was playing in at the time. He said it was a student violin, and not really worth much. (He was a sweet little old man, and a wonderful teacher, even after Libby threw up on his shoes at one lesson. She said she was sick, but I've always suspected she didn't really want to play violin.) Anyway, I've subsequently found that the Strad label is the most counterfeited label in history, and the violin was almost certainly mass-produced in Germany. My mom was the one who was right, because she always said the violin Fahta played was made to the exact specifications of a Strad by Otto Migge, and it has a Migge label inside.

Chapter 11   Holland, Marriage, and a Close Call

Armand accompanied me to the Gare Saint-Lazare where I boarded a train. Traversing the second time in a year the serene rural countryside of France, Belgium, and Holland, my thoughts were fixed upon the new life awaiting me. Would this new country finally be the congenial resting-place for me after all the years of my straying hither and yon?

At the railroad station in Amsterdam my fiancée's warmhearted reception made such a deep impression upon me that my doubting-Thomas attitude vanished like a fog in the midst of the all-conquering sun. At her home we found Miss Repelius occupied with putting the finishing touches on an appetite-inspiring lunch which was served in the high-ceilinged 16th century-styled dining room, decorated with valuable paintings of that period.

Our lunch finished, Marie led me outside to a light carriage and told the driver where to take us. It was a pleasant ride along the calmly meandering Y river, with borders of each shore adorned with farmhouses situated cozily amidst profuse shade and fruit trees, giving one the impression of calm, uneventful living. A 10-mile ride brought us to a halt at one of these farms.

In the main house, bordered by tall poplar trees, the farmer and his three grown children lived, while a much smaller house occupied the other side of the drive—this dwelling my fiancée had rented for me. It consisted of three snug, immaculate rooms which were simply but tastefully furnished. My stay there would be for two weeks. At the end of that time our wedding would take place.

These two weeks of leisure were only interrupted by an hour or two of study each day, the remaining hours were filled mostly with reading and hunting around the place, and I shot several wild pigeons. I had ample time to get acquainted with a Holland farmer's family life. The quaint habit of the family members never entering a room with their clumpjes (wooden shoes) on their feet surprised me; I learned that every Holland peasant leaves his clumpjes outside his door.

For expedience, the cow stable was connected with the kitchen; 12 animals were kept there. The space between the double row of bovines was brick laid. The cows' stalls were of slanting cement construction with a gutter at the lower side to take care of spills. Cleanliness reigned. No displeasing odor was tolerated. The walkway was strewn with white sand. Everything was also warm. Extreme winter temperatures were hardly felt inside these comfortable animal quarters. Life is tasking for the dairy farmer though: up at three a.m. milking, feeding the animals, loading milk on a dog-wagon, transporting it to town, then back by eight a.m. An hour's rest at noon, work, work, work, followed by a very early greeting of Morpheus (the Greek god of dreams).

My dear doctor, her days' extensive work very tiring, nevertheless paid me several visits. She, being 32 and I nearing my thirtieth year, both serious strugglers against life's unruly whims, we discussed very thoroughly our plans for the shaping of our future together. One proposition to which I found it difficult to give my approval was relayed to me from Miss Repelius as she wished us to begin our married life in her home. Only the fact that Marie's office was established there allowed me to accept the offer. An exceedingly important problem kept crossing my mind so I finally decided to discuss it with Marie. I felt that a discussion on the subject might eliminate any dispute later as she was a Mennonite and her yes was yes, her no was no, her word was always strictly binding; that was her creed.

"If our marriage should come to an impasse, let us end it," I suggested. She found this proposition reasonable and both of us were willing to accept its consequences should it happen.

My two weeks' recreation, augmenting my weight by several pounds, ended, and I moved back to Amsterdam to pass the few days before our marriage at the home of the generous sisters Heineken once more.

The civil marriage ceremony took place at the Amsterdam City Hall. An old friend of the doctor's family, an industrialist, and her uncle, Mr. du Saar, were our witnesses. Afterward Miss Repelius invited all of us to an excellently prepared Holland lunch after which my bride and I departed for a little village in the heather country. How is that? Heather country in Holland? Yes, there existed at that time in northeast Holland thousands of acres of uncultivated land covered with up to four-feet high heather interspersed with groups of low pine trees.

The little house in which we spent our honeymoon was built so that the second floor could accommodate from two to four guests. The owners were sturdy, hospitable, and discreet people without children who often rented their upper rooms to visitors. The lady of the house served typically tasty Holland meals. The two weeks we stayed there, in the heart of this unpretentious, sympathetic oasis were a valuable preparation for our unfolding marriage.

We took long walks daily, breathing deeply of the pure air which was gently scented with the fragrance of heather abloom. When the high temperature of the noon hour approached, the atmosphere was drier than at other times of the day, and my wife always became fatigued and short of breath. She would immediately sit down and try to relax, and confided to me that her heart was not robust and needed to be coddled a little. (Her humor, which she displayed even when speaking of her own health issues, was always refreshing.)

These days, enjoyed in happy unison, flew by. Back to Amsterdam we went to the challenge of a new morrow. My wife had of course already mapped out her professional future but I had now to create a new chapter once more.

Amsterdam is the home of one of the globe's finest symphony orchestras, the Concertgebouw, founded by Willem Kes, an outstanding organizer and a good conductor. I acquired a subscription for my wife and myself for all the concerts being given during the upcoming year as only subscribers gained admittance to these concerts, no separate tickets were sold. It was and still is today of the high rank established by Kes who, to the end of his life, held highly honored positions in several other countries as well.

Always striving to attain a worthy conductor's position, the outlook for me was not in any way promising. Through my dear doctor's efforts, several blossoming violinists applied for lessons with me. I then began to direct my thoughts toward the possibility of forming a string quartet. Among the members of the Concertbegouw orchestra, I knew three ardent chamber music enthusiasts and invited them to my home to discuss my idea. They were agreeable and we decided to start rehearsals the following week. In a short time we developed a closely-knit ensemble.

Meanwhile, as Marie was the head of the City Clinic and spent at least half of each day there, we acquired a tricycle for her daily transportation. Usually my feet powered this as she was not strong enough to keep pedaling in the regular rhythm needed.

In the second month of our marriage my wife fell seriously ill with typhoid fever. She had passed through a siege of the same disease some years before and now had to combat this dangerous enemy for the second time (a rare occurrence). She lost much weight and needed a long period of recuperation thereafter.

During this episode, a deputation from the male chorus "Zanglust" visited me, offering me the position as leader of their troupe, and I gladly accepted this opportunity to conduct again. After inquiring, I discovered the reason why I was chosen the leader of this oldest male chorus in Amsterdam—the former leader, an accomplished musician from Haarlem, had filled this position for 23 years. In Europe, singing societies always compete in international song festivals. Starting the first year in the lowest classification, a chorus only advanced to a higher one by winning in that lower division. All were eager to attain the highest class, the "Division d'Excellence". "Zanglust" had tried for the past seven years to reach this goal but always in vain. A few months hence there was to be held another of these international festivals in Amsterdam's Palais of Volksflyt, a large building with a seating capacity of about 10,000, which served as a hall of exposition in the last World's Fair in Amsterdam.

When the conductor of "Zanglust" did not succeed in winning the battle of the choruses in the course of seven successive trials, I was told the committee of the society came to this conclusion: "Because we all want to win the competition this year we must get a new conductor. We might try that ambitious young fellow, Hammer. With him we may finally arrive at the top of the ladder." This then was the reason for my engagement.

At the first rehearsal, which occurred while my wife was convalescing, I found the singers to be disciplined and willing hard workers—all of them were members of the Diamond Cutters' and Slypers' Union. The competition was to consist of two parts. First, the group would sing an acapella composition of its own choice of about 10 minutes' duration. Then they must sing an opus of the Belgian composer, Tilman, called "The Wrath," also acapella. This was a complicated piece with dramatic accentuation. We rehearsed both compositions with great zeal and care, until two weeks before the festival when I fell victim to a rather severe influenza. My wife and personal physician did everything to combat the ugly fiend, but stubbornly my suffering persisted. Daily, committee members of "Zanglust" visited me, everyone clamoring for my return. A very capable assistant leader took good care of the now almost daily rehearsals, but everybody wanted me to hurry and get well. Unfortunately, these visitors were not conducive to my recovery and actually aggravated my sickness. A few days before the festival, just out of bed and still very weak, I said to my wife, "This evening I am going to rehearse the chorus. Call a closed wagon, help me down to it, bundle me in some woolen blankets, and send me to the rehearsal hall."

"You'll kill yourself!" she protested.

"Alright, let me die on the field of battle."

When I arrived at the hall, members of the chorus carried me up to the second floor and put me upon the conductor's chair. Weak as I was, the thundering applause of the 150 members revived me a little, and, enlivened by the sonorous, spirited voices, I totally forgot my weakened state. The perspiration ran in streams over my whole body as I concluded a satisfactory two hour-long rehearsal, after which I was carried down to the wagon, bundled in as before, driven quickly home, and rushed up to my bedroom where my anxious doctor put me to bed. I slept for 18 hours.

The competition was a formidable one, giving little hope of a favorable result for us. In our class were the "Männercher" from Cologne and the "Choral" from Brussels, both 200-strong and famous for their fine work. The tonal quality of the Brussels chorus was far superior to ours. They were mostly young men; 90% of mine were much older. My group's voices, often having been carelessly used, had lost that fine, velvet-like quality. However, the prize composition as stated before was one of inspiring dramatic force, and was particularly well-suited to my singers. There occurred a phrase in the piece, the "pointe de culmination:" "Bow down! That, never!" requiring a powerful fortissimo. I made my men not sing but effectively proclaim the words, "Boigen dat oit!" As the contestants were not allowed to be present at the performances of their rivals, none of us knew the outcome that day. But the following day the judges of the contest gathered on the stage of the big concert hall to present the trophies to the winners. What joy overwhelmed me when the presiding judge announced, "Zanglust is the winner of the first prize—500 guilders in gold and a gold medal". As soon as these words were uttered, the entire throng of my singers surrounded me, uproariously waving and gesticulating, lifting me upon their shoulders and carrying me around the hall in triumph.

This perfect reward had a profound and exhilarating influence upon me, and also upon Marie's unstable health. To restore her, I proposed to use the unexpected financial windfall for further ministrations to her body with a few weeks' sojourn in Switzerland. She knew of a place, Spiez, where she had passed a very satisfactory vacation before. Writing to the home in which she had lived then, we received a favorable reply. Preparing for the departure was a short process and, soon, we were off.

It was springtime and this trip became a second honeymoon for us. High-spirited and carefree, we traveled along "Vater Rhein" toward Switzerland and my first visit to the country where, in later years, I would find rich satisfaction in the fulfillment of my fondest dreams.

We arrived at a plateau in view of the mountain giants, Eiger, Mönch, and Jungfrau. The house in which we found lodging was in the midst of this scenic vista. A panorama of surpassing grandeur surrounded us; in every direction such enchanting views! Lakes at our feet, sun-saturated mountains encircling them. Wherever we looked, grandeur was the keynote. As we were the only guests in this peaceful and spotlessly-clean farmhouse and the owners were eager to grant all of our wishes, this was the ideal setting to restore to my wife her former buoyancy. We took long walks around the area, enjoyed simple and nourishing food, and lazed about, unencumbered, day after day.

The apex of this blissful period came when, one day, the letter-carrier arrived with a small package from Belgium addressed to me. What did it contain? The membership insignia in the form of a beautiful order and first class medal of the "Académie Belgique du Hainaut." Imagine our joy and surprise at this unforeseen honor being received from the "Académie's" council! Just a week later I received my nomination for membership in the "Accademia Humanitaria di Roma"—only persons of outstanding accomplishment are ever made members of these honorary organizations and I was understandably proud. A few days later, we left Switzerland after thanking our kind hosts, sorry to be departing though both feeling refreshed and my wife entirely her former self again.

Picking up loose ends where we had left them had its slight difficulties upon our return home. However, we mastered them quickly and, with renewed vigor, the doctor started her clinic work, my pupils came for their lessons, and rehearsals for the chorus and string quartet resumed once more.

A letter from the secretary of the School Teachers' Singing Society in nearby Haarlem arrived asking me to conduct their group. A short while after I began rehearsals with them, I received another letter from The Hague's "Euterpe," a mixed chorus, offering me the directorship of this unique singing society—it was composed of members of the court circles of Queen Emma. Kammerherr, Count Hogendorp, was the society's president. The mayor of The Hague and his son (a lawyer and excellent baritone) were also members, and the Mayor's daughter was the accompanist at our rehearsals, a most accomplished pianist of an artistic nature.

Every rehearsal was a festive occasion, the ladies in formal dress and white gloves, the gentlemen elegantly attired in evening clothes, and each was a trained singer. It was a pleasure to conduct such a body of well-disciplined musicians. Always when I arrived at The Hague to conduct a rehearsal, a chauffeur was waiting for me at the railroad station which would take me to the home of one of the chorus members for dinner and from there to the rehearsal. After one month's work with the chorus I was asked to take over the leadership of the chorus of the church Valon, the Queen's church, facing the palace. Many of the members of "Euterpe" were also in the church chorus. French was the language used in the church. My activities in The Hague sixty years ago evoke pleasant memories today, even all these years later.

The string quartet had arrived at the point where

[22] **Joseph Willem Mengelberg** (28 March 1871 – 21 March 1951) was a Dutch conductor. In 1895, Mengelberg was presented with the honourable request to become conductor of the Concertgebouw Orchestra in Amsterdam. This ensemble had been founded in 1888 and had acquired a good name under the conductor Willem Kes. Kes, however, had found an improved position in Scotland. Mengelberg came to stand before the Concertgebouw Orchestra as a young man of twenty-four. His first years in Amsterdam cannot have always been easy for him. Complaints were made about his changing ideas about some scores, the members of the orchestra sometimes behaved in a difficult manner and his health was not everything it might have been. Yet Mengelberg's popularity grew steadily. (Frits Zwart, Willem Mengelberg Dirigent Conductor, Haags Gemeente Museum, 1995.)

our ambition was justified. We began our public career with a successful concert in Amsterdam and continued by playing in the provinces. Many re-engagements followed. I know of no more satisfying task in the realm of art than performing chamber music with congenial and gifted partners.

In 1895, the conductor of the Arnheim Symphony Orchestra had resigned to accept another post in Germany. I was asked to be one of its guest conductors in order to compete for his position. I won the competition, but when the authorities discovered I was not a native of their country, they told me they were sorry but they wanted a Hollander, not a German. Another competition for Hollanders alone was arranged and one of them was appointed. This was my first setback in Holland.

Very soon another one occurred. Willem Kes, the founder and capable conductor of the Concertgebouw Orchestra, was called to Glasgow and I applied for his vacated spot. But Mengelberg[22], another Hollander who was a fine pianist but inexperienced conductor, was chosen. Another frustration. You might have taken it for granted that I led a contented existence in Amsterdam, but I constantly felt the urge to get back to my beloved orchestral conducting. These two successive disappointments removed all my hope of finding a satisfactory conductor's position in Holland.

My resultant musings about other possibilities were interrupted by several noteworthy events. We left our residence in Miss Repelius's home and moved to a

[23] **George Hendrik Breitner** (1857-1923) was born in Rotterdam. In 1876, he enrolled at the academy in The Hague. Later, he worked at Willem Maris's studio. In this early period he was especially influenced by the painters of the Hague School. Breitner preferred working-class models: labourers, servant girls and people from lower-class neighbourhoods. He saw himself as 'le peintre du peuple', the people's painter. In 1886, he moved to Amsterdam, where he recorded the life of the city in sketches, paintings and photos. (Rijksmuseum.nl)

two-story house, as the recent occupant, the famous painter Breitner [23], had relocated to other quarters. This house was situated across from the anatomic laboratory of the Queen Wilhelmina hospital, one of the largest in the world at that time. I was present with my wife at the dedication of this magnificent edifice to the young Queen Wilhelmina, then just 12 years old. (Further development of this autobiography will show you how inscrutably Destiny weaves her thread.)

My first son, Ernst, was born the 11th of November, 1893, in our new home. His birth nearly claimed the life of his mother, who was attended by her friend, Doctor Catherine van Tussenbroek[24], who would go on to become a professor of gynecology at the Amsterdam University. The head of the child was so large that it took five full hours before its passage. I was present during all these torturous labor pains Marie suffered as she endured so bravely. When all the dangerous and fear-filled hours had elapsed, a blue, wizened little being finally appeared and the climax of the poor woman's agony was completed. The child weighed 12.5 pounds and his birth executed a ruinous influence upon the health of his mother. The baby cried lustily as he greeted his new surroundings. We embraced and, in our happiness, forgot the arduous struggle. I went out then and, like an unbalanced madman, ran aimlessly around the house, overcome with the indescribable thrill of being the father of a newborn son!

Marie's long convalescence thereafter strained the patience of her active nature. Luckily, through the persuasiveness of our old loyal servant, Louise, her mistress remained

[24] **Catharine van Tussenbroek** (4 August 1852 – 5 May 1925) was a Dutch physician and feminist. She was the second woman to qualify as a physician in the Netherlands. She set up as a GP in Amsterdam in 1887. An appointment in 1890 as assistant gynaecologist in Amsterdam gave Van Tussenbroek security and a grounding in a specialist field. [She] moved to obstetrics and gynaecology; microscopic research, hygiene and public health, health of the school child, [and] medical ethics all featured amongst her work and interests. (Rudolf Dekker, ed., Curing and Insuring: Essays on Illness in Past Times: the Netherlands.)

confined a few critical days longer than her doctor had required of her. The arrival of Ernst—named for my grandfather—put another burden of responsibility upon my wife's already heavily-laden shoulders.

About this time, Mr. Falkenburg, another well-known painter and one of our neighbors, asked me to sit for a portrait. I did so faithfully but I never saw it after it was finished and I do not know what became of it. Ernst continued to be a big, strong baby, prospering under the care of doting parents. Louise, who called him "my boy," loved him as if he were her own. (She was 60 years old and unmarried.)

Our regular routine work carried on, but life as it was did not satisfy me. I saw no possibility of ever attaining in Holland what I was sure I could accomplish in other countries. Furthermore, the status of a musician in Holland is not to be compared with its equivalent in other places—instead I was simply the husband of Dr. Marie Cornelia du Saar. My wife loved me dearly and it was our happiness which kept my champing at the bit at a minimum. Loving my art deeply, it is self-evident that I attended with great care to my chorus work, and with apparent success I may say.

We often visited the Rijksmuseum (Ryks Museum) with its tremendous wealth of some of the world's most valuable paintings. Rembrandt's "Nightwatch," containing the portraits of 500 burghers (citizens, typically members of the wealthy bourgeoisie), is so large that Cuyper, the renowned architect of the museum, was assigned to build a special annex for this masterwork. Miss Repelius was a welcome guide on all of our visits and she also encouraged me to invest some of my earnings in acquiring master paintings.

Mengelberg, like many "soi distant" (would-be) conductors before and after him, was the pupil, not the master of his orchestra. When he finally passed his apprenticeship after painful experience and many mistakes, he began to treat his colleagues, the members of the orchestra, hitherto his teachers, like a slave driver treats his negroes. He was indeed a good pianist. I once heard him give a satisfactory interpretation of Liszt's Piano Concerto No. 1. His orchestra gave well-prepared programs although somewhat tinged with sentimentality. He was now the conceited master, backed by all the members of the steering committee. Nine of the best musicians of the orchestra, embittered, complained to the committee—but these grumblings were all ruthlessly dismissed.

On my trips to Haarlem where I conducted the school teachers' mixed chorus, I often went to the Frans Hals Museum and the City Hall exposition. Whenever I could in the springtime, I went to the outskirts of Haarlem to gaze at the hundreds of acres of tulips, narcissi, jonquils, gladioli, daffodils, iris, and other bulb flowers, every field containing just a single color of blooms. A plot of several acres of vivid blue always gave me the impression of a piece of the clear firmament having fallen to the earth. Haarlem is the center of the world's bulb-flower trade.

My daily work lessening with the approach of summer and nearly ceasing entirely with the advance of the season, I had long idle intervals in which to thoroughly explore my thoughts, my desires, and my motives regarding my career. The personnel of the string quartet had changed several times, always followed by the tedious task of again molding four souls into one, a very tiring and nerve-wracking process. The road to the fervently hoped-for conductor's position was basically closed. The blues frequently took hold of me when my thoughts ran in this direction.

One more trial: I must make one last effort to find out if somehow I will be able to hold on to the art which has filled my life entirely. For the past month, Jean Syckes, an industrious young piano virtuoso, and I had enjoyed playing some ensemble music together. One time after playing Grieg's C Minor Piano-Violin Sonata we were led into a discussion of Scandinavian music in general which ended with my telling the story of my life in Sweden. At the conclusion of my tale, I found I was longing to see Sweden once more. This gave birth to the idea that this could easily be accomplished if Jean and I could make a Scandinavian concert tourneé (tour). My wife's approval of our project enhanced our commitment to this new goal as Jean liked the idea, so we arranged a series of dates for the concerts.

We departed on our way with anticipation. First concert in Malmö—reminiscent of The Mikado—up the coast to some small towns, then Norrköping—recalling my first orchestra playing—then to my beloved Örebro. Entrée triumphale! Carl and all my old friends gave a big feast for us after our concert there. We played in a few small cities and then went to Sundsvall where, on an impulse, I visited the jeweler whose store I had saved from plundering when the town was destroyed by fire. He remembered me well. You recall he promised to give me the rings when I married. As this was already a past occurrence, he presented me with a brooch set with a large Wisby stone, a gift for my wife. We gave several concerts in high-northern tuberculosis sanitariums attended by the liveliest audiences of our whole trip. Our last performance of the tourneé was in Bergen. From there we took a steamer to Antwerp.

For our first dinner on board ship we were served the finest apples I had ever tasted. I inquired with interest about their origin. The captain told me they were Gravensteins, grown in Denmark.

Outside the Norwegian harbor we encountered a terrible fog. The next morning at five o'clock I was thrown out of my upper bunk to the floor by a tremendous jolt. Running up to the deck in my pajamas I saw that a ship had rammed us. Its nearby bowsprit was contorted unrecognizably and ripped sails were flapping madly in the foggy wind—a ghastly sight. I asked the captain if I had time to dress.

"Hurry up!" he yelled.

Returning to the deck I saw the first officer, an elderly gentleman, just coming out of his cabin. He looked around, his hands shoved in his pockets.

"I was nearly killed," he said in a matter-of-fact tone to me, like he might say he had just eaten.

I saw the other vessel was rocking aimlessly in the rough sea. Its captain called to us for help, in German. Our captain did not speak German, so I translated the message to him and stated my willingness to go over to the other ship in one of the small boats with him. As our steamer was also very badly damaged, he said, "Tell him we are badly hurt and cannot help him." I called out the message and the ship was slowly swallowed up in the impenetrable fog. In the midst of all this, I glimpsed Jean standing on deck clutching his life preserver nervously. Earlier I had helped the captain to clear the lifeboats, but luckily they were not needed. The anchor of the other ship had torn a large hole in the first officer's cabin, just above his head. It was astonishing how soon the crew succeeded in bandaging the steamer with an enormous piece of sail cloth which prevented an excessive amount of water from entering the hold. We arrived in Antwerp one day late and only once there did the captain disclose to us that we were carrying twenty tons of water in the hold! Again I seem to have been lucky in a scrape with death.

Chapter 12   Country Life

Back in Holland, my wife and I attended a lecture by former Lieutenant Colonel Rosenthal which gave me new food for contemplation. The guest speaker was president of the Holland Hyde Matchappy (Holland Heather Association), the goal of which was to profitably cultivate the hundreds of thousands of acres of heather, a crop which was only used for sheep pastures at that time. After the lecture, we talked to the ex-Lt. Colonel and he elaborated upon the association's work, providing us with more details. The ex-soldier's personality and the zeal he displayed in describing their efforts made a favorable impression upon me.

Coming home, we discussed at length the prospects of the heather project. My pioneer spirit was alive again. (I have often regretted that I was not born 400 years earlier so I could have become one of those daring and hardy pioneers of the New World.) A few days later, after a serious discussion of pros and cons with Marie, we decided to buy a piece of land from the Heather Association with a plan to cultivate a part of it plus build a house there. Notifying Lieutenant Colonel Rosenthal of our intention, I asked him to show us some of the parcels for sale.

We took a train to Apeldoorn, the summer residence of the Queen-Regent, Emma, and met him at the station. He drove us several miles on the main road to its termination at the heather acreage where another main road crossed. He showed us a piece of land at that juncture. It was a nice flat, square field, dense with small heather bushes, and was about eight acres. We bought it, the very first one we saw, and advanced to land ownership in Holland.

The lonely, barren surrounding countryside was populated by only a few widely scattered farms, the owners of which extracted a meager living raising sheep which found scant sustenance from the poor vegetation—these environs certainly formed a vivid contrast to the more popular and prosperous parts of Holland. Our nearest neighbors lived about a mile away, occupying acreage on the same road across from our newly-acquired parcel. They were a childless couple of middle-age, hospitable and helpful; they lived on a fixed income and were not sheep owners. Returning to Amsterdam, we made plans for the cultivation of our land and for our future home.

About this time, a conveyance man came to my house with a large barrel for me. I told him I had not ordered anything, but he said this would cost nothing. On opening the barrel, I discovered about 200 pounds of Gravenstein apples from the captain of the wrecked ship, apparently a token of his gratitude.

I used to practice my violin two hours a day in my study. The room was furnished entirely with rattan—a settee, a table and chairs; these were a set I had bought at an exhibit of this type of furniture which was very much in vogue at that time. A large bookcase holding an extensive library took up one side of a wall. One of the largest volumes, an anatomic atlas, attracted Ernst's attention. He was then two years old, a quiet and serious little chap. One day, to satisfy his demands for the book, my wife took it out. Sitting upon the soft rug, she opened it and showed him some of the colored plates of sections of the human body.

"Dad is de book met bones," she told him. ("This is the book of bones.")

"Book en beene," he repeated as well as he could.

Every morning from then on, when Marie went to the clinic, the little prince would sit down on the rug and eagerly ask for the "book en beene." The first time I gave it to him reluctantly. But he sat very still, so absorbedly scanning the pages, turning them carefully, not damaging anything, that I had no further qualms. For two hours each day he would sit there perfectly fascinated by his "book en beene." He sometimes would look up and watch me for a moment, seeming to enjoy the melodies I was playing. I am sure it was here that my little boy laid the foundation for his future brilliant career as a great anatomist.

The arrival of another member of the Hammer family was in the offing. My dear doctor, our household's unifying force, absolutely refused to release her tasking obligations at the clinic, the hospital, or at home, until a few days before our second child's birth was imminent. This delivery of a seven-pound, rosy little girl was a normal and thankfully unperilous procedure, greatly aided by the valiant attitude of my courageous Marie. Her recuperation was also of astonishingly short duration. Off she went again in her energetic manner to attend to her pressing duties not long after our daughter arrived, making our family a foursome.

One work-free day thereafter we went to Apeldoorn to analyze the composition of the soil of our newly-acquired land. We found an underlying two feet of iron ore one foot below the surface. To cultivate the land successfully, it was necessary to break this two-foot layer. We therefore decided I should move to Apeldoorn, engage a work force, and have the men prepare the acres we intended to work. A few days later I moved to an apartment in town.

As at that time one could almost always find the necessary number of diggers needed for a job, so it was easy for me to put together a crew of 32 men to tackle my property. I bought a bicycle to peddle the eight miles I had to cover daily. On an appointed day at six a.m. I met my crew at the field to begin the project. Each of the men was the owner of a plaghock (a hoe about a foot square of strong construction). With these implements they would, with forceful motions, cut foot-square pieces of ground with the adherent heather plants. A man would gather these chunks onto his wheelbarrow and deposit them on the boundary line of the section intended for cultivation in such a way that the cut sod eventually would form a fence around the entire area. After the completion of one layer around the square, a layer of un-slacked lime was laid on top, then a second layer of sod, a second layer of lime on top of that, and so on. The lime, slacked by rain, would disintegrate the heather and would form the humus so necessary for fruitful agriculture. I followed each digger with a five-foot iron rod, measuring the depth of his work, to see if he had attained a three feet penetration into the earth. Eight hours a day for several weeks we continued this strenuous labor. My wife came out on weekends and, together, we looked over the expanse of completed work and chose the site on which to build our house.

After the finishing of the humus-producing fence, I returned to Amsterdam to continue my musical activities. The days of that winter were uneventful and prosaic. As a result, my dissatisfaction with my situation grew. At last I decided to end my musical work there entirely, being convinced that I could never accomplish my goals while in Holland. My dear wife loved her work, and being a renowned ophthalmology specialist and an experienced Doctor of Medicine, could look with pride upon the satisfactory remuneration her practice provided. Therefore, it would be unwise for us to leave Holland in order for me to look for a satisfying appointment in my field.

After long, calm discussions we came to a conclusion: I should go to Apeldoorn to supervise the construction of our house and, after its erection, should stay there and attend to the development of the soil.

The following spring I started my new full-time task after approving the architect's sketch of our abode-to-be. The house was begun under the surveillance of the builder, a stout, skilled craftsman. Upon a solid concrete foundation, a brick building of sound proportions steadily arose. A sufficiently large living room, comfortable dining room, and the kitchen formed the ground floor; a small cellar could be reached by a trapdoor in the kitchen. The second story contained two spacious bedrooms and a maid's room. Adjacent to the kitchen was a large wagon-house at the end of which a door led to a scientifically-constructed horse stable; next to that was a great stable with a big square space above for chickens. The horse stable slanted downward to the rear wall where a convenient trapdoor opened into a deep cement manure pit, covered with a large double door which kept the nitrogen from escaping. All these innovations were installed after my extensive study of agricultural science.

As the house was built of brick and covered with a thick coating of cement, it took some time before it dried thoroughly. I slept there in one of the second-story beds. A slight attack of rheumatism punished me for my temerity. When the house passed the drying-out period, my wife came with Ernst. She stayed a few days and, upon her departure, left Ernst with me as a soothing solution for my loneliness. It was a great joy to have the little fellow for company. He exuberantly explored the area around the house and played with a kitten the neighbors had given him. It was interesting to watch his antics with the cute little four-footed creature.

One day, these antics took on a cruel aspect. I noticed him digging a hole in the ground with his little spade. Then he grabbed the tiny animal, shoved it in the pit he had prepared and tried to bury it, covering it with dirt. The kitten resisted, crying. Ernst angrily squeezed it hard into the bottom of the hole, determined to have his own way. At that instant, after having been curious to see how far he would go, I interfered. I administered a few sound whacks on his backside, the only whipping I ever gave him, and ended with stern moral admonitions. After this event the cat was taboo; Ernst ignored it entirely.

The next time my wife came to Apeldoorn she informed me she was pregnant again. Meanwhile I intended to start the cultivation of the previously spaded ground. To this end, I ordered the fence material, as now, through the action of the rain, rich humus had formed which was spread over the field. I wanted to plant lupine and had learned this needs to be inoculated with Bacilli Wagneri, a bacillus which filters nitrogen from the air and, in so doing, makes it unnecessary for the planter to buy this most expensive fertilizer. So I bought a large amount of the Bacilli Wagneri, used pails filled with water, put a quantity of bacilli in each pail, and sprayed it over my field. This process was just recently made public, and was extremely successful in my case as in others. After the ground had been prepared, I had yellow lupine planted. Why yellow lupine? It is a cousin of our common blue lupine, but superior in two essentials; it is a stronger, heavier-blossoming plant and exudes an indescribable mignonette-like scent. Many times I have urged agriculturists to introduce this fine "papilionacea" to the United States, but my pleas have always fallen on deaf ears.

A deep green, the sprouts of the new "lupinus odorata" soon covered the planted field and, after two months' growth, strong, healthy, four-foot-high plants with four to six-inch flower stems of bright yellow bloom saturated the air a mile in circumference with their delicate perfume, a feast for both nose and eyes. Unfortunately, the field must be mowed for a more practical use. The cut lupines were plowed under, forming another thick layer of humus, this time saturated with nitrogen. It will be easy for you, dear reader, to convince yourself of the existence of the useful Bacilli Wagneri if you dislodge one of the "papilionacea" plants—beans, peas, clover or acacia. Adhering to its roots you will find several knots. These knots are the domiciles of those minute soil improvers.

The field work completed, I went back to Amsterdam to inspect my little garden plot behind the house where I had planted all kinds of fruit tree seeds. They were now developed, forming small two-year-old trees, ready for transplanting. Back in Apeldoorn, having laid out one acre for fruit culture, I replanted the young trees. After satisfactory growth of these saplings I grafted them. In one or two years we would be blessed with a good deal of fine fruit. I sowed the rest of this field with clover to augment the amount of nitrogen.

This was a mistake. As soon as the clover appeared above ground, it seemed as if all the rabbits from miles around were rendezvousing at the Hammer clover field for supper. The Holland hunting laws at that time were the worst on earth as the Queen was the only person who had hunting rights in my district, which extended approximately 100 miles. A landowner inside this area was not even allowed to destroy the obnoxious animals on his own property. When I saw the rabbits invading my clover field, I got my gun and sneaked forward to get in shooting range, very much aware of my disregard of these laws.

My long shot, the distance diminishing its force, only wounded the rabbit. He ran laboriously toward the road. Just then I saw the letter-carrier coming down the road on his delivery route. I knew he would meet the rabbit and I feared he would denounce me for non-observance of the hunting law; but when I saw that he dispatched the rabbit with a strong kick of his wooden shoes, I knew he was my friend. I then fetched the animal and prepared a tasty dinner for Ernst and me. Several times I repeated these same tactics, trading my clover for fresh game.

Ernst and little Marie (whom we called Sis) were two fine strong, healthy children thanks to their mother's excellent care. Ernst, now four years old, Sis, two, saw each other once a week when Mother came with Sis to Apeldoorn. Both children had great fun romping around the big fields, and my wife was enthused about our place and its wide views. Sometimes we would picnic in an adjoining pine wood where a clear view of the Queen's Castle was the main attraction.

Marie was to have the newest baby in about six months. My decision to quit music entirely had been strengthened by this new expectation. She and I were completely in unison concerning life in the country and its advantages for the children's education. Marie now came to live at our farm full-time, and we had all the furniture moved from the city house. If necessity called for us to augment our income, she could easily start a practice in the nearby town of Apeldoorn. MD's in Holland must also pass a pharmacist's examination, so country doctors there are always prepared to fill prescriptions, which side-issue also nets a financial increase. So, n'en despaire, we did not need to worry.

Not willing to lose contact with the musical world entirely although I was no longer one of its citizens, I wrote several scientific articles for some of the leading professional periodicals, including some of a controversial nature like that concerning Lucy's "L'Anacrouse" and Jaques Dalcroze's[25] Eurhythmics. Another impressive "call to arms" was released when the Bohemian String Quartet gave a concert in Amsterdam. What a revelation! There was never before, nor ever will be, such a perfect ensemble. It was a true melting pot with four personalities beautifully melded into one. Hoffman, the first violinist, Suk, the second violinist and son-in-law of Dvorak, and Nedbal, the outstanding viola player, were all students at the Prague Conservatory of Music where Professor Hanush was teacher of violoncello. He was the founder and indefatigable mentor of the quartet. These four remarkable artists took the world by storm, giving four successive concerts to "sold out" houses in Amsterdam, yours truly attending all of them, not missing the occasion to tell them of the deep gratitude I felt for their marvelous performances. The four virtuosi were then invited by President Diaz, the tycoon of Mexico and a great music-lover, to come to Mexico and play for him. He enthusiastically kept them there a whole month, playing for him daily. Upon their departure he gave each an enormous share of his highly valuable silver mine stock, representing for each of the four

[25] **Émile Jaques-Dalcroze** (July 6, 1865 – July 1, 1950) was an Austrian composer, musician and music educator, who developed Dalcroze's Eurhythmics. "Dalcroze's method teaches musical concepts, often through movement. The variety of movement analogues used for musical concepts develop an integrated and natural musical expression in the student. Turning the body into a well-tuned musical instrument—Dalcroze felt—was the best path for generating a solid, vibrant musical foundation." (V.H. Mead, "More than Mere Movement – Dalcroze Eurhythmics", Music Editors Journal: 82(4): 38-41.)

a sizable capital investment. Theirs were never simply concert tours but triumphal marches around the globe. More of this unique foursome later.

Chapter 13   Coal Dust

With apprehension I became aware of Marie's seemingly declining health. When I spoke to her about it she confirmed my suspicion and confided her doubt concerning the regular course of her pregnancy. As an MD, she knew there was something wrong, and she expected a probable abortion. As she was with me in the country at this time, she suggested calling the Queen's physician who lived nearby who had been one of her co-students at Amsterdam University.

One of the following days the letter carrier brought me a great surprise. He handed me a letter postmarked Bochum, Germany. Strange! What could I be receiving from Bochum? It was a call to come to that city for a meeting with the committee of the town's symphony orchestra—they needed a conductor. Our friend, Miss Repelius, was with us at the time I received this communiqué. My wife urged me to go to Bochum to learn of the conditions and details of the position in question. I was very reluctant to go at this time as I was anxious about her condition and wished to hear the doctor's diagnosis. She was adamant and reassured me; and her old friend would be there with her. Reluctantly, I departed for Bochum. The conferences there lasted only a few days, but my further inquiries extended the time of my stay.

On the last day of my sojourn in Bochum, I received a telegram from our friend: "Hasten your return. Betsy Repelius." I was dumbfounded upon receiving this startling note and hurriedly left for Apeldoorn. When I arrived, no one was at home. Taking the train for Amsterdam I found the children in Miss Repelius's care at our original home. This is what Miss Repelius told me. "The day of your departure for Bochum your wife prematurely gave birth to her baby. It was a girl and was born dead. The following day when the doctor visited her, your wife complained of peculiar pains. He assured her she would feel better the next day. However, the next morning, after a torturous, sleepless night from which she emerged exhausted, she was convinced her condition was serious. She asked me to hand her a mirror. She examined herself and then told me that she was certain the doctor had carelessly brought her childbed fever from another woman's delivery. 'It's a deadly sickness,' she said. 'If you do not get me instantly on a train for a hospital in Amsterdam, I will die.' I went quickly to the nearest neighbor and used their telephone to call the railroad inspector. I told him of the emergency and he said that one hour later a freight train was to start for Amsterdam. That was the earliest train possible. Your wife, the children and I went in the neighbor's tea-wagon to Apeldoorn. We boarded the train, your wife on a stretcher. In Amsterdam, an ambulance took her to the Catholic Hospital as she wished. The doctor reported to me shortly thereafter she was extremely ill and added that for some time it would be absolutely impossible to visit her."

That same afternoon I saw the consulting chief physician of the hospital and asked him about the consequences of Marie's malady upon her future. (His manner would influence my reply to Bochum, which I promised to send as soon as possible.) Frankly and earnestly he told me she probably would never again have the strength to follow her professional career.

As it was now up to me to fill the breadbasket, I went back to Bochum and accepted the position of conductor of their Municipal Symphony Orchestra. I rented an apartment, not wishing to live by myself in a large house. Before coming to Bochum I had arranged for our city home to be sold. Our two children stayed in Miss Repelius's home and I faithfully kept in daily contact with her regarding their welfare. After about a month, she informed me that the day before she had been granted a 10-minute visit with Marie in the hospital. She wrote, "Our dear doctor has suffered so much; she is a different person. Speaking still seems difficult for her. When I carefully told her of your new position she wept, but at the end of my visit she seemed composed and asked me to tell you to write to her and, if possible, to come to see her."

Luckily, Bochum was not far from Amsterdam, so the next day I departed with haste to see my poor wife. On that first visit I was convinced that the chief physician's diagnosis was right.

Returning to Bochum thereafter I plunged energetically into a difficult task; the entire rearrangement of the orchestra, personnel, and composing and balancing of the season's programs. Leaving the assistant conductor to continue with the outlined work I again spent a day in Amsterdam and found my wife's condition slightly improved. This time we were able to have a few minutes to discuss our future.

I visited her every week and, after several weeks had elapsed, her progress was steady although very slow. She was finally able to leave the hospital and return back to our peaceful farm home and the children, accompanied by Miss Repelius and the maid. In these restful surroundings and again near her beloved children, her recuperation advanced more rapidly with the sympathetic care of her friend as well as the maid. With the tranquil beauty of the countryside and the view of the brilliantly blooming field of yellow lupine with their delightful scent, her old serene spirit returned. Her body's strength, however, did not keep pace with her spiritual recovery, and to my great sorrow I must admit that never again, to the end of her life, did she regain her former physical vitality. The physician had been right—it was an absolute impossibility for her to ever again take up a regular practice as an MD.

During these months of her recuperation I lived my old bachelor's life in Bochum, visiting Marie and the children every weekend. To make one of my visits to Apeldoorn a real surprise, I bought from a friend a handsome, well-nourished pony, a really spoiled family pet. I intended to arrive this time on horseback. That surprise was rudely spoiled by my miscalculations. I started at an early morning hour in order to finish the day's journey at the Holland boundary line. Everything proceeded smoothly; the best of oats and several rest periods seemed to keep my steed in fine shape. But upon nearing Holland, I began to feel I had underestimated both horse and rider's physical powers. Near the entrance of a little village the knees of my poor tired pony buckled and both of us went down. Not enough strength was left in my own knees to stick to the saddle—I flew over the front of the horse head first. My face went into the coal dust which covered the street and my glasses were pressed against my cheekbones; luckily they did not break but left under each eye a cut filled with coal dust. I took my slightly limping horse to the railroad station, dispatching him to Apeldoorn. The next day I arrived at the farm with my nice new pony "per pedes apostolorum" (by the feet of the apostles). On my subsequent visits to Apeldoorn, we had great pleasure taking refreshing trips with our willing pony who seemed to enjoy carrying us along in the little wagon I acquired. I carried two black marks on my face for a long time thereafter.

When we felt Marie was well enough to move, I found a spacious apartment and engaged a middle-aged lady who'd been recommended by trusted acquaintances to serve as Stütze der Hausfrau (a housewife's helper) and hired two well-qualified servants as well. (In Germany, a servant must possess a book in which are inscribed testimonials of persons in whose homes the servant has been occupied.) My wife liked this arrangement which eliminated any physical exertion on her part. Everything proceeded smoothly under the experienced direction of the Stütze der Hausfrau.

Bochum was an industrial center surrounded by an imposing number of large coal mines; a prosperous city without a single jobless person. But oh! oh! that coal dust! You could wash your white curtains immaculately— always within one week following the washing they would change color again. As our apartment was located in the center of town, the only available place I could find at the time, I constantly kept watch to find an abode near the Stadtpark and finally I succeeded. In a newly-built, architecturally well-conceived apartment house, I was fortunate to be able to rent pleasant quarters on the second floor which were appropriate for my family's needs.

Upon moving to this new home, my wife began to take over the direction of the servants' work. As untiringly and as well as the lady who was my wife's assistant performed her duties, Marie, with her Holland training, could not restrain herself from taking an active role in the management of the household.

Years earlier on one of her vacations spent in Tyrol, my wife had made the acquaintance of the family Neuber from Vienna, consisting of Field Marshal Neuber, an instructor at the Austrian War Academy—an institution where the officers of the general staff are prepared for their duties—along with his wife, a charming, motherly lady whom Marie called "Aunt," and their three daughters. Marie's acquaintance with this family had ripened through the years into a deep friendship. We now had more room in our home than before and it was a natural impulse on my wife's part to invite the Neubers to Bochum for a visit. The 85-year-old Field Marshal and his wife came first and, two days later, one of the daughters arrived who was Marie's best friend. We all spent a pleasant week together during their stay.

One day the Field Marshal and I visited the immense Bochum Ironworks, famous for its production of church bells and railroad material. As I knew the chief engineer of the factory well, he was our guide throughout this highly instructive tour. At one point, he demonstrated to us the tremendous crushing power of a colossal hammer weighing many tons and told us the following story about it, having once guided the old Emperor Wilhelm through the works. At that time, he told the Emperor the manipulator of the hammer was able to stop the enormous thing, no matter how swift the fall, at a fraction of an inch above an object to be crushed. The Emperor calmly took his precious gold watch and chain and put it on the large iron plate under the hammer, urging the attendant to prove his cleverness. The hammer moved upward to a considerable height, dropped like lightning and halted at a nearly imperceptible distance above the watch. The Emperor, astounded and pleased with the workman's skill, handed him the watch and chain as a souvenir—a royal gift indeed!

At one of the concerts I conducted in a nearby town, I met the owner of the hotel in which I stayed over-night. We were pleasantly surprised when we discovered both of us were ardent hunters. He told me of his weekly hunting trips to a place near the Holland boundary line. He and three of his friends had rented a hunting territory comprising the property of many farmers in the area, a few thousand acres in all, adjacent to a count's extensive properties, as it was a custom in Germany for the farmers to conjointly auction the hunting rights of their land. Seemingly enthused by my spirited patter about hunting, he invited me to the following week's hunting party.

At the railroad station I met the hotel owner and his three friends. After an hour's traveling, we arrived at a small clean village and entered a solidly-built and thatch-roofed Westphalia country inn. We absorbed a sub-stantial portion of country-fresh scrambled eggs with the famous Westphalian ham. What a hearty breakfast to prepare a hungry hunter for his arduous task—onward to the hunt! We were out all day, then returned back to the inn where we consumed a satisfying dinner, enjoying a peaceful sleep thereafter. Dinner cost 30¢, breakfast 20¢, and a night's lodging 15¢. A whole day's rich living for 65¢. (Just like today.) Hunting-coats filled with game, we returned home, refreshed and ready for the week's work ahead. After another hunt with the congenial four, I begged of them to make me a participant in their venture, paying my share of the rent. I became No. 5 and remained active in these outings with them through my five years in Bochum.

Sometimes, after hunting, we called upon one of the local farmers providing us access to his land. In these farmers' kitchens were hung the world-renowned Westphalian hams on long poles in front of a generously-sized fireplace, waiting to be smoked. We were able to purchase some five or six-pounders for three marks (75¢) each. And when we wanted a chicken, we were told to just shoot one of the roosters strutting around the yard!

These recreational excursions exerted a beneficial influence upon my health. Coming back from a strenuous hunt, I would always sleep so restfully, and with renewed energy the following day, I would return to my duties thoroughly refreshed. In the succeeding years right up until today, I have as much as possible incorporated these life-giving hunting days. So please, dear reader, do not upbraid me if now and then I leave the common track and entice you to follow me on some surprisingly exciting hunting trips.

From hunting to Bach's "Passion of St. Matthew" may be a startling jump, but I am recording sequential events here and must adhere to the facts.

A large mixed chorus had been divided into two separate parts, and, under the direction of the city school's Superintendent of Music, he took the tremendous job in hand of studying the "Passion of St. Matthew." This composition demands a larger number of performers than anything composed before Bach. Two mixed choruses, two orchestras, a boys' chorus, and four soloists comprise the large infrastructure necessary for its performance—a dreadful task for even the best of conductors! Apparently the work involved was too weighty a burden for the over-ambitious conductor who frantically strove for an early presentation of the noble composition. Likely due to the strain, he contracted a severe neurasthenia (nervous exhaustion) necessitating a strict period of rest.

The final rehearsal, to which the public would be admitted for an entrance fee, had already been advertised when the conductor, by doctor's order, had to quit his work. What a calamity after nearly two years of strenuous rehearsals! Frantically, the unfortunate chorus leader sent telegrams to Germany's foremost conductors asking them to take over his conductorship for the general rehearsal and performance of the "Passion." None would accept the proposal unless they were given time for three rehearsals beforehand. As the day of the general rehearsal arrived, a messenger came to me asking me to accompany him to the conductor's sickroom for a conference.

Arriving at his home, I found the pale, emaciated leader in great distress. He explained what I have related above, and pleaded with me to help him. I must confess I had never been fortunate enough to hear the work performed and had never seen the score. I did know very well it would be difficult to conduct, but, full of confidence in my ability—young egotist!—I calmly assured him I would make a great effort to honor his good work in preparing his chorus for a performance of one of the greatest masterworks of all times.

That evening I entered the concert-hall with unbound optimism. I began by separating the choruses and orchestras and arranged one chorus and one orchestra upon the left side of the stage and the other two upon the right side. The four soloists I put in the center and the boys' chorus with their leader in a balcony above the whole ensemble. I opened the score, lifted my arms, and began the orchestra prelude. (For the first time, I conducted without the customary baton, feeling it would be an advantage in this case. I never used one again, and for many, many years I was the only conductor to do so. Others later followed my example.)

I am one of those happy souls who is gifted with a faculty for reading an orchestra score easily at sight, like reading a book, and if I had had any doubts at all, they were quickly dispelled after a few bars. The members of the chorus stood in a rather justifiably dejected attitude, their heads down, eyes only on their music. I gave them the sign for their entrance, but at best, the attack was a ragged one. Heedless of the fact there was an audience of approximately 3,000 in the auditorium, I stopped the proceeding.

"Ladies and gentlemen, I am up here," I admonished the chorus. "Please look at me and not at your music. You have been studying this for two years; you ought to know it by now."

For a while, with my encouraging gestures, everything went satisfactorily—until the leader of the boys' chorus began to lead his boys the way he wanted to without so much as glancing in my direction—however a sharp remonstrance on my part brought him to rights. After that, things went much more smoothly, but it took almost five hours for me to satisfy myself that the next day's performance would be a successful one. The entire audience remained with us for the entire five hours. At the end of this preview "performance" I received a rousing demonstration, with the male members of the chorus lifting me upon their shoulders and carrying me triumphantly through the concert-hall. I was elated at the turn of the situation and considered the successful conducting at sight of the "Passion of St. Matthew" a sort of passing of my final examination to become a true symphony orchestra conductor.

The first performance in Bochum of Beethoven's Ninth Symphony which I conducted was also a successful venture. The following criticism by Robert Luther of the Bochum daily newspaper bears witness:

"In the directing of Heinrich Hammer, all the details a sincere conductor should observe are united; a broad, clear perception, exhaustive knowledge, warm sentiment, and the force to impart his knowledge to others; an authoritative grip upon the fundamental idea of the work to be performed, and the utmost care in its preparation and execution."

Many music-lovers from the nearby cities of Essen and Dortmund were season ticket holders for our symphony concerts.

I was keenly interested in the newly-formed "Allgemeiner Deutscher Musiker Verband," a kind of musicians' union, and was chosen to be one of eight members of its national committee. The General Assembly was held that year in the 2,000 year-old Hansa City, Hamburg, which is one of the largest harbors in the world. Several hundred representatives of the musicians' unions of Germany gathered there and labored valiantly to remedy various union laws and improve the positions of their fellows, and I made several speeches to further good propositions. While I was there, I met an old friend from Amsterdam, the manager of the Concertgebouw Orchestra. We went to an old, old Rathskeller to empty a bottle of old, old red wine in toasting the memory of old golden times.

Passing along the Alster Basin one day while still in Hamburg, I spied in the window of a well-known piano store a concert grand, just the hue of our furniture in Bochum. Entering the store, I tried the instrument and liked its tone and construction, purchased it, and ordered it sent to Bochum. This good piano, after many lengthy transportations, finally found a resting place in Amsterdam where Ernst, who was by then a fine amateur pianist, made good use of it.

Back in Bochum I plunged with renewed fervor into my work but soon I received a call from Apeldoorn. I was asked to bring my orchestra there and give a symphony concert in honor of Queen Wilhelmina's birthday. We were warmly welcomed and the whole orchestra was invited to a sumptuous supper after the greatly-lauded performance.

To keep the members of the orchestra interested in both their work and world affairs, I arranged for some of the free evenings in our schedule to be devoted to educational lectures, given by prominent persons or myself. These lectures, attended by the orchestra personnel and their families and friends, were well-patronized. I also instituted a fine system for latecomers: five minutes late, a twenty-five pfenige fine; ten minutes, fifty pfenige, etc. The money accumulated was deposited as a fund for the annual orchestra festival, which always culminated with a lively ball. These yearly gaieties, strongly supported by the citizenry, would fill the auditorium in the Stadtpark to overflowing.

There were two special attractions for me in the city park, near which we lived. The first were the enrapturing songs of several nightingales who seemed to be residents of the park; their melodies filled the night air with lyrical beauty. The other attraction was the fishing in the park's small lake. A few times I passed moments of complete relaxation at the edge of the lake, sitting in the lush grass with a simple fishing rod, an earthworm on its hook in the water, waiting for a bite (I am sorry to say the wait was never very long). One needed no license to fish in the park, but when one became the proud possessor of a two to five-pound carp, the lucky fisherman was always willing to march to the park caretaker's cabin where the fish was weighed, then paying a very small amount per pound for his dinner. Being a hunting rather than a fishing enthusiast though, I recall with amusement these few hours by the little lake in the park.

Speaking of sports, I might as well entertain you at this point with a hunting story. A friend in town was a member of a hunting club which rented a large wooded territory in the Sauerland, a picturesque valley in which almost every inhabitant owns a small iron industry, forging and manufacturing small tools in his typically very primitive smithy—it was a smoky country indeed as a result. He invited me on a hunt and we met the other members of the party who awaited us in large wagons at the railroad station. We drove with these boisterous, congenial companions and all our dogs a few miles inland and stopped at a cozy country inn. From there we marched to our hunting ground where we started a rabbit drive.

I had just been posted on top of a small hill when a rabbit, evidently not scenting my presence, came running toward me. The fellows below the hill hollered at me, "Shoot! Shoot!" I loathed and still loath to shoot downhill, as almost anyone doing so will overshoot. Excited however by my fellows' urgings, I shot—and missed. Then the fun began! One of the hunters, a big fat owner of a brewery, started it by saying, "Well, how can you expect a Musikdirector to hit a rabbit?" The jokes began flying back and forth. As we crossed through a young oak grove the brewer behind me was still joking about this inept musician. Just then a wild pigeon flew over us. "Shoot!" the brewer yelled.

"I don't want to miss again. Too far."

The brewer threw his gun up, shot and missed. The pigeon came soaring back on the wind stirred up by the shot. Quickly I sent my own shot after the bird. It dropped to the ground. I picked it up and presented it to the brewer, who looked crestfallen. And, voila, I was a laughingstock no more.

We then went to the blinds to shoot love-sick cocks, and I was crouching, watchfully waiting for one of the Auerhans (of the Swedish Orre species) when one landed near my hiding place and started his burlesque antics. His queer clownings made me laugh so hard I could not raise my gun to end the life of the gay gallivanter. Not wishing to again be made a target for jibs I kept quiet about this latest incident.

At nightfall we returned to the inn where the game, piece by piece, was auctioned off among us, the money used to pay for drinks. I bought two rabbits and was given the pigeon as a trophy. I went to bed immediately after supper, exhausted, but the rest of the party disturbed my sleep for hours before they decided to greet Morpheus too.

One afternoon after a serious rehearsal, I took up my trusty fiddle again to study Spohr's Eighth Violin Concerto as I was to play it at the next week's symphony concert. After a few hours of study I went into the living room, and at that moment a visitor was announced—a bandmaster, Urban. That name recalled the time in Örebro when I had engaged a 17-year-old youth by that name as first trumpet player. He had been a tall, light-blond, beautiful youngster, a ladies' delight, but also an earnest and splendidly gifted musician. These memories still rummaging in my mind, there enters my old Urban, trim and neatly attired.

He was near 30 now but still the same good-looking fellow. He told me he had volunteered for service in the pioneer regimental band and was sent to the bandmaster department of the Royal Academy of Music, and this was the nature of the uniform he wore. He had stopped in Bochum on a tour with his band and had come to ask me to conduct the Tanhauser Overture in a rehearsal while they were in the city. I willingly complied and found a fine pliable spirit so I was able to carry out my wishes easily—a pleasurable experience and a testimony to Urban's artistic ability.

Then came my appearance as soloist in Bochum where I played and conducted simultaneously. Much praise crowned the orchestra's and my own endeavor. At the last concert of the winter season we gave another performance of Beethoven's Ninth Symphony; this concert was the most outstanding of the entire concert series. The well-trained chorus of the "St. Matthew Passion" formed the background of this masterwork of masterworks.

My wife's health at this time showed marked improvement. When the Paris World Exposition was announced—during which the inauguration of the Eiffel Tower was to take place—I asked her if she wanted to go. She expressed an eagerness to see our old Paris again. We stole a week and off to Paris we went! We found a quiet place at rue Blanche, near Uncle Richard's home, and called upon him to pay our respects. We passed every day at the Fair, enjoying the glorious view from the height of the Eiffel Tower, ordering one of those fascinating French lunches to fill our empty stomachs. On a visit to the Russian fur exposition, my wife saw a fur coat she especially admired. I bought it for her as a remembrance of our second visit to Paris. She wore this coat through all the years of our married life. We passed a marvelous week in this unique metropolis and went home carrying souvenirs to our children and friends.

And then there was the winter season upon us again! At one of the first symphony concerts a young friend of ours, the daughter of Mr. Landgren (who had been one of the witnesses at our wedding) played the Beethoven Emperor Concerto with great success.

The children, still continuing their education at Mrs. Koch's private school, liked their teacher and the teacher returned their affection, a circumstance which is bound to produce satisfactory progress. For example, their German was now without a trace of foreign pronunciation. Marie, who spoke it as well, was not however pleased with our Bochum surroundings. So when we passed a two weeks' vacation in Godesberg near Bonn, she became even more desirous of moving. The comparison was too great for her Holland spirit of cleanliness; the contrast of the fresh spring air of the Rhein country completely crushed the coal dust of Bochum.

I could appreciate her feelings and I had also had some difficulties in the city; it had been impossible for me to obtain more money for a larger orchestra as I wished, so I gave notice of my resignation to the Bochum municipal authorities. Reluctantly it was granted me.

We chose to live in Bonn, as it is a renowned center of learning. We attended to the packing and shipping of our furniture, however the farewell to my beloved orchestral family was a difficult one. A number of players who had entered the orchestra with no past experience had grown up in the art of symphony playing with only this one conductor, yours truly. Some had climbed to positions of leadership in their sections and I promised them my abiding interest in the furthering of their careers. Several of these worthy artists also followed me through many years thereafter as members of my orchestras.

We found a well-located, solid two-story home on the Kirschen Allee, across from the old Bishop's Palace where Beethoven's father was once a tenor singer. Ernst was now ten years old and entered the Gymnasium, Sis was eight and was enrolled in the elementary school. Our domestic life, with the aid of one of our Bochum servants, soon became routinized, and everyone breathed freer in this healthy and vigorous climate.

A pleasing interval was a visit of my dear friend, Roderich von Moisisovich, then Director of the State Conservatory of Music in the city of Graz, Austria. We enjoyed long walks in the surrounding woods, discussing all phases of our artistic careers. When I returned from the railroad station where I had seen Roderich off, Marie handed me a letter which had just arrived from Lausanne, Switzerland. It was from the president of the cooperative orchestra there, asking me if I would be willing to become its conductor. I asked Marie for her opinion on the subject.

"As much as I like Germany and its excellent schools," she said, "I must confess I like Switzerland better than any other country I've seen—except Holland, of course. If you would like to accept the Lausanne proposition, I will gladly go with you."

I, myself, had also been impressed with the country and its sturdy inhabitants while passing through on my way to Italy so many years ago, as well as more recently on our vacation in Switzerland. Also, I was very proud of the fact my own colleagues had chosen me as their leader. I sent a letter accepting the position and, by return mail, my acceptance was acknowledged. I was invited to take up my new duties the first of the following month. Marie wished to finish the term of rental at the new Bonn home, so again, as earlier in Bochum, I would have to live a bachelor's life until the arrival of the rest of the Hammer family. As I was a real "pater familias" (father of the family), I would have much preferred to go "tout ensemble" (all together) to Lausanne, but I knew my wife's plan was the wiser one.

Chapter 14   Frustration in Lausanne, Switzerland

Entrance into another foreign country required the children to acquire another tongue, this time French, which luckily their mother and father spoke fluently. As is the custom among professional people, I was received at the station by the person responsible for my journey. The president of the cooperative, a dignified elderly gentleman of German descent, offered me a hearty "Willkommen" and guided me to the entrance of a tunnel where we boarded an electric train, called a funicular, which ran swiftly along the steep incline of the tunnel to the center of the city. From here we walked over a long, beautiful bridge to a nearby street which wound upward. He then escorted me to the large apartment house where lodging had been arranged on my behalf.

Allow me to make you acquainted with the peculiar construction of this well-known city. It is built upon three steep hills, the first rising from the shore of the Lake of Geneva, the church Saint-Francois sitting atop its crest. The famous University of Lausanne crowns the second hill, and below the bridge I mentioned (which connects the first two hills) can be seen an enormous marketplace far down in the valley below, hustling and bustling with life. The third and highest hill which reaches 1100' and dominates its summit is adorned with a simple yet imposing cathedral. A continuous snake-like road leads from the lake to the top of this highest hill. Here, about the cathedral, are grouped the state, city, court, and office buildings. The view from this point embraces a wide swath of Switzerland: the entire Lake of Geneva (the south side of which is French territory); the towering Alps with their giant Mont Blanc, the highest mountain in Europe; to the east the majestic, continually snow-and-ice-covered Dent du Midi, and the enchanting valley at its feet—what a panorama! Excuse my enthusiasm, but let me urge you, if you ever visit La Suisse Romaine (Lausanne is situated in its center), don't miss ascending to the cathedral to enjoy this thrilling vista.

It was a rather arduous task to put the somewhat spoiled orchestra members to rights. Years of easy existence made possible by continuously-ensured occupation was the understandable cause of a certain laxity among the players. The symphony concerts were more "pro forma" affairs than artistic events up until this point, so I devoted my initial efforts to changing this deplorable state of affairs. As many of the members of the orchestra were also past middle age, it was not easy to guide them out of lethargy and up into the realms of pure enjoyment of classical beauty. With daily rehearsals and strict adherence to details, we were able to give a decent account of ourselves and register a successful performance at our first concert. Criticisms were favorable and the spirit of the orchestra brightened accordingly thereafter.

After the close of this concert, a gentleman, Dr. Anton Suter[26], former counselor of the Swiss Embassy in Berlin, spoke to me, expressing his thanks for the well-chosen program and the satisfactory performance of it. You will hear of this extraordinary gentleman in succeeding accounts.

The termination of the period of rental of the Bonn house neared and I inspected many a house in Lausanne to find a suitable future home for my family, but without luck. Finally in the city newspaper I found an ad: "For rent, Villa St. Pierre, second story and roof, garden, etc.." Hurriedly I traveled to the address and found it to be the property of the city building inspector, who lived on the first floor. The apartment was well arranged and spacious so I rented it. The view from the apartment, located on a corner upon the second hill of the city, was wide and lovely. Below it was a small city park, planted densely with sycamore trees, pruned so that the tops of them made the pattern of a lawn as seen from our window. Much of the city, the lake, France on the far side, and Mont Blanc glistening above the mountain range completed the magnificent scene, which was further enhanced when enjoyed from the little rose garden on the rooftop.

Enthusiastically I described all this in a letter to Marie. Two weeks after my happy find, my family and our furnishings arrived in Lausanne. Marie seemed to be very satisfied with her new home. Both children were again placed in a preparatory school to learn French.

[26] **Anton Suter** 03/02/1863 in Wil (SG) 20.11.1942 in Lausanne. Studied law at Bern, Lausanne and Leyden doctorate in Berlin (1890). Embassy attaché in Berlin and Vienna. Based in Lausanne in 1900, Suter was a pioneer of the cooperative movement, originally consumption Cooperative Society Lausanne Region (Chair until 1935). Co-founder of the house of the people of Lausanne (1899). Patron and musician, he supported the Symphony Orchestra of Lausanne which he founded in 1903. (Historisches Lexikon der Schweiz - Fabienne Abetel-Bequelin)

Lucky children. We say "like a duck to water," and so it was with them. In less than three months they were admitted to the city schools. Here it might be said that the Swiss educational system is probably the best in the world. It is not aimed at the masses but truly at individual development. Classes never contain more than 16 pupils, which actually creates a mandate for the teacher to see each pupil as an individual; they are instructed to be painstaking guides to every young scholar.

The servant question in Switzerland is a complicated issue. They are very independent by nature here and "handle with care" must be the motto for employers as a result. Their salaries are high and their Swiss national pride equally so. A middle-aged lady took care of us and the apartment the first year. I am afraid if my wife had not been the excellent housekeeper she was and had not spoken the language of the country so well, our household's sailing would not have been as smooth as it was.

During my stay in Switzerland I was fortunate to become acquainted with several outstanding individuals to whom I became deeply attached. I must tell you their well-known names: Dr. Suter, whom you have met, Henri Marteau[27], Max Reger, Émile Jaques-Dalcroze whom I knew simply as Jaques, Émile-Robert Blanchet, Professor Stilling, pathologist of the University of Lausanne, René Morax, a great Swiss writer, Hans Huber, composer, Mme. Annie Simrock, a fine pianist, the daughter of the publisher Simrock of Berlin, and Ernest Schelling. I kept in contact with each of these individuals until their deaths. Nowhere, in any country,

[27] **Henri Marteau** (March 31, 1874 – October 3, 1934) was a French violinist and composer. "Marteau was remarkable both for his individuality and for his development. His debut was made when only ten years old, at a concert given by the Vienna Philharmonic Society, conducted by Hans Richter. A tour through Switzerland and Germany followed. A year later Charles Gounod selected this young violinist to play the obbligato of a piece, Vision de Jeanne d'Arc, composed for the Joan of Arc Centenary Celebration at Reims, where he also performed, before an audience of 2500 people, his teacher Léonard's Violin Concerto No. 5". (History of Seven Days, The Illustrated American. Chicago: Illustrated American Publishing Company. 13 (154): 121–122. January 28, 1893.)

have I found such a company of true brotherhood. I gratefully look back after these many years upon the unselfish devotion of these people to me, their friend, and the many beautiful hours I spent with each of them.

Henri Marteau was like a loving brother to me and my home was his home. Numerous were the occasions we performed the world's musical masterpieces together, he as soloist, I as conductor. One of the great violinists of his time, he was to give two performances of Jaques-Dalcroze's violin concerto, which was dedicated to Henri, one in Lausanne, the other in Geneva. I was to conduct the first in Geneva, Jaques the second in Lausanne. I did not know the concerto. When the orchestra parts arrived the day of its performance I quickly sight-read the work with the orchestra; discovering six glaring misprints in the parts, even two bars of a two-clarinet solo missing. We had hardly finished the sight-playing when Henri arrived.

"Have you played this concerto before?" I asked him.

"Yes."

"There are six mistakes in the parts," I informed him.

"No! How could that be?" he asked, astonished. "Jaques conducted it himself in Berlin."

When I showed him the mistakes, he was dumbfounded.

A little later, when Henri played the entrance theme of the work, I felt it necessary to stop him.

"I'm sorry, Henri," I said, "but you are playing that theme too slowly."

"Oh, no," he said. "Jaques wants it so."

"Jaques is wrong," I said. I explained my reason for the change and he played it the way I suggested. When I tell you that Jaques, conducting the second concert in Lausanne, took the same tempo we had taken at the Geneva concert, I am sure you can picture my astonishment.

Some of the orchestra members, the older ones, could no longer sustain the continuous effort necessary to uphold and heighten the prestige of the group as a whole. As the individual incomes were very satisfactory, I proposed to the president that they engage a few more artists (he was the first flutist, formerly a fine artist, but now rheumatic and somewhat deaf, his intonation suffering as a result of this handicap)—not to replace the older ones, but to improve the tone quality of the orchestra. My proposition was rejected.

Dr. Suter was an excellent amateur pianist, a proficient sight-reader and avid ensemble player. We played sonatas together often. Once he surprised me by playing several pages of the difficult César Franck Sonata for Violin and Piano by heart. He was also a multi-millionaire. His mother, a countess, owned much valuable property; his father was Consul-General of Holland in Switzerland. Dr. Suter's wife was the sister of the six-times President of Switzerland, da Motta. Dr. Suter was also highly interested in my efforts to improve the status of the orchestra. I told him about the suggestion I had made to the president of the orchestra and its negative result.

"You tell the president I will pay the salaries of any players he may wish to engage to augment the orchestra," he said to me.

This royal offer I submitted enthusiastically to the president, explaining to him again the profits to be gained by the cooperative through the employment of additional musicians. The next day I was informed that this new proposal was also unacceptable.

At the next morning's rehearsal I addressed the orchestra.

"Gentlemen! Your rejection of my two propositions has shown me clearly that you are afraid of new blood and are allowing that unreasonable fear to stand in your way of making finer music. To me the latter comes first. Therefore, you will please accept my resignation at the conclusion of our contract term."

Absolute silence.

The next day, the news of my resignation had reached the press and, as usual in such cases, a multiplicity of opinions was voiced everywhere. Dr. Suter met me after the following not-exactly-inspiring rehearsal.

"I am astonished that affairs have taken such a turn," he said to me; he paused reflectively. "No!" he replied emphatically, "You will not leave Lausanne. You engage the orchestra you want and I will pay the costs."

What a surprise to me! This fine sympathetic soul and fervent lover of music was willing to stand sponsor for such a costly enterprise in order to realize an ideal.

The following morning I told the orchestra of the impending change, of the aims of the new orchestra, and of its non-competitive operation. The present orchestra would keep its position in the city and its income (derived in the main from concerts in hotels). The new one would only play weekly symphony concerts in the "Maison du Peuple," a concert hall Dr. Suter had built a year ago and donated to the people of Lausanne. The old orchestra held its rehearsals in the basement of this building. I declared further to the members of the orchestra that those who wished to be part of the new organization should make their applications now. Only four of the original Lausanne Symphony applied for positions. All were accepted.

Maison du Peuple

From now onward the cooperative spirit dwindled to nothing. At one rehearsal shortly thereafter difficulties arose. It happened that the first French horn player, a rather insignificant being but a fairly good hornist, made a glaring mistake during the rehearsal of a piece, an unusual occurrence. I patiently repeated the passage, but he made the same mistake, apparently willfully, and on a third trial did it once more, obviously attempting to rile me. At that point I spoke calmly to the president, asking him to talk to the horn player. The president rose and loudly called out to the culprit, "Behave yourself! I'll fine you a hundred francs for this!"

The weakling was crushed and sank low in his chair, tears rolling down his cheeks.

"No," I said. "The fine will harm his family more than him. If he does his duty hereafter as becomes a gentleman, I will forgive him and forget this regretful episode."

It was not easy sledding to lead the uncooperative cooperative to the end of my contract term. One threatening incident bore witness to the general spirit of the older members of the orchestra in particular. A mediocre double-bass player, a stocky fellow about 55 years old with a real Bolshevik nature, seemed to have been chosen the leader of the opposition. One day he took advantage of the intermission of the rehearsal to address some nasty remarks to me. The calm but biting answer I gave him aroused his hot anger. Menacingly, he advanced toward me with clenched fists. I was standing next to the percussion instruments and quickly grabbed one of the heavy drumsticks. I had my back to the wall.

"All right, come on," I said.

Hesitatingly, he looked around. When he saw several "loyalists" ready to pounce on him, he quickly changed his advance to a retreat. This was the last disturbance.

I finished my duties with the cooperative and took over the leadership of the new Philharmonic Orchestra, a fine assemblage of capable artists. The concertmaster, a rising young violinist, a pupil of Joachim (at that time the master of violinists and President of the Royal Academy of Music in Berlin), was a valuable leader of the string section. The assistant concertmaster was also my assistant conductor, one of my loyal band from Bochum, several of whom had joined me in Lausanne after I had notified them about my change. My first flutist was a great artist, a pupil of the famous Parisian flute school.

Dr. Suter was proud of the newly-launched institution he had championed and he expressed his satisfaction with the outcome of the first concert by inviting the members of the orchestra to a lavish meal at a first-class hotel afterward. There, in well-chosen phrases, he spoke of the favorable reception of the program and performance and his hope that this new venture would prove to be a valuable asset to the city of Lausanne.

As time went on, other music enthusiasts offered their thanks for the pleasurable evenings the orchestra had given them. Among them were several of those persons I mentioned before, acquaintances which had ripened into pure friendship. One was Emile Blanchet, the great piano virtuoso, composer, and indefatigable mountain climber, having accomplished 50 first ascensions of Swiss peaks. His book telling about these hazardous experiences was crowned by the French Academy (he was probably the only pianist who ever accomplished such feats).

He and I would often take long, exhausting walks together. Occasionally, he and his little dachshund were also my companions on hunting trips. One of those trips was the source of one of our undying jokes.

Early one morning we took the train to Morges and climbed eight miles up to Apple from a point near Paderewski's home, where one of my hunting friends lived. From there, we hiked through two feet of snow—which was hard going for Emile who was clad in his heavy fur coat and accompanied by his little doggie who got lost repeatedly in the deep soft stuff. Emile stopped a few feet ahead of me, his legs wide apart, apparently looking for the dachshund. As I took a step, something slid out from under my foot. It was a scared rabbit, covered with snow; he dived right between Emile's legs and I shot. In front of a surprised Emile dropped a dead rabbit. This rabbit lived for years in Emile's letters to me. He never would forget to mention the droll incident. Thanks, my dear friend Emile, for the many unforgettable hours we spent in both philosophical discussions and silent companionship during our long and always-invigorating walks.

Henri Marteau was Professor of La Classe de Virtuosité at the Conservatoire de Musique de Genève. A number of eminent violinists were called upon yearly to be judges of the skill of the contenders for the virtuoso diploma. For several years in succession, I served as one of these judges. One year, I was asked to compose the music for the sight-reading examination. I composed a tricky little number, and only one of the future virtuosi played it without mistake. He was a Mr. Brand, an American I met many years later in Washington D.C. at a performance by the Metropolitan Opera. He was one of the first violinists in its orchestra.

At another year's examination, Paul Viardot, son of my former vocal teacher, was one of the judges. At the time, he was conductor at the Grand Opera in Paris. After one of the examinations, Henri, Paul, and I drove along the Lake of Geneva, stopping at a small restaurant which was well-known to a discerning clientele who appreciated its fresh trout dinners. When we ordered trout, the proprietor of the place, a fishnet in hand, bustled down to the lake, fished a few live trout out of his underwater fish cage and returned quickly, then setting about preparing them for us. We held a lively conversation, full of pleasant memories.

"Paul, how is your uncle?" Henri asked at one point. "I know he is very old."

"Oh, him? He's only 99." Paul's eyes twinkled. "He just came back from Africa with his valet." (He, like his sister, was a distinguished singing teacher. He had lived in London for years and I later learned that, on his 100th birthday, King Edward gave a brilliant dinner for him.)

The centennial festival commemorating the birth of Schiller was near. I was appointed director of the great dramatist's historical play, "Wilhelm Tell", and I composed a suitable aria for soprano and orchestra for the occasion. The role of Tell was played by the director of one of Lausanne's foremost educational institutions, a splendid male specimen with a dressy brown beard adorning his face and an energetic personality. A rather comical incident occurred during one of the rehearsals. A serious scene was being enacted by the hero. "Through this deep canyon he must pass," Wilhelm Tell acclaimed loudly.

"Tell, telephone," a stentorian voice behind the stage suddenly called.

The fine pose of Tell went flat and the entire cast roared with laughter.

Ernest Schelling, the prominent American pianist, lived at the home of the Mayor of Lausanne where he was treated like a son of the house. The wife of the Mayor was one of several pupils who studied ensemble playing with me. These lessons were a great help in providing me the opportunity to keep up my violin playing.

Schelling was a pupil of Paderewski who, as often as his numerous concert engagements would allow, passed his time at his home in Rion Bosson near Morges. It was a unique dwelling on an 80-acre estate situated high above the Lake of Geneva. King Edward had made him a present of a number of sheep which grazed in the succulent pastures there. A large greenhouse erected by Paderewski provided lovers of the luscious Ribier grape with the fine fruit for which he charged a costly five francs per pound. Schelling played Paderewski's "Fantaisie Polonaise" at one of our concerts. His mentor was present and elated to hear one of his cherished compositions performed. After the concert he came into my director's room and broke out excitedly, "It was perfect! You will hear from me!" We talked for a few minutes and then he left. As he had promised though, I did hear from him. To express his appreciation for our "perfect" performance, he gave a special concert every year, the proceeds of which were allotted to the members of the orchestra—a noble thanksgiving indeed!

On the lakeshore at Ouchy, in a grandly-proportioned mansion surrounded by acres of garden space (which were under the meticulous care of a French master-gardener) lived Mme. Annie Simrock. Her ancestors were the first publishers of Beethoven's compositions. Many were the times my friends and I spent in this congenial home playing piano trios, quartets, and quintets to our hearts' content. So many delicious fruits were harvested under the gardener's care that I equally looked forward to partaking of these riches of nature to which we were always treated.

The celebrated sculptor, Hauschild, was a guest at her home while he worked on the design and creation of the monument which she commissioned to be erected upon the grave of her father who had been buried in the cemetery of Lausanne. A large block of white Carrara marble was the material which the skillful hands of the artist formed into an enlivened allegory: a life-sized angel sitting upon a pedestal playing the harp and casting an inspired countenance to the sky. It was truly a masterwork of pure lines. Many visitors to the cemetery bide a little at this statue, enthralled by its beauty. Through many years, Hauschild and I kept in close contact. On one of my visits to Berlin as guest conductor he was my congenial host in the Grünewald Artists Colony where he lived as a bachelor in one of its quaint studios.

One pleasant traveling experience we shared was en route over the Gemmi Pass going to visit Mme. Simrock and her sister in her sister's summer home in Aathal. We took the train from Lausanne to Bad Leuk, situated at the foot of the Gemmi. We entered the famous bathhouse there where a lively crowd of men and women sat steeping up to their necks in the healing waters of the pool, each provided with a small floating table, most of them cluttered with newspapers, coffee cups, cakes, and various other such items. As soon as they noticed our presence, they greeted us by wickedly splashing us with water. Hastily we retreated, barely avoiding a complete drenching. The remainder of the day we spent exploring the little town.

Early the next morning we prepared our rucksacks for the tramp over the Gemmi, an extremely steep climb, one which I could not repeat today. Halfway up, we met a one-armed, middle-aged Swiss man carrying a large and deep willow basket on his back, his son who looked to be about 12 at his side. We entered into conversation with him and he told us he was an Edelweiss picker. (Edelweiss is a composite plant, growing exclusively in the high Alps. It has a unique woolly foliage, is difficult to find, and is sold at a high price per single little grayish flower.) He told us he and his son climbed to the heights and scanned the steep sides of the mountains for the flower. Often the father, a rope around his middle, was lowered by his son down the side of the mountain to pick the flowers from the precipices—a dangerous occupation for a person possessing all his limbs, let alone a man with only one arm. As he only received ten centimes—two cents—per flower, hustling was required to keep a family alive on such earnings. He offered to carry our packs in his basket. We protested emphatically but he insisted, saying he often carried much heavier loads. Nearly at the top of the Gemmi he showed us a little side path and told us a few plants of edelweiss were growing some way down the path. Eager to pick some ourselves we followed him and found the plants. The flowers were small. (Our guide had to find larger ones.) Nevertheless, our enthusiasm grew, and seeing a party of three ladies coming up the trail, we shouted like children, "We've found some Edelweiss here, come and pick some too!"

They hastened toward us and were as overjoyed as us to pick a few of these rare specimens. To the end of the trail and to the foot of the majestic glacier atop the mountain, we kept company with this group, a mother with her two daughters. Our guide told us that formerly a few travelers who were unable to climb the Gemmi trail had made it on donkey-back. Several of these people had perished when, going back down the steep trail, their donkeys slipped and plunged with their riders over the 4,000-foot precipice. One summer, an English countess and several others paid with their lives for this hazardous adventure, and thereafter it was forbidden to use any medium of transportation but one's feet.

We stood at the base of the silvery glacier, marveling at the colors dancing off the numberless facets of glistening ice. The ladies stayed there longer than us as our destination was now near. Our guide and his son lost themselves in the awe-inspiring mountain labyrinth and bid us a resounding farewell. Full of life's vigor, we marched down, down, down into the darkly wooded Aathal, where the sun's rays cast iridescent lights here and there through the dense pines, arriving at the Simrock summer home at evening time. We were very tired but had enough spirit left to tell all the details of our trip from our departure from Lausanne till the hour of our arrival in this peaceful valley. Our eager listeners did not however forget to ask the cook to prepare a substantial meal for us which we gratefully consumed.

The meal finished, lively plan-making took place. The unavoidable reaction: two tired pilgrims not willing to stop the conversation and seek relief for their weary limbs in a soft bed. But finally we bade our compassionate hostesses good night. I dreamed of the grandiose panorama that had unfolded to us lucky fellows on our sojourn to this lovely setting.

All too soon, the sun sent his morning greeting into our room. Refreshed and anxious to explore our new environs we stepped into the dining room where we found our hostesses diligently preparing the breakfast table. The new day soon found us filling our stomachs in anticipation of tasking adventures. It was decided we would spend the day exploring our surroundings, finishing with a visit to the Blue Seeli a few miles away.

The house occupied by Mme. Simrock and her sister was situated on the main road from the Gemmi to the

Vierwaldstättersee. Towering heights bounded the house on two sides. The pinewoods were a delight, covering the giant mountains with their warm, deep green. We discovered small cached brooklets at intervals, these forming foamy cataracts which contrasted strongly with the plethora of the massed pines. Saturated with all this beauty, we went home to the more mundane exercise of eating. After a little rest and sustenance, off we went to see the Blue Seeli, a small lake of an extraordinarily deep blue hue. The water is so transparent that when a person sits on a boat he can see every plant and stone at the bottom of the lake and feels that all he needs to do is reach out and touch them with his fingers. Even the needles on the pine trees lying at the bottom could be counted. It was not easy for us to leave this fascinating "little lake."

The next day, Mme. Simrock, Hauschild, and I left the idyllic Aathal in a comfortable transport for Interlaken. There, Hauschild and I took rooms in a hotel, and Mme. Simrock promised to be our guide for our last sightseeing tour the next day. In the few remaining hours of daylight, we strolled through the renowned Swiss town built in the center of four surrounding lakes, this explaining its geographical name, Interlaken, i.e. between lakes. Mme. Simrock, good scout that she was, arrived early the next morning in a smart open landau (convertible) to treat us to an invigorating ride, the vivid memory of which is still with me. Dreamily lolling in our luxurious seats we viewed miles of lovely, thoroughly Swiss scenery, Mme. Simrock's knowledge of the area providing enhancement to our enjoyable tour. Sadly, all good things have an end though, and so must our vacation.

Ernst, at the end of his first school year in Lausanne, came home with an exceptionally outstanding report. With the idea in my mind of showing him how pleased we were with his scholarship, I asked Marie if she would like to take a vacation with the family, visiting some of the places I had recently admired. She said that she herself had already seen all those locales several times, and was also concerned that if she went, we would have to ride all of the time. She felt it would instead be much better if Ernst could have a real outdoor experience, so it was decided the two of us would go alone.

So with our rucksacks, in typical Swiss fashion, we went on our way to Interlaken. From there, we toured much of the territory around the four lakes and saw Tell's Chapel, where the Swiss national hero was supposed to have jumped from the boat in which he was being kept prisoner to the shore, escaping his captors. Ernst's enthusiasm knew no bounds. At glaciers he would stand enthralled and ask numerous questions. To him, just then in his early teens, beauty was a sort of god which he worshipped profoundly, a trait completely inherent in his nature.

Henri Marteau told me in a letter of a recital he and Victor André, a composer and conductor of the Zurich Philharmonic Orchestra, were to give in Lausanne, playing André's Sonata for the Piano and Violin. He asked me for the privilege of rehearsing the sonata at my home. I told him of the pleasure it would be for me to hear the first playing of the opus—and I was not disappointed. The rehearsal itself was flawless and the concert thereafter a tremendous success.

As a member of the Allgemeiner Deutscher Musikverein, I attended its music festival in Essen. Several of my friends' compositions were programmed, among others, Hugo Kaun's String Quartet in F, its premier performance, which was warmly received. Henri's composition for soprano and string quartet was given successfully at one concert, he playing the viola part and Eva Lessman, the daughter of the publisher of the "Deutsche Musik-Zeitung," singing the soprano part. The overture, "Cyrano de Bergerac" by the Hollander, Wagner, also found a warm reception. The pièce de resistance was Gustav Mahler's Fourth Symphony. I wrote an extensive and positive criticism recapping the festival.

At the concert hall, I met Mr. Ziegfeld, Sr. [28], the President of the Chicago Music College. He asked if I could recommend a pianist to fill a teaching post at the college. I told him of Mr. Weismüller, an excellent pianist and teacher from Amsterdam whom I knew. I then spoke to Mr. Weismüller, telling him of the offer and asked him to give Mr. Ziegfeld an example of his skill. He was unwilling to play in the concert hall so I asked both of them to come to my lodgings in the home of the gracious Dr. Richter, an ardent music friend who had been a regular attendant at my symphony concerts in Bochum and who had now requested I be his guest during my stay in Essen. Mr. Weismüller gave Mr. Ziegfeld a fine sample of his virtuosic playing on Dr. Richter's concert grand piano. Ziegfeld was rightly impressed and offered Mr. Weismüller the vacant position in Chicago. My friend then asked about the salary. "Three thousand dollars fixed with the liberty to give private lessons," Ziegfeld answered.

"No, I cannot accept your offer," Mr. Weismüller laughingly replied. "I make twice as much in Amsterdam."

So, later on, I recommended my friend Ernesto Consolo for the position—he was eager to learn something about the United States and not hampered by financial considerations and stayed several years in Chicago. His successor was Rudolf Ganz, who became President after Mr. Ziegfeld.

Never was my life so crowded with events as when I was in Lausanne. After the Boer War, a number of Boer generals made a tour of Europe to give details of their participation in this regretful affair. As there resided in Lausanne a number of prominent Hollanders, the Boers decided to visit there and I was chosen president of the reception committee. Among the soldiers was General Rey, an outstanding hero. He told an appalling story about being wounded 40 times and then being captured. Ignoring his ravaging wounds, the English had put him in chains and thrown him upon a truck to transport him the many miles to a prison camp. He spoke perfect English, but his hatred for that people was so strong that he never spoke one word of it for the rest of his life.

28 **Florenz Ziegfeld, Sr.** "Ziegfled, Sr. spent much of the late 1860s trying to establish himself in the musicbusiness. He had a rickety music school above the Crosby Opera house, published music and sold instruments with Ziegfeld, Gerard, and Co., and finally opened the Chicago Musical Academy in 1867. [He] became one of Chicago's leading citizens, his Musical College the most successful and elite of its kind in the area". (Eve Golden, Anna Held and the Birth of Ziegfeld's Broadway.)

Chapter 15   Between Berlin and Lausanne

A very important event took place for me in the year 1903. A letter telling me of my appointment as conductor of the Hector Berlioz Centennial Festival in Geneva both aroused my pride and kindled my humility. In spite of being German-born, I had been chosen to conduct the greatest French symphonist's centenary! Henri played the solo viola part in "Harold in Italy," and the gala festival was acclaimed an eminent success. Allow me to cite here the critic of (newspaper) Geneva: "Harold in Italy was the pièce de résistance of the Berlioz Centenary in Geneva and we must congratulate Mr. Hammer on the splendid results obtained with his orchestra. It was a magnificent performance."

From Blanchet, I received this letter:

"Dear Heinrich: Yesterday evening thy work was all-surpassing, gripping. I will never forget the deep emotional impression I received from 'Harold.' I was exhausted, broken by emotion afterward. Berlioz would have been elated—thou understand him; thou feel him. Yesterday thou wast Berlioz himself. I must express my deeply heartfelt thanks for this great enjoyment. It was the first time I became in reality acquainted with thee.

"It was a gigantic task thou accomplished with thy orchestra. Not one moment was I aware of the presence of four personalities: thou, Berlioz, Marteau, and thy instrument. No, only one was there for me: the idea of Berlioz! And thou hast made it understandable for me, through thee, it gripped me as never before.

"Man, thou art a great artist. Even the Philistines felt it. Once more, thanks! And remain my friend. Thy Blanchet."

Soon afterward I was called to conduct my first concert in Berlin, the famous Philharmonic Orchestra being my interpreter. Miss Harriet de Muthel, a prominent former pupil of von Bülow whom I had coached through the season, was to play Liszt's E Flat Piano Concerto. Her technique was brilliant, but her nerves the contrary, "ûnzûverlâssig" (unsteady) like the Germans say. My program contained Berlioz's "Harold in Italy" again.

A peculiar incident of a disturbing character surprised me the evening before my appearance upon the Berlin podium. Dr. Karl Muck, the ex-conductor of the Boston Symphony Orchestra conducted that evening. His program also contained the Berlioz number. Desirous of hearing his performance of this masterpiece, I went to the concert. I was disappointed to the highest degree with his interpretation which was entirely void of the scintillating French spirit so necessary for its correct performance. I was sorry it was also to be on my concert. The composition as directed by Muck was received with only lukewarm applause.

The next morning, filled with misgivings, I held my rehearsal. Starting with "Harold," I addressed the artists.

"I am very sorry you played "Harold" yesterday. If our programs were not already printed I would omit it on this concert; but circumstances force us to go ahead. Gentlemen, knowing your artistic standards, I am confident of explaining my procedure in only a few words. I take the andante twice as slow as Dr. Muck did and the allegro twice as fast."

Here I had occasion to see if my studies in Paris would bear fruit. They did in reality. Those fine musicians exhibited a magnificent disciplinary spirit and deep understanding, holding the inspiration with which Berlioz's works always blessed me, wide awake, and thus they were able to follow my lead well. The performance that night was a worthy tribute to the genius of Berlioz. The viola soloist, Klingler, was the first chair violist in the orchestra, a brother of the former concertmaster. The concertmaster at that time was Anton Witeck and the solo cellist, Malkin, a highly talented young Russian. Both of them later on occupied the same positions in the Boston Symphony.

I was asked to give two more concerts in Berlin. My second concert was an all-Beethoven one. The last number of my program was the Seventh Symphony. It challenges description how the orchestra sustained its productive powers to the last—its day's work had been unusually severe, consisting of my strenuous rehearsal, an afternoon concert and then an evening concert. The

[29] **Ferruccio Busoni** (1 April 1866 – 27 July 1924) Ferruccio Busoni was the only child of two professional musicians: his Italian/German mother a pianist, his Italian father a clarinettist. They were often touring during his childhood, and he was brought up in Trieste for the most part. He was a child prodigy. He made his public debut on the piano with his parents, at the age of seven. (Bach Cantatas Website; bach-cantatas.com)

finest praise could not do justice to the splendidness of artistic power and force they displayed in the Seventh, Beethoven's ode to gaiety. The calls of "Wiederoomen" (Come back! Return!) and "Hoch! Hoch!" from the audience packed in front of the stage would not end. I went out seven times; yet they kept on calling.

As I was heading back to my director's room, elated, I noticed a gentleman leaning nonchalantly against the staircase. His face looked familiar to me, but I could not place him. He came toward me, took my hand and introduced himself, "Busoni [29]. You are a great artist." A wonderful compliment from the King of pianists! I entered my room and there sat the wife of Ambassador Rooth of Switzerland, the man who dared to defy Bismarck. He wished to invite me to dinner at the Embassy. Another beautiful lady came toward me with outstretched arms, apparently about to kiss me, but (I was sorry) she did not do so in the presence of Mme. Rooth. Enthusiastically, she uttered the same words as Busoni. She was the Queen of the pianists: Mme. Teresa Carreño [30]. While I remained in Berlin I was a constant guest in her home.

The soloist for this concert was Miss Agnes Gardner Eyr, a young American and pupil of Leschetitzky. She played the Concerto in G Major. When she had played the same concerto in Lausanne, all the lights in the hall went out just as she began the cadenza. Without stopping she gave full justice to it and, at the end, the lights went on again. It was a courageous feat for a comparatively inexperienced artist.

[30] **María Teresa Carreño García de Sena** (December 22, 1853 – June 12, 1917) pianist, was born in Caracas, Venezuela, the daughter of Manuel Antonio Carreño, a Venezuelan minister of finance, and Corinda García de Sena y Toro. Although the young Carreño exhibited musical talent as a toddler, she did not begin studying the piano with her father, a talented amateur, until she was six. Manuel Antonio devised clever technical and musical exercises for his precocious daughter, which included improvisation, harmony, and variation techniques. In July 1862, the political situation in Venezuela became untenable for Manuel Antonio and he moved his family to New York. It was there, on 25 November 1862, that Teresa, not quite nine years old, made her piano debut at Irving Hall. In March 1866, with her reputation firmly established in the United States, Carreño and her family moved to Paris. By May of the same year, she had become the darling of the French artistic community. In 1868 she was introduced to Anton Rubinstein who, as a master teacher and devoted friend, guided her career. (American National Biography Online; anb.org)

A few words about the Philharmonic in Berlin may be injected here. The Philharmonic, a complex of buildings covering an entire city block, was entirely dedicated to the musical realm. There were four separate concert halls, the largest seating 5,000. This was used for the popular Sunday symphony concerts, filled to capacity every Sunday night by music-loving workingmen with their families. (Mother would typically carry a basket filled with food for supper. She would order a cup of coffee for herself, glasses of milk for the children and Father would drink his beer.) The waiters wore felt soles on their shoes and stopped serving as soon as the first note of music issued forth. All movement ceased, there was a reverent silence; every ear closely attuned to the message of music. The entrance fee was only about 20¢!

On one of these evenings I was entering the hall in the company of the owner of the Philharmonic. There, a bright-eyed, corpulent little gentleman was leaning against the door jamb.

"Do you know this gentleman?" my companion asked me as we approached the little roly-poly fellow.

"No, I don't," I replied.

When we came up to him, he introduced us: "Mr. Hammer, this is Leopold Godowsky [31]."

So, "between door and angle" I met one of the geniuses of our time, who seems today nearly forgotten.

In the intervals between these concerts in Berlin, I also paid some calls. An interesting one was my visit to Mme. Simrock, the mother of my friend in Lausanne. I was received there like an old friend by the amply-proportioned, dignified but amiable last link to a remote generation, the significance of the name and the august interior of her home relaying its past grandeur. The white-haired, convivial Mme. Simrock showed me her Böcklin salon, a very large room, all four walls of which were covered with Böcklin's masterworks, representing a great fortune in terms of their monetary worth. I can't help but wonder, what became of all this wealth when Berlin was reduced to shambles in World War II?

The third concert I conducted in Berlin was dedicated to the works of Brahams: Tragic Overture, Violin Concerto, soloist, Professor Markes, assistant to Joachim as Director of the Imperial Conservatory of Music, and the Third Symphony. Again happily a successful venture.

Every evening and even after my concerts, my friends, Hugo Kaun, Dr. Ertel and others insisted I go with them to the Leipziger Hof to have din-

Leipziger Hof (Hotel), Berlin

ner, and usually from there to the Bairischer Hof, the largest, most luxuriously-equipped restaurant I have ever seen, complete with a full-fledged symphony orchestra entertaining its guests, the bairsch beer an agreeable bonus. From there, we would go to one of the renowned coffeehouses, and on it went until at least three a.m., a very unusual hour for me to turn homeward. My friends told me Hugo Kaun, who had spent a number of years in Milwaukee and had, at the time of my Berlin activities, reached the top of the artists' ladder when he was nominated a Senator of the Berlin Academy, was always the instigator of these long-drawn-out jaunts as he liked to remain up until all hours at night. Not I. So, after returning home from my two weeks in Berlin I needed much recuperative sleep. I was happy to carry the highly favorable criticisms back with me. Each member of my dear family received a suitable present bought for him or her as a souvenir from Berlin.

When I returned to my old friends at the orchestra, I was honored at a lavish banquet which Dr. Suter had arranged to welcome me home. A few weeks later, at the end of the season, I received a letter from him in which he expressed his thanks for the last year's task I had carried out successfully on his behalf, and as my summer vacation was now here, he wished I might find new inspiration for the coming winter season's hard work. As a tangible sign of his gratitude he enclosed a thousand-franc check and said he hoped the Hammer family would enjoy a pleasant holiday. Time and again I had occasion to admire Dr. Suter's unselfish attitude and

[31] **Leopold Godowsky** (13 February 1870 – 21 November 1938) was a Polish American pianist, composer, and teacher. One of the most highly regarded performers of his time, he became known for his theories concerning the application of relaxed weight and economy of motion in piano playing, principles later propagated by Godowsky's pupils, such as Heinrich Neuhaus. He was heralded among musical giants as the "Buddha of the Piano" and was probably the most astonishing instance of a self-taught performer and creator in the history of art. (The International Master Institute of Music "Leopold Godowsky", Inc. godowsky.com)

constant readiness to help where help was needed, and was frequently touched by his generosity as well.

He brought up his three children efficiently, not as spoiled offspring with a considerable inheritance await-ing them, but as simple, well-educated youngsters who, when circumstances demanded, would be able to take care of themselves. All three of them are independent self-reliant citizens in good positions today, not mighty financially, but intellectually. Dr. Suter, a convinced Social Democrat, spent his entire fortune doing good. At the end of his life he was living in moderate circumstances in a small castle at Lutry, an inheritance of his wife, surrounded by a small vineyard.

The following winter season brought a great surprise. Max Reger, who never traveled much, came to Lau-sanne to play his Violin-Piano Sonata with Henri, a first performance in that city which was greatly lauded. The next summer at another Allgemeiner Deutscher Musikverein music festival in Frankfurt he played the same sonata (while I turned the pages for him). That critical audience also liked the work and they generously applauded it.

At one of the intermissions, I met Mrs. Wurmser, the wife of the famous Parisian pianist. She was the only concertizing chromatic harpist (an instrument invented by the famous harp builder, Lyon, in Paris). Here she was trying to get a chance to exhibit the possibilities of her instrument to these most prominent of the world's musicians assembled in Frankfurt—and yet not knowing how to accomplish her desire, so I promised my help. Gathering a number of colleagues, among them Richard Strauss, our President, Max von Schillings, Nicode, Dr. Obrist, Dr. Neitzel, Max Reger, and Henri, I introduced Mrs. Wurmser and her instrument to them, and she played the Beethoven Piano Sonata in F for us—a feat impossible to execute upon the common harp. She played it flawlessly and with spirit, excellent artist that she was. Everyone was astonished and warmly praised her performance.

At Frankfurt, I made the acquaintance of Chabrier, the composer of "Louise." One of his compositions was performed in Heidelberg where the members of our association were the honored guests for one evening of the Heidelberg Municipality for the inauguration of the new music hall in which the innovative stage was movable (we often traveled during these festivals). Professor Dr. Walfrum began the concert with the orchestra seated as usual. For the second number, the stage—musicians and all—was hydraulically lowered, and the lights turned down. In this mystical atmosphere we heard the music with extraordinary enjoyment, unhindered by the faculty of sight. After this impressive performance, we visited the classical ruins of the old Heidelberg castle with its colossal wine vat, big enough to accommodate a horse and its rider. A fine group picture was taken of some members in the courtyard of the castle.

Back to Frankfurt and from there to Manheim to listen to the first performance of Jacques Dalcroze's quaint opera "Onkel Ikasumal," which was written in a light, humorous manner and pleased the audience. Again we returned to Frankfurt. There I saw my old student, Max Kaemfert, who, after his studies in Paris had been called to the concert-mastership of the Münich Kaim Symphony Orchestra and, later, when Felix Weingartner left, had become its conductor. From there he went to Eisenach and then Frankfurt as conductor.

Mentioning Weingartner reminds me of a droll incident which occurred years before when, under his leadership, the Münich Orchestra toured Italy and Switzerland. Henri and I were about to leave Henri's home in Geneva for Weingartner's concert there when the doorbell rang. The servant announced Mr. Weingartner. He entered, greatly agitated, and told us his luggage had not arrived, leaving him without his evening clothes.

"Oh! That's too bad," Henri said. "But never mind. You may use mine."

Hastily the metamorphosis was accomplished and we jumped in the waiting carrosse (coach) which took us to the concert hall where an anxious audience awaited the conductor's entrance. It was not the "Tirer à quatre épingles" (dressed to the nines) gentleman who walked on the stage that night (as Weingartner was known for his impeccably correct attire), but a rather strangely "overdressed" one, as Henri was about six inches taller than Weingartner! Regardless of the slight incongruity of his garments, the concert was the best I ever heard conducted by Weingartner. The audience seemed in accord with me.

On returning to Lausanne from Frankfurt, bad news awaited me. Mr. Iso, the owner of the apartment house in which we lived, had informed Marie of the impending marriage of his only daughter, and as it had been decided she should occupy our apartment after her marriage, we must now look for another. Speaking to my friend Blanchet about this sudden announcement, I was told that friends of his had just evacuated a villa in the English garden at Avenue du Theatre. He recommended it highly and said that his friends, the Grand Duke of Mecklenburg had lived there previously. He gave me the address and Marie and I immediately went to see what the place was like. We found an old, solidly built house, three stories high, including a big basement with large coal and wine cellars. It was comfortably encircled by a beautiful garden, a grand catalpa tree in full bloom on the east side, a dense hedge enclosing the house, and an old wisteria vine, covered with hundreds of large white flower clusters which reached to the second floor balcony, covering it fully. The trunk of the plant was about four inches in diameter, and it was simply magnificent. Being impressed with everything about the house, we rented it straightaway and felt ourselves very lucky to get it.

As it happened, the wisteria once rendered me a useful service. I went to one of Dr. Suter's convivial orchestra suppers, but forgot my house key. I lost track of the time while there and when I got home it was very late. I rang the rather soft doorbell several times without results. Unluckily, the servants slept on the third floor and Marie on the second. Finally, desperate, I went around the house and calculated the chances of the wisteria's aiding me. Gripping its trunk, I hoisted myself up to the second story where the door of our bedroom opened onto the balcony. Marie screamed when I knocked at the window, thinking I was a burglar. I reassured her immediately of course, and when she opened the door we had a good laugh about the comical role I had just played; a gentleman in tails climbing like a monkey up a wisteria vine in the dead of night.

About this time, more serious happenings entered into my already overcrowded schedule of giving lessons, writing, rehearsals, concerts, etc.

Emánuel Moór [32], who lived down at the Lake of Geneva in Ouchy, commissioned me to write the li-

[32] **Emánuel Moór** (19 February 1863 – 20 October 1931) was a Hungarian composer, pianist, and inventor of musical instruments. His best-known invention was the Emánuel Moór Pianoforte, which consisted of two keyboards lying one above each other and allowed, by means of a tracking device, one hand to play a spread of two octaves. (UnsungComposers.com)

bretti for two of his operas, "Andress Hofer" and "Columbus," which he could easily afford to have printed and produced as he was married to a very wealthy lady from Ireland. I wrote the libretti and earned his praise, but had great difficulty getting my fee. In the end, I received only about a fourth of the contracted sum.

The weight of continuous activity needed a strong counteraction to keep it light enough to carry. As you have seen, sport was always a beneficial influence upon both my body and soul, especially so when I was most burdened with work. Horseback riding in Switzerland is not such an exhilarating experience as it is in other countries with gentler terrain; but hunting provided an excellent opportunity. The fee for a hunting license is high there but the amount accrued through fees is used to buy a crop of game from Hungary every year to be released upon their depleted hunting grounds. My wife, my constant doctor-guardian, encouraged me to hunt one day a week for recreation. Therefore, I introduced a free Monday for the members of my orchestra and a hunting day for their boss.

I owned a fine Anglo-Swiss hunting dog, Fino, a peculiar character, at war with every one of his kind, big or little. As there was no transportation to the hunting territory and the distance to it was significant, it meant our poor feet had to accomplish this task, which consumed from two to four hours. Another period of hours for hunting and then the march home made for a day of constant walking. Half a loaf of bread, a sizable hunk of Swiss cheese, and a bottle of café au lait would take care of the day's nourishment. After the homecoming a refreshing bath, the recital of the day's happenings and a substantial meal in the family circle, then to bed and sleep, sleep, sleep. The "morning after" I always felt thoroughly invigorated, raring to go. Fino, who on the hunting trips covered at least five times more territory than I, also slept about five times longer than I afterward.

A certain day's hunting trip brought an unforeseen decision with it which gave a settled habit a sound uprooting. I always smoked a pipe when I was hunting and it was a discreet companion which seemed to add some zest to the adventure for me. That day, like many days before, Fino was off giving voice in the direction of a fox near the precipitous mountain cliffs where those destructive fellows often have their dens so they will be secure from hunters. Fino stubbornly chased this fox for hours, but I never saw the sly creature, as usual, which was annoying. My thoughts were interrupted by the approach of an old Swiss fellow, gun astride his shoulder. After a friendly "bonjour" he expressed his admiration of my dog.

"Yes," I said, "the dog is good, but his master isn't. As I have still never shot a fox though I have often hunted them."

Grinning, he pointed at my pipe. "You will never shoot one with that thing in your mouth." And thus a longtime habit was duly uprooted.

I conducted a concert Henri gave in Berlin. He performed a remarkable feat, unique in music history. He played three compositions on three different instruments. He played the Brahams Concerto upon his big Maggini violin (inherited from Hubert Léonard), "Harold in Italy" on his rare Amati viola, and the Schuman Concerto on his Stradivari violin (formerly owned by Beethoven). Otto Lessman, the well-known critic and owner of the "Deutsche Musik-Zeitung,"(German music newspaper) wrote this about the event:

"Concert of Henri Marteau with the Philharmonic Orchestra of Berlin, conducted by Heinrich Hammer . . . it goes without saying that soloist and conductor received an ovation in which the orchestra participated."

Back in Lausanne, I received a note from Ollaio Morales, the music critic from Göteborg, Sweden, informing me of his arrival in Lausanne and his wish to see me. He brought me greetings from Teresa Carreño, his piano teacher, and then told me that a Maecenas (generous patron) had left half a million kronor to the city of Göteborg for the establishment of a symphony orchestra and he had recommended me to the executive committee for the position of organizer and conductor. He had evidently been quite confident of my skills to make such a suggestion. I was impressed but wary of leaving my easy path in Lausanne, although the orchestra would be larger there and my salary higher. Morales wished to take some conducting lessons with me, so he and his wife rented a cozy little house near the charming woods on the outskirts of the town and he came to the daily orchestra rehearsals for instruction.

The widow of the former Russian Ambassador to Weimar now lived in Lausanne and she was an ardent music lover. Through the summer, she lived at the Oeschinensee, high in the Alps in view of the legendary St. Bernardine Mountain. Alongside her home she built a number of bungalows to be occupied by the guests she invited for summer vacations, and I was one of her guests this summer. The young Brazilian pianist, del Carrillo, was also invited and we took the train together, then climbing up the steep ascent to the retreat where we were warmly welcomed by our hostess, her family, and their guests. The baroness was the mother of three sons and one daughter. The oldest son was a first lieutenant in the Kaiser's guard regiment. (A great music enthusiast, he had been at most of my Berlin concerts.) His younger brother made a stately figure in the uniform of the Bavarian Dragoon regiment. The youngest was 16 and tutored by a Doctor of Philosophy who was also a guest. The daughter was a beautiful girl, 18 years old. I was surprised to find Mr. Denereaz, the distinguished organist of the Lausanne Cathedral, among the people at the baroness's home. That evening, del Carrillo and I retired early and were lulled to sleep by the strains of gay dance music played by a mademoiselle from Paris.

The next morning, we were up early and had a short dive into the icy cold waters of the Oeschinensee (lake) which fronted our little colony. The sons of the family, hardened by daily bathing, were actually able to swim a little in the freezing water. About 300' from our bungalows was a steep, broad precipice from where we had a splendid view of the St. Bernardine Mountain and the convent of the renowned life-saving dogs. We passed pleasant days in these majestic yet peaceful surroundings.

Two other guests were the Colonel and Mrs. Schwenninger. He was the colonel of a German pioneer regiment and brother of Professor Schwenninger, Bismarck's personal physician. Evenings always ended with dancing, with many of the guests, even Colonel Schwenninger, playing the tunes. Mr. Denereaz and I took great pleasure in playing four hands extemporaneously, either he or I improvising the melodic line, wickedly slipping from key to key trying to lead the partner astray. What fun that was, and what elation for the dancers, moving to unknown music.

One day the oldest of the baroness's sons invited del Carrillo and me to ascend a nearby mountain which is visited yearly by thousands who watch the sunrise on its summit. Each of us carried about 40 pounds of camping equipment on our backs; the lieutenant probably had more, as his anxious mother had filled his pack with provisions. The climbing on this trek was exceedingly tiring. Our goal should have been reached in from four to four-and-a-half hours, but we were now past the six-hour mark. Del Carrillo and I were miserably tired and surmised that we had lost our way. Darkness descended, though the starlit sky still permitted us comfortable vision. Looking around us, we saw a feeble light glinting in the darkness high above us. Our guide, seeing it, confided his error: "That light is from the hut on the summit. I somehow missed the road back there."

Being a trained soldier, he was perfectly able to take a livelier march tempo, but we two, though somewhat enlivened by the inviting glimmer, could only follow him slowly. Finally, literally exhausted, we arrived at the lonely hut where del Carrillo and I sank down on the straw-covered floor. The room was filled with men who had come to watch the next morning's sunrise. The lieutenant, probably attempting to compensate for his mistake, boldly edged himself, cooking pot in hand, through the crowd to the hot stove and soon was able to make his way to the fire and prepare a meal for we three hungry wolves.

That night was one of the most uncomfortable I have ever spent. That mass of males was packed on the straw like pickles in a jar and a chorus of snores "made the rafters ring"—needless to say, not much sleep! An hour before sunup there was a grand rush to wash basins. (Water is the only comfort you find at heights; everything else has to be fetched from below and carried up by human backs and hands). I heard the sounds of feminine voices and was told there were as many women on the floor above us as we men below. We grabbed a quick breakfast and ascended the highest peak to watch the sunrise.

A dense crowd was already gathered when we came. Many of you, dear readers, have probably seen sun-ups at sea; or from the lower mountains, but it is another sun-up altogether when viewed from the supremacy of the Alps. Here at sunrise the panoramic vista defied the greatest painter's brush. Attuned to nature's language, a shower of ice-water seems to flood your body; awestruck, you feel like voicing softly your thanks for the privilege of witnessing the visual spectacle occurring before you. It was not easy to leave this sacred mountaintop. But that we must: so down we went to the little mountain hut again. There, we packed and hiked back to our trail (this time the right one). After a two-hours' tramp, we finished the rest of our provisions at the side of a small gurgling brook, and two hours later were back once more at our bungalow.

On a Sunday one day before the end of my two weeks' vacation, the youngest son of the baroness (a first lieutenant), his tutor, and I decided to visit a glacier some seven miles away. At about the midpoint on our journey there was a tiny settlement consisting of a few houses and a small inn. We planned to meet the baroness's daughter, the Parisian pianist, the Dragoon officer, and del Carrillo at this inn for lunch upon returning from our hike. They had not been interested in joining our trek but did want to have some sort of outing. Soon after the four of us had passed the settlement on our way up, we discovered a fork in the road and we could not seem to agree upon which road to take. The tutor said the upper road was the nearest one and the others concurred with him; I felt the lower road would be shorter.

"Alright," I said, "you take the higher one; I'll take the lower. We'll see who gets there first."

I went my way. I could see the three mounting the road I judged would not lead to the glacier, which in fact, I saw about two miles ahead of me. Along my way, I met a little girl and a boy tending to a few grazing goats. Briskly I walked along though the going was not easy as the entire valley was strewn with heavy boulders, all ejections from the powerful stream gushing out of the tremendous glacier tunnel ahead. Coming nearer, my enthusiasm gradually increased. High on the road I saw the three figures. Loudly I called to them, though I was fully aware that even my boisterous hollering could not be heard over the thunderous stream.

My excitement over this grandiose sight—the enormous opening in the great milky glacier out of which the foaming stream rushed, the luminous ceiling of the tunnel sheathed in its wondrous icy blue, and the primeval surroundings consisting of massive boulders grouped around the stream's exit—was so great that I exclaimed aloud in admiration and began jumping from boulder to boulder like one possessed. Too caught up in the overwhelming emotion of the moment, I entirely forgot to watch my step. Swift punishment followed my carelessness. Jumping from a rather slippery rock to the next one, I missed my aim and fell down between the two big blocks of granite. Great pain began coursing through my right foot and I thought it was broken. Examining it, I discovered an ankle sprain. Here I was, alone and helpless, unable to make myself heard because of the boisterous roar of the surging waters. I raised myself on one foot from between the boulders.

Looking around, I found a long thick tree branch on which to support myself. It was three and a half miles back to the inn. Hopping slowly along, it seemed an eternity to me before I reached the place where I had met the two children. I asked if one of them would show me the shortest way to the inn, giving them both a few coins. The little girl wanted to assume the role of guide; her brother promising to take good care of the goats. Off she went at an oblivious trot. Poor me, struggling along on my makeshift cane I could not possibly keep up with her. It took quite some explaining before she realized I could not go as fast as she could. After another long mile, which seemed like ten to me, we finally arrived at the inn. The seven people assembled there were greatly astonished at my late arrival, but seeing my condition showed deep concern—it turned out the three had returned without seeing the glacier except for a glimpse from high above it.

I needed the help of the lieutenant to remove my boot. With the excruciating pain still mounting, the dinner was not an enjoyable one for me. The worst, however, lay still ahead—the long march home. Those last three miles were three miles of internal groaning and suffering. As the day was to be concluded with a picnic that evening in the meadow with the view of St. Bernardine Mountain, I asked my companions not to tell the baroness of my mishap, knowing it would greatly disturb her. As soon as we arrived at the meadow I sat down on the ground, and when the baroness came over to me I excused myself for sitting by saying I was tired after the long walk. But her youngest boy was eager to tell his mother the news and gave me away. Immediately the fine lady came to me and expressed her concern and asked if there was anything she could do. As soon as Colonel Schwenninger heard the story, he came over to me too.

"Why didn't you tell us right away what happened to you, Mr. Hammer?" he asked. "Cases like yours need immediate attention."

He sat down next to me and started at once to give my hurt foot a strong massage, which he kept up for a full agonizing hour. Later, after I had crept tiredly off to bed, Colonel Schwenninger came to my room and gave me another hour's massage, preparing me for my next morning's five-mile walk to the railroad station. I had bid everyone farewell that night and thanked my hostess so I could leave early the next day. The five miles' hike downhill, hobbling as best I could on my "cane" was no pleasant one. Thereafter, the railroad journey to Lausanne and the taxi ride home were only a matter of a few hours, during which I recuperated somewhat.

Marie and the children gave the "pater familias" a fine welcome, but our reunion was dampened when they caught sight of my swollen, bootless foot. Luckily, Morales was conducting the summer concerts, granting me a month's relief. We used several days for picnics, visits to Évian-les-Bains across the lake and to the surrounding vineyards where we saw the winemaking process at the wineries.

Morales came to see me and said how stupid my foot was to misbehave so. He brought a book with him by Verner von Heidenstam [33] "Harold and the Drake." He asked me to prepare a German libretto from this well-known Swedish novel, as he wished to compose an opera on the subject. After we signed the contract for our opera "in spe" (future), I rented a comfortable two-story farmhouse at the foot of the Glacier du Diable where I could take my task in hand without interruption. Miss Repelius came with us and we all passed the remainder of my vacation happily. I wrote on a large second-story balcony in view of the glacier. One day I saw 32 gems (a species of mountain antelope) passing along the snowline of the mountain—an inspiring sight indeed. It was raspberry time in the wooded part of the country near us, and throughout our stay at Les Diablerets, we were supplied with an abundance of this fine fruit, going every few days to pick a gallon of it.

About this time, I received a letter from my old friend Arthur Abel, the European representative of the Musical Courier, in which he promised to visit me in the near future as he lived in another mountain village, about six miles south of us. I sent him directions for getting to our place and arranged to meet him at a designated spot. Ernst and I went to the site to await his arrival (I was still using a cane.) No Abel. After some time, Ernst and I loudly called his name. No answer. Over and over we repeated our calls, which in this serene morning hour would naturally be heard at quite a distance. At last we heard a feeble answer far down in the valley and, after a long interval, a tiny figure came into sight below us and waved a greeting. It turned out my friend Abel had lost his path as wide roads are non-existent in wooded mountain areas in Switzerland. We spent a rich day reminiscing and just conversing. After a satisfying Swiss-Holland dinner we walked to the station where he took the post-wagon to Lausanne. This had been his last day in the mountains for the summer.

Our vacation was at an end and the libretto for Morales was finished. Ernst had grown so fast the past year he had adopted a habit common to fast-growing youngsters—hunching his back, probably in subconscious protest against becoming conspicuously tall—resulting in a slouchy walk. His mother was disturbed about this, so when we came back to Lausanne she consulted an orthopedist. He prescribed a six-by-four-foot plank, with a hole in one end large enough to hold the head; below this aperture was a movable contrivance to adjust the plank to any desired angle (the same sort of installation found on hospital beds.) On this plank with his head down, Ernst had to lie several hours a day. He soon was perfectly able to study his schoolwork and read books in this uncomfortable position. After a few months his walk and posture were completely corrected.

The invention of eurhythmics by Jaques Dalcroze, subsequently providing the foundation for modern dance, aroused my lively interest. Often I visited his classes in Geneva where he was a professor at the Conservatoire de Musique. I wrote several articles on the subject for the monthly publication, Leipzig Musik Zeitschrift. This new science kindled the valuable interest of the King of Saxony who invited Jaques to form a colony for students of eurhythmics at Hellerau in Saxony. Jaques passed a few fruitfully happy years there, but the war was the death knell for his dream's paradise, after which he returned back to his beloved Geneva.

[33] **Carl Gustaf Verner von Heidenstam** (6 July 1859 – 20 May 1940) The Nobel Prize in Literature 1916 was awarded to Verner von Heidenstam "in recognition of his significance as the leading representative of a new era in our literature". (Official website of the Nobel Prize; nobelprize.org)

Chapter 16 And On to Sweden

In the spring of 1905, a letter arrived from Göteborg (Gothenburg), Sweden, inviting me to conduct a concert there. From Morales's explanation of the circumstances, I was aware I was the seventh of a series of guest conductors of whom eventually one would be chosen as the permanent conductor of the orchestra which would later be officially organized there. I decided I did not want the position if I was chosen, but I could not resist the thousand kronor payment for the concert.

I traveled to Berlin and from there in a wagon aux lits (wagon with beds). My train brought me to Copenhagen early the second morning, and from there to Karlskrona, Sweden, and from there I was off to Göteborg. Welcomed by the committee members of the orchestra association, I was provided lodgings at the Grand Hotel.

The next morning was my first orchestra rehearsal. The orchestra was not a permanent institution yet but instead one formed "aux bonne hazard" (by chance). This presented an issue as it was not easy for me to create technique where it was non-existent. But with goodwill and patience one sometimes can create marvels. My program of Tchaikovsky, Wagner, and Beethoven was difficult to perform well, but with the genial cooperation of the orchestra personnel, I was able to present it satisfactorily, receiving numerous compliments after the concert. At the performance's conclusion, my colleagues in the orchestra presented me with a large laurel wreath draped with a wide red silk ribbon inscribed, "The grateful members of the Symphony Orchestra to Kapellmeister Heinrich Hammer." After the concert, the president of the committee asked me if I would accept the position of organizer and conductor of the future orchestra. I asked about the conditions of the office. I was told the orchestra would be engaged for the winter concert period.

"I am sorry," I said, "but I would never put myself under a contractual stipulation founded on only six months' engagement for the orchestra members." (In Europe, the orchestra is almost always engaged on a yearly basis so the conductor will not have to reorganize it at the beginning of every winter season. However, this does not mean the conductor must also direct the summer concerts; in fact, as a rule, a prominent conductor in Europe always uses the summer months for studying scores and constructing his programs for the next season and his assistant conducts the summer concerts.) I had momentarily wavered from my earlier decision but now I was glad I had another reason for keeping my dear Lausanne orchestra position.

Upon arriving back home, I told Dr. Suter of my Göteborg experiences and he was glad I had refused the offer. A few days later, I received a letter from Göteborg's Orkestra Foröningen asking me to conduct another concert. Returning once again to the Grand Hotel, I found the committee members and reporters from the Göteborg newspapers who greeted me with an unexpectedly warm welcome. The president made the announcement that the committee had unanimously decided to accept my condition of a full year's contract for the orchestra personnel and they had signed a contract with the municipality of Marielyst in Denmark (the Danish King's summer home) for a summer season's engagement for the orchestra. This generous offer so surprised me that I replied I was unable to make a hasty decision. At my appearance on the stage to conduct this second concert, the public and members of the orchestra accorded me a clamorous greeting. The execution of the program found the same favor as that of the first concert and, afterwards, a reception was held at the home of the treasurer of the committee, a congenial, devotee of music and number one bank director of the city, Herman Manheimer.

The next day I went back to Lausanne and told Marie of the proposition offered me and asked her counsel. After long and earnest reflection she drew the obvious comparison between Lausanne and Göteborg—Lausanne, small orchestra, 3,000 francs less salary than in Göteborg; Göteborg, large orchestra, higher salary.

"But I must tell you that I could not go with you if you accept the Göteborg offer," she said. "After living in foreign countries so long, I am sorry to say I am still not able to acclimatize—I am nothing but a genuine Hollander. If you go to Sweden, I will go back to Holland to live and let the children finish their education in their home country. I would visit you now and then during the winter season and, as you would be free after April, you could pass the entire summer with us."

This was a weighty argument for my going as I had not realized the extent of Marie's dissatisfaction. When I told Dr. Suter of the difficulty of my position he made a proposal so much in keeping with his personality that I should almost have foreseen it.

"Dear friend," he said, "I don't want you to leave Lausanne. I will pay your salary as long as you live. I cannot guarantee you an orchestra all that time, but your salary will be deposited in trust."

But even with such an offer I was still undecided. I could not have the orchestra I wanted in Lausanne, though if I had been bold enough to ask Dr. Suter I am certain he would have given it to me, and I had informed the Göteborg committee before that I must be allowed to choose my players from all over Europe, to which they had also consented. I tried to put other obstacles in the way of my going to Göteborg too. For instance, I knew the city boasted of a well-trained choral society conducted by Liljefors, a brother of the renowned painter of the same name. To make my appointment impossible I wrote to the president of the orchestra association that wherever I was a symphony orchestra conductor I was also leader of a large mixed chorus and if I could not also be the conductor of the choral society in Göteborg, I would not leave Lausanne.

A few days later a letter from the president declared his regret that the leadership of the chorus could not be changed. Fine! I had succeeded in keeping my pleasant position at Lausanne —but no! Shortly thereafter another letter from the president followed, bringing the surprising message that I was to be installed as leader of the choral society as well. This position carried with it another salary income of 2,000 francs. The yearly income in Göteborg was now 5,000 francs—more than my emolument in Lausanne. Also I felt highly honored by the apparent eagerness of the Göteborg committee to satisfy all my stipulations so they could procure me for their city's orchestra. So…destiny ordered my return to the country of my adoption.

I signed the contract, returned it and made preparations for moving my family back to Holland.

In Leyden lived two old aunts of my wife; one, 84 and the other 86, the last members of the proud family du Saar and Marie decided to live there. Ernst was well advanced at the Lausanne gymnasium, furthered greatly in his studies by his last teacher. Before I left Lausanne, to show my admiration for the splendid work of this outstanding instructor, I instituted a yearly stipend for the best scholar of his class.

Dr. Suter was greatly disappointed when I told him about my decision. He reluctantly accepted my resignation and expressed his profound regret at my refusal of his proposition. I thanked him again and asserted my sincere admiration of him for the gracious help he had always tendered the orchestra, benefiting both me as well as so many other artists. Was I an ungrateful friend? Should I have stayed in Lausanne though my wife was unhappy and my children were being educated in a foreign country? Was my ambition the deciding factor? How can we poor humans be sure we are choosing the right direction when arriving at a puzzling crossroad? Even now, after the elapse of almost 50 long years, I am not able to give enlightened answers to these perplexing questions.

The newspapers were agog about my resignation. A number of letters also begged me to reconsider. Thanking them one and all, I stated my case clearly, saying that retreat was an impossibility. About a week later, I met Dr. Suter again. "I have paid your fine," he said simply in the midst of our conversation.

Only such an unselfish individual as humble Dr. Anton Suter could provide such an example of true friendship. I had entirely forgotten the paragraph in my Lausanne contract which stated I must pay a 1,500 franc fine in case of breach of contract.

Freed from my Lausanne responsibilities, I gave my full attention to the removal of my possessions. We needed the biggest railroad freight car available to accommodate them, but still had to leave an overflow of belongings behind. My true old guard, the musicians who had followed me from Bochum to Lausanne would have to cross a whole continent to follow me again this time—which they did. When it came time to part with all my dear friends, the members of the orchestra and my pupils, I wondered with a sudden, piercing sorrow, why was I really leaving them all?

We nevertheless departed for Holland where we passed a relaxing vacation at the seashore at Noordwyk on the Sea. Ernst and I would take our watercolor paraphernalia and traverse all over sketching what we liked. He was gifted with an extraordinary sense of artistic perception and was always more successful in the reproduction of objects we selected to paint than me. Later on, he filled his free days sketching a series of old castles and buildings. For years I kept some of these sketches, and how I later lost them, I do not know.

Noordwyk is an old Holland town of a few thousand inhabitants located behind high sand dunes which shelter the land before them for miles. These dunes are crowded with rabbit dens. Wandering along the dunes as we reached the top of one, hundreds of rabbits were to be seen scurrying in haste to their dens in the large kettle-like depression between that dune and the next. It was a hilarious sight.

We had rented a little villa behind the dunes, at the outskirts of the town. A fine, sandy beach led to the water. The bathing was wonderful, a great pleasure for the children. One evening as I was reading in the living room, Ernst rushed in, excitedly exclaiming "Father! Come see the glorious sunset!"

I went out with him and we climbed the dunes. In full validation of his statement there was a glorious sunset indeed. Sitting down to watch it, the fiery vermilion ball slowly descended to rest on the lap of the sea whose rolling movements gradually diminished until only soft, rhythmic splashes on the shore gave voice to its vast heartbeat. The sun then changed to a deeper hue and appeared to expand its circle, an occurrence peculiar to Holland sunsets, and then slipped down behind the sea to fulfill its next day's duties at the antipodes. As always in the presence of the majesty of nature I was left awestruck and nearly breathless. I was so inspired that a creative passion took hold of me. Returning back to our living room, in a half hours' time I had written the entire sketch of my symphonic poem, Sunset at Sea. In the following days I finished the orchestration of this new work.

The end of school vacation necessitated our going on to Leyden where both children started their Holland education. I traveled northward to visit Stockholm where I advertised for musicians to audition for membership in the new Göteborg Symphony, holding an audition thereupon my arrival from Stockholm. A few of the better musicians from the hastily-organized orchestra I had conducted before applied. Among them was a dignified gentleman, about 60, who had come with Smetana to Göteborg. (The latter lived many years there, although he never was able to satisfy his artistic ambition to organize an orchestra capable of performing his compositions.) The old gentleman played a difficult Kreutzer etude for violin flawlessly for me, though he was applying for a viola chair. I did not have him play more; he was engaged. Of the other Göteborg musicians who auditioned, all were capable and were hired. Now I began to travel to pick the rest of my orchestra.

From Göteborg, I went to Copenhagen, then to Berlin, Leipzig, Dresden, Prague, and Vienna. Here I found the small-sized but big-hearted Leschetizky still sending sprouting talents on their way. From there I went on to Zurich, Basel, Paris, Brussels, and Amsterdam—where nine artists auditioned for me, unwilling to continue under Mengelberg's leadership. I engaged all of them. Hamburg and Bremen were the last two cities in which I held auditions.

Back in Göteborg two bassoonists, brothers who were members of the Milano Opera orchestra, wrote to me for positions. The older brother said he had been sole clarinetist during the summer season in the Spa orchestra in Belgium. From their background, I knew they were better musicians than the bassoonists I had, so I engaged them and was not disappointed—they turned out to be the two finest bassoonists I had ever heard. They were equally skillful artists and often exchanged their first and second parts. Droll fellows they were too; fine, nice boys. But they complained continuously about the Swedish food. "Who can eat macaroni cooked in milk?" was their constant lament. After six months they begged for their release. As I had other aspirants for their positions I reluctantly let them go. Nineteen different nations were now represented in the orchestra. As a result, I had to use six languages to achieve the desired results in communicating my instruction to them. The concerts held on Wednesdays and Sundays were warmly supported by a grateful public there.

During the many years of a symphony conductor's career, a calling which necessarily involves human relations, awkward circumstances are bound to arise now and then. One of these was a crossing of swords between a diva and conductor. Mme. Ellen Gulbranson [34], the great Bayreuth Brunhilde, was engaged for a single appearance. I programmed a Wagner Festival with Brunhilde's Farewell from Wotan, and Isolde's Liebestod. When Mme. Gulbranson arrived at the rehearsal—and with the whole committee present—she said to me, "I am not going to sing Isolde's Liebestod; I will sing the Tanhauser aria."

"Mme. Gulbranson," I said carefully, "if you sing the Tanhauser aria it will be a Gulbranson Festival; if you sing Isolde's aria it will be a Wagner Festival."

"All right," she snapped. "We might as well call the whole thing off."

"Suit yourself," I replied.

She hesitated noticeably, probably thinking about her nice fee. "Please, let us start," she then said abruptly.

She sang Brunhilde's Farewell with such deep understanding and fineness of expression that tears wet my cheeks. When the piece was ended she exclaimed enthusiastically, "You have a wonderful orchestra! I'll sing Isolde."

I was glad she had decided to perform what I had programmed. But I soon discovered the reason for her original refusal. When we rehearsed the Isolde aria she had to follow the orchestra score closely and she made several mistakes. I could see she had never sung it before. This was explainable; her Junoesque figure (tall and shapely) was certainly not suited to the role of Isolde. However, when she sang the aria at the Festival concert, she in fact embodied the true Isolde, and received the thundering approval of the audience.

My dear old friends of the Bohemian Quartet [35], concluding their second triumphant world tour in Scandinavia, arrived to give a concert in Göteborg. Afterwards, Herman Manheimer invited them and some friends to his home, including myself. A smorgasbord supper awaited us and that treacherous Swedish punch, its delicate sweetness tempting

[34] **Ellen Gulbranson** (4 March 1863 – 2 January 1947) Her real name was Ellen Norgren. First she received her education at the Royal Conservatoire in Stockholm by Julius Günther, then went to Paris, where she became a pupil of Mathilde Marchesi de Castrone and Ellen Kenneth. She made her concert debut in 1886 at Stockholm. In 1889 she made her stage debut at the Royal Opera in Stockholm as Amneris in "Aida". She became known internationally an excellent interpreter of part in operas of R. Wagner. (forgottenoperasingers.blogspot.com)

[35] **The Bohemian Quartet** (Czech: České kvarteto; known as the Czech Quartet after 1918) were a Czech string quartet of international repute that was founded in 1891 and disbanded in 1934. (A. Eaglefield-Hull, A Dictionary of Modern Music and Musicians; Dent, London, 1924)

you to overindulge, was generously served. The Bohemians were unsuspecting victims of this devious punch, faire le diable a quatre, ("the devil with four", a French expression for something that causes lots of noise and disorder) which soon exerted its influence upon them. My poor friends, saturated with the sweet ravisher, had to be put to bed and were lost for several hours. Finally we aroused them and took them to their hotel. The next day, after a short visit, I accompanied the quartet to the station and wished them Godspeed. It was the last time I saw them. Several more years' traveling ended when Nedbal, the viola player, eloped with the wife of the first violinist, Hoffman.

Artur Schnabel [36] was one of the soloists on our concert series. After his concert, we went to a friend's home where Artur played one Strauss waltz after another, the ladies sitting upon the floor around the grand piano admiring the enthusiastic young artist. It was three a.m. when this animated session finally closed.

Henri Marteau came to Göteborg and gave us an exquisite performance of the Brahms Concerto. He told me that Joachim had chosen him as his successor at the Imperial Conservatory of Music in Berlin. In order to have time to talk with Henri, I took him home with me. That night he slept in my bed, and I on the sofa.

I must foist on you again some hunting stories. The committee in Göteborg did everything to make life agreeable for me. One of the members was the director of the large Carnegie sugar and ale factory; he owned a magnificent estate, two hours' travel from the city.

Artur Schnabel

[36] **Artur Schnabel** (17 April 1882 – 15 August 1951) Artur Schnabel was born in Lipnik, Moravia (at the time a part of Austria) on April 17, 1882. At the age of seven, he was taken to Vienna to play for Professor Hans Schmitt (1835-1907), with whom he studied privately from 1888 to 1891. From 1891 to 1897 he studied with Theodor Leschetizky (1830-1915) and his assistant, Annette Essipoff. He received his theoretical training from Eusebius Mandyczewski (1857-1929). Schnabel made his debut in Vienna in 1890, but began his concert tours in Europe in 1896. He moved to Berlin in 1900 and made this city his home for thirty-three years. (Schnabel Music Foundation; schnabelmusicfoundation.com)

Knowing I was fond of hunting, he invited me to hunt on his grounds whenever I wished to do so. It was exceptionally fine game territory—with moose, deer, rabbits, and birds in abundance. The moose hunting was strictly regulated in Sweden. Every year the animals were counted and a certain number designated to be shot each hunting season. This method assured a continuously stable herd.

One of our soloists was Hugo Becker [37], the great cellist. After his appearance, we sat together philosophizing. When I mentioned my hunting hobby, he confessed his own enjoyment of the sport. I told him I would be going hunting the next morning on the committee member's estate and invited him to join me. He was eager to do so and early the following day we started out, he clad in a thick fur coat, I more practically, in my lightweight hunting outfit. When we came to the field, difficulties arose. The snow was about three feet deep and ditches filled to the brim. Hugo, not familiar with the terrain, would step right in the ditches and several times was buried in the snow with only his head and fur cap protruding. But he took all these hindrances blithely and even seemed to be having a lot of fun.

Soon, directly in front of me, a rabbit stuck his head out of the snow. He ran as fast as he could and, after a few dunkings in the deep softness, came to a four-foot high stone wall; here he made a mighty leap and while he was in the air I shot him, dropping him atop the wall. When Hugo came up to me, dragging his feet behind him, he asked, "where is the rabbit?"

[37] **Hugo Becker** (born Jean Otto Eric Hugo Becker, 13 February 1863, died 30 July 1941) Hugo Becker was a prominent cello teacher of the early twentieth century, who had studied as a youth with Piatti, and the infamous Grutzmacher in Dresden. (Grutzmacher is the "author" of the Boccherini B Flat Concerto, in its most widely seen form.) Becker was born in 1864 in Strasbourg in Alsace, the son of a famous violinist. His father started teaching him the violin at the age of six, but he loved the cello, and switched over at the age of nine. He was a child prodigy of sorts, and by the age of 15 had become a leading cellist in the Court Orchestra in Mannheim. He also toured with a string quartet made up of his father, sister, brother and himself. Becker was appointed solo cellist with the Opera Orchestra in Frankfurt in 1884, and the following year became the leading cello teacher at the Hochschule in Frankfurt. He also did extensive touring in other countries, including the United States. He played in a trio with Ysaye and Busoni, which was well received. He was personally acquainted with Brahms and Schumann. Becker owned two Strads: The "Cristiani," dated 1720, and one made in 1719, now known as "The Becker." He is most remembered as a teacher. He did much research in the areas of physiology and anatomy with regard to playing the cello. Among his many students were Mainardi, Grummer, Beatrice Harrison and Herbert Walenn. He died in 1941. (Hugo Becker, Cellist; Internet Cello Society; cello.org)

"Find him," I said.

After he had searched all around in the snow without result, I showed him where the rabbit lay. He said what I thought, "this is the first time I have ever heard of a rabbit being shot in the air!"

My recreation days in Lausanne were Mondays; in Göteborg I changed them to Sundays. As I wished for Morales to acquire the necessary routine of an orchestra conductor, having returned to the city to be my assistant, I assigned him to lead the Sunday concerts. Three of my friends and I rented the hunting rights on an island from its inhabitants where game was plentiful. One of my friends had a well-trained pair of hounds, fox and badger hunters. Another of us owned a big Gordon setter. The cashier of Herman Manheimer's bank was the owner of one of the best-trained dogs I have ever known, a fine English Setter. When the four of us came back Sunday evenings we always "brought home the bacon." The cashier and I typically hunted behind his setter. The dog would stand poised near a covey of partridges and we would flush them. My friend would shoot to the right—two birds down; I to the left—two birds down. This procedure could almost always be carried on until each of us had gathered at least a dozen trophies for the day. A few rabbits and maybe a passing duck would fill our rucksacks. Those were hunting days! Sweden at that time was a hunter's paradise. The American ambassador to Sweden married a lady of that country and, when he retired, stayed in Sweden to enjoy the hunting there.

Eugen d'Albert [38] was another of the soloists en-

[38] **Eugen (originally Eugène) Francois Charles d'Albert** (10 April 1864 – 3 March 1932) was a Scottish-born German pianist and composer. Eugen d'Albert made extraordinary progress as both a pianist and a composer, and after several appearances at the Popular Concerts, was the soloist in Robert Schumann's Concerto at the Crystal Palace in London (February 5, 1881). On October 24, 1881, when only 17, he played his own piano concerto at one of Hans Richter's concerts, arousing great enthusiasm. The press compared him to Mozart and Felix Mendelssohn. He received a Mendelssohn fellowship and went to Vienna. Later he studied in Weimar with the elderly Franz Liszt, who was greatly impressed by his technique and often referred to him as "the young Tausig." D'Albert can be heard in an early recording of that composer's works. (Bach Cantatas Website; bach-cantatas.com)

[39] **Carl Wilhelm Eugen Stenhammar** (February 7, 1871 – November 20, 1927) was one of Sweden's most important composers at the turn of the 19th century, and one of the finest Swedish pianists of his time. He was elected onto the Royal Swedish Academy of Music in 1900. After studying in Stockholm and Berlin (1887-93) he became a prominent figure on the Stockholm music scene before being appointed principal conductor of the Gothenburg Orchestral Society in 1907. (Swedish Musical Heritage; swedishmusicalheritage.com)

gaged by our committee. He played the Emperor Concerto by Beethoven in his persuasive, unsurpassable manner. To also honor him as a versatile composer, I chose his Improvisator Overture for the program and asked him to conduct it. Just before the piece was to be played my tympani player suffered a collapse. To save the situation, I played his part myself. After the performance—a grand success for the composer—d'Albert approached me.

"Have you done that before?" he asked me in his high falsetto voice (he kept his soprano boy's voice till his death).

"Why, no," I answered.

"Well, one would certainly think you had," he said. "You did well."

Stenhammar[39] , then the foremost Swedish composer, played his own piano concerto in one of our concerts under the conductorship of Tor Aulin [40] —Sweden's most outstanding violinist. Aulin had conducted the composition before but, at one point, lost entire control of the orchestra which faltered for several bars. However, the well-trained musicians found their way back, and with them Aulin. Both Stenhammar and Aulin had been among the seven contestants for the conductorship of the orchestra. Stenhammar was my successor after my resignation. He was also esteemed in Sweden as the foremost interpreter of Beethoven, but the members of the orchestra and I had a different opinion about it. He played the Emperor Concerto with us in a very mediocre way and even said he hoped to do it "better next time."

Tor Aulin

[40] Tor Aulin (10 September 1866, Stockholm – 1 March 1914, Saltsjöbaden) was the most prominent violinist of his time in Sweden, one of the foremost conductors and a champion of chamber music. His oeuvre contains three concertante works for violin and orchestra, incidental music, songs and chamber music. In 1887 he formed the Aulin Quartet. Between 1889 and 1902 he was concert master for the Royal Court Orchestra, after which he formed and led numerous ensembles, including the Swedish Musicians' Society Orchestra (1900), the Stockholm Concert Society (1902-09), the orchestra of the Royal Dramatic Theatre (1907–09) and the Southern Sweden Philharmonic Society (1907-08). He was conductor of the Gothenburg Orchestra Society from 1909 to 1911 and became a member of the Royal Swedish Academy of Music in 1895. (Swedish Musical Heritage; swedishmusicalheritage.com)

At mid-winter, Marie paid me the promised visit. The day of her arrival was a beautiful but bitingly cold one. We were invited to the family Pratt's home that evening, but before we departed for our visit she complained of a severe headache. Probably resulting mainly from the headache, we had a slight dispute about some unimportant subject and our frame of mind was not conducive to a pleasant evening. Today I am still deeply sorry that this evening of reunion, my wife attired in a very becoming black velvet evening gown, found us in a discordant mood. Her headache increased at the party and she wanted to go home, but she insisted I stay. So Herman Manheimer took her home and I remained until he returned. After a few minutes, I left the Pratt's and walked home where I found Marie still suffering. The next morning she went to see Herman's brother, Dr. Manheimer, for treatment. Somewhat relieved, she was able to go with me to the art galleries where the main attraction was the valuable Furstenberg collection of paintings. We took a short tour of the city, and a pleasant walk through Kings Traegorden concluded our day. She stayed a week with me. She heard two concerts in which some of her preferred compositions were performed. I felt that this was the highlight of her visit and had made the journey worthwhile for her.

[41] **Roderich Edmund Ladislaus Anton Julius Mojsisovics of Mojsvár** (*10. May 1877 in Graz ; † 30th March 1953 in Bruck an der Mur) was an Austrian conductor, composer, music and playwright. (Revolvy.com)

Shortly hereafter, my friend, Roderich von Mojsisovics [41], appeared with his Alpen Symphony in his satchel. His stay in Göteborg was only of a few days' duration so I had not much time for the rehearsal of his difficult opus, but it found favor with the musicians and public, and Roderich was kind enough to give this occasion a prominent place in his autobiography which was printed in the Deutsche Musikzeitung.

Roderich and I paid a visit to the island of Wisby, Sweden's popular west coast summer resort. We two old friends, desirous of bringing each other up to date on the happenings of the intervening years, still did not have enough time to philosophically ruminate about their hows and whys. But the Graz music festival was not too far off and this would enable us to spend more time together, delving into the past which we always loved to do.

Spring made its triumphant arrival in Göteborg. A present as fine and beautiful as I ever received came to me with the visit of my dear old friend, Carl Årman. I had invited him to come to Göteborg to see me, and gave a concert in his honor, asking him to choose the program. After the concert, Carl came to my director's room. Tears obstructing his view and in a faltering voice he spoke to me, "Heinrich, the passing of the years brings heavy burdens; but if I could more often listen to music like your orchestra played for me today, they would be easier to carry."

I was aware of a rare gladness at having pleased him so. Carl was then 78; rheumatism and gout ruled him to such an extent that he was unable to any longer satisfy his constant desire to commune with his lifelong friend, the concert grand piano, the instrument which formerly enabled him to bring the greatest masterworks to life. When Carl started his homeward journey to Orebro the next day, our farewell awoke in me profound emotions— as we knew it was our last. He embraced me tenderly and said, "You have been a very dear friend to me; my last greeting before I close my eyes forever will be sent to you, with my blessing."

Unable to speak in reply and in tears our eyes met, our words miserably inadequate in scanning our thoughts of the future, and we parted.

Events followed events, weeks passed, summer arrived with its welcome vacation, and the music festival in Graz where Roderich was director of the State Conservatory of Music was near. After a week's rest with my family in Leyden, I was off to Graz, one of the pearls of Austrian towns where, that year [1905], the festival of the Allgemeiner Deutsche Musikverein was to take place. All the greats of the European music world were there. I had been a member of the organization for years past and attended every one of the festivals. Sometimes, on request, I wrote the reviews of the performances.

At a welcoming supper, the municipality of Graz was host to the members of the association the first evening. Max Reger [42], my old friend from Lausanne and Frankfurt, sat with me and was browsing around old territories when the governor of the province rose to make his "welcome" speech. As he began to speak, Max began speaking also. Throughout the speech Max, acting like a naughty little boy, continuously threw clearly audible nonsensical remarks into the slight pauses between the Governor's phrases. My frequent remonstrances to him were of no effect. He continued his senseless stupidity to the end of the address. Everyone was obviously incensed. At the end of the oration, the diners arose, a few at a time, and went up to the Governor to clink glasses with him and our President Max von Schillings as is the custom in Germany. When Max and I performed the ritual, von Schillings said severely to Reger, "You are a great musician, but a gentleman you are not."

A remark of this kind means an unavoidable duel. On our way home Max, now uncomfortably aware of his misbehavior and its consequences, said anxiously, "What shall I do, Heinrich? I have to play tomorrow."

I promised I would speak to our President about postponing the affair and expressed confidence in my success (as I was on friendly terms with the President, having written an opera libretto for him, Die Beiden Hexen). But von Schillings sent no word about the immediacy of the duel and I did not feel I should speak to him before he did.

The next day's program included the first perfor-

[42] **Johann Baptist Joseph Maximilian Reger** (19 March 1873 – 11 May 1916) was a German composer, musician and teacher. He is counted among the most influential German composers of his time. A multi-faceted personality, he is especially well-known for elaborating on the stylistic traits of Johannes Brahms, and leading the transition of German music into the 20th century. He was also an organist and conductor and had made important contributions to music in these roles as well. (The Famous People; thefamouspeople.com)

mance of Max Reger's piano composition, Variations on a Beethoven Theme. A raging thunderstorm was in progress outside and lightning flashes and powerful rumbles greeted Max when he sat down to play. One of these mighty thunder rolls shook the whole building, but Max, undisturbed, played his fine wide-dimensioned opus masterfully, with deep emotional accentuation, his full, almost orchestral tone pervading every corner of the hall. The tumultuous applause following this perfect presentation of a great work surpassed even the roar of the thunder. Later I saw von Schillings shake hands with Reger and Max told me he had said the performance "Was magnificent!" Thus the otherwise foreboding duel episode ended satisfactorily.

Roderich and I had ample time to not only spend our meals together but to discuss philosophical quandaries. One pleasant afternoon, the members of the association were guests of a countess at her castle in which Franz Schubert had composed his quaint country dances while a guest. The occasion was a German "Kaffeeklatsch" called "Schnause" by the Austrians. The society ladies of the town served the refreshments, clad in colorful Austrian peasant costumes. A number of the men, impressed by the beauty and friendly grace of these members of the feminine sex, started flirting with them (and seemingly successfully) until Roderich, by the grapevine method, apprised them of their errors. I wonder if the ladies were not a little disappointed?

Some students of the university provided several gay musical numbers upon the queerest combination of instruments I ever saw—harmonicas, zither-like contraptions, and I don't know what-all. Max von Schillings invited me to his table where one of the guests was Willem Mengelberg from whom I only received some annoyed glances. He could not forget the desertion of nine of his fine artists from his orchestra to mine.

Chapter 17   Ambition Strikes Again

"Les bon j'our d'Anjoux sont passe." The beautiful hours of Graz belonging to the past, Holland waited for the return of the pater absent for such a long time from his family. I was pleased that their installation in Leyden seemed agreeable to them. Marie's health had improved and the children grew like well-fertilized tomato plants. Ernst was already over six feet tall and Sis a strong well-grown girl. Miss Repelius, who was a frequent visitor to the Hammer home, came and invited us again on a summer vacation.

This time we traveled to Bussum, a short distance from Amsterdam. Across from the comfortable house Miss Repelius had provided for us lived "Onkel Kruger"—so called by the Hollanders—the ex-President of the Transvaal Republic who lost to the British after the Boer war. He retired to this distinguished little village and later died there.

We made many a fine excursion into the surrounding countryside. The weather in Holland is very changeable and not many sunny days squeeze in between the foggy and cloudy ones. But we passed comfortably pleasant hours in our family circle, including paying a few visits to Rijksmuseum in Amsterdam with Miss Repelius as our expert guide. The Night Watch (Rembrandt) aroused my admiration to a higher degree each time I saw it. Our restful stay in Bussum exerted its beneficial influence upon us all.

In Leyden again, the children began preparations for returning to school while I prepared to return to Sweden. Ernst's term in high school would end in two years and my wife wished to move back to Amsterdam at the end of that time as Ernst intended to take up his mother's profession and she was very familiar with conditions there. I agreed and thought this a sound way to further our boy's education.

Only a few replacements in the Göteborg orchestra personnel were necessary this season. My new assistant concertmaster was a very young Hollander—Snook was his name—a pupil of Seveik. This young genius was the master of a brightly polished technique and an unreserved interpreter of the classics, which made him a valuable addition to the violin section. The old guard was happy, like myself, to start the winter season's work again, though all of them had enjoyed the summer season in Marielyst in Denmark. One of my oldest followers, Johansen, the first double bass player, returned from Denmark, his native country, a full-fledged landscape painter. He showed me some small oil paintings which clearly displayed his fine sense of artistic talent.

Two distinguished visitors who attended a few of our symphony concerts were the wife of the former American Ambassador Thomas and her sister, both living in Stockholm. On one of their visits, Mrs. Thomas told me that a Mr. Kohlsaat, manager of the Ter-Centennial World Exposition of Norfolk, Virginia, would be holding the event the following summer to memorialize the arrival of the first pilgrim there in 1607—and he had asked if she knew a prominent conductor whom he could engage to program a number of international concerts at the exposition. She had given him my name and he told her that before his return to the United States he would see me in Göteborg.

The following week I had the pleasure of meeting Mr. Kohlsaat at the Grand Hotel. He described the magnificence of the exposition he was planning, then asking me to name my conditions, if any. I told him I would conduct 20 international concerts for $20,000. He accepted and asked me to come to Norfolk about the end of April. Unexpectedly then arrived the means of fulfilling one of my long cherished desires: to visit the great U.S.A.! During this winter season, I often discovered my wandering thoughts were exercising a disturbing influence upon my actions as I pondered and speculated about what my experiences might be in that huge, and unknown, country. I rejuvenated my quite-rusty English, searching the library for useful reading material and, whenever possible, tried to get my friends to converse with me in English, which they spoke better than me.

One of my closest friends in Göteborg was Hugo Alfven, the composer of Midsommervaka, based upon the Swedish festival of that name. This season, we performed several of his other compositions—his first, second and fourth symphonies—all fine works. Shortly afterward he accepted the leadership of the world renowned Uppsala University male student chorus which repeatedly made triumphant appearances in the United States.

Coming or going from our hunting trips we were often molested by a Great Dane belonging to one of the houses in a little village on our way. He would snarl and follow us, barking, his excitement growing when my friends threatened him with their guns. One day I was passing the dog's home alone. His owner also seemed to hold a grudge against us—for no reason I know—for he was standing unconcernedly in front of his house when the animal followed me, growling ominously. Being a great friend of dogs myself and never afraid of them, I proceeded calmly on my way, but suddenly, sneaking up on me, he bit me on the rear, drawing blood. I turned around and, pointing my gun at the dog, called to his owner, "If you don't call your dog back I'll shoot him!"

He sullenly told the vicious animal to return to him.

"If he comes after me once more it will be the end of his life," I said angrily. Two weeks passed before I could sit down in comfort again.

The season's work progressed satisfactorily and included a performance of Mendelssohn's oratoric, Elijah. Hugo Kaun [43], my old friend from Berlin, sent me the score of his new symphonic poem, Falstaff, and we commenced our rehearsals. I later learned the performance, the first in Europe, was slated for the same day Theodor Thomas, conductor of the Chicago Symphony Orchestra, had planned to give it for the first time in the United States. But on the day on which both these premieres were to be given, Theodor Thomas died, so what would have been a strange coincidence was instead eliminated by a tragedy.

Delightful hours were passed at the home of my dear friend, Herman Manheimer. After a concert, his wife would sit down at the piano and play passages from compositions she had heard there, flawlessly—she was a marvelous music talent. The second floor of Herman's home was occupied by his wealthy father-in-law who was the happy owner of a well-equipped billiard room where we often enjoyed a stimulating after-dinner game. And so another season neared its close.

[43] **Hugo Wilhelm Ludwig Kaun** (March 21, 1863 – April 2, 1932) was a German composer, conductor, and music teacher. Kaun was born in Berlin, and completed his musical training in his native city. In 1886 (or 1887), he left Germany for the United States and settled in Milwaukee, which was home to a well-established German immigrant community. As the conductor of local choral societies such as the Milwaukee Liederkranz and the Milwaukee Men's Choir, Kaun quickly acquired an important influence over the city's musical life. He also taught at the conservatory, where his colleagues included Wilhelm Middelschulte. (Hugo Kaun; World Heritage Encyclopedia; worldbooklibrary.org)

PART 2

UNITED STATES
1907—1952

Chapter 18   Off to America

I made a reservation for a cabin on a Hamburg Lloyd steamer on which I would make my trip to the United States. When I arrived at the Lloyd's office in Hamburg the day of my sailing, I was greeted by some bad news—the ship I was supposed to board was being held up by a strike.

"There is a steamer second class, carrying only second and third-class passengers, which sails tomorrow morning," the manager told me. "You can exchange your first-class ticket for a second class and go on board right away if you wish."

My luggage was transported to this ship and I mentally made a tour of places familiar to me from my two previous visits here. That night, I took refuge in my cabin; it was nice to be alone there for a while. With the soft sloshing of the Elbe on the sides of the steamer, its waters journeying to Hamburg, we passed the places where I spent my early youth and in which I had enjoyed many an invigorating swim long ago, the rhythmic sound now lulling me to sleep. After a refreshing shower and breakfast the next morning, I went on deck, and here, like ants bustling around me were officers, sailors, porters, and passengers, each preparing for the departure of the big ship Batavia on its transatlantic voyage. A few hours later the ship's bell sounded its last warning and a few stragglers came running up the gangplank to fill the ranks of those already onboard. Anchors aweigh! The chains rattled and the heavy iron anchor which held the ship securely to its mooring was lifted high out of the water. Slowly, the engine forced the monster into a crawling forward motion and, helped by a tugboat, we left the inland harbor and traveled along the wide-armed Elbe to the North Sea. It was here our first dinner was served.

I was seated at the captain's table—his name was Schmidt and he was the senior officer of the Hamburg Lloyd Line—and there I made the acquaintance of a Mr. and Mrs. Drexel from Philadelphia who, like myself, had exchanged their tickets from first to second class. Toward evening, the weather roughened; a cold, sharp wind had arisen and most of the passengers seemed eager to reach the salon where many a place was empty, their occupants having left to pay an unexpected tribute to Neptune. I could not believe that I would very soon imitate them! When, before going to my cabin, I looked hastily out of the salon's window, I could see the raging sea's high waves and valleys wreaking havoc upon our poor vessel. Thrown into a valley, it would go satisfactorily, but when it was wrested atop a wave's crest, I could see the propeller leave its element and spin uselessly above it. This would cause a shudder and trembling throughout the ship, making restful sleep impossible.

Great speed was also impossible in the midst of such conditions. The next day, still an exceedingly stormy one, I had lost my appetite, and did not partake of any of the meals, but subsisted on fruit and lemonade. The storm continued for a number of days, but toward its end, I finally felt better and dispatched my five meals a day in true German fashion. These were the meal stations on the Batavia, one of the oldest ships of the Hansa: breakfast at 6:00, second breakfast at 10:00, dinner 12:30, kaffeeklatch 4:00, and supper at 8:00. No wonder the sailors, free from seasickness, gain weight on such a voyage! Every morning Captain Schmidt invited Mr. and Mrs. Drexel and me for an appetizer—that strange name!—in his cabin. He was a master cocktail mixer, never leaving this sacred process to his cabin boy.

Another passenger was the painter, Paul Knauerhase, who was returning to America from his studies in München (Munich). He was the merrymaker of our little group; decidedly bowlegged and the possessor of an abnormally large nose, and both of these anomalies were often the objects of his own droll jokes. He had a pleasing baritone voice and gladly entertained the crowd with popular songs. Everyone liked him, including yours truly. The First Engineer Officer was an ardent music lover and we also often relaxed in his cabin enjoying lively discussions, always enriched with a few glasses of excellent red wine.

Days flew and a number of us were unconcerned about our extended crossing. We arrived in New York two days late but it did not matter to us, though everyone was happy to at last behold this magnificent metropolis. At that time, one could travel anywhere in the world without a passport, outside of Russia, so as free beings we entered a free country. On our arrival, Paul Knauerhase took care of me, escorting me to a coffee shop where I tasted my first American pie —although it happened to be a sour, poorly-made rhubarb pie and I decided I did not care for this facet of American desert; thankfully I was treated to the real kind later.

From there, Knauerhase took me to the home of his parents, as both his father and mother were immigrants from Germany. One of Paul's younger brothers was a dentist, the youngest still a high school pupil. Regarding his own professional efforts, Paul's work grew until he became an outstanding painter; some of his paintings are in the Metropolitan Museum of New York.

His was a congenial family and his mother was a fine German cook. The fortunate circumstance of my entering straightaway into a circle of such friendly and hospitable folks eliminated at once the typical difficulties of a stranger who had just arrived in a giant city the size of New York. During the big family dinner at his home, Paul counseled me not to go to a hotel but to instead rent a convenient room or apartment temporarily until he could find something more comfortable for me—he then found an ad in the newspaper for a room on Washington Square. We went to inspect it and found a large, comfortable space so I took it, paying two weeks' rent in advance.

It was the year 1907; automobiles were still rare at that time, so I hired one of the old cabs and, with Paul's help, transported my luggage to my new living quarters before sundown. Everything settled, Paul and I took a stroll around my new neighborhood, the quaint, and previously fashionable section of the city where old, solidly-constructed houses three to five stories high attested to the wealth of the patricians who had built them. Paul informed me that the aristocracy, with a few exceptions, had now left this quarter and painters and other artists had taken possession of it.

After our refreshing walk, I asked Paul to have dinner with me and asked him to choose a good restaurant. He knew a place, frequented by artists, where original French dishes and real French wine were served by French waiters. As good as it sounded, I would have preferred to try an American meal; but as he was my gracious host, I deferred to my new friend's suggestion. I certainly didn't regret his choice as the genuine French atmosphere awoke sweet memories of my days in Paris for me. Home and to my first sleep in the United States; but I was still slightly troubled by imaginary tosses of a fantasy ship lolling beneath me.

Unpacking the next morning, I found, among other things I had not remembered having, six pairs of woolen socks my mother had sent me when I first went to Sweden. Across the street from my room I saw a sign: "Chinese laundry," so I took my six pairs of socks over to be washed. The owner of the laundry spoke a strange language, an almost unintelligible mixture of what I thought was Chinese and English. I did not know that every word he spoke was a form of English. I gathered that in a few days the socks would be ready.

During the following days, I repeated the system I always followed when coming to a new town. I rode all transport lines, buses, trains, elevated, etc. to their farthest points and back to survey as large a territory as possible in a short time, plus acquire a certain knowledge of the various sections of the city.

I returned to the Chinese laundry to obtain my socks. But instead of socks I got shocks. When I asked for my property from this same man I'd originally given them to, he innocently answered, "We no got."

I did not understand. I repeated my demand. Same answer. I still was nonplussed. "I brought my socks to you a few days ago."

"We no got," he replied for the third time.

Angrily I walked out, looking for a policeman. I hailed one nearby and told him my story. "Did you get a receipt?" he asked.

"No," I answered.

"Was there a witness in the room?"

"No."

"Then you're out of luck," he told me. "We get all kinds of stories like yours and we know there are lots of scoundrels like that fellow; but they know their tricks and play them so cleverly that we can very seldom catch one."

This was the first robbery of which the innocent and trusting German was the victim. Many more were to come later in this "land of opportunity."

Note from Melinda...

I think "naïve" is maybe a better word than "innocent" trusting German. My mom always said he trusted everyone on no sturdier foundation than a good handshake!

For two weeks I stayed on Washington Square and my time here was usefully spent. Besides learning a great deal about the city's geography, I saw its slums near the Bowery, the section occupied by "the 400," [44] institutes of learning, Madison Square Garden, the tremendous library, opera houses, concert halls, the great harbor with its incessant ferry services, and Victor Herbert's [45] new work, The Red Mill.

At that performance, in which Montgomery and Stone were the main hilarious attraction, I met Victor Englander. Afterward we went to a nearby restaurant where we discussed past and present conditions of our métier (occupations). At that point, Englander was a well-liked composer of operettas and popular compositions. When I mentioned my experiences in writing opera libretti he quickly took hold of the information, then asking me eagerly if I would like to write an operetta for Anna Held (the wife of Ziegfeld, Jr. at that time), offering that he would write the music for it. I gladly said yes and finished it in two days. Informing him of its completion, he arranged a meeting at Ziegfeld's home.

While we were discussing the operetta, Ziegfeld's wife returned from a lunch given in her honor by the officers of a warship anchored in the harbor. She stood in the center of the room embracing large bouquets of costly flowers, chattering like a young girl, and looking like one too, given her diminutive stature, telling of the glorious time she had had on the battleship among the admiring sailors. After a very animated conversation led primarily by Mrs. Ziegfeld, we gave her the script for her perusal and left in a hopeful state of mind. These hopes were shattered like so many others of mine afterward. The book we had submitted was too tame for Anna Held. With an expression of regret and a "thank you" it was returned to Victor. He spurred me for another effort but I declined, feeling that I had not yet mastered the American spirit so necessary for writing something of that kind for U.S. audiences.

Paul came to see me several times during those two weeks. One day he told me not to pay any more rent as he had found a better place for me. It was in Mont Vale, a little town where he used to spend many weekends. Ferry and railroad, plus half an hour's walk brought us to an idyllic place, a large house pleasantly located halfway up a hill entirely covered with dogwood in full bloom which, when seen from a distance, gave one the impression of a snow-covered landscape. The house was owned by a friend of Paul's, a middle-aged lady of German descent who lived there with her 86-year-old father and a younger sister, a piano teacher who was unmarried like herself. The father, Mr. Busse, a handsome old gentleman with a big and beautiful white beard, had been the mayor of a little German town as well as a photographer by profession before he emigrated to America 40 years before with his family. I immediately rented one of the

44 **"The 400"** - A U.S. idiom meaning a select group. It was created (1892) by Samuel Ward McAllister (1827-95), a U.S. socialite, when, in shortening a list for a ball, he boasted that there were 'only about 400 people in New York society'. (New Webster's Dictionary and Thesaurus)

VICTOR HERBERT.

45 **Victor August Herbert** (February 1, 1859 – May 26, 1924) was an Irish-born, German-raised American composer, cellist and conductor. Although Herbert enjoyed important careers as a cello soloist and conductor, he is best known for composing many successful operettas that premiered on Broadway from the 1890s to World War I. He was also prominent among the tin pan alley composers and was later a founder of the American Society of Composers, Authors, and Publishers (ASCAP).

large rooms in their house.

The food was good, a sort of combination American and German style. Saturdays and Sundays the house was crowded to capacity with old friends of the owners who seemed to like to spend their weekends exclusively at this place. Very soon I knew them all quite well.

One Sunday I was greatly astounded to see a Negro gentleman at the dinner table. Asking Paul—both he and his brothers were among the weekend guests—about the Negro's presence, he told me there was very little segregation in New York. I learned that the very clever and fashionably dressed gentleman had been educated at the court of Weimar where his father had been valet to the Grand Duke.

The time for my engagement in Jamestown neared. I traveled first by train then ferry to New York City and then by train to Baltimore. There, being unenlightened about the extent of racial prejudice in the South, I entered a car which I noticed had only Negro passengers. Before the train started, the conductor came in. "What are you doing here?" he asked harshly when he saw me.

"I have my ticket for Norfolk," I said, surprised.

"Can't you read?" he said, pointing to a sign. "This car is for Negroes only!"

This was my first graphic comparison between the state of the Negro in the South and that of his brother in the North. Why are these conditions still prevalent 40 years after the supposed abolition of slavery?

It was a great pleasure to traverse southern Maryland, a country so different from that I passed through on my way to Baltimore. This was very serene country—pastures, woodlands, small cozy farmhouses, and here or there one of the old mansions of former slaveholders. Additionally, small fishing villages and historic towns were all sights which made a vivid impression on me. My lively fantasy, nourished in this case by my knowledge of the history of the United States, (acquired in my school years mainly because of my keen interest in cowboys and Indians), easily led me 100–200 years back in time, and I saw in my mind's eye the mansions and towns in their original dress, a stately south Maryland tableau of unusual pictorial quality.

My first crossing of the broad Potomac and down the Chesapeake Bay to Norfolk was invigorating and particularly memorable. A cold high wind was blowing and had apparently put the old King of the Waters in a bad humor for he shook us poor humans aboard the steamer mercilessly. Hundreds of ducks were restlessly switching back and forth between air and water, seemingly undecided about which was the lesser of two evils.

From Norfolk I went to Jamestown where I took lodging in a reputable boardinghouse. At the supper table there, the upcoming exposition was one of the subjects of discussion. I discovered with apprehension that the tones of the diners' voices and their words were rather more derogatory than approving. I am sorry to say that the next day I was fully in accord with the judgment of the critics. When I arrived at the fairgrounds, I was astonished to see the buildings only half-finished and an insufficient number of workmen half-heartedly busy on some of them. I entered the main office, also unfinished, and announced myself. I was led to the gentleman in charge to whom I gave my name and of my verbal contract with Mr. Kohlsaat.

"Where is your orchestra?" he asked me.

Dumbfounded, I stared at him. "My orchestra?" I said. "I am engaged as guest conductor and not supposed to bring an orchestra with me. Where is yours?"

"Why, we have none," he said in surprise.

"What are you going to do?" I countered.

"I don't know," he said slowly.

"There seems to be no way out of this impasse, or is there?" I asked.

"This is an awkward situation," he said. "And, at present, there is no capital available to rectify it."

"What is your counsel concerning my position?" I asked him, feeling progressively more incensed.

"Even to that question I have no answer," he said rather uncomfortably.

"As you have no answer to any of my questions, I will return to New York. Here is my address; I'll await your answer there."

With these words I left the office, went back to the boardinghouse, and left Norfolk that afternoon. The next morning I was back in New York City.

As I was passing Carnegie Hall I noticed a placard announcing that evening's recital by Ernesto Consolo, pianist. What a coincidence! Here was my old friend who had played the Schuman Piano Concerto with my Lausanne orchestra in Vevey, Switzerland, under peculiar circumstances. Throughout the entire first part of the concert there had been a strange continuous clattering noise emanating from the piano. Finally, I could stand it no more. I stopped the orchestra and looked into the piano where I saw an iron key like those holding the piano strings lying on the tuning board in such a spot as to be easily rattled by the vibrations. I asked a stage attendant for a pair of scissors and, as the audience patiently waited, carefully removed the mischief maker. These proceedings made the soloist nervous and in the last part of the concerto he made a great mistake, leaving about 20 bars unplayed. Although he lost his way, my well-disciplined orchestra jumped the 20 bars with him and the audience was none the wiser regarding our impromptu musical acrobatics. After the performance, behind the stage, Ernesto embraced me impulsively.

"Thank you, thank you, Heinrich; I will never forget this," he said fervently.

At the period of his recital in Carnegie Hall, Ernesto was head of the piano department at the College of Music in Chicago. I had recommended him to Zeigfeld, Sr., its president, as you will recall. I naturally went to the recital that evening and, at the intermission, went to Ernesto's room. A great surprise awaited me there. A number of my old acquaintances and friends were gathered inside congratulating Ernesto—Ernest Schelling, Victor Herbert, and Arthur Hartman among others. They were all surprised to see me. After yesterday's debacle, it was especially heartwarming to find so many of my old friends from Europe together; after all I was thousands of miles away in a foreign country to which I had just arrived and was virtually a stranger. We all enthusiastically talked at once and the little room seemed about to explode. Finally someone asked, "Hammer, what brings you here?"

I recounted yesterday's story to them and what a guffaw followed my recital! They knew more about conditions in Jamestown than I did.

"You seem to be one of the many unfortunate victims of that affair," Herbert said to me. "It's rumored that bankruptcy is near. There will probably be no chance for you to collect."

"Another punishment for my careless handling of business transactions," I said. "But never mind. I have always wanted to see America. This gives me the opportunity to see a bit of it before I return to Europe."

"I am going to give a concert in Berlin," Arthur Hartman broke in. "Will you conduct it?"

"Certainly . . ."

"Oh, no!" Herbert interjected. "Reginald de Koven[46] has just left Washington D.C. as conductor of the orchestra there. I think you should go there and take over."

"I'll think about it," I said, interested; but I did not have time just then to ask him for more information.

Later, after the performance, we gathered for a French supper which held our little group pleasantly together for a few hours, and there I asked him some questions. I learned that the orchestra had flopped financially but that made me eager to go. With all my successes in Europe behind me I felt I could do anything and wanted to show my prowess in the United States. I went back to Mont Vale without disclosing my near-decision to Herbert because I felt I should think it over a little more. But my ponderings did not change my desire and the final result was a definite decision to go to Washington.

This was further strengthened by a conversation I had with the eldest sister of the owner of the house in which I was staying. Her name was Mrs. Schwaneke and she was the widow of an M.D. of German descent who had been a well-liked physician with a busy practice in the Bronx. Mrs. Schwaneke had an 18-year-old daughter who had been studying piano with her aunt but wanted a better teacher so she could become a professional accompanist to artists. When Mrs. Schwaneke told me all this I said I would be glad to help her daughter toward her goal if Mrs. Schwaneke would be willing to assume the position of housekeeper in my future home in Washington D.C. As her financial status would not allow her to pay for lessons from a prominent teacher, she gratefully accepted my offer.

Yet a mishap unavoidably extended my stay in Mont Vale. A dark green hedge of copious growth about five feet high, the foliage of which was unknown to me, had greatly interested me since my arrival. Inquiring of Miss Busse about its name, she told me it was poison ivy, a "great nuisance." "We'd like to eradicate it," she said, "but nobody dares to touch it."

"I'll do it for you," I told her. She warned me of the dire consequences but I had never heard of such a plant and her warning went unheeded. That same day I procured the necessary implements and started the destructive task—and it was indeed a real task! It took a whole week of hard labor to complete it. Everyone who saw me at work cautioned me of the calamitous effects the obnoxious plant would exercise upon me, but not a thing had happened so far, so I just laughed at their warnings.

He who laughs last, laughs best? Not in this case! My destruction had left in its wake an enormous heap of brush. What to do with it? As always the man of impulse, I decided to simply burn it. Quick judgment was meted out to this stupid German. The heat of the

[46]**Henry Louis Reginald De Koven** (April 3, 1859 – January 16, 1920) was an American music critic and prolific composer, particularly of comic operas. in 1888, he composed his first opera, The Begum, written with librettist Harry B. Smith. The following year he again teamed with Smith to compose the opera Don Quixote. From 1890 through 1920, De Koven introduced over 450 popular songs through his operas and operettas (the equivalent of a Broadway production in the 1950's). De Koven's operas include Robin Hood, The Knickerbockers, The Algerian, The Fencing Master, Rob Roy, The Highwayman, The Little Duchess, Maid Marian, Red Feather, Happyland and The Beauty Spot. Throughout the years, De Koven was also a renowned music critic for several periodicals including Chicago's Evening Post (1889-1895), Harper's Weekly (1895-1897) and New York's World (1898-1900, 1907-1912). In 1902, he organized and conducted the Washington DC Symphony. (Songwriters Hall of Fame; songhall.org)

burning brush released the oily substance of the leaves, saturating the air and attacking my half-naked body so that soon I was almost entirely covered with blisters—a whole week's suffering was the result of my recklessness. Through the years, I have tried to avoid poison ivy and poison oak plants as much as possible—the slightest touch of them was and still is exceptionally injurious to me.

Let me give the reader a few words of caution as well as a remedy in case you are subject to the influence of poison ivy. If you feel a strong itch after touching one of these plants, on homecoming wash the itching portions of the body thoroughly with soap, but do not use a towel to dry the washed parts, for if you do you will probably infect all the other parts of your body. This procedure has always helped me to quickly localize the scourge. While I was first-aid chief for 350 mountain-road builders and a Deputy Boy Scout Commissioner, this simple treatment helped many a victim to a quick recovery.

Chapter 19   Capital Struggle

At last I journeyed to the nation's capital in Washington. Feeling brazenly confident of myself, the first thing I did was to rent a three-story brick house with a basement on North Euclid Avenue. Acquisition of furniture, concert grand, etc. took some time, but they were the basis of a comfortable home, one which I hoped my family would soon also make theirs. In fact, I took for granted they would, and I only very slightly alluded to it a few times in my frequent letters to Marie and the children. One half of my lifetime had passed when I came to the U.S. as I am 90-years old at this writing. I had to turn my habits and actions upside down to conform to American customs—a rather difficult task for a 45-year-old man!

When Victor Herbert suggested in New York that I go to Washington D.C. to take over the leadership of the symphony orchestra recently disbanded by de Koven's departure, I was very eager to follow his counsel for another reason beside that of my egotism. The ebullient life in the great city with its melting-pot population had fascinated me from the moment of my arrival. I liked its aspects—the enormous buildings, bearing witness to a restless energy and unending daring, the large-scale living. I liked this country and felt that my pioneer spirit was akin to those who, in the short space of 150 years, had built this colossal nation, and I fancied myself a co-builder. Here I was in Washington D.C.! And I would see what I could now build.

The enormous differences between New York with its uninterrupted 24-hour hustle and bustle and Washington were both striking and pleasing to me. Washington was a calm, residential city in which the only outward sign of useful activity was the daily influx of thousands of government employees to the city's center, near which I lived, which was followed by their noon recesses when they streamed out of the massive office buildings and then in again, concluding with their exodus at the termination of the workday. Everything was then calm again; no industrial turmoil. However, even here at the U.S. heartbeat, there was a segregationist spirit. The Negro did not enjoy the privilege of equality which was granted him in New York.

My first steps after those I took to buy my house were directed to the headquarters of the Musicians Union where I inquired about the condition of the symphony orchestra. The information I received was utterly discouraging. Reginald de Koven, in his earnest endeavors to improve the positions of the orchestra members, had not only spent a considerable amount of his capital, but had seemingly gained nothing but broken-down health for his trouble. It turned out the orchestra committee had been dissolved and further questioning uncovered their unwillingness to rebuild the organization. Simmering in depression, I finally chose a side road by which I could obtain a means of livelihood until I could organize another orchestra, which I fully intended to attempt. I ordered the printing on fine Holland paper of three hundred small double-paged circulars announcing the establishment of the "Institute of Musical Art, Heinrich Hammer, Director" and secured a large bronze plate with this inscription to the wall next to the entrance to my studio. I addressed the three hundred circulars to the "haute vole" (high fliers) of the town. Not a single response resulted. A few pupils, however, appeared from the neighborhood. No one there knew of me except Oscar G. Sonneck [47], the head of the music division of the Library of Congress, himself a pianist, composer, and one of the globe's eminent musicologists. Our informal meeting in the Library one day paved the way for a warm and lasting friendship, one which was strengthened by our weekly musical sessions at his home which included browsing through newly copyrighted piano-violin sonatas, etc. We always ended with an English dinner. His wife was English and the owner of two dogs, a fox terrier and a small bulldog, who shared our meals with us, each occupying his own chair at the dinner table like well-behaved gentlemen.

My efforts to form another symphony orchestra in Washington were successful but this had to be done with my own money. I called it the Heinrich Hammer Symphony Orchestra. Our first concert was an artistic triumph, but not a financial one (resulting in yet another dip into my own resources).

After another concert of a more encouraging char-

[47] **Oscar George Theodore Sonneck** (October 6, 1873 – October 30, 1928) born in Jersey City, was a U.S. librarian, editor, and musicologist. For thirty years he studied philosophy and musicology in Germany at the universities of Heidelberg and Munich. From 1902 to 1917, he was head of the music division of the Library of Congress, creating a significant music library. As a writer, he specialized in the history of early (before the 19th century) American music. He died in New York, aged 55. (from "Notes" by Otto Kinkeldey, Vol. 11, No. 1 [Dec. 1953], pp. 25-32; pub. Music Library Association)

acter, I was asked to lead the Washington Choral Society which had fallen into disrepair. With the help of Sonneck, Bernhard R. Green, superintendent of the Library of Congress, and other music lovers, I brought the Choral Society to life again. The performance of Gounod's Redemption was the first fruit of our diligent work.

"**The Washington Choral Society** . . . second concert, given on February 17, introduced the new leader, Heinrich Hammer, a man of unusual eminence as a conductor, as readers of The Musical Courier know. The local orchestra, which appeared for the first time, played the purely instrumental portion with much precision and assurance, and with a delightful regard for the marks of expression in the score . . . the work chosen was Gounod's 'Redemption', without cuts, which was prefaced by 'Blessed Are They', from Mendelssohn's 'St. Paul', given in memory of Father Stafford, one of the best beloved priests in this city, who died recently.
(The Musical Courier, Volume 56, March 11, 1908, page 30)

I then decided to produce the nine Beethoven symphonies in consecutive performances. I wrote a "vada mecum" (a program guide) to the symphonies and employed the Choral Society and the four soloists from the choir of the pro-cathedral which I had recently been called to conduct. These concerts also found appreciative audiences, but again not sufficient financial returns. At last my efforts, aided by continuously favorable mentions in the capital's newspapers, aroused the truly music-loving population of the city who then clamored for the solidification of a Washington D.C. Symphony Orchestra organization. Sonneck, Mrs. Wadsworth, a noted music patron, Bernhard R. Green, Mr. Riggs, ex-president of the Riggs Bank (the bank of the President of the United States) and a few others, along with Mr. Scranage as the very industrious secretary, formed the committee of the now-reborn orchestra. But they encountered great difficulties in getting even a semblance of sufficient capital in hand to enable them to acquire the necessary players for the establishment of an orchestra worthy of the name of the capital of this great nation.

As proof of the admiration I felt for the United States, I composed a large work for mixed chorus, orchestra, narrator, and two soloists: Columbia Triumphant in Peace. The story was written by Dr. Henkels of the Carnegie Peace Organization. The performance of the work featured David Bispham as narrator and main soloist (at the apex of his career), the orchestra, augmented by members of the U.S. Marine band, and the Choral Society, and took place in the Belasco Theater. The work encompassed the tale of American history, and I regret to say, my faith in the patriotic spirit of our people was not justified as the enterprise was to become a costly one for me. Not familiar with the customary method of backing in the U.S., I carried the responsibility of it on my personal risk. A loss of eleven hundred dollars was my recompense.

Ode to Peace Triumphant

Washington D.C., May 26 – Last night Washington heard the premier presentation of "Columbia Triumphant in Peace", a national ode by Theodore Henckels, set to music by Heinrich Hammer of this city. The solo parts were artistically delivered by David Bispham, baritone, and Helen Donohue De Yo, soprano, while the ensemble numbers were sung by the Washington festival chorus, with the Washington Symphony Orchestra accompanying and Heinrich Hammer directing. Both the ode and the musical setting of "Columbia Triumphant in Peace" deserve praise. (Musical America, Volume 22, June 5, 1915)

One of my many mistakes in my new environment was my avoidance of society life. Now my work almost always took up a full day and usually my evenings as well, for I had the orchestra, the Choral Society, the church choir, the Sängerbund (a German male chorus), plus spending three half-days a week teaching at Miss Madera's School for Girls, besides having my private pupils—so when I occasionally had a free evening I felt no inclination to spend it in idle chatter. Unpleasant as it is to mention it, this probably cost me the financial and verbal backing of some of the influential residents of the city.

At one of the concerts, my symphonic poem, Sunset at Sea, the birth of which you will remember took place at the seashore in Holland, had its first performance in the United States.

Miss Fletsher and Miss Frances Densmore, both Smithsonian Institute researchers in the field of Indian music, approached me thereafter and asked my help in publicizing their findings by writing an orchestral work based on Indian themes. After my study of Indian lore at the Institute, Dr. Hodge, who was then chief of the Indian division there (at the time of this writing, the 85-year-old director of the Southwest Museum in Los Angeles) enthusiastically encouraged the project. I studied with deep interest the Sioux Indian music which Miss Densmore had gathered on Gramophone discs. The melodies used for the Sioux Indian Sun Dance, a ceremony lasting a week and comprising a great number of well-developed songs, seemed to me to be suitable for an Indian Rhapsody. I used the 16 most important songs of the dance as the foundation for my First American Indian Rhapsody, and dedicated the composition "to the American People." It was not my intention to distort the melodies as done by most composers who have written music of this genre, but I wished to conserve the original form of the pure Indian music, underlain by simple versus modern, harmonization. It was published by the Boston Music Company.

Just after its premiere performance (which I conducted at one of my regular symphony concerts), I was surprised to see a group of Indians mount the stage. They were a delegation from the North American Indian Brotherhood and presented me with a gold medal and an honorary membership in their organization. As the publishers neglected to give the composition the necessary promotion through publicity, the whole amount of the royalties I received for my work was $13.50. I regret that this opus, which was warmly received wherever performed and very suitable for high school orchestras as educational material, is not more widely known. About this time, I also wrote a Te Deum and Nune Dimitis, both published in New York.

Published Music Based on Themes Collected [by] Frances Densmore

Chippewa Themes: Unpublished (Both of these were successfully performed)
Winona – Opera by Alberto Bimboni, based on Chippewa themes; publication uncertain
Chippewa Indian Rhapsody for Full Orchestra, by Heinrich Hammer
Sioux Themes: Sioux Indian Rhapsody for Full Orchestra, by Heinrich Hammer
  NOTE: Both the Chippewa and Sioux Indian Rhapsodies were performed by the Washington Symphony Orchestra, Heinrich Hammer conductor. It was my impression he said both were either published or to be published in score and parts by Fisher, but copies are not filed in the copyright section of the library of congress. SOURCE: Typescript by Densmore, Frances Densmore papers, Library of Congress Archive of Folk Song, box 17. (www.news.minnesota.publicradio.org)

A constant attendant at rehearsals and concerts of the Sängerbund was Samuel Gompers [48], the founder of the American Labor Union, who became a good friend of mine. He was a remarkable man, empowered with a lofty intelligence which enabled him to make extemporaneous speeches of any length using perfect English, a feat which never failed to impress me.

A group of society ladies, having heard of my work with the choruses and choir, engaged me to conduct their "Friday Morning Music Club." This small singing society became my best group. Each of the ladies had already studied singing so it was a joy to work with them, and we met in private homes for our rehearsals. When I had been with them for a year, they presented me with a small gold lyre pin, which I have to this day, a token of their gratitude.

A Brief Account of the Long History of [the] Friday Morning Music Club Chorale

  "The Friday Morning Music Club is a remarkable organization, perhaps unique in this country for its longevity, independence, and selfless promotion of music. The FMMC played key roles in the founding of the National Symphony Orchestra and the Washington Performing Arts Society. The Club's nurturing of young artists helped propel Jessye Norman and Evelyn Lear onto the world stage . . .

"Membership was generally in the twenties in this period [1900-08], but something must have happened in 1911. The Chorus was suspended and reorganized in 1912 with Mr. Heinrich Hammer "a prominent Washington musician" engaged as director . . . During World War I the Chorus sang five times for troops, no doubt raising their morale before shipping overseas. Mrs. Dean was again Director following Hammer's resignation, possibly because of anti-German feeling . . ."

By Alan T. Crane, 2005 – Friday Morning Music Club, Inc. (fmmc-chorale-director.weebly.com)

The ranks of my pupils increased. Among them was the beautiful little eight-year old daughter of the English Ambassador Spring-Rice. Four of my pupils formed a male quartet which sang on several occasions. One of the members, a baritone named Raymond Moore, eventually became one of Washington D.C.'s outstanding vocal soloists. Leona Kidwell, a gifted soprano, reached the concertizing point but instead married a newspaper man and ceased her musical pursuits. I had several piano students too, of which some were pupils at Miss Madera's School. The newly-formed Washington Piano Teachers Association chose me to be its president. For our monthly gatherings I always arranged for a lecture

[48] **Samuel Gompers** (January 27, 1850 – December 13, 1924) Samuel Gompers was the first and longest-serving president of the American Federation of Labor (AFL); it is to him, as much as to anyone else, that the American labor movement owes its structure and characteristic strategies. Under his leadership, the AFL became the largest and most influential labor federation in the world. It grew from a marginal association of 50,000 in 1886 to an established organization of nearly 3 million in 1924 that had won a permanent place in American society. In a society renowned for its individualism and the power of its employer class, he forged a self-confident workers' organization dedicated to the principles of solidarity and mutual aid. It was a singular achievement. (AFLCIO.org)

and a soloist. At that time the Washington schools offered no credits for music studied outside school hours. The Association's insistence that the school board grant scholars credit for taking private music lessons finally produced this innovation in the schools' academic system.

In spring of 1908, a representative of the Colorado-Yule Marble Company showed me some samples of their white marble with gold veins and asked me to buy stock in this valuable enterprise situated in Colorado's Gunnison County. He told me that a mountain 3000' high and to a depth of several thousands of feet beneath the ground was one solid mass of this precious marble. Marble City was the seat of the company. I knew that Carrara in Italy was no longer able to fill the world's demand for white marble and I liked the idea of investing in a promising American enterprise, so I risked a great amount of my European-earned capital for the privilege of being a stockholder in the Colorado-Yule Marble Company—alas, the company went bankrupt and I lost every penny of my investment!

Note from Melinda...

Another example of Fahta's lack of business acumen. Good instincts, bad follow-through. The Colorado-Yule Marble Company was in the midst of a boom when he bought their stock with contracts reaching $1M dollars and marble shipping to both east and west coasts. If he had paid attention to his investment, he likely would have done well. Difficulties within the company did indeed lead to their bankruptcy in April 1917; however, they subsequently recouped and supplied the marble for exterior of the Lincoln Memorial as well as the Tomb of the Unknown Soldier, and are still operating today.

At one of our sonata evenings in September 1908, Sonneck asked me to go with him to Fort Myer the next day where Orville Wright was to pass a government test with his new invention, the aeroplane. On the parade grounds at Fort Myer a dense crowd of about 100,000 people had formed, eagerly awaiting the history-making event. The plane was of the simplest construction possible—the early double-wing with its propeller, everything in the open, including the engine, with the pilot seated on a simple seat, his feet resting on a thin iron bar, maneuvering the gangly structure via the simplistic steering apparatus and control panel in front of him. Sonneck and I found a place in the front row where we could easily watch the proceedings. When Wright and a Lieutenant Selfridge entered the primitive machine, a thunder of applause encouraged them. After its propeller was spun by hand, the aeroplane's engine started with a great noise and the monster then rose and began its epochal flight.

The space inside the ring of spectators within which the flyer had to remain was not wide enough for him to make an easy turn, so when he made his second bank almost directly in front of Sonneck and me (he flew very low), his plane turned over. As it fell we saw Lieutenant Selfridge jump out. The engine landed on his face and crushed his head, killing him instantly. Sonneck and I along with everyone else ran to the wreck where two army medical corpsmen hurriedly took Wright out of the plane and put him on a stretcher.

"How is Selfridge?" I heard him ask.

Wright suffered a double thigh fracture; Selfridge might have lived if he, like Wright had stayed with the plane. An army airfield bears his name in memoriam.

The Wright Bros., 1903

The postal service carried weekly messages between the United States and Holland and back. As I have said, I assumed my family would soon emigrate from Holland to my new home in Washington and at first I only very spasmodically touched upon the subject in my letters. But then, seeing no mention of it in any of Marie's notes in reply, I asked her what she intended to do. She still remained silent for a while but finally gave me a somewhat definite answer. I received a letter which contained these sentences:

"As I told you after we had moved from Holland to Germany, from Germany to Switzerland and back to Holland, I am tied to my mother country. The strongest reason compelling me to stay where I am, however, is Ernst's education. You know how greatly I can help him in medicine here, which I could not do over there. As you intend to come over in the near future, we will have ample time to give the subject a discussion of the necessary pros and cons."

The yearly festival of the Allgemeine Deutsche Musikverein was to be held in Zurich, Switzerland. As an old member of the association and not having missed one of these important events, I resolved to go to Holland to see my family and, from there, to the grand reunion with all my dear old friends in Zurich.

I took passage on a Russian steamer, the former yacht of the Russian Czar, a small but fine ship with a large salon and only a few passengers aboard. Our meals were served in the captain's large cabin—and they were substantial ones—I slept every night on deck and had a wonderful voyage. Every evening a brass band of eight Russian sailors played for us; oh, how it revolted my ears, accustomed as they were to decent music. The captain asked me to write the Holland anthem for the band to be played upon our arrival at Rotterdam. I did; but how those eight sailors murdered that beautiful anthem to an unrecognizable atrocity is indescribable! I am sure they were unable to read notes. As a result, the listeners on the quay that evening must have taken this noise as some crazy Russian thing.

My whole family comprised my reception committee. Happy to see one another again we went to Leyden and the cute little house in which they lived. To sit peacefully after a long absence, once more with your family around you is a real blessing to those who know the value of intimate relationships among the members of their household, and ours had always been a close family. Yet at present this was in danger of being broken. All of us had to choose whether to follow the old or the new road. "Enfin," (in short) don't let us spoil our happy reunion by introducing this subject now. There were so many others to pass in review that the entire first day was spent in conversation concerning the interval of my absence from home.

I had unwittingly chosen an eventful time for my homecoming as the Rembrandt triennial year was being commemorated in Leyden. I count everyone who visited this extraordinarily complete exhibition of the heritage this great master left to humanity an exceptionally privileged individual.

I have been an eager lay student of art during my long, long passage through life, and never missed visiting museum exhibits whenever I passed through a town. This Rembrandt exposition was a new testimonial to his abundant creative power. One very large, exquisitely bound volume, owned by a wealthy Frenchman, contained over a thousand designs of every species of four-footer known to man. Rembrandt had the unique opportunity to study animals at the zoo in Amsterdam which contains one of the world's finest aggregations of wildlife. Through the East India colonial possessions, the zoo is able to procure and replenish its resources. The valuable Rembrandt sketch book was insured for one million guilders. A great number of etchings, their striking, rare lucidity, masterly choice of subject and design, equaled the compositions of his virtuoso creations in oil. I paid my respects to Rembrandt every free moment I was able to do so. Another special attraction in the city at the time of my visit was the Lustrum Festival of the University of Leyden, an open air performance of an elaborate national play, enacted by students in 16th Century array, another artistic gem.

A pleasant interruption was when I was called upon by my pupil and friend, Edwin Borchard[49], Law Librarian of Congress, who, as secretary to then Secretary of State Mr. Rooth, had come to Holland to rectify errors in the western world's fishing laws via committee, with several other judges forming an international tribunal.

[49] **Edwin Montifiore Borchard** (October 17, 1884 – July 22, 1951) professor of international law, was born in New York City, the son of Michaelis Borchard and Malwina Schachne. His father was a prosperous Jewish merchant, and Borchard enjoyed  the benefits of a highly cultured upbringing. Even before completing his Ph.D., Borchard embarked on a distinguished career in international law. In 1910 he advised the American delegation during the North Atlantic Coast Fisheries Arbitration at The Hague, Netherlands. He served as law librarian of Congress from 1911 to 1913 and from 1914 to 1916. In between, he was assistant solicitor for the Department of State. He worked as an attorney for the National City Bank of New York from 1916 to 1917. (Michael S. Mayer, American National Biography Online; anb.org) Borchard's other interests included music. He was first violinist in the New Haven Symphony Orchestra and president of the Orchestra Association. (Humanities and Societies Net, www.h-net.msu. edu)

We passed a few hours together and also went to the Rembrandt exposition together.

Before I left Leyden it was decided definitely by Marie that she and the children would remain in Holland, to my great sorrow.

Leaving Leyden, I stopped twice in Germany, in Cöln (Cologne) and in the Saar district. The Reich was at that period an exceedingly prosperous, peaceful country. In Zurich, I took lodgings in the Hotel Baur au Lac, where Richard Wagner read for the first time his Tristan and Isolde story to his friends. There I found many of my old friends: Max von Shillings, Dr. Obrist, Dr. Marsop, the aesthetician, Traugott Ochs, the famous Berlin conductor of the Sing Academy Chorus, Max Reger, his wife, and many others.

The hotel was also the headquarters of the Swiss army commander as the maneuvers of the Swiss army were being held near Zurich. The commander of the army was Colonel Bourgaux (the highest rank in the Swiss army at that time was colonel)—only in wartime would the supreme commander be a general. It was at his table my old friend Gustav Doret was sitting when I entered the hotel garden at noon that first day. Both of them were from Lausanne, the colonel a famous lawyer there and an old acquaintance of mine. (All soldiers of the Swiss army are civilians for approximately ten months of every year. Maneuvers are held for only about two months in the summer.) He invited me to dinner, and while we three sat devouring the delicious meal, adjutants came and went with various reports on the progress of the maneuvers. I noticed that some of my friends at the other tables in the garden were visibly curious about all those military officers running up to our table.

The concerts brought interesting first performances, among them Max Reger's Variations on a Mozart Theme. I consider this the best and it seems to be the most successful of his compositions for orchestra. It is the only one of his works which is not contrapuntally overcrowded.

Dr. Obrist and I went to a fair outside of town and enjoyed the change of scenery. We reenacted our boyhood years by riding the merry-go-round, eating heisse wurst (hot dogs), and chewing on candy sticks, with stove-pipe hats covering our pates. Refreshed and rejuvenated, we went back to Zurich.

On our way home, Obrist greatly surprised me by telling of his impending marriage. He was then 40-years old and told me his story. Being General Musik Direktor at the Royal Opera at Stuttgart, he went to Vienna to hear a prima donna there, intending to engage her for his opera. He was successful and she came to Stuttgart where her debut was a great triumph. He fell deeply in love with her and she likewise confessed her love for him—an easily understood situation. Obrist was an imposing, manly representative of his sex, tall, elegant, his face partially hidden behind a fine brown beard, "bien soignée" (well cared for).

However, knowing well a few attributes common to most prima donnas and their unfitness for married life,

I made certain to warn my friend of possibly unhappy consequences. His was a highly sensitive, crystal-clear soul and I knew if he were to take a miscalculated step it would inevitably incur dire results. He was anxious to go home immediately after the close of our last concert and asked me to write the criticism of the festival which he was supposed to do. I promised him I would.

That afternoon in Zurich, the members of the association paid a visit to the Wesendonck villa, the annex of which was an attractive little house, the asylum of Richard Wagner, where he wrote his songs for voice and piano (with words by Frau Wesendenk of Tristan and Isolde). The next day we were invited on an excursion across the Lake of Zurich to see a castle occupied by a Polish count. In the library of the castle I saw three very interesting letters written to an ancestor of the count by George Washington. At our arrival in Zurich a band awaited us to lead us to the concert hall. Max Reger, his wife and I leading the group all returned to the hall where our last concert took place.

As I wished to go back to Holland as soon as possible, I quickly finished my evening meal and sat down at the desk in my room to write the promised critique. I was interrupted by friend Obrist, who in haste informed me that his train would leave in 30 minutes and he had come to say "au revoir." I sent him off with warm wishes for a happy future. We too often forget how little we know of our future! His assistant conductor later told me that Dr. Obrist, arriving home, was eager to pay a surprise call on his fiancée and when he did, found her in a negligee—sitting at the breakfast table with the tenor star of the Royal Opera. He went home and shot himself.

Note from Melinda...

He did not go home, or only shoot himself. According to a translation of a German newspaper:

"On June 29, 1910, the police report in terse brief reports: 'Yesterday morning was found shot dead a lady and a gentleman in a home of Schubartstrabe. It is murder and suicide . . . two people, standing at the level of life, richly talented, destroyed abruptly by the storm of passion, the opera singer Anna Sutter and former Kapellmeister Aloys Obrist. A great tragedy of the Stuttgart cultural life.'" (Stuttgarter-Zeitung.DE)

Obrist studied music in Weimar and Berlin, he received his doctorate in Berlin in 1892 in musicology. Then he was appointed as Kapellmeister at the Stadttheater Augsburg. From September 1895 to 1900 he was royal Württemberg Kapellmeister at the Staatstheater Stuttgart , where he [made] great contributions to the modernization of the repertoire of the subscription concerts of the court orchestra. 1901-1907 curator of the Liszt Museum in Weimar. He married Hildegard Jenicke. Obrist was known among other things by the jealousy murder of the opera singer Anna Sutter followed by suicide."

The Violinist, Volumes 14-15
Article: **Will Congress Aid Music at the Capitol?**

"Music in all of the European nations gained its strongest support in the beginning through wealthy patrons and royal subsidies. We all know that the Royal Opera in Berlin, London, etc., the schools of music under the patronage of the government in St. Petersburg, Leipzig and many of the capital cities and other methods used by the royalty or government for furthering interest in music and musicians have been the mainstay of the advancements made in this form of art.

"Our states have done little, and the national government practically nothing (outside of its wonderful library) for the practical encouragement of music. And it has looked as though, between the question of national or state rights in this matter, all government assistance would be lost to our profession.

"There is a project on foot whereby the capitol city may receive musical support from its governing body. This is in the form of a bill for the establishing in Washington of a permanent international exhibit. Such a project has been presented to Congress at various times in the past, but the matter has recently taken a more serious aspect. Especially does this seem encouraging in the light of the appointment of Heinrich Hammer, choral and symphonic conductor and composer, as chairman of the music committee of the permanent international exhibit. He has selected, as his associates, Charles Tittman and Edwin M. Bouchard.

"In an interview on this subject Mr. Hammer states his pleasure and encouragement in the prospect of the passage of this bill before Congress to establish a permanent international exhibit. 'This,' said Mr. Hammer, 'seems to me to present the only means of assuring the city a symphony orchestra and a choral society. With the government as a guarantor, success will be definite. My plans of procedure are by no means formulated; but, depend upon it, there will be no cause to decry Washington as not being a musical city. It will be my intention to give frequent, perhaps daily, concerts and it will be my effort to use local talent. There are plenty of musicians in this city to furnish artistic programs as soloists with orchestra and chorus for a long time to come. I want to give these artists a chance. Given the opportunity Washington can make a big musical showing and this is its opportunity. The city is interested in this project and the country is interested and there is every reason to believe the plan will soon be an accomplished fact." (The Violinist, November 1912, George Mortimer Brush)

Chapter 20   D.C. Disappointments

Only one week was left of my stay back in Holland. Unable to resist, I once again tried to persuade Marie to come to America with me. But she still held firmly to her decision to remain in Holland, also saying that after Ernst's graduation from high school two months hence, she planned to move to Amsterdam to act as his special mentor during his medical training. Ernst also expressed his desire to stay in Holland.

What was there for me to do? I had found a new field of activity, though not as yet entirely satisfactory as far as the orchestra situation was concerned. I was however full of hope in improving that condition, and felt I could not come back to Holland and again commence another experiment. My poor wife's health would not permit her to again take up the strenuous duties of the medical profession, but thankfully I was amply able to provide for my family's needs. The future was a Gordian knot and there was no Alexander the Great to cut it. This then was the situation when I returned to the United States, again a lonely man.

This time I took the new Holland steamer Amsterdam for the crossing. It was a well-equipped, comfortable ship, and the captain and crew were conscientiously attentive to the passengers' needs. Arriving at New York harbor, I very proudly used my first citizenship papers as identification. Back in Washington D.C., I felt a little less lonely when I was eloquently welcomed home by my housekeeper and her daughter. I then plunged into lively activity.

A project on which I hoped to expend additional working hours was a proposed permanent exposition showcasing the musical resources and accomplishments of the United States. A general enthusiasm was aroused for this new plan. The instigator of the project was a man with wide experience and great push-power, and he was indefatigable in his efforts to bring the abstract "exposition" into concreteness. I was selected to be chairman of the music committee by the two commissioners of the District of Columbia. The project, which would have created a unique institution attracting world-wide interest, did not unfortunately find Congressional approval and was subsequently abandoned.

All my efforts to organize a symphony orchestra on a sound financial basis were in vain. I even fostered the thought of combining the Washington D.C. and Baltimore orchestras, but after a thorough canvassing, my attempt was thwarted by selfish motive. Our symphony concerts were steadily frequented by many ardent music lovers and a few Midas's, but none were interested enough to offer some of their shekels to establish a first-class orchestra.

Intending to make the United States my future home country, I was dissatisfied with the lack of the right to vote for the citizens of Washington D.C. I liked Maryland, so on my hunting trips there, I began looking around for a piece of land on which I could build a little house for myself. One day I found a beautiful section, comprising three elevations, a little brook coursing between two of them, and a number of fruit-bearing chestnut trees, several hundred hickories, huge walnut trees, and on one hilltop, a dense pine population and some fine oaks of respectable periphery and height. Of all the parcels of land I had seen, I liked this idyllic Maryland landscape best, and purchased 20 acres. I then bought the lumber which was used to build the stands for President Wilson's inaugural parade. When a hotel was dismantled, doors and windows of perfect workmanship and intact, I acquired them also.

As summer vacation was starting and the materials for home-building were ready, I decided to use the experience I had gathered from the carpenter lessons long ago in Friedrichstadt for the creation of my country house. I decided to build it all myself, with no help whatsoever.

I laid the foundation on top of the middle hill next to the acre of pines. At the bottom of the hill meandered the clear little brook which was to be my source of water. Many hours had to be spent removing the mass of nails from the lumber of the inauguration stands; but the wood was clean and dry. Now to the erection of the beams. I enjoyed my work immensely. The most difficult task was placing the roof joists. I had to tie a rope around a beam, mount a ladder, and draw the timber up by the rope—a tricky manipulation, especially single-handedly. When Mrs. Schwaneke, my housekeeper, watched me at this stage of my work, she offered her help in guiding the beam from below. Although I felt I did not need her help, she insisted. I mounted the ladder with rope in hand and cautioned her to be careful. She held the heavy beam straight, below me, but in a moment of inattention she let it slip. The beam moved in the wrong direction and came down on her thumb. Luckily the damage was not serious. This was the only help (?) I suffered in the process of my house-building. The erection of the four-room home took four months. It was a comfortable country seat, with a south porch and a large pine tree in front. The electric train passed below my property, situated between Lincoln and Bell stations. It was a 10-minute walk to each of the stations, and about four miles to the next village and railroad station to the south, Glendale.

Back in Washington, I had bought a house in the northern part of the city, on 15th street near the junction of 15th and 16th streets—the latter now Presidents' Avenue. This property, three stories and a basement like the Euclid house, was located near the most recently-developed part of town. When my little country house was finished, we moved there and I rented out my property on 15th Street. I took the electric train from there every day to attend to my business in Washington D.C.

About this time, I formed a string quartet, with the first cellist of the orchestra, the first violist, the assistant concertmaster as second violinist, and myself as first violinist. Bahá'í Ulla, the nephew of the founder of the Bahá'í religion, came to Washington on a tour of the United States. He was a guest in the home of one of his fellow followers and my string quartet played at his solemn reception. His beautiful long white beard and hair and dignified apostolic countenance in combination with a sermon he delivered flawlessly aroused my admiration.

At the home of my friend, Henry Bush-Brown, the renowned sculptor of Arabian horses, my string quartet performed for another private reception. Later, his wife, a well-known portrait painter, did a nearly life-size portrait of me. Another was painted by Nanette Craig and was displayed for several years in the lobby of the Columbia Theater. Both portraits are now lost, and my extensive efforts to locate them have been fruitless. When I went to Florida, I stored each of them along with two large packing boxes at the home of my friend, Walter Sharp, but when both he and his wife died, only one box was delivered to me. The portraits and the other box containing a number of my compositions and other materials were lost.

Another concert took place, one of high artistic merit, but it accrued very poor financial returns. This was not my orchestra but was the first appearance of the Minneapolis Symphony Orchestra, and was led by Emil Oberhofer, its founder and conductor. First performances of strange artists or orchestras seldom played before a sufficiently large audience. I was ashamed that my name was on the program as one of the patrons. But such is the public attitude in Washington. The most prominent citizens of the town are usually government people who, though they actually live in Washington most of the time and enjoy its culture, are unwilling to support that culture because they instead choose to help the orchestras in their "hometowns." The assistant concertmaster of the Minneapolis orchestra looked very familiar and during the intermission he came up to talk to me. It turned out he had been one of the first violinists in my Göteborg Symphony Orchestra. After the concert, I thanked Oberhofer for the excellent presentation of the fine program regardless of the nearly-empty hall.

Dr. Herman Hase, the owner of the international firm, Breitkopf and Härtel, the largest private printing establishment and music publisher in the world, paid me a visit as he was on an inspection tour of the firm's music stores in North and South America. We dined together and conversed about present-day conditions in his business. I accompanied him to the Government Printing Office where he inspected the machinery thoroughly and observed the employees at work with great interest. Our guide was astonished when Dr. Hase told him he was the employer of 5,000 workers. After our visit, he told me much of the machinery we had seen was obsolete and that his establishment had installed the newest time-saving equipment.

I then took him to the National Museum, the capitol, Library of Congress, Smithsonian Institute, Corcoran Art Gallery, and on a general tour of the city, which the fine, erudite gentleman seemed to appreciate. We talked of Germany and he spoke about the favorable conditions there and of the country's expanding industry and commerce.

The Philadelphia Symphony, Leopold Stokowski [50] conductor, gave the first concert in its yearly series in Washington. I believe it was at that first concert that I spoke to Stokowski. In the course of our conversation I asked, "Why don't you discard the baton, Mr.

[50] **Leopold Anthony Stokowski** (18 April 1882 – 13 September 1977) was a British conductor of Polish and Irish descent. One of the leading conductors of the early and mid-20th Century, he is best known for his long association with the Philadelphia Orchestra and for appearing in the film Fantasia. He was especially noted for his free-hand conducting style that spurned the traditional baton and for obtaining a characteristically sumptuous sound from the orchestras he directed. (Theodore Presser Company; presser.com)

Stokowski? I have done without it for many years. I can talk more effectively to an orchestra through the medium of my hands and fingers than with a stick." It took him many years before he followed my counsel. At present he is stick-free and what a plastic figure he is.

The Boston Symphony also presented a series of concerts in our capital. Dr. Muck, formerly conductor of the Berlin Imperial Opera, was at that time its leader. Ah! These superb orchestras compared with mine. During the intermission of the first concert I gave in Washington, the fine pianist, Miss Alice Burbridge, a pupil of Teresa Carreño, came rushing into my director's room. "Mr. Hammer, how do you do it?" she cried. "You create technique where there is none!"

This was a fine compliment to me but it also speaks lucidly of the insufficiency I had to contend with in my orchestra. Though that was my own symphony, the situation was almost identical when the orchestra officially became the Washington D.C. Symphony. Even when I was fortunate enough to have a first-class symphony orchestra under my command in the United States, I was usually given very little time in which to prepare a program. To name only one occasion: when I conducted my second symphony with the Los Angeles Philharmonic Orchestra, I was given only 45 minutes—just enough to read it through once—*no time for rehearsal!*

One day I received a letter from the Catholic high

Ad from

school in Washington asking me to act as judge for a contest to be held for violin pupils of the music department of that institution, a sort of final examination. The outstanding student of that contest was a young lady of 17, Miss Lilian Milovich. On my recommendation, she received the first prize, a silver medal. After the contest she came to my studio and asked if I would teach her. She was a talented scholar, gifted, and with a fine sense of musical values.

Note from Melinda...

Miss Lilian Milovich will shortly become my beloved grandmother, Munna. She and her older sister, Bess, played music for the silent movies shown in Washington D.C. theaters; Munna played violin and Bess piano. Some years ago, for my birthday, my husband took me to spend the day at the de Young Museum in San Francisco. There's a painting there which I took a picture of (of course I completely forgot to check the name of the artist), showing two young women in gowns of silk and tulle, one seated at an upright piano, and the other next to her holding a violin and bow in one hand while she turns a page of sheet music with the other. One day I'll make a copy of that painting and call it 'Lilian and Bess.' According to newspaper articles back in the day, Munna also played many engagements around the city with other aspiring musicians. Family lore has it that she played violin in Washington's Symphony Orchestra, conducted by Fahta, but he doesn't mention that, so I may be mistaken.

Another prominent music publisher from Germany—Leipzig—was the publisher of one of my less-important works (a composition for women's chorus with piano accompaniment) and their Mr. Sanders arrived in town and called upon me. He was a lively, youthful gentleman whom I had met years before at one of our music festivals. We passed some mirthful hours on our sightseeing tours here and there. While he was in town we attended the opening ceremonies of a new joy palace, a sort of permanent carnival on the large second floor of a big building. There was a restaurant, all kinds of booths, tricky things, and most interesting of all, a large disc about 15' across placed horizontally on an axis, upon which it spun, powered by electricity. The fun of it was to sit on the table and stick to your seat as long as you could while it was spinning. The centrifugal force would not allow anyone to keep his seat for very long—in fact, most were dispatched in no time.

Mr. Sanders, eager to show his prowess, thought he could put the physics law to shame. He took his seat in the center of the contrivance and stayed longer than anyone before him and thought he was surely going to win the prize that was magnanimously offered to anyone who could remain on the whirring disc. But he was duly confronted with an inexorable law of nature and soon realized the impossibility of his attempt. Slowly he glided outward, marking a larger and larger circle until even he was off the plate. But he was not yet convinced and repeated the experience twice before he finally was.

Another quite different event was the arrival of the London Philharmonic with Arthur Nikisch [51] as conductor. Nikisch was the acknowledged foremost conductor of his time. (He was for many years conductor of the Berlin Philharmonic and, after he left this position, Dr. Strock, musicologist and critic, recommended me as Nikisch's successor, but Dr. Kunwald, assistant conductor of the Berlin Philharmonic, forestalled my appointment. He was later chosen to be conductor of the Philadelphia Symphony.) When I saw Nikisch in Washington the day of his concert, he was not well. I told him I would gladly conduct the concert if he was too ill but he answered, "That is impossible, Hammer; when the London Philharmonic comes to Washington, the public wants Nikisch not Hammer to conduct it."

I asked my friend, Dr. Williams, to see Nikisch. The doctor's care made it possible for him to successfully

[51] **Arthur Nikisch** (Hungarian: Nikisch Artúr; 12 October 1855 – 23 January 1922) was born to a Hungarian father and a Moravian mother, and was a typical case of a young boy whose musical talent showed itself early. At the age of seven he heard the William Tell and Barber of Seville overtures for the first time. When he got home he wrote them out from memory. In 1889 he was engaged to become the conductor of the Boston Symphony Orchestra. He stayed there until 1893, and toured the United States, which was then in the midst of an explosion of new symphony orchestras. In 1893 he became director of the Budapest Opera, keeping that post until 1895. In 1895 he was offered the directorships of both the Leipzig Gewandhaus Orchestra and the Berlin Philharmonic. He accepted both positions (the two cities are not far apart) and later added the Hamburg Philharmonic Orchestra in 1897. He returned to America on tour with the London Symphony Orchestra in 1912, and made other successful appearances there over the years. (Joseph Stevenson; allmusic.com)

present his well-chosen program and he electrified the Washington audience. The next morning, Arthur not feeling too well, Dr. Williams and I accompanied him and his dear Elena Gerhardt to the railroad station; she was the greatest lieder (romantic) singer of her time and a worthy companion for Nikisch.

Returning to my multitudinous duties, several careful rehearsals prepared the Choral Society well for its first performance in Washington of Chadwick's Christmas Oratorio. The composer honored us with his presence and expressed his satisfaction and thanks for our efforts. Shortly after this event the Boston Symphony's conductor resigned. I wrote to Chadwick asking him if he would advise my soliciting for that conductorship. "No," he answered. "It is unfortunate, but the committee will not even consider a German, and they probably never will."

Carrying on my pioneer work in Maryland, I bought hundreds of purebred Plymouth Rock chickens, some Peking ducks, and several large incubators, and called my farm "The Hammer Great Poultry Park." One day as I returned home from a necessary trip to Glendale, an acrid smell assailed my nostrils. Coming up to the house I saw that the entire breeding building was burned to the ground; smoke and ashes were all that remained. Five hundred eggs in the incubator and 200 four-day old ducklings had been lost. Start from the beginning again! What courage is needed to meet all these mishaps of life with equanimity.

At the east side of the house I laid out a good-sized garden in which I planted six kinds of grapevines, logan and blackberries, currants, gooseberries, and raspberries and a few two-year old fruit trees. On the hillside I planted several acres of black-eyed beans. They grew copiously and delivered throughout the summer an abundant harvest of the tenderest green beans. I planted several hundred ever-bearing strawberry plants and a full acre of assorted young fruit trees. For hunting purposes, I prepared one-half acre of buckwheat. In the fall hunting season I would go down there with my fine setter at precisely 3 o'clock in the afternoon, the hour the quail always arrived to feed on their beloved buckwheat. He would point, I would flush the quail, and I would shoot enough birds for the evening meal. Rabbits and squirrels were also plentiful on and around my property.

One of my neighbors was Daniel B. Lloyd, Jr., one of the six official stenographers of the United States Senate. He owned a 200-acre place with ideal hunting grounds. We enjoyed much hunting together.

One day an aeroplane, still a quite primitive contrivance, flew over my house only about 30' above it. A few minutes later I heard the engine stop, followed by what I then thought was a crash. I quickly grabbed a pail full of water and pieces of linen for bandages and ran out. Nearby, on my friend Lloyd's place, the plane had landed in a clover field. The occupants, a lieutenant and a sergeant, had been forced down through engine trouble, but were unhurt. The landing had been auspicious, but even after the elimination of the mechanical trouble, the take-off was defeated when the pilot, apparently inexperienced, turned the nose of the craft downward, boring it into the ground and breaking the propeller. A truck from the nearest army camp carried the wreckage away the next morning.

My friend Lloyd and I commuted every day on the electric train to Washington; his son and daughter accompanied us as they were students in the city schools. His youngest child, Harriet, then five years old and already a budding pianist, attained an enviable position as soloist and teacher in her later years. (She is still the possessor of the Steinway piano I sold to her father when I left Washington.) My friend served the government longer than anyone—60 years! I was proud of Daniel Lloyd's friendship. What wonderful subjects filled the substance of our discussions on our daily commutes to the city. His was a fine, humanitarian soul. His wife had a lively intelligence, and was the understanding mother of his three fine children; theirs was a well-knit and happy family. His immaculate dress and immaculate behavior were two of the sources of Lloyd's Congressional nickname, "the 96th Senator." He died at the age of 85. His last letter, written the evening before his death, was to me. The next morning, arm in arm with a Senator friend, while striding into the Senate chamber, he collapsed, a powerful stroke ending his life.

The Choral Society chose Handel's oratorio, Judas Maccabeus, for its main winter performance. I decided to perform the work exactly as Handel wrote it, using the small orchestra and clavicembalo (harpsichord) which was not usually done. Our clavicembalo player was Arnold Dolmetsch [52], the artist-founder of a famous old-instrument trio consisting of his wife, another lady, Miss Solomon, and Dolmetsch. They performed concerts in the United States and Europe with great success, playing compositions written by old masters for nearly forgotten instruments. Judas Maccabeus, in its original form, well-executed and openly accepted by the sizable audience, was a new incentive for the introduction of lesser-known compositions in Washington. When I stepped down from the podium after the performance, our president, Bernhard R. Green motioned me to stay. The members of the chorus and soloists had not left their places. Surprised, I turned to the president again and saw him holding a long horn-of-plenty filled with a mass of flowers, in the midst of it the gleam of a tiny iron ring. He presented it to me. It was quite heavy. Puzzled about its contents, I pushed some of the flowers aside and uncovered a fine .351 automatic rifle for big game hunting. On the butt, a silver plate carried the following inscription: "The grateful Choral Society to its beloved conductor, Heinrich Hammer." The happy recipient ended his day in the happy society of a few friends at a happy dinner.

An interesting event took place at this time. At the small park in front of the White House, the statue of Lafayette occupied the site across from the Belasco Theater. On the opposite side of the park in front of the Carnegie Institute, the statue of von Steuben, the Quartermaster General in George Washington's army, had just been erected. Its inauguration was planned with President Taft as speaker and I was asked to conduct the musical portion of the program. About 500 German singers from all over the United States who were members of various German male choruses assembled in Washington to sing at this unveiling. The U.S. Marine Band was also to be under my direction. I will never forget the power of those solemn chords of Kreutzer's This is the Day of the Lord carried by that full-toned and inspired chorus of such mighty strength. President Taft's speech was full of eulogies for the German people, and specially emphasized the word "gemüthlichkeit" (geniality) which visibly impressed the audience and elicited a thundering applause. That eve-

[52] **Eugène Arnold Dolmetsch** (24 February 1858 – 28 February 1940), was a French-born musician and instrument maker.  "[He] was a pioneer in the late 19th- and early 20th-century revival of interest in the study and performance of early music and the manufacture and restoration of historic musical instruments. Dolmetsch's growing reputation in both performance and instrument manufacture eventually took him to the USA where he collaborated with the Boston piano makers, Chickering (1904-1911), working on keyboard instruments, including clavichords, harpsichords and spinets, and early stringed instruments such as violas da gamba. When the 1910 economic downturn caused Chickering to close its early instruments division, he left America to work with another piano maker, Gaveau, in Fontenay-sous-Bois outside Paris. Returning to London in 1914, he completed and published his ground-breaking work, The Interpretation of the Music of the Seventeenth and Eighteenth Centuries, the following year." (Horniman Museum & Gardens; horniman.ac.uk)

ning there was a celebration at the Willard Hotel. I sat at the table of honor next to President Taft's aide.

This reminds me that the Librarian of Congress, Mr. Putnam, graciously extended me the distinction of being the guest at one of the famously exclusive round table sessions at the Library. Once a month, a pleasant evening was passed in the Germania Club, an organization of prominent Germans. Count Bernsdorf, the German Ambassador—who was married to a member of the California Spreckels family—and his staff were members. But politics was taboo at these meetings. Every club gathering brought a lecture by one of the members. Literary and scientific subjects were discussed and, on some occasions, a "gemüthliches" (pleasant) dinner was arranged. Count Bernsdorf was often one of our more brilliant speakers.

At Hammer's Great Poultry Park the replenished feathered denizens grew in number. The ducks, regardless of changes in temperature, would drop their eggs anywhere. Repeatedly I gathered eggs in the snow. They were excellent layers, but Washington was not a market for their eggs. After unsuccessful trials, I concluded that duck-raising on a small scale was not profitable; so I made arrangements to discard them. But an interesting scientific problem demanded solution. I had heard of an exceptionally small turkey gobbler owned by one of my neighbors and went to see it. I had the inkling of an idea and bought it from the farmer and put it among my other gallinaceans. I observed his continuous lovemaking to a small Plymouth Rock hen, a prolific layer. I gathered her eggs and incubated them. Picture my satisfaction when out of one of her eggs emerged a tiny chick with a turkey's bare neck. I pampered the little fellow and it developed into a little brown hen. After her maturity I bred her to my finest Plymouth Rock male. The ensuing eggs, incubated and hatched, produced a number of what I called Hammer Barenecks, and the rest Plymouth Rocks. Now I had clear sailing for my intended scientific work, namely to bring into being an important variation of the chicken. The difficult work lay ahead however. These little chickens were not pure Plymouth Rocks and that was my goal: a Plymouth Rock with its fine meat and laying propensities, plus the valuable leather-like neck to prevent it from contracting the croup. I now bred those who were of a decided Plymouth Rock type together and, after five years of alternating joy and trouble, I succeeded in producing an excellent bare-necked chicken. At a poultry exhibit, my chickens received a first and second prize and I thought I was to be the master of a great fortune. A judge of the exhibit wanted to buy several trios from me, but his offer was so inadequate that I refused it. "For Sale" advertisements brought no results and my neighbors and visitors found the birds so queer looking that they called them turkey buzzards. I was so disgusted that when I left my country place I gave them all to my neighbors. Today these same chickens are all over the United States and are called turkens.

Naked Neck chicken (Turken)

Illustration by Danny Martin
www.DannyMartinArt.wordpress.com

Ernst, now an inspired student of medicine at Amsterdam University, asked me to send him a bullfrog, writing that he wanted to study its brain. I was well acquainted with the director of the National Museum and asked his help in the matter. He willingly procured a huge frog and prepared it for transportation. When we went to the post office to dispatch our parcel, we were informed that fluids could not be sent by mail. My friend then dried the frog and we were able to send it off to Ernst.

It was not easy for me, who, since my marriage, had been an ardent homebody, to carry on this bachelor's existence. I made a few last pleas to Marie to transplant the family to the United States but made no headway, especially since Ernst had entered the University. The recollection of our early verbal contract entered my musings now and then, and finally I decided to speak of it in one of my letters. I reminded her of our agreement and the impossibility of a future reunion, asking her to engender divorce proceedings. In her reply she spoke very sorrowfully of the impasse in our marriage, but said she saw that my demand was inevitable. She took the necessary steps and finally her lawyer sent me the papers for my signature. So ended an important phase in my eventful life. Twenty years of a nearly-flawless marriage ended by quiet mutual consent. Caused as it was by outside influences, we kept ties of friendship until her death (including with the last of the entire Holland branch of the family) many years later.

[53] **John Frederick Wolle** (b. 4/4/1863 – d. 4/4/1933) Born Bethlehem, Pennsylvania, April 4, 1863. Graduated from the Moravian Parochial School in 1879, and began teaching in Bethlehem. Organist of Trinity Church, Philadelphia (1881-84) and a student there under David D. Wood. Studied with Rheinberger in Munich, 1884-85, and after returning to America was organist of the Packer Memorial Church at Lehigh University (1887-1905). Organized the first choral societies in Bethlehem and Easton. With the Bethlehem society, presented the first complete performance of Bach's St. John Passion in 1888, the St. Matthew Passion in 1892, and the B-minor Mass in 1900. In 1905, moved to California, where he taught at the University of California (1905-11) and was organist of the First Congregational Church, Berkeley (1907-9). Returned to Bethlehem in 1911, resumed administration of the Bach Choir, and was organist at the Salem Lutheran Church. He died in Bethlehem, Pennsylvania, on his seventieth birthday, April 4, 1933. (Hymnary.org)

Chapter 21   A New Country Beckons

In 1912, my first five years in the U.S. came to an end and, with it, the end of my non-citizenship status. Bernhard R. Green and Mr. Wickle (the piano dealer from whom I bought my concert grand) were my witnesses, and Judge Gould the deciding factor. Now I was at last a proud citizen of this great country and a legal voter in the state of Maryland.

That state's representative, Senator France, one of the most erudite men who ever graced a seat in that august body, was a much-adored friend of mine. He carried the titles M.D. and Ph.D. and was so widely admired that he was asked to run for the Presidency of the United States, which he did. Had he been elected he would have been a wise leader, proficient, kind, and just. He gave me a permanent visiting card to the Senate which I still highly cherish. Another member of Congress who was a dear friend was Congressman Barthold, a record-breaker of 40 years of service as one of our lawmakers, a man beloved by members of both parties; his pure purpose always was, "My country first." He was in the Germania Club and many a time provided us with inside glimpses into life at the capitol.

Another of my true friends in Washington was Dr. Williams, a Scot, who was also an admirer of my work. Many a pleasant dinner was enjoyed amidst his sympathetic family, evenings seasoned with interesting conversation, and this companionship helped me surmount an otherwise lonely hour.

The Bethlehem Bach festivals, conducted by the energetic John Frederick Wolle [53], were interrupted by his summons from the University of California at Berkeley to serve as head of their music department. He stayed there two years, continuing his apostolic work for his musical idol Johann Sebastian Bach. Upon his return to Bethlehem, he founded the Moravian Bach Society, and this time was able to procure the help of the Philadelphia Symphony in giving larger and better three-day Bach festivals enjoyed by overcrowded houses every year. The fame of these festivals crossed the oceans and Dr. Williams invited me to attend one with him. We heard an unforgettable presentation of the giant masterwork, the B Minor Mass.

In 1914, the First World War began. Everything changed in the U.S., although we were not involved. Of course our military forces had to be increased and a considerable number of bandmasters were needed, but seemingly not available. I was summoned to the office of the Secretary of War, Baker, to confer with him about the matter and I expressed my opinion freely.

"Mr. Baker, the bandmaster's position in our army today is an untenable one. A young man with only a high school education and a very short period of training in an officers' camp may become a lieutenant. But a bandmaster, after years of daily, difficult study, has no standing in the army. He might become a corporal and the highest rank he may attain, with a few exceptions, is master sergeant—but his education should entitle him fully to an officer's rank. You are not able to get any bandmasters simply because there is no incentive for them to join the army."

Secretary Baker seemed impressed with my argument and personally led me to the office of the Adjutant General March. However General March said he did not think my argument was valid, but Secretary Baker argued that a competent committee of three would make a report on the situation. He appointed the president of the New England Conservatory of Music, Mr. Goodrich, Mr. Hamner, a lawyer, and me to confer and put our conclusions before him. We did and, as a result, all bandmasters were promoted to the rank of lieutenant. Nevertheless, that lasted only as long as the war. At present the bandmaster is the only position whose rank is not defined by military statute. I have seen a private conducting a 200-man band, whereas in every other case, 200 soldiers are always under the command of a captain.

A number of French and English military staff officers began arriving in Washington at this time. The English officers seemed to feel at home in our country, but the French were like lost sheep. No one spoke their language and most of them did not speak ours. One day, as I sat in the train, a French major entered the car and sat next to me. His face carried a rather forlorn look. I addressed him in French and his dismal countenance changed to an agreeably surprised one. When he asked me about my nationality I naturally answered that I was born in Germany, but was now a citizen of the United States. Again his face altered into that somber expression. I tried to put him back to his better mood, saying,: "I am an artist—conductor of the symphony orchestra here, and dislike this war as much as you do."

"You are an artist?"

"Yes."

"I have a Swiss friend who is a composer," he said.

"What is his name?" I asked him.

"Ernest Bloch."

I laughed loudly. "Why, I know him well. His first symphonic work was given its premiere performance by my orchestra."

His face and guarded attitude now changed entirely and, later, sitting together for dinner at Harvey's, we exchanged reminiscences of past, carefree times.

Mrs. Schwaneke, the housekeeper, and her daughter, my pupil, who wished to try her wings as a soloist and accompanist in New York, left Hammer Crest. After their departure I lived alone for nearly a year.

I was becoming more and more disturbed as the United States appeared to be drifting closer and closer to entering the war. When I would come back to my dear farm toward evening I was greeted by my two faithful four-footers, Treu, my wonderful setter, and Speck, the beagle who was my indefatigable rabbit hunter. Then, sitting on my porch with these two furry friends at my feet, I would let my thoughts wander. Often they formed themselves into sorrowful ponderings over the miserable conditions of war brought about by greed and misunderstanding while people talked of the brotherhood of man.

I received a very good offer for Hammer Crest and sold it, furniture and all, and moved back to Washington, setting up residence in a divided apartment in the Brunswick Apartments. Major Cameron, secretary of the newly-created Air Force, lived in the other wing of the apartment to which we shared a common entrance. The Major was a friendly neighbor with a fine sociable nature. Every so often he asked me to make a short flight with him. As I was continually tied down by my duties, I had to refuse his kind invitations until one day when I had some free time, I told him I was eager to take a refreshing flying trip and agreed to go up with him. "Oh, I'm sorry," he said, "it's too late. We aren't allowed to take civilians anymore."

As yet I have never entered an airplane.

The United States declared war on Germany in 1917. Everything crumbled. Count Bernsdorf had to leave his post as Ambassador, the Sängerbund building was confiscated by the government, the Germania Club discontinued its meetings, the members of my male quartet were all drafted for service in the army, the ladies of the Friday Morning Music Club chorus took on activities in the Red Cross, orchestra concerts stopped, and private lessons dwindled to just a few pupils.

The pall of loneliness weighed heavily on me. Was there nothing which could guide me back to a regular family life? And then suddenly I had an answer. One day I was invited to dine at the home of my pupil, Lilian. During the meal, her sister happened to relate a story about Lilian and a young man who had taken her on an outing to Great Falls, a very popular and magnificent place on the Potomac. Coming back, Lilian had talked almost continuously about "Professor Hammer," and the young man had told her sister he would never take Lilian out again.

I then remembered how she had always seemed to admire me and certain little incidents when she had displayed this, though, at the time, I had not perceived the obvious. This story provided a valuable tip for me. When, after some time, I asked her if she would marry me, she said yes. We kept our engagement secret, knowing that it would be a hard task to get her mother's assent as I was not a Catholic and of course much older than Lilian. After some hesitation, we finally decided to marry secretly and planned to make a honeymoon trip to Florida.

To this end, I bought a Ford car with a Columbia top. At that time no one had to take a driver's examination; he simply paid a small amount for his license and he was off to the races. I had never taken any driving lessons and the owner of the car only superficially explained the workings of the machine to me, but once I had bought it, I brazenly drove away by myself. I drove right up steep Thirteenth Street—and half way up, my car refused to proceed. A man on the sidewalk yelled, "put 'er in low," but I had forgotten how. I asked him to show me, which he did, and I proceeded on. I leave it to my reader to guess how many shenanigans I committed while behind the wheel during our journey south to Florida.

 Note from Melinda...

This prosaic declaration of his intention to marry my grandmother, Munna, was a real disappointment to me. When I was barely a teenager, there was a perfume called "Tabu", and the magazine ads showed a woman in a ball gown, seated in front of a grand piano, a man in a tuxedo standing on her right, violin and bow aloft in one hand, the other embracing her waist, drawing her up for a passionate kiss. *That's* how I always imagined Fahta's proposal.

And here's the family legend: Munna's mother and her sister and brothers were totally against their marriage (her father died when she was very young), not only because Fahta wasn't Catholic, but because he was 27 years older than Munna and a divorced man. Their subsequent elopement caused somewhat of a scandal. Nearly 60 years later, when Aunt Bess was ill, my Aunt Lillian decided she was going to take Munna back to Washington D.C. so the sisters could see each other. (They had not been together since Munna eloped, although they did exchange letters.) When Aunt Lillian called Aunt Bess to tell her of the impending visit, Aunt Bess exclaimed, "*Oh no!* You can't possibly bring her here! What would the neighbors say?" The visit never happened.

We started with a very heavily-loaded sedan and had to return from Alexandria to Washington D.C. to unload half of our freight and leave it in storage. Off again. I had acquired a tent as we intended to make it a real camping trip. Each day we drove till about three o'clock in the afternoon with a short rest at lunchtime. When we stopped in the afternoon, I would put up the tent and cook our meal. We avoided restaurants as much as possible because we wanted to "rough it." It was not a matter of finances—I had sold my property in Washington for a fair price in cash. But the beauty of the outdoors was far more appealing to us than the so-called comforts of civilization.

Roads at that time were generally in terrible condition. Inundations here and there caused by the raging downpours often necessitated horse or mule power to help us through the high water. It strained the nerves, but was romantic amidst the beautiful countryside backdrop. At one place, we were forced to drive upon a very narrow elevated road, built for the purpose of saving cars from the water-filled road below it. But this was like going from the frying pan into the fire. The road was muddy and slippery, and then suddenly one side gave way. The car tipped far over and stopped. Luckily the wheels sank down into the water-soaked earth, preventing us from toppling. The mud was up nearly to the axles and engine power alone could not move the car. In front of us was a farmhouse, and out plowing his field with a very badly matched pair of mules was a tiny, aged farmer, who called out to me "Ah'll come out and help you, suh!"

He brought his mules, one very small alongside a much bigger one, and for an hour or so see-sawed without success. All the while these useless proceedings had been going on, a little boy, about 12 years old, with a big mule, had nonchalantly watched. Finally he stated matter-of-factly, "My mule can do it, suh."

"Alright, go ahead and show us," I said.

With characteristic southern slowness, the boy proceeded to hitch his mule to our front bumper, while the farmer politely regretted his inability to help and led his mules back to the field. The boy, with an encouraging word to his mule, took the line in hand and the animal with a remarkably effective "Grrrrrruk!"—which I can hear clearly today—hoisted the car right out of the mud.

Only a short distance from the place of this mishap a more serious one awaited us. Driving down towards a river, we could see that the unceasing rains had inundated wide portions of the shore. We had to pass over some very precarious, primitive bridges which were composed of loose tree trunks laid across treacherous places. I do not know yet how we got across them. Arriving finally at the edge of the river, we had to drive up two narrow planks which were laid from the shore to the small ferry sitting a ways out in the river. The ferry itself was so short that I nearly ran overboard. But the crossing of the river did not end our troubles by any means. On the opposite shore, we immediately came to a steep hill which was impossible to climb by our own car's power. The two ferry men and I used all our physical strength to push the vehicle over the hill. As we entered the woods on the crest of the hill, we beheld a large glittering water surface resembling a shallow lake, but which was in reality only another inundation. The muddy water reached up to the axles of our car. Suddenly we went up and over a big log lying unseen across the flooded road and hung there with the center of the auto resting on the log, unable to move either forward or backward. Here we were, solidly anchored in the midst of a wilderness and night was approaching. We had to stay in this position while we waited for eventual travelers to help us get out of our predicament. We ate a cold supper and sat, resting as best we could, through the night. The next morning a shiny new Cadillac limousine came sloshing through the water directly in front of us and stopped. The man at the wheel, a big prosperous-looking individual accompanied by his wife, a society lady of the bluest blood, and a little fat boy in the rear seat, asked me to clear the road. I told him of our dilemma and asked him if he would lend us his help. "I cannot do that," he answered me roughly.

I begged him to try but he was unwilling. This exchange was interrupted by the arrival of an old jalopy out of which three woodsmen emerged. They came up to me and, seeing my unhappy position, approached the man in the limousine, telling him to pull us out. Of course he told them he did not want to, but the three men, their axes slung ominously over their shoulders, began using threatening phrases and commanded him to free our car. Reluctantly he fastened our chain to his bumper. The big limousine seemed to say, "Come on little baby, I'll get you out," and without any visible effort it rolled our car over the log and we soon stood in the middle of the road. The man in the Cadillac was so angry that he did not look behind him, and lo and behold! The same thing happened to his car that had happened to ours. He had, by his turning aside to a higher dry spot, also straddled a big log, and now his precious car rested atop a tree trunk. The three lumberjacks, without hesitation, took their axes and chopped the log in two and freed the car. I admired their action, the impulse of helpful, unprejudiced souls, giving the owner of the Cadillac a good example of a fine Samaritan spirit.

We drove on to Baxley where I discarded the too-heavy, useless self-starter which I had had installed in my car at great expense and went back to the old cranking method again.

Note from Melinda...

Apparently, Fahta's driving skills never improved. My mom remembers many hunting trips to the desert in Southern California when Fahta would take all six kids with him in order to give poor Munna a little peace and quiet. Off they would go, jouncing across the desert sands, in search of a likely place to pop a rabbit or two. If Fahta ran up against or over any sort of impediment — large rock, big cactus, whatever—he would merely say, "Randolph, get out and see if we can make it over" while the rest of the kids huddled in the backseat, holding their collective breath.

Also, in Ontario, there was the obstacle of Euclid Avenue, the main drag, a divided street running through the business section of town. Being a thoroughly logical soul, Fahta could never understand why he had to cross traffic in order to turn onto a street on the other side of the road; so he merely drove down the wrong side until he could make the turn he wanted while whatever kids he had with him hid in the backseat so their friends couldn't see them. And if the kids misbehaved while he was driving, he made them run along behind. (They may have been grateful for that!)

The heavy rains stopped and the South displayed its true amiable aspect. Traveling had once more become a pleasurable experience. It was a joy to behold the beautiful, constantly shifting scenery and pass through quaint, at that time still-sleeping, towns. From Tampa to Fort Myers great vistas opened up—the infinite sea on one side and the vast, luxurious fields and woods on the other. There were good roads along the coast and friendly people.

One 40-mile trip through pines and palmettos brought some surprise. Passing a picturesque little creek surrounded by a multitudes of colorful flowers, we stopped at its shore and prepared our lunch. Inspecting the creek, I saw great schools of fry-able fish in the very shallow water. I cut a stick, put a fishing line with a hook on it and caught one of the numerous grasshoppers for bait, asking Lilian to catch some more. I threw my line and got an immediate bite. The fish must have been deprived of food for a long time. This was not angling but rather unsportsmanlike murder! It was line in, fish out, as quickly as you could pronounce those words, and our lunch consisted of a great portion of freshly caught and fried fish. Yum, yum! We had hardly finished lunch when one of those short daily rain and thunderstorms started. Our car was drenched and a postman's auto was stalled on a nearby bridge. He asked me to tow him, which I did, exacting from him a promise of his help if we needed it. He promised, but when he had crossed the bridge, he defaulted, leaving us helpless, my car having stopped temporarily, a circumstance I'd feared. After our car had dried out in the ensuing sunshine, we then continued on our journey. It went badly however and soon we were stalled again—the transmission having failed.

It was dark and we had no lights. We could do nothing but remain there for the night. About four o'clock the next morning we awoke and saw a settlement of a half dozen houses or so a few hundred yards ahead. On the side of the road was an inviting pool of crystal clear rain water. Clothes off and a cool dip was only a matter of a few minutes and we felt new-born.

Note from Melinda…

I find the phrase "clothes off and a cool dip" pretty startling—because, you see, my grandmother was the biggest prude you could imagine. There used to be an old TV show called "Burke's Law" starring Gene Barry, and part of the theme song was a woman saying in a breathy, sexy voice "it's Burke's Law." Whenever she heard it, Munna's mouth would purse up and she would say, *"Disgusting!"* in a disapprovingly patrician tone of voice. We used to tease her mercilessly by copying her any time we thought it appropriate.

A man was coming down the road toward us. As he drew nearer I recognized him; it was the faithless letter carrier. When he saw us he looked extremely embarrassed. I approached him and explained our new predicament to which he, seemingly anxious to exonerate himself for his recent discourtesy, effusively assured us he would send help. He told us the tiny settlement was Myakka and was his home. After a short waiting period, a young man came with his car and towed us to an abandoned farmhouse where we could make ourselves at home, as he put it, until he finished fixing our auto. He lifted the car by a chain hung over a strong branch of an oak tree in front of the house. After inspecting it, he explained he would have to drive 40 miles to the next town to get the necessary repair parts and that, as it was Sunday, he would have to wait till the next day to make the trip.

Again we were stranded in the wilderness, but this time with better shelter than a car and surrounded by the friendliest neighbors one could find anywhere.

Across from our new abode was a large farmhouse, occupied by a middle-aged couple. The wife of the farmer, a charming and sociable lady, came over to us at noon, bringing with her a well-prepared dinner which we ate with gusto. The next day, an elderly lady who said she was the mother of the young man who was repairing our car, brought us a pail of sweet potatoes and the lady from across the way kept us abundantly supplied with milk, fruit, and dinners. What an unsurpassable spirit of hospitality was displayed by these good-hearted people!

A fine rabbit dog belonged to our food suppliers and a splendid camaraderie developed between the two of us in the course of his running a good number of rabbits for me, providing some fresh game for our table. The affectionate creature was seemingly as fond of me as I of him and I was really sorry when, after a few days, the repairs on our car were completed and we had to leave him and our other new friends.

We drove through 45 miles of pines and palmettos before reaching another grouping of human habitation. The pine woods in Florida are rather ugly, every tree being severely slashed along the trunk and pails hung below the slashes in which to accumulate valuable turpentine. However Central Florida, with its small sparkling lakes, prosperous farms, and lovely tranquility was altogether delightful. We traveled along the west coast to Punta Gorda where another discouraging repair of our car was handled by brothers, expert and honest mechanics, a rare case among Florida's garage men, the majority of them having caused us much trouble.

The leisurely continuance of our trip brought us to Fort Myers, the city where Edison and Henry Ford sojourned during the winter seasons. Fort Myers is a clean, industrious city, sitting by the side of a broad river which empties into the Gulf of Mexico. It also had a nice climate. We decided to end our trek right there, attracted by its friendly, distinctly appealing character. We went to a real estate office and inquired about a home, whereupon the agent showed us several houses, one of which both of us found best suited to our needs. We moved right into this well-furnished, comfortable, two-story residence with nice front and back yards, its flowers and fruit trees forming a special attraction for us. A big tank on a high platform, a wire screen fitted on top as a sieve, caught the rain water from the roof. This is done all over Florida to take care of domestic needs for water. In our rear yard's cultivated ground were several orange trees and a kumquat—a miniature citrus fruit of a bright orange color—loaded with ripe fruits and in healthy condition. Kumquats comprised our daily breakfast food, eaten right from the tree, skin and all.

I planted a few watermelon seeds and potatoes. The growth of one of the melons was preposterously fast. We watched it every day and imagined we could see it grow. I weighed it one day and it pulled 35 pounds on the scale! One of our neighbors saw these proceedings and said, "You ought to pick it."

"We have so much fun with it while it is on the vine; we want to see how large it will get," I said.

"You will regret it."

"Why?" I asked him.

But he only replied, "You will find out," rather forebodingly.

How true was his prediction! Only a few days after this exchange the first summer thunderstorm occurred. A furious rain, accompanied by rumbling thunder and vivid lightning flashes, drenched everything. After half an hour's flash and crash, the clouds disappeared as though they had been wiped out with an eraser and the sun in fervid splendor sent her scorching rays to reinstall calm and order. This kind of weather became a daily spectacle, and after a few days, when we again inspected our watermelon, it was wilted, cooked. The hot sun rays, coming as they did immediately after the rain, had spoiled it entirely. We also had baked potatoes. This taught me that you cannot raise common vegetables in this torrid climate; in fact, I saw nothing but peppers and beans in the vegetable gardens of Southern Florida.

Long ago I had cherished the idea of writing a eurhythmic drama, embodying my old friend, Jaques-Dalcroze's creation. When I first knew Jaques in Lausanne he was beginning to formulate his plan for interpretive body movement to music which he called eurhythmics. Though Dalcroze always emphasized that his invention was not a dance, his eurhythmic was assuredly the forerunner of Modern Dance. I started the scenario of my drama soon after we moved into our new home. I worked assiduously to finish it as I had the touch of an idea about its future and wished to carry it out as soon as possible.

Now and then we took short recreational trips into the surrounding countryside. On one of these excursions we visited Naples, a little town south of us on the Gulf, where we saw a number of fishermen on a long pier diligently trying to catch some of the beautiful mackerel you could clearly see swimming leisurely around all the nicely baited hooks. Not one was caught during the time we watched.

I had finished the scenario of my work and began to compose the music for it, but the inhospitable summer heat made concentrated work impossible. In consequence, I was not progressing satisfactorily. Lilian complained of headaches and I suspected something more than the heat might be responsible. I asked her if she would like to move to another place with a more favorable summer temperature, for instance, Canada. She liked my suggestion, so in a conversation with the spritely 85-year-old gentleman from whom I had bought the Fort Myers house, I asked him if he might possibly be willing to take the house back. To my great surprise he told me that he would gladly do so, as he and his wife were dissatisfied with the rented home they were living in at present. That simple agreement settled, we left our sedan at a used car dealer's for him to sell on a commission basis and made preparations for changing our domicile. It was as scorching hot as ever when we left Fort Myers and this heat kept up until we reached Chicago. After a few days' rest and inquiries about conditions in Canada, we decided to make Winnipeg our goal.

Canada. Quite a trajectory: Washington D.C. to Florida, Florida to Winnipeg.

The change of climate, with its invigorating effect in the clean, crisp air served as an ebullient energy-creating magician, seeming to electrify us and command: "On to new deeds."

It was astonishing that under these stimulating conditions I could sit for hours working on "Faustina," my eurhythmic drama. Another favorable influence upon my work was the fact that we found an apartment in Fort Rouge, a quiet suburban section of Winnipeg, away from the noisy business district. The apartment had been occupied by a law professor at the University who sub-leased it to us for the duration of his three months' vacation. It was tastefully furnished and boasted a good piano. We liked the kind, helpful neighbors and peaceful surroundings. The River Rouge was nearby, and the serene aspect of it was flanked by enormous wheat fields and groups of northern trees which tapered into an unending, clear light-blue horizon, instilling in us a growing respect for this big country-in-the-making. I worked hard every day till late afternoon; then we would take an energizing walk, a fine health-sustaining habit which I still follow.

I soon made the acquaintance of several music-loving people in Winnipeg, among them a professional soprano who took some coaching lessons with me. Once she invited Lilian and me to a musicale in her brother's home, and there I met some influential members of Winnipeg society who became excited with the idea of my organizing and conducting a Winnipeg Symphony Orchestra with their financial help. But subsequent discreet inquiries disclosed the fact that another gentleman, with a powerful local following behind him, was eager to form an orchestra also, and I was not willing to disturb the busy bees.

"Faustina" grew fast. The clean, refreshing atmosphere almost demanded that I buckle down and do something worthwhile and I did buckle down; whether what I accomplished was something worthwhile must be decided by posterity.

One sunny day we chose a relaxing outing to Lake Winnipeg where we pumped enough ozone into our lungs to last us for days. Who would have thought our joyful spirit would so soon turn to a contrary direction? On our return to Winnipeg an incident took place which nearly brought this beautiful day to a tragic end. My wife and I sat on the first seat in the railroad car next to the door facing toward the front. About halfway home a sudden tremendous jolt threw us off our seat. My head was forcefully thrown against an iron rod in front of me and blood streamed down my face. Lilian grabbed my handkerchief and wound it around my forehead, stemming the blood temporarily. My wife was only two weeks away from childbirth at this time and I was relieved to see she was unhurt. We were told to leave our car which had bolted the rails and stood at a dangerous incline. The three cars behind ours were derailed and lay on their sides and, as the passengers came pouring out of them, we were all directed into the only upright car besides the locomotive, an old freight car into which we were packed like cattle. I was the only passenger who had been hurt; I had bled profusely and felt weak, but the train personnel seemed to have lost their minds. So although one of the conductors saw my crudely-bandaged head, no one ventured to take care of me. This behavior aroused my anger, and what with the repulsing odor of the densely-packed crowd and the almost complete lack of oxygen, I began to feel nauseated. I was near fainting and asked for a glass of water. No response. At last a lady near me, having heard my plea, indignantly called out, "Someone give this gentleman a drink of water! He is fainting!"

A conductor arrived with a bottle of Coca-Cola and I quickly swallowed some. I came back to a fairly normal status, but a seething anger gripped me. The attitude of these nonchalant attendants, seeing me wounded and not making the slightest effort to give me first aid, was revolting to me.

As soon as the partial train arrived in Winnipeg, about 11:30 p.m., Lilian and I went to the office of the president of the railroad and asked the man at the desk to take me to the hospital; he indicated his inability to do so but I was insistent. Finally, he phoned the president's chauffeur, ordering him to take us to the hospital in the president's limousine. At the hospital, an intern and a nurse attended to my needs. The somewhat clumsy intern put pure arnica on my wound and started bandaging my head, but I, with years as husband of an M.D. behind me, perceived his inexperience as a first-aid helper. I felt relieved only when the older, better-equipped nurse took over and bandaged my head correctly. It was now one a.m. when the limousine arrived at our house. Shock and loss of blood inducing a deep dreamless sleep kept me in bed for two days.

The railroad company seemed to have forgotten my case entirely. As we contemplated leaving Canada shortly, I wrote a letter to the president of the railroad, indignantly stating my dissatisfaction with the treatment I had received. Two days later, an employee of the railroad came to our apartment and spoke in a rather insolent, legère (sleazy) way about my case, whereupon I cut him short, telling him that I wanted to have an interview with their chief counselor. I was subsequently invited via a letter to an appointment at the counselor's office. Arriving there, a very young gentleman received me and spoke to me in the same manner as the visitor to my apartment. "Are you the chief counselor?" I asked him.

"No, I am his assistant," he said.

"I asked to see the chief counselor," I replied firmly. "Will you please arrange an interview with him for me?"

He uttered a few words of protest but a couple of days later I received notice that the counselor would see me the next day. At his office I was greeted by the quite sympathetic counselor with the declaration that Canadian law contained no provision for restitution to Canadian travelers on Canadian railroads. I countered by telling him that I was an American citizen and demanded to be treated as such. "Well then, we have to ascertain the seriousness of your injury," he said. "You will have to submit to an X-ray test."

I told him I was willing, so he telephoned an X-ray institute and made an appointment for me for the following day. I came to the institute the next morning and was there for an hour, having to answer numerous questions and having repeated X-ray photographs taken. The next day my hair began to depart. With thumb and fore-finger I could grab a lock and simply remove it. When I went again to the counselor's office the first thing I did was reach up to my head and lift from it a lock of hair which I held out to the lawyer who turned as pale as snow. He forthwith told me that he had received a very favorable report from the X-ray institute. I said that I intended to leave Canada soon and wanted to have my case settled; I made it clear to him that it was not a case of money but of principle and asked a thousand dollars for the injury I had suffered. He naturally acted in the interest of his company and said, "I have no authority to sign a check for that amount, but will give you $750."

I reiterated that it was not the money but the principle—the right of an American to expect the same treatment in Canada that he would receive in his own country, and I then accepted the $750 check, thus terminating the meeting.

A week later at 5 p.m. I brought my wife to the hospital and, under the care of a Miss Smith, who had been the only female military surgeon in the war, a baby girl was born at 7 p.m., a healthy, fine dark-haired girl whom we called Lillian, after her mother.

Note from Melinda...

I had to laugh when I read this about "baby." My Aunt Lillian never got over her love of speed, driving a series of Thunderbirds, Cougars, and various other muscle cars well into her senior years. Faaaaast.

Two weeks later, we were on our way to Hollywood with the aim of having "Faustina" produced as a movie. Baby had a very peculiar habit. At every train stop she would cry but as soon as the train moved, she was quiet again. We stopped for a month in Chicago where we had to rent a tiny room with a kitchenette for $100, being unable to find any other vacancy.

There I made the acquaintance of Professor Schütze, head of the German language department at the University of Chicago. He invited me to a concert of the Thomas Symphony Orchestra (later the Chicago Symphony, but then still carrying the name of its founder). The former first viola player and assistant conductor had been promoted to conductor when Thomas died but he could not come up to the standard set by his predecessor. The second Brahms symphony he did not perform to my satisfaction; Brahms' spiritual idea and the light touch demanded in this splendid opus of bubbling surprises was absent.

I met an old friend from Oldenburg, Elmar Vente, a poet and writer, who submitted a libretto for an operetta to me, asking that I compose the music for it. When I happened to mention to Professor Schütze that it was very difficult for me to accomplish this task in my tiny apartment with the baby crying as they are wont to do, he generously offered me the use of his home to complete my composition. His wife, a painter, was absent and he was occupied all day at the University. His was a quiet home in a select neighborhood and it took me only two weeks to finish the score for "The Mayor of Podunk."

I sent it to my friend in Kingston, New York. He tried to place it for production in New York City, but his efforts were fruitless and I never heard anything of our stillborn effort afterward. Vente later took up residence in Germany where he married a newspaper reporter.

I knew Mr. Cherwonki was settled in Chicago, so I looked him up (you will remember him as concertmaster of the Minneapolis Symphony Orchestra). One evening he gave a recital in my honor at his quietly elegant home. He played the second Bruch Violin Concerto for me, a fine, sympathetic work, inexplicably neglected. Hofmester, the former solo clarinetist in the Concertgebouw Orchestra of Amsterdam and afterwards in my Göteborg Symphony Orchestra, had also chosen Chicago for his home, a fact which demanded I visit him. Our stimulating reminiscences encompassed the span of many years, and, if only for that, I was glad I had come to Chicago. That month was one of the shortest of my life, what with composing, reminiscing with old acquaintances, attending shows and concerts, and sightseeing. Every moment was filled to overflowing and the days passed by swiftly.

Chapter 22   Hollywood, Here We Come

In early 1919, with accommodations in a comfortable "roomette" aboard a train, mother, baby and pater traveled to Hollywood. After much strenuous house-hunting, we bought a small but nice home in West Hollywood on a 60' x 200' lot with five orange trees, a fig, a plum, and a peach tree in the backyard, and a winter Nellie pear tree on the neighbor's property with half its branches kindly living on our side of the fence. The rear of the lot was like a well-built fortress, quite able to hold off an enemy, consisting of a densely-entangled blackberry hedge, its richly blooming whiteness giving promise of an abundant harvest come summer.

It was not easy to find suitable furnishings for our little house due to the extremely high cost of many things and the non-existence of many other necessary items in the stores, it being not long after the war had ended. So to buy our furniture I had to rent a truck and drive to the row of buildings on Adams Boulevard in Los Angeles where auctions are held.

After this fatiguing process I had to give serious thought to finishing "Faustina," the composition of which had been so abruptly interrupted by the Winnipeg railroad accident. My happiness at having finally settled into a home of our own again in one of the glorious artistic centers of the globe (I thought so then), the climatic superiority of sunny S. California, and the fact that physically I was once more in condition to work, were powerful incentives for me in completing my cherished project.

To introduce the newly-arrived Hammers, we gave a joint recital in our community. Afterward one of the audience, an elderly lady, expressed her thanks to us for the pleasure the concert had given her and, in further conversation, we learned she was of German origin. When she told us she came from Krakow, near Magdeburg, this aroused my curiosity, as we schoolboys from Friedrichstadt were always fighting the boys from Krakow. At one of these skirmishes, one of my gang threw a stone which hit a Krakow boy in the eye, causing the loss of his sight. Imagine my astonishment when she told me that she was the wife of the schoolteacher in whose class this boy was a pupil when he was injured, an incident she remembered vividly.

How large is our earth in fact? Here in California two persons meet who, 6000 miles away and nearly half a century before had been actors in the same drama, yet unknown to one another. The son of this lady is the wealthy Mr. Ecke [54], small in stature but large in enterprise, who has made a fortune in poinsettias, sending them all over the country in great carloads from his vast fields in Encinitas, California. An article in an issue of the *Reader's Digest,* published several years ago, told about this unique business.

"Faustina," at last finished, required my efforts to promote its production. As M.G.M. was at that time known to be the outstanding moving picture studio and backed by powerful financial interests, I went there. I was directed to the office of Paul Bern [55], Producer. We had a long and friendly conversation and I was very much impressed by his affability and intelligence. He read the summary of my scenario but told me, "I like the story, but we have no synchronization and cannot produce it."

At that time, the studios used only atmospheric music so large orchestras were never required. He asked me to come back and see him any time which I did and we became good friends. In fact, I received a gift from him every Christmas until he took his life many years later.

As I was passing through the studio I came upon a group of five musicians rehearsing. I struck up a conversation with their leader, Victor Schertzinger [56], who later became a top movie conductor and producer, and was informed that their task was to play while the movies were being made, thus exercising a stimulating influence upon the actors working under the torture of the hot, brilliant Klieg lights. I showed my piano score to him and he said he wished he could perform it, but of course it was impossible. I had come, full of hope, from Canada to California and found nothing but a will'o-the-wisp. However, having all my life made a new, vigorous start after any maligning setback, I now looked around me for new fields to cultivate.

[54] **Albert Ecke** - The story of the modern day poinsettia in America is really the story of the Ecke family of Encinitas. Originally from Germany, Albert Ecke emigrated to the U.S, in 1906 and settled in the Hollywood area. The family lived off the land growing fruits and vegetables but were also, by 1909, selling cut Poinsettias at a stand on Sunset Blvd. Poinsettias grew wild in the area and son Paul Ecke (Paul Sr.) had the idea that the ruby flowers would sell well around Christmas. This turned out to be so successful that in 1915 Albert Ecke bought five acres in nearby El Monte to grow poinsettias. By 1917 the Eckes were shipping plants to customers in New York and Chicago. (PoinsettiaDay.com)

[55] **Paul Bern** (December 3, 1889 – September 5, 1932) was a German-born American film director, screenwriter and producer for MGM, where he became the assistant to Irving Thalberg. He helped to launch the career of Jean Harlow, whom he married in July 1932; two months later, he was found dead of a gunshot wound, leaving what appeared to be a suicide note. Various alternate theories of his death have been proposed. Film producer Samuel Marx believed that he was killed by his ex-common law wife Dorothy Millette, who jumped to her death from a ferry soon afterwards. (Wikipedia)

Exploring various branches of musical activities, I found no opportunity there whatsoever and focused my attention on the real estate business as a means of earning a living. At that time real estate was booming. The end of the war brought about as its healthy consequences a new spirit of enterprise which, in California, found its main expression in a lively building boom. I studied the business carefully, using a well-known book for my teacher and when I was ready for my examination to become a broker, I passed it. I had become acquainted with the owner of a cleaning establishment and, having been unable to secure office space due to said boom, I persuaded him to let me use an empty front room of theirs as an office.

About that time, I was chosen as one of the directors of the West Hollywood Chamber of Commerce and, in this organization, I met several other real estate brokers. In some shop-talk discussions with them the possibility of forming a real estate board which would give its members the coveted title of "realtor" was seriously considered. Nine of us applied for a charter and, after it was granted, formed the West Hollywood Realty Board.

Across from the car barn was a small building occupied by a fruit and vegetable business and owned by Town Marshal Moore. I needed an independent office and here was one. I bought his contract and all his mer-

VICTOR L. SCHERTZINGER
M.P.D.A.
Now directing Mabel Normand
Goldwyn Studios

[56] **Victor Schertzinger** - A violin prodigy, an early film scorer, and the composer of standards including "I Don't Want to Cry Any More," "I Remember You," and "Tangerine," Victor Schertzinger was born in Mahanoy City, PA, in 1890. Classically trained from early childhood, Schertzinger began appearing with orchestras (led by Victor Herbert and John Philip Sousa) from the age of eight. He toured America and Europe as a teenager and after moving to Los Angeles, he worked as a conductor for theater orchestras, often composing his own music to use as backing for silent movies. After the silent era came to a close, Schertzinger began composing music to be used in early talkies. (John Bush, allmusic.com)

chandise from the fruit vendor, and for two weeks I was both realtor and green produce merchant. Then I cleaned the small room thoroughly, painted it, equipped it with modern business furniture and had my new office.

A very important event took place in the midst of all these happenings. Another member of the Hammer family announced his entrance into the world with a lusty cry, aided by a capable lady M.D. of Russian descent. When he was born, the doctor placed his tiny hands upon her index finger and lifted him up in the air. Greatly surprised, my wife and I saw him grip and hold the finger firmly. The doctor held him this way for about 30 seconds. This act reminded me of the old unwritten law prevalent among ancient tribes which said that every newborn baby was to be thrown into a body of water; if it could swim it was worthy to live, but if it could not it was allowed to drown. Mark, as we named him, entered life as a strong baby and grew up to be a strong man. Mother and son, under the care of a German graduate nurse, fared well, relieving me from anxiety and enabling me to spend more time on the development of my business.

After the surveying of hundreds of acres of open country, a real spurt of construction started in West Hollywood and my little office was stormed by car motormen and conductors from across the street. Entering the office, their first greeting would be, "I want to buy a lot."

I would take up my map and ask, "Where do you want it?" but they would always say, "Never mind, here is a $50 deposit. Any lot will do."

That went on all day every day and I felt that I had gone into the right business. A small parcel of property, a few acres, formerly occupied by a nursery, was subdivided and, in a few days, the plot was sold and ten of the lots I sold three times over with nearly a 100% profit to the seller. The influx of newcomers to California grew and grew, and lot sales and building went on in continuous succession.

I opened a main office on Santa Monica Boulevard near Fairfax Avenue and hired four salespeople, among them a young ex-army officer who had lost his hearing in the war. I had recently been appointed by the government to help rehabilitate professional musicians just returned from the war, along with Dr. Gowen, a friend from the realty board, in reestablishing their skills and enabling them to again take their place as worthy members of their profession.

One of these ex-G.I.s, Narnjy, a talented violinist, who had served in the Navy artillery under Pershing, told me he would rather get into the real estate business than continue his violinist career. I counseled him to take the real estate salesman's examination, and when he had passed it, I took him on as salesman in my first small office and left him there as manager when I opened the main office.

The West Hollywood Realty Board now boasted a membership of over one 100, a lively agglomeration of wide-awake businessmen. Our highly effective, intelligent president was George Schmutz who, at present, is the official appraiser for the City of Los Angeles and the Edison Company. I was then chairman of the membership committee and chairman of the "Own Your Own Home" committee of the California State Realty Board.

One evening I spoke in Pasadena at the state meeting of the California Realty Board. During the dinner a fine little orchestra played, led by an excellent violinist. The program gave his name as Henri van Praag. The first viola player of my orchestra in Göteborg had carried the same name, so when I congratulated Mr. van Praag on his good orchestra I asked him if he was related to his namesake in Göteborg. "Yes, he is my cousin," he replied. He then scrutinized me, lay his violin down and threw his arms around me, tearfully exclaiming, "You are my old teacher!"

Then I remembered the talented little chap, van Praag, who had taken lessons from me in Amsterdam. He took up his violin again and played one of my old compositions "Bagatelle," which he had studied with me so long ago. He invited me to visit him which I later did and was surprised to see not an ordinary house but a mansion. His orchestra furnished the music for all the five hotels in Pasadena and he was also the conductor of the Pasadena Fireman's Band.

In 1922, the Community Chest [57] institution was still in its infancy when I was chosen Colonel of a Division in Hollywood. It was a great pleasure to me to be called into a type of work which had held an abiding interest for me since my own childhood. It was no easy task for a head of a Division to gather a sufficient number of solicitors together to collect the capital necessary to stem the needs of the numerous sufferers who must rely on our organization. The structure of a Division was formed after military order: a colonel, lieutenant colonel, four majors, each major over four captains, each captain over two lieutenants, each lieutenant in charge of as many workers as he could gather. An imposing regiment. Everyone was a volunteer and gave his services to the organization without remuneration. Each worker, provisioned with subscription sheets, made tiresome walks from house to house but were very seldom, at that time, received cordially. If a worker's sales talk was ineffective, his immediate superior would attempt to collect and if he was unsuccessful, his superior would try and so on until it was necessary for the colonel to obtain the subscription, which he always did.

Divisions No. 12 and 13 occupied the same headquarters on Hollywood Boulevard. Mrs. Atherton Irish [58], at present General Manager of the Barnsdall Foundation of Hollywood, was my colleague—Colonel of the 12th Division. The Colonels had to stay all day at their task of counting the amount gathered in order to hand it over to a representative of the Society. Often it was necessary for me to urge some of the delinquent financially who were able to donate. At the end of the first year's drive I examined my lists, and found that the sister of Bill Hart [59], the movie actor, had not given anything to the Chest. When I went to Bill's home—I was acquainted with them as I had given French lessons to his wife—and told him of his sister's neglect, my forwardness was excused when he told me she was sick, but he gave me a $50 check in his sister's name, though he had also signed for a larger amount himself. For two consecutive years I was engaged in this exacting but immensely satisfying work.

Houses grew like mushrooms. The scantily-settled parts of Hollywood and miles of previously untouched surrounding territory were now filled with new buildings. The fields where a big part of West Hollywood is now located were hunting grounds at the time of my arrival there. It was there that I shot my first jackrabbits in the United States, and I also shot a great number of snipes with Town Marshal Moore, one of my enthusiastic hunting companions. An old friend, who still lives in the same large home on Sunset Boulevard in which he lived when I came to California, used to go hunting with me at five o'clock in the morning to shoot a few cottontails which came up from the meadows of Beverly Hills to settle in the hills above Sunset Boulevard. All this territory was entirely wild country, but in the short

[57] **The Community Chests** in the United States and Canada were fund-raising organizations that collected money from local businesses and workers and distributed it to community projects. The first Community Chest, "Community Fund", was founded in 1913 in Cleveland, Ohio by the Federation for Charity and Philanthropy. The number of Community Chest organizations increased from 39 to 353 between 1919 and 1929, and surpassed 1,000 by 1948. By 1963, and after several name changes, the term "United Way" was adopted in the United States, whereas the United Way/Centraide name was not adopted in Canada until 1973–74. The Community Chest was promoted on several old-time radio shows, including the H. J. Heinz Company–sponsored The Adventures of Ozzie and Harriet show, the S. C. Johnson & Son–sponsored Fibber McGee and Molly show, and the Chevron-sponsored Let George Do It show. (Revolvy.com)

[58] **Florence Atherton Irish** – "always referred to as Mrs. Leiland Irish, was one of the three founders of the Hollywood Bowl and was its director for nearly thirty years." (www.allanellenberger.com)

[59] **William Surrey Hart** (December 6, 1864 – June 23, 1946) was a successful Broadway actor who became the silent screen's first western hero and one of the biggest box office stars of the 1920s. The larger-than-life actor made more than 50 silent films between 1914 and 1925 and went on to write western novels, as well as the 1929 autobiography "My Life -- East and West." (Myrna Oliver, Times Staff Writer; LA Times May 25, 2004)

period of three years, civilization moved in and covered the former swamps, meadows, and hills with homes. In the far west of California was the Mecca for the modern pioneer.

In 1913, during my time in Washington D.C., the American Boy Scout Law was enacted. After long talks with a prominent and well-regarded lawyer, Mr. West, President Roosevelt was persuaded to accept the position of National Executive of the Boy Scouts of America. I was greatly interested in this movement at the time but found no occasion to take active part in its development. Now the time was propitious to lend my help to this worthy cause.

This is how I began my experiences with the Boy Scouts. Across from my home, in the basement of a church, a small group of boys were making futile efforts to start a Boy Scout troop, but no leader was available. I owned a Scoutmaster's Handbook and had familiarized myself with its contents, so at the boys' next meeting I went down to the basement and spoke to them. Then I led them through a real Boy Scout exercise and let them choose their patrol leaders, secretary, and treasurer. One older boy, about 16, was elected assistant scoutmaster. As it was impossible to get sponsors for the troops at that time, we decided to have each boy pay 10¢ at each weekly meeting, the money going toward purchasing the troop's necessities such as uniforms, a flag, writing materials, etc. Our troop was adopted by the Crescent Bay District Counsel, headquartered in Santa Monica, and very soon afterward I was nominated Deputy District Commissioner by the American Boy Scout Counsel of the United States, headquartered in New York.

My district comprised Beverly Hills, Sherman Oaks, West Hollywood, Sawtelle (e.g. west Los Angeles), Inglewood, and Culver City. I have the honor to have been active in putting four of these cities on the map in scouting.

My most difficult task was finding scoutmasters. Beverly Hills suffered most from this calamity as no one there seemed interested in scouting. One energetic boy, then 14, a fine natural leader but only a tenderfoot (the lowest grade in scouting), tenaciously held a small troop of 12 together, though they did not even have a permanent meeting place. They moved from school to school so that on my inspection rounds I usually had to search to find where they were holding their meeting that night. One time, I was unable to find them, so I decided to ask at various homes near the last school I'd visited, thinking someone might possibly know where they were. The first house I went to brought me unexpected success. When I asked the friendly gentleman who opened the door if he knew where the Boy Scouts were meeting that night, he said, "I don't know but I am sure my boy does." He called the boy, a lively little 11-year old who had apparently heard my question for he immediately said, "I'll show you."

We jumped into my car and he guided me to one of the schools in the area where we found Lehman, the leader, with his troop. My little guide, who said his father was the well-known architect, Kaufmann [60], the designer of both the Los Angeles Times buildings, stayed to watch the meeting which he followed with avid interest. Afterward, he attended every one though, at that time, a boy had to be 12 before he could be admitted into the scouts; however, now the age has been lowered to 11.

To give the scout movement in Beverly Hills a better impetus, I gave lectures to the Lyons and Kiwanis clubs and arranged a scout Court of Honor which would pass judgment as to the promotion of members of the troops to higher grades. I asked Mr. Kaufmann to be its president and Mr. Roberts, a prominent realtor, became its secretary. Young Kaufmann had just turned 12 and at the first session of the Court of Honor, after all the aspirants recited the Boy Scout oath, he took his tenderfoot tests with the others and passed summa cum laude. Tears ran down Mr. Kaufmann's cheeks as he watched the ceremony and heard the recitation of the moving oath. Afterward he came up to me and exclaimed with gusto, "I never knew the significance of scouting!"

This Court of Honor session marked the beginning

[60] **Gordon Bernie Kaufmann** (19 March 1888 – 1 March 1949) was an English-born American architect mostly known for his work on the Hoover Dam. He arrived in California in 1914 and during his early career he did much work in the Mediterranean Revival Style, which had become popular at that time. He was also the initial architect for Scripps College, a liberal arts women's college in Claremont, California. While gaining recognition for his work on the Scripps campus, he was also hired by California Institute of Technology in 1928 to design the complex of dormitories now known as the South Houses, and the building for the Athenaeum, a private club located on the school's campus. Later in his career, Kaufmann worked primarily in the Art Deco style, with a personal emphasis on massively thick, streamlined concrete walls which gave his buildings a very distinctive appearance. Kaufmann's buildings as a result took on a very "mechanical" appearance, often resembling huge versions of old-fashioned appliances. *The Los Angeles Times'* headquarters is a perfect example of this. Kaufmann was active in the Boy Scouts of America and served as President of the Los Angeles Council of the Boy Scouts of America in 1948. (PCAD; PCAD.lib.washington.edu)

of the steady improvement of scouting in Beverly Hills, and Mr. Kaufmann's enthusiasm for the movement was the incentive for his acceptance of the presidency of the District Counsel, a post he held for the next 15 years until he moved out of the district to South Pasadena.

When the U.S. Army Air Corps ordered six fliers to make a flight around the world under the command of Major Mitchel, 150 Boy Scouts under my supervision were honored to police Clover Field, the point of their departure. There were no police officers present, and although a spirited crowd of about 100,000 surrounded the airfield, the ring of diligent scouts was able to keep perfect order. Major Mitchel told me he was astonished; he never would have believed that the crowd would obey boys as they would policemen, and asked to pose with me for a photograph, congratulating us on our success. Four of the fliers completed the tour but Major Mitchel and his pilot lost their plane in the tundras of Alaska where, after two weeks of hardship, they emerged on foot and succeeded in returning to civilization.

On my inspection tours, Colonel Frank, a staunch warrior recently returned from duty in Europe, was my constant companion. He was an ardent Boy Scout supporter. He had served for years in the Philippines where he was wounded 15 times. A strong-fibered soldier he certainly was as evidenced by his telling me of the time had had to submit to an appendectomy at the Sawtelle Military Hospital—when he was brought to the operating room and saw they were preparing him for an anesthetic he said he didn't want "any of that stuff."

"I want to see what you fellows are doing," he told them. "Give me a cigar."

The medical staff attending him complied rather unwillingly and he calmly watched while a surgeon removed his appendix.

He and his chum, Colonel Bartlett, opened a real estate business together and were successful realtors when I knew them. Two more of my realtor friends were the former majors Fitzmorris and Holl who had had equally good fortune. Fitzmorris had been one of the United States' first six fliers; although he lost an eye in the service and had to return home, he now lives a satisfactory bachelor's life in Pasadena. Major Holl still lives in West Hollywood. Once in a long while we see each other and reminisce about old times together. The two colonels both passed away years ago.

One day our little house on the big lot was visited by a young real estate salesman who told me a client of his liked my home very much and wanted to buy it. Later, he came again with the potential buyer herself, a Mrs. Mary Belcher, who showed a seemingly genuine interest in the house and the large lot, offering me $6,700 for it. She said she would give me $200 cash and $6,500 worth of shares in the "Fidelity Mortgage Company," the entire amount payable after 30 days. I considered it a good price and the next day gave her the deed for the $200 and the certificate from the mortgage company for the shares. I visited the large and sumptuously furnished, three-room office of the mortgage company in the Bank of Italy—now the Bank of America—building, where the manager, a portly and congenial fellow, effusively declared that the Fidelity Mortgage Company was built on a very solid basis and he could assure me that the $6,500 would be paid out to me after 30 days.

He came to my office a few times and one day invited me on a trip to Arlington, near Riverside, where he said he intended to buy an orange grove. When we got there, I sat in his limousine while he entered the house; after awhile he came back and told me he had bought the orange grove. He also told me that day that in two weeks I would receive my $6,500. The two weeks passed and I went to the office to get my money. I was surprised to see the office closed, but then I remembered it was a Saturday; I had forgotten.

But the next Monday when I went again it was still closed. I inquired about it at the adjacent office. What a shock I received when I heard that two of the men of the "Fidelity Mortgage Company" had been arrested on charges of fraud. And Mrs. Belcher had disappeared; I could learn nothing concerning her whereabouts. However, I elicited the following fact: as soon as Mrs. Belcher had received my deed for the property she sold it to a businessman in town who was now building a bungalow court on it. My home was irrevocably lost.

Note from Melinda...

My mom always said that Fahta would have been a lot better off if he would've let Munna manage the family finances. I've heard tales of lost masterpieces, oil wells, real estate. It seems that Fahta, a man of impeccable honor, just assumed everyone else was the same, and you know what they say about "assume." That little thing about making an "ass" out of "u" and "me"?

We had rented another house, and there Constance, another fine baby, greeted the world, seeing her first light of day. I had acquired an agglomeration of property, all on shoestrings but all in the hope of profitable sales. I owned a large house in Beverly Hills, a duplex in West Hollywood, 80 acres near Victorville, and a 25-year lease on a corner lot at Santa Monica Boulevard and Doheny Drive running through to Melrose Avenue. The monthly payment on this lot was gradually raised from $150 to $300 per month. To add to my financial burden, I moved my family to a newly-built home on Coverly Drive for which I paid $65 per month after a sizable down payment.

At this time, slowly but unavoidably, the Depression began creeping upon the country. Real estate was now a nearly stagnant business, an inevitable consequence of over-building. I turned to a branch in the real estate field which afforded the only possibility of our keeping afloat. I put a blackboard in our Realty Board office on which I advertised to our members the pieces of property clients had offered me for exchange, a new method of dealing which saved me for a while. In fact, when I began working in exchanges I wrote an article about it for the California Real Estate Journal. I bought a lot in Wilmington for which I paid $13,500 cash. A first mortgage of $5,000 was attached but, as a railroad ran across it, I judged it to be an excellent investment for my purpose which was to eventually build a bonded warehouse on it. A large street bond issue drew extremely high monthly payments on my extensive lot and that, added to taxes and the seven percent interest on the mortgage, brought the monthly cost of carrying it to about $110.

Mercilessly, the Depression droned on and I began losing one piece of property after another. I could have made a sizable profit on the corner lot on Santa Monica Boulevard if the promise to put a railroad switch onto it had been fulfilled, but the railroad commission would not allow that now as traffic had grown too heavy.

One little gleam of light in the darkness was my appointment as appraiser for the Pacific Electric Railway Company. General Sherman, who had settled in Los Angeles after the war, had a dispute with the County of Los Angeles over some Santa Monica Boulevard frontage. I won the case against the county in court for them for which I received the sum of $440 accompanied by a letter of gratitude. The Depression's powerful flow inundated the country. "Sauve qui peut!" (a public stampede) was the cry everywhere. Property was not sold for anywhere near its value, if it was sold at all. The holders of second trust deeds lost their investments as the happy first mortgage holders unpityingly foreclosed and took over the properties for the price of their simple mortgage money.

If I had received the amounts rightfully owed me—about $14,000—I could have been able to sail successfully through the raging sea of circumstances. For instance, I closed one large deal in a manner far from anticipated. A $150,000 apartment house was to be exchanged for several pieces of property valued at the same amount. When the owner of the apartment house gave me a check for $1,000 as a partial payment of my commission, the owner of the mixed parcels of property, having used all the finest manipulations to convince me of his honesty and hearing of the check from the apartment owner, made me believe that the deal could not be closed if I did not lend him the $1,000 until it was accomplished. Again I was the dupe of my now-vanished German belief that everyone is honest. I gave him the money, eager to finish the transaction, and the exchange was made. But when I asked for the return of the loan and my commission all I received were excuses and, as time went on, more excuses. In the end I was forced to conclude that I had been cheated. I sued him, he declared bankruptcy, and that was that. I lost all the property I owned except that in Victorville, a fact which pointed boldly to the value of paying cash for everything you buy if you can.

Note from Melinda...

The 80 acres in Victorville is still jointly owned by the six brothers and sisters or their heirs. My mom's been paying the property taxes on it since Fahta's death.

I now had only enough money left to put a down payment on another new house in West Hollywood at the boundary line of Beverly Hills. Here our fourth child, Patricia, was born.

Note from Melinda...

My mother, Patricia, fondly known as "Aunt Pitta" by her numerous nieces and nephews.

The same capable lady M.D. attended the birth who had delivered Constance. She lived in West Hollywood with her 99-year-old mother who, thanks to her daughter's fine care, was in an excellent state of health, having only a little deafness. Soon after this birth, a small knot appeared on one of my wife's breasts and we soon learned it was malignant. We saw nine cancer specialists and all said the breast must be removed. As a last resort we went to our trusted lady M.D. who immediately said that in the approximately six weeks allowed her before an operation would be absolutely necessary she would attempt to cure her. And that is just what the fine woman did. There has been no recurrence of the dreaded disease.

I exchanged a few pieces of property here and there, thus keeping the wolf from our door, but an accident interfered with my daily routine, now more strenuous than ever. One day after lunch, having sat down in my easy chair, the children began making a deafening racket. I quickly jumped up to find the reason of the turmoil. My feet slipped on the finely waxed oak floor and I fell heavily, landing on my right shoulder. It dislocated and severe pain followed. Lilian phoned our family doctor but he was not in his office. She called another one who came with one of his colleagues and, both working together, put me through half an hour's excruciating pain to set the bones. But after their departure, when I tried to put the palm of my right hand upon my left shoulder, I found it impossible; hence I knew my shoulder had not been set as it should have been.

For a week I carried my arm in a sling and still, after discarding it, I was not satisfied with conditions; yet contrary circumstances in the real estate business claimed more and more of my time and exertion to secure even half a livelihood. But as the pain in my right shoulder increased day by day, I finally went to the newly established X-ray clinic in Hollywood to get a picture of the trouble. When it was developed, it showed the bones to be an inch and a half apart! I went to our family doctor and showed him the picture. He said so much time had elapsed since the dislocation that there was little hope for a complete setting. Nevertheless, he and his assistant spent quite some time trying to help me, using all the strength they could muster, without effect. Just as they had nearly given up, Dr. King, our dentist, happened to pass by the open office door. He was a big man, weighing about 250 pounds, and was immediately asked to lend a helping hand. He put his weight to the task and by the combined efforts of three men, the bones were set right; my right hand could now touch my left shoulder; but a certain stiffness of the arm has remained.

Note from Melinda...

I think it worth nothing that Fahta was 64 at this point in his life.

Another mishap occurred at this time to a member of my original Boy Scout troop. One of the directors of the Chamber of Commerce, an old friend, offered me his cabin in the Arroyo Seco for a weekend with the scout troop. What joy erupted when I mentioned his good deed to the scouts! A well-furnished cabin with enough cots for all welcomed us. After a busy afternoon of testing followed by suppers cooked over open fires among the big boulders, Boy Scout songs and spooky stories brought a happy day to a blissful but rather spine-tingling end. The bugler's morning greeting rallied the boys to vigorous freshening up. After breakfast, more tests and firewood chopping from gathered dead timber (Boy Scouts may not mutilate growing trees) and the well-filled time flew.

Of two brothers in the troop, the eldest, fifteen, six feet tall and very awkward, though a good scholar, would always be involved in some clumsy nonsense on a camping trip, and here he was again. "Leonard has hurt himself!" someone cried. As I came running up, Leonard held out his right hand. The tip of the middle finger was badly crushed right down to the first joint. The boys told me he had tried to lift a heavy stone from its place and it smashed down onto his finger. I quickly bandaged his wound and ordered the assistant scoutmaster to take care of the troop and clean the cabin and surroundings before going home. I then departed immediately with Leonard in my car at a very quick tempo, speed laws unheeded, to our Boy Scout doctor who used 14 stitches to bind up the shredded flesh. Scout life can be exciting, and the right kind of leading is bound to make a man of a scout. Our motto is: "Be prepared." A first-class scout can take care of any emergency. I am so fond of scout work; I could talk about it constantly.

Chapter 23   A Farmer Once Again

One of my acquaintances owned an orange grove in San Joaquin Valley, which he could not care for alone so he asked me to exchange the property for him. Inquiries about the grove gave me favorable information about its location and the value of the last year's crop. The real estate business was at such a low ebb that our board membership had dwindled down to only a few members, and we even had to give up the rental of our board office. As an exuberant friend of nature I was strongly inclined to take the orange grove in exchange for our home. My present lack of profit in real estate and the desire to bring my children up in the country were other compelling reasons. So I made an offer to my client which he accepted.

As the harvest time for oranges was imminent, I asked him to give me the name of the person who had been taking care of the grove for him for the past year. I since had every reason to be sorry for this action. The man who did this work for me owned a dilapidated grove across the street from mine. His trees bore very little fruit and what they did bear was not good; mine were young, full-bearing, and the quality of my fruit was excellent. He mixed his oranges with mine and cheated me out of $400. When I had moved to my new property, people told me he had also loaned the almost-new tractor I had acquired from the former owner of the grove to everybody who wanted it and always left it out to the mercy of wind and weather, as a result of which the costly machine was nearly ruined. Needless to say, I dispensed with his "help" and, in turn, acquired a confirmed enemy.

How happy we were in these new surroundings, from a realtor to a hard-working orange grower! I have always been a joyously busy individual. When work was not pressing, I went hunting to provide the necessary protein for my sizable family. Hunting was an exciting experience in San Joaquin County. There was lots of game—jackrabbits, cottontails, quail, and doves in droves. I owned a clever, ardent hunting dog, Fritz, a dachshund, who was an avid pursuer of the ground squirrels which were plentiful around our grove. They were so destructive—picking good-sized green oranges and feasting on them in their dens—that I had to ask agricultural agents to get rid of them for me. If Fritz found a squirrel in the grove he would always outrun and kill him; however, this occurred so infrequently that it didn't even make a dent in the hundred others who plagued me. The agricultural agents were able to exterminate most of them, but the next season they were back again.

The most difficult work on the grove was irrigating for which I had to dig ditches four to five feet wide and four feet deep. Three times a year I was allowed to irrigate from the water company's big canal; this service cost $32 a year. There was not always enough water, as the canal level was not constant. My own water was provided by a 40' well (which twice had to be deepened, as the water was rapidly receding). At the beginning of our stay at the grove I used tractor belts for power, but belts would break, stopping irrigation. To circumvent such hindrances, I installed an electric pumping plant. I also had electricity put in the house and added a bedroom, bathroom, and porch to make our home more livable.

Our two eldest children, Lillian and Mark, now had to climb the first rung upon their ladder of academic education. We took them to the nearest schoolhouse, two miles away, where a congenial lady principal welcomed them. All the necessary steps for the children's entrance into the new little schoolhouse completed, we walked back through abundant vineyards and orange groves, passing for the first time the little Lake Wahtoke at the end of the big canal.

With the two oldest now in school, Constance and Pat were left to themselves at home. Constance developed a useful talent for storytelling, relieving mother of many hours of care by keeping her little sister's attention from troublemaking with her quaint fictional inventions.

Note from Melinda...

Oddly enough, I don't remember my mom ever mentioning she was at any time an instigator of troublemaking! She did, however, remark numerous times that Aunt Connie 'snacked' her (I gather 'snacking' was a kind of thump on the head with a knuckle or two). My husband always got a kick out of my mom's strange expressions. There was 'chik it up' – e.g. to loosen something up, a cross between chipping and chiseling ("...chik up that ice and put some in your glass"); and 'faunching around' – e.g. to throw oneself about in high dudgeon when told to do something you didn't want to do ("...quit faunching around and clean up that room!"). I guess she came by it honestly: her particular favorite was Fahta's exclamation of disgust ("Ach! You sheep, you!") when someone did something stupid. The other favorite was 'shortskin' – that's when you sneeze and fart at the same time (as Fahta explained it, "your eyes squeeze shut when you sneeze and there's not enough skin to cover").

The entire care of the orange grove rested upon my shoulders as it had for the prior owner whom I'd relieved. It was not an easy life. When irrigating, I had to walk in gummy, adobe ground and my rubber boots repeatedly sunk so deep in the mud that I had to hoist them out with my hands. From deep plowing, a hard layer of dense plow-core had formed under the surface of the entire 20 acres and I had to break it up to loosen the soil again.

The first crop, harvested with the help of 30 pickers, was a good-sized one, though.

A few words here concerning the San Joaquin navel orange might not be amiss. It is the earliest orange, reaching the market six weeks ahead of the rest of the Southern California crop, and is the finest flavored specimen in the United States. Those in the West never have occasion to taste it however, for all the oranges harvested in the San Joaquin Valley are instead sent to the East. Even the orange tree in the Valley is different from all others. Whereas the southern orange blossoms in the winter, the northern takes a rest at that time; the leaves lose their color and the whole tree has a discouraging-looking appearance. Its awakening starts with the spring sun's warm rays. Then how fast the tree goes to work! Buds and blossoms quickly appear and, by April, speedy growth is on its way. The extremely high temperature of summer heightens the ripening of the fruit and kills predatory insects. Thanksgiving is usually the end of the season's labor and all the navel crop is in the packing house by then.

An orange grove is an expensive possession. It cost me about $100 per acre to keep it in good productive condition. One senseless loss I suffered could have been avoided. It had rained heavily and the adobe ground was muddily soft. Nineteen field boxes of A-1 oranges had been left in the grove and I asked my man, Hendrix, to bring them in with his two-mule wagon. He thought it would be too difficult to accomplish this task given the mud and proposed to bring them to the shed the next morning. When I went out the following morning the oranges had disappeared, stolen! A police search was fruitless—literally! I suspected with ample reason my "friend" across the street, but was unable to prove it.

Despite this setback, the financial report from the Sunkist packing house—I was a member of the Sunkist Association—was very favorable and my A-1 crop was profitably sold. We entered our second year full of hopes for an equally satisfactory income, but were deceived. The orange growers are one of the fruit growers' group who, still today, have not created one single all-embracing organization like the apple, nut, and other fruit producers who are able to profitably control the prices of their produce through unified policies. That is why the price of oranges fluctuates continuously. Our second year's crop, of the same quality as that of the first year, left no capital margin above the necessary amount for the sustenance of the ground.

As the birth of another baby was now near, we needed capital. I therefore was forced to put a second mortgage on the property for the amount of $2,000. One early morning at five o'clock, I brought my wife to the hospital in Dinuba and at six a.m. we had another little girl to love, and gave her the name of Elizabeth. Lilian recuperated in a week and came home, again to take up her heavy duties. But there was now more fun for four-year old Constance who was quite the little mother and could now count on another listener to her stories. She was an invaluable aid to her mother.

Lillian and Mark were mischievous little devils. They were always happiest when they could recruit their two little sisters, Pat and Constance, to share in their fun. One day as I was busy with irrigating, I noticed all four leave the house and disappear behind a row of trees. I was preoccupied at the main ditch when suddenly the water diminished abruptly. I could not imagine what had caused it and walked up and down the ditch examining it. I could see suspicious puddles all along the upper edge and then, at one place, I found the dirt wall of one side entirely demolished and the water inundating an entire section of the grove. When I came back to the main ditch, there, jubilantly screaming and laughing, were the four pranksters, all in Adam's costume, plastered from head to toe in brown-red dirt.

Should this happen today, I really think that scene would find me feeling the same hilarity they were enjoying, for I have improved my understanding of things since then, and it truly was a comical sight. But my entire irrigation system had been temporarily spoiled and, at the time, I was angry. I gave them each a few telling swats and ordered Lillian and Mark to clean the whole gang and go back to the house.

Note from Melinda...

I'm now close to the age Fahta was then, and I can't imagine dealing with five small children at this point in my life — I'm afraid you'd see me running down the street screaming at the top of my lungs and tearing out handfuls of my hair! But my mom has wonderful memories of his patience and kindness. At every child's birthday, they would come down to breakfast to find their place at the table carefully decorated with flowers around their plate, and the entire day was made special for them. (She did say, though, that Fahta was a stickler about finishing their meals—if they didn't, the next day they had it again for breakfast, and lunch, and dinner . . .) She said he was great at helping with schoolwork because he had such an inquisitive nature and was interested and knowledgeable about everything. The only time they were expected to be quiet was when he was composing. And, I just now realized, for a man who spoke eight languages, none of his children spoke anything other than English.

It seemed as if people had lost their taste for oranges; they were now a drag on the market. The cost of producing a box of oranges at that time was 75¢. Transportation and commission added would bring the total to about $1. Even that price was absolutely unobtainable at that time. It was a terrible trial to see the beautiful fruit ripe on the trees and be powerless to market it at even a small profit. One could not get capital from the banks as they felt it to be a risky proposition to lend money to orange growers. The grower who had started many years before had been able to put aside enough reserve capital to carry him through less prosperous years; the newcomer did not have this advantage. A private loan of $2,000 carried us through another year and a good harvest slightly augmented our reserve funds.

The orange market gave no promise of a speedy recuperation. The owner of the second mortgage, a real money-monger, had acquired the first mortgage on our property and now threatened foreclosure; he made me an offer of a few hundred dollars to save himself the trouble of the long court procedure. We accepted his offer and moved to Fresno where we found a comfortable apartment. The four eldest children entered school there. This orange grower morphed back into a musician and tried to form a symphony orchestra. I spent many hours combating the apathy displayed everywhere when I attempted to make the people of this prosperous town of 45,000 inhabitants orchestra conscious—but all my efforts were in vain. The San Francisco Symphony Orchestra, Alfred Hertz conducting, gave three concerts in Fresno and I wrote preview notices of them similar to program notes for the leading local newspaper, the Fresno Bee.

On one occasion the Music Teachers Association gave an evening recital in my honor at which Agnes Gardner Eyre performed with a violinist the F Major Sonata by Grieg—she had previously played Beethoven's G Major Concerto in Berlin with the Philharmonic Orchestra under my direction.

A gleam of light penetrated the horizon when an orchestra manager in Santa Monica engaged me for eight Sunday afternoon summer concerts with the Los Angeles Philharmonic Orchestra, to be sponsored by Dr. Wagner, the owner of the large ballroom in Santa Monica in which we gave the concerts. The Los Angeles Times stated in part, "The concerts, which are sponsored by Dr. F.J. Wagner, due to Mr. Hammer's fine leadership, have become musical events of importance, bringing musicians from the whole county to Santa Monica."

A belief in fatalism has inevitably become mine.

Whenever I undertake a new move, no matter how earnestly and fervently I strive to make it successful, some insidious force seems to thunder, "to here and no further." And try as I may, I am powerless to surmount the opposition. So here again, a few days after our fourth concert in Santa Monica, Dr. Wagner was found dead on the floor of the hall; the result of a stroke. His wife decided against continuing the concerts and I saw that without court action I would not receive the $2,000 owed me according to my contract and decided to give it up.

My wife was again expecting another child but felt this time somewhat uneasy about it. An examination by the doctor disclosed the fact the baby's position in the womb was not as it should be. When the time of the accouchement was near, we went to the same hospital where Elizabeth was born. A further examination showed that a Caesarian operation would be necessary. Amidst Lilian's great suffering and loss of blood, the baby, a strapping boy, was liberated. Her fallopian tubes were tied and the possibility of any further pregnancy eliminated. That made us then the parents of six children, who still today meet the promise given at each of their births of being strong, healthy people. All have married well and fulfill their duties as loyal American citizens. The last of the Mohicans we named Randolph.

To stay any longer in Fresno would be useless. We moved back to Southern California, to Hollywood, and the four oldest children entered the Laurel School, two blocks from our new residence. The Depression had now reached fatal proportions and it was exceedingly difficult to carry a family of eight through these trying times. And to augment our worries, the children, one right after the other, came down with the measles. None suffered a serious attack, but poor Mother was incessantly being called to the bedroom by one or the other of them, and every evening she was exhausted. While the measles period mercifully ended, Constance, coming home for lunch one day, tried to open the front door by pushing hard on the glass instead of using the door knob. Her hand went through the glass window, lacerating her wrist badly. Sixteen stitches were necessary—doctor bill, $14. Elizabeth, by now a wild, obstinate little girl, added more trouble. One day she ran away, and Constance followed after her. When she got to Fairfax Avenue, always a heavily-traveled street, she ran out to the middle and stretched out on the asphalt while Constance screamed on the sidewalk. Luckily, traffic was comparatively light just then, but one lady, coming along and seeing Elizabeth, surmised she was badly hurt. She stopped her car and, with it, the rest of the traffic, got out and carefully lifted the little girl up. Like lightning, Elizabeth pulled the lady's hair! Constance, happy that she wasn't hurt, brought the little dickens home.

Another time, I was standing outside the Laurel School talking to an acquaintance while a festival was going on inside the grounds. I had Elizabeth with me but became absorbed in our conversation and forgot to watch her. Then I looked around and realized she was not there. As I scanned the area, there high atop the 10' wire fence surrounding the playground stood my daughter, just getting ready to go over it. With my heart in my mouth I reached up and took hold of her leg and told her to come down. She was having the time of her life, but if she had gone over the fence she would surely have fallen.

Note from Melinda...

This was my Aunt Libby, who died of a brain tumor when I was eight. She and my mom were closest in age and shared a room on the second story of their house. When they got mad at each other, they'd open the window and throw the other one's belongings out, which would land all over the yard. Once, after my Aunt Connie had just finished sweeping the living room where Fahta was composing at the piano, Aunt Libby came in dribbling cracker crumbs all over the floor. Aunt Connie snapped, "Get those crackers out of here!" and Fahta, distracted and now irritated, barked, "cracker!! You crack her and I'll crack you, you sheep you!"

After a year in Hollywood, the restless spirit which was my constant companion when I could not earn enough to decently keep my family prompted me to seek a change once again to other more promising territory.

So we moved to Burbank, a rapidly growing city, where we occupied a new and well-situated house. Finally, after getting nowhere for so long, I turned to the W.P.A. which seemed to be the panacea for our ills. Sixty dollars a month was not a great amount on which to keep a large family in even modest circumstances. An exceedingly intricate system of economy had to be evolved but our efforts were insufficient. As a musician of some standing, I thought I might find a position with a higher salary. Picture my astonishment when I was put on the rolls as a digger on a mountain road! I reported to the timekeeper at seven a.m. the first day and, along with several hundred other men, had to climb 300' up to the road site. A lucky circumstance saved me from digging however. I saw no first aid station so I asked the foreman about it. He said there was none. I told him that as I was a former Deputy Boy Scout Commissioner I'd be glad to install one. He was amenable in accepting my proposition and ordered a little shack erected for that purpose.

My work was confined to poison ivy cases. That obnoxious plant grew in profusion all around us. One workman suffered so terribly from this scourge—his legs were covered with large wounds—that he had to be hospitalized. Only one case needing a doctor's care occurred during my stay as first-aid man in the mountains. A reckless young fellow, a water carrier, fell down from the edge of the road and broke his leg. It was a hard task to carry his exceptionally heavy body down the steep trails after I had put splints on his leg, but we succeeded in bringing him down safely.

What a wealth of human knowledge was assembled here among my co-workers who had resigned themselves to the work any unskilled laborer could do! There were two bankers, a lawyer, several moving picture directors, businessmen, etc. All of them could have been placed in much more useful positions, but the W.P.A. was still new and had not yet hit its stride.

Stories of financial losses and misery were told as we visited among ourselves at lunchtime—heartbreaking events in family lives; countless plots were narrated, enough to satisfy a story writer for a long time. The hard labor all this intelligentsia were now performing seemed to exercise a beneficial influence upon their bodily welfare, regardless of the skin peeling off their hands as a result of the continuous strain of manning shovel and spade. All arrived pale-faced and dejected; but after one week's work in the refreshing mountain air and interaction with individuals in circumstances equal to their own, healthy countenances replaced the pale faces and they became more willing to assume the new duties destiny had dealt out to them, many arriving at a better philosophy of life. I also took new courage personally and was convinced this was only a transitory period. Some say that darkness is always followed by light. That was true in my case, but before this beneficent light was to shine for me, fate willed that I pass through a long period of darkness indeed.

Chapter 24   W.P.A. Blues

The work upon the mountain was completed and I, like some of the rest of the men, was sent to the city's eugenics office where I was assigned with a number of others to sweep the streets of Burbank! Were the many thousands of marks spent for my education to lead to such an end? My life in Europe had never traveled in a descending but always in an ascending direction as my success had steadily increased. At the time of my arrival in the United States, most of the noted conductors here had come via the route of conducting the Berlin Philharmonic Orchestra, but every one of them had employed an agent, something which I was too proud to do. I see now how that would have helped me. As it was, all my broad knowledge of the music literature of the Western World, which should be heard in my adopted country, led to nothing.

And then began the gradual decline in my financial status though, with it, came a deepening of my nature through pondering profound thoughts—in the end a far more important thing.

Fortunately, the street-sweeping episode only lasted a few days. A cooperative of workingmen and some businessmen, all victims of the Depression, was formed in Burbank, aiming to afford its members better support. The members had strict working schedules and divided the goods they received in payment equally. I was elected secretary of this new organization. The work was divided in the following manner: skilled workers were sent to do the kind of jobs they were experienced in, for example a baker assisted several hours a day in a bakery, his pay consisting of a certain number of loaves of bread; a carpenter did odd jobs and the money he received was used to buy groceries for the cooperative; unskilled laborers helped on farms and received vegetables for their work. Some of the members were sent out to visit private homes which boasted fruit trees to ask permission to pick the fruit for the cooperative. It was a life-giving organization, though some members had to be carried along by the others. Complaints were uttered here and there about these drones, a situation which probably will never be avoided in any cooperative. Canning season kept many of the members' wives busy. At its end, about 12,000 cans of fruits, tomatoes, beans, and other vegetables filled the shelves in the old Armory where the cooperative led its bee-like existence.

Thinking about these dire times of the cruel Depression, I remember so many cases of suffering that my heart aches all over again. My dear old friend, Richards, who was the secretary of the Chamber of Commerce in Burbank and who should be honored highly in that town for the outstanding work he did for the development of its industry and business, often asked me to take baskets of food and clothing to needy souls. I visited many homes of the poorest people who were living in pitiful squalor—I do not know how some lived at all. I remember one case especially in the Mexican quarter. My directions took me to a shack about 10' square, a deplorable little hovel. Inside, an old lady, literally skin and bones, was huddled before a tiny iron stove with a fire sputtering and smoldering in it, her frail hands spread wide in trying to absorb some of its pitiful heat. It was raining heavily outside and her roof was leaking uncontrollably, soaking the bare, earthen floor and forming puddles all around the miserable old woman. My heart was deeply stirred. I went back to the cooperative and asked two carpenters to take some of the old lumber from our pile in the yard, install a wooden floor in her little shack and repair its roof. In a few hours the hut was turned into a fairly decent living room. I gave her a basket of food, and the poor woman was so sincerely thankful for everything that, knowing no other way to express it, she took an old guitar, and accompanying herself, sang with great feeling in her agreeable voice some old Mexican songs. Do you wonder that tears rolled down my cheeks in response?

The cooperative lost a number of members who, through their continuous efforts, had found more remunerative pursuits. I too was no longer a member when I heard of its dissolution.

About this time, it seemed as if the authorities had finally discovered me. I received a letter from Mr. Dahl, President of the Los Angeles Department of Recreation, asking me to assume the leadership of the W.P.A. Symphony Orchestra which rehearsed at the Shrine Auditorium.

When I arrived there, the orchestra was rehearsing under a very incompetent young man. Just as he was nearing the conclusion of the piece and I was getting ready to take over, a messenger approached me with a note from Mr. Dahl, asking me to come to the Department headquarters. He told me I was needed as the Director of Music for the Recreation Department and that was more important than the conducting of an orchestra. This was a good group and I had been very happy about having an orchestra again, but orders were orders. My new job was to create orchestra groups in all the branches of the Department. My salary, though small, $90 a month plus all my car expenses, enabled me to finally take better care of my family without constant fear. And, in a sense, I was a free man again. Mr. Dahl was released from his president's position as my new position commenced and Mr. Hjelte, a capable and more well-liked gentleman, took his place.

Those days were filled with useful activity. The circuit of my work was far-reaching—from Reseda in San Fernando Valley to the 1000 block on Harvard Street in Los Angeles to Hollywood, North Hollywood and

Eagle Rock, a vast piece of Southern California.

In Reseda and some other smaller branches, there were not enough amateur musicians to form an orchestra so I established mixed choruses instead. My best orchestra, containing remnants of the disbanded Businessmen's Orchestra, gave concerts in the different Department branches to encourage aspirants to join their own community orchestras. As most of my days were filled and I held my rehearsals in the evenings, I had very little time to spend at home, but every Sunday, my one free day each week, we used to take a trip to the country, hunting and picnicking together as a family.

One aspect of my work was rather discouraging. As soon as I had organized and established an enthusiastic group of amateurs who were eager and able to display their musical skills in public, I had to leave them to form another orchestra in another branch. The well-grounded orchestra was entrusted to a young man ignorant of the task imposed upon him. The excuse for this action was that every Tom, Dick, and Harry claiming to be a musician (which in most cases he was not at all) rushed to the W.P.A. for a job, and the heads of the departments, who were inadequate judges of these applicants' capacities, put them wherever they thought some good might be accomplished by them, often in the wrong place. No probationary period was imposed upon these quasi-conductors and if it was shown after a short lapse of time that one was incompetent, the only action taken was by the best players in the orchestra who would quit, leaving only a small fragment of the once-effective body remaining. This same process was repeated several times, giving me a disheartening sense of futility.

In the midst of these disenchantments, I received an order from the Music Department of the W.P.A. to take over the conductorship of the Pasadena W.P.A. Symphony Orchestra. From the Berlin Philharmonic and my fine Göteborg Symphony Orchestra to the discouragingly incomplete instrumentation of the Pasadena orchestra! What a declining state of affairs for my erstwhile career! Not enough stringed instruments and, of these, only the first violins were capable players; only two double basses, both mediocre. In contrast, I did have an excellent flutist and first clarinet, but no oboe, no bassoon, and only two French horns; among the brasses there was only one decent trombone and a good tuba player, and the timpanist was good. I later acquired an oboe and then a bassoon but the oboist left when the bassoon came. At no time did I have a complete orchestra. How difficult it was for me to conjure up all the missing parts as I listened to their collective efforts, while at the same time trying to actively not notice so many of the false tones produced by the numerous incapable players! Nevertheless, one of my strictly adhered-to rules is, "Whatever you do, do well," and I tried to do as well as possible under these trying circumstances. In fact, it was rather a challenge to me.

Our prescribed public concerts were warmly received; my enthusiasm seemed to communicate to both the orchestra and the public. The greatest enjoyment of my stay in Pasadena revolved around the approximately 200 concerts we gave in all the public elementary and junior high schools, accompanied by lectures given by myself or the Superintendent of Music in the Pasadena schools, Dr. John Henry Lyons. The children in these schools, along with those in other cities for whom I later conducted, were, without exception, the most attentive audiences I have ever had. For two successive years these concerts were a source of pride and joy to the musicians and their audiences. The children of the Linda Vista school liked the concerts so much they arranged a sort of tea with all kinds of refreshments after the last concert we performed for them.

Near the beginning of my Pasadena period, Lilian's mother died, leaving her $8,000 plus a monthly income of about $40 from property. Soon afterwards we moved to Pasadena. We bought a spacious two-story home with eight rooms, situated on a large lot, 60' x 200' feet which boasted many fruit trees for only $5,500.

There, in my few leisure hours, I experimented in raising vegetables by chemi-culture (e.g. hydroponics). I fabricated two 10' long boxes, waterproofed them, and filled them with water. I put wire netting over them, covered this with a small layer of leaves and dirt and seeded it on top with different vegetable seed. The plants grew very quickly and healthily and my work with them gave me great pleasure.

Two large avocado trees grew on the lot, one of them a Fuerte seedling and the other a seedling with small black, valueless fruit. I discarded the latter one and erected in its place a grape arbor, 16' long, and planted a number of varieties of grapes around it. I also planted a currant and a gooseberry bush and, from these, I was soon able to propagate enough plants to mark 100' of my boundary line. The other 100' were covered with several kinds of guavas, miniature fuchsias, and roses. A large pineapple guava tree grew in the rear of the lot along with a passion fruit climber, a peach tree, a lemon tree, and a Satsuma (Japanese) plum. In the empty lot behind us grew a fine Chinese Saturn peach tree, loaded with delicious fruit. As every member of the family was a hearty consumer of fruit, our harvest gave us great satisfaction. A persimmon and a walnut tree which I planted—I always chose two-year old trees for planting—each bore fruit the next year. I refer to all these recreational occupations to give you an idea of my love of fruit culture, an absorbing source of gratification for me. No drinking, no smoking, and useful hobbies in nature's realm have helped me to nicely balance work and joy and keep robustly healthy.

Following my two years in Pasadena I was then sent to conduct the Long Beach W.P.A. orchestra. That group needed a serious awakening as the lamentable instrumentation was poorer than that in Pasadena. By this time, I had been promoted to the status of supervisor, salary $140, an advance I had awaited for a long time. A greedy head supervisor whose name I will not divulge later took this increase away from me. Just before that he had highly lauded my performance of Brahms' second symphony.

The work in Long Beach required two hours for driving every day, 30 miles each way. In the springtime, the fog was often so dense I had to drive five miles an hour for miles to avoid mishaps. It has always been my aim to be punctual for appointments. Only once in all my adult years was I not one of the first to arrive at a rehearsal. This occurred on one of those foggy days when, not far from Long Beach, a tire puncture detained me long enough so that I arrived just barely in time.

There the same procedure was followed as in Pasadena. We gave concerts in all the public schools. The principals and teachers were all kind, helpful people, grateful for our efforts to bring this educational feature to their little scholars. In one school I was invited to be a permanent lunch guest of the principal and teachers. The best orchestra I had all this time was a combination of the Long Beach and Pasadena orchestras. We gave several successful concerts with soloists in the Polytechnic High School auditorium in Long Beach.

The authorities heading the Music Department of the W.P.A. at no time emphasized the existence of a fundamentally sensible policy. Instead of using the ability and experience of a conductor they felt was too old to instruct young aspirants (as I did a few times earlier), they simply replaced him with a young man, no matter how inexperienced he was in the art of conducting. I was nearing 70 but was vigorous, healthy, and fully capable of conducting any first-class symphony orchestra— just as I am today at nearly 91 years—but I was removed and my job taken by a talented-but-green young man. Then, illogically, I was placed as a lecturer and instructor of composition and music theory. After a few months of giving classes at churches where I had hardly any pupils, I resigned.

During that last year with the W.P.A. I had also conducted the Swiss Harmony mixed chorus which rehearsed at the International Home. One of the Harmony's rehearsals happened to fall on the evening of my seventieth birthday. It ended in the same jovial spirit as always, and then, as I was taking my overcoat and hat and getting ready to depart, the president of the organization took my arm and asked me to stay a bit, leading me into the hall next to our rehearsal room. To my great surprise, the entire chorus had congregated there and in the center of the room was a long table, festively arrayed with plates and refreshments. Everyone called out, "Happy Birthday!" The president made a congratulatory speech and then uncovered a unique, foot-high cake— it was an inimitable piece of art, the likes of which I have never seen. My fondness for hunting was well known as I often went hunting with the cashier of the society, a former resident of the Swiss canton, Graubunten, where a Latin dialect is still spoken. We even went out with another Swiss one day and shot 27 rabbits for a Hasenpfeffer dinner which was prepared by the ladies of the chorus. Thus, the intricate, six-inch sugar figure atop the cake was a well-proportioned hunter, properly attired and equipped with gun, rucksack, and a rabbit hanging from it. Around the hunter's feet were figures of all kinds of game and other wild animals; likewise, the sides of the cake were decorated with dogs, other animals, and plants, all in realistic colors of nature. It was a wonderful masterpiece, displaying the exceptional talent of the society's president whose profession was cake decorating. This extraordinary cake was for some time a subject of conversation among my family. A photograph was taken to keep the memory of it alive but I am sorry to record it has been lost. However, this precious remembrance of father's seventieth birthday remains.

After a few years of conducting the Swiss singing society for a paltry sum, doing it more for love of it than money, I was informed they would have to pay me even less. I then felt it would sadly not be worth my time any longer and resigned.

In Los Angeles at that time there were many, many excellent musicians unable to find positions. With their needs and mine in mind, I procured an interview with the busy Mr. Kühne, former solo clarinetist with the Minneapolis Symphony, during which we spoke of this calamity and decided to gather some of the finest of these players together and try to alter our financial status using a cooperative basis. Fortunately, my wife's inheritance enabled me to look with greater confidence toward the future than most of these men.

I regret to say the orchestra was sponsored nominally vs. financially by a great number of prominent persons in Los Angeles. It made its successful debut at the inauguration of the famous Greek Theater in Griffith Park. This orchestra was one of the finest I have conducted. Uscher, the foremost critic in Los Angeles, compared it with the Philharmonic, but in many ways it was superior. We gave concerts on two successive Sundays, attracting an increasing number of music lovers. At one of the concerts, John S. McGroarty , the California poet laureate and writer of the Mission Play, spoke impressively to the audience saying, "If I were a rich man, the first dollar I would spend would be for a symphony orchestra."

If these concerts could have continued weekly with the profits gradually increasing as I am sure they would have, the orchestra's existence might have been secured. The Recreation Department, however, had already contracted other programs for all the season's calendar of Sundays. We gave an original concert in the Philharmonic Auditorium consisting of a program presenting only Mexican composers with Mme. Nietz, the famous Mexican nightingale, as soloist. The audience included the consuls from all the Central and South American Republics and the event was fairly remunerative. Then followed some broadcasts over KFI (radio), but we could not find a sponsor and had to discontinue them. We did receive over a hundred heartening letters praising our performance. These were so welcome in this time of dejection that I would like to quote a few:

". . . Express heartfelt gratitude for an hour of truly exquisite pleasure today in listening to the beautiful, painstaking and supremely artistic renditions of the orchestra under your masterly direction." L.R. Deane, Los Angeles

". . . My heart was delighted to hear such an extraordinary performance over the radio. I am unable to put into words my appreciation for your excellent interpretation of Schubert, Wagner, and Liszt." Mrs. N. Burkhardt, Los Angeles

". . . Your directing was superb. There was something so sympathetic, imaginative, poetic about your conducting that I cannot resist telling you a little of my appreciation." B.K. Downing, San Diego

At Bovard Auditorium on the campus of the University of Southern California, we played several more concerts, among them the last one of our organization. We were only allowed to charge 25¢ entrance fee and although we had a packed house for each concert, we only received a few hundred dollars each time, not sufficient to keep our otherwise successful orchestra alive. Regretfully we disbanded.

In the years since I composed my "Sunset at Sea," I had harbored the idea of composing a counterpart to that piece: "Sunrise at Sea." One morning, about an hour before sunrise on a deer hunting trip to Topeka Canyon, I walked along the ocean shore to my destination. The sky was exquisitely clear and, as I walked, the horizon became flushed a rosy pink, then transformed into bright vermilion streaks radiating from and enhancing their fiery parent, the venerable old sun which was now peeking over the horizon. The same sentiment of deep awe filled me as was the case in Holland when I had conceived the idea of "Sunset at Sea." That had happened by the side of the North Sea and this was on the shore of the Pacific Ocean, far, far away. Coming home, I tried to distill my impressions into music. But the orchestra parts were never copied, thus it was never performed.

Max von Schillings came with the orchestra and personnel from the Berlin Imperial Opera to Los Angeles to perform a week of Richard Wagner's dramas at the Shrine Auditorium. I was his guest for all of these magnificent productions. Ours was an acquaintance of long duration and it was good to see him again.

Two well-known conductors, Tyroler, formerly with the Metropolitan Opera, and Blechschmidt, from the

Imperial German Opera, had successively been conductors of the Ellis Club, the finest male chorus in Los Angeles. After Blechschmidt left, I was called to take the position. I received a fairly good salary and had the pleasure of working with outstanding singers. Two concerts were given each year in the Philharmonic Auditorium.

Artur Rodzinski was at that time conductor of the Los Angeles Philharmonic Orchestra. One day I showed him my second symphony which I had completed a couple years before. He only scanned the first page of the score before declaring, "We will play it."

I was given only 45 minutes in which to rehearse it, but when I conducted my work for one of the regular Philharmonic concerts, it was seemingly to the satisfaction of both the audience and the critics.

Many years have passed since I have spoken of the members of the Hammer family in Holland. At his mother's alma mater, the University of Amsterdam, Ernst was an ardent student of medicine, especially interested in microscopic anatomy. At the age of 25, he was made assistant to Dr. Shoo, director of the University's pathological-anatomic laboratory. While he held this position he wrote a treatise on microscopic anatomy, a number of articles which were published in French, German, and Holland medical periodicals, as well as his doctoral thesis on liver cirrhosis. When Dr.

DECEMBER 21, 1930.—[PART III.] 1

ANGELENOS WILL HEAR COMPOSER

BARITONE T(BE HEARI NEXT WEE

American Singer Con to Los Angeles Af Success in East

Next Sunday afternoon Ge Houston, baritone, appears as s ist with the Philharmonic Orcl tra on an all-Russian program. Houston has been signed by Metro-Goldwyn-Mayer Studio musical productions. His mus education has been a thorough, having studied violin and piano composition as well as orches conducting under Eugene Goos Having been with the Ameri Opera Company for six years, m ing his operatic debut with company in 1925, singing the role in "Boris Godounov," under baton of Eugene Goosens Mr. H(ton was the first American to this Russian role. For his app ance with the Philharmonic cestra he will sing a monolc from Act II "Boris Godounov" Mousorgsky, which will be gi first hearing at these concerts. Other numbers programmed Glazounow, Overture Solemn Op. 73; Tschaikowsky, Symph No. 4 in F Minor, Op. 36, prog closing with the Suite f "Christmas Eve" by Rimsky-Kor kow, which will also be given hearing at these concerts.

Heinrich Hammer

BY L. M. J.

Heinrich Hammer, for years the conductor of the Washington Symphony Orchestra and of the Washington Saengerbund, will be heard again in Los Angeles this winter in his own compositions. He is known among the musicians of this country as a man of broad education and attainment.

Born in Erfurt, Thuringia, Hammer broadened his thorough German music education with French training with Marsick in violin, voice with Viardot and Garcia and theory at the Sorbonne in Paris. Later he augmented this with study in Florence. He began conducting orchestras when he was 20 and for years was a guest conductor in demand all over Europe. The famous composers and performers of the world are his friends. He has been professor at the l'ecole laique in Paris, a member of L'Academie du Hainaut and of the Academia Humanitario in Rome.

During his residence in Geneva where he was associated with Dalcroze, Hammer conducted the Berlioz Centenary and was conductor of the Lausanne Symphony for five years.

Throughout his honorable career in music, Hammer has had much to do with choruses, having conducted the Choral Society of Sweden, three male choral societies in Amsterdam and the French Choral Society at The Hague. In Washington, D. C., Hammer conducted an entire Beethoven symphony cycle including the Ninth, with the Washington chorus he had trained.

Afternoon and Evening Classes Will Be He

Five late-afternoon and even classes in music will be given the winter quarter of University (lege, University of Southern C fornia, which opens January 5, n In charge of the regular facu these classes will be held at college of music, 2601 South Gr avenue, Los Angeles.

A Monday evening course in no. class instruction, will be charge of Adelaide Trowbridge I ry, head of the normal-training partment at the Trojan college music, from 7 to 9:20. At the hour Horatio Cogswell, chairma the voice department, will cond a group in voice and class inst tion.

Miss Julia Howell, head of harmony department, will be charge of a class in harmony Ti day nights, from 7 to 9:20.

On Thursday afternoons a c in ear training and dictation be conducted by Miss Julia How Miss Pauline Alderman and I Mabel Woodworth from 4:10 to 6 On Thursday evenings from 7 9:20 Horatio Cogswell will be charge of a course in voice, c instruction.

Registrations are now being ta at University College for these (ning classes, which grant full t versity credit.

Shoo became ill, Ernst took over his work and, after the director's death in 1921, he succeeded him. The laboratory was at the large Wilhelmina Hospital across the street from the house in which Ernst was born. What a complete cycle: to find the summation of your professional accomplishments at the place of your birth! In 1930, Ernst's laboratory was moved to the Amsterdam City Hospital. He was renowned as a liver cirrhosis specialist and received the French decoration, Officier de la Legion d'Honneur.

Sis had meanwhile passed her examination to be a household director for which she had taken intensive training, and she found a fine position as such in a private school. During all these years, Marie and I had kept a continuous correspondence. She was in fairly good health and seemed to be in good spirits. Her pride in our children was boundless as was evident in her letters being almost entirely about them.

As I continued my chorus work and private lessons, a peculiar listlessness took hold of me. A loss of appetite and, concurrently, weight, irritated me, but I was unable to discover the reason for these symptoms. Even so, I did not go to a doctor. After I lost about 25 pounds, Lilian took action by calling our family physician one Sunday evening. After a thorough examination he stated grimly that I had a ruptured appendix and ordered my immediate removal to the hospital for an emergency operation. At midnight I lay on the operating table; the clock was in front of me and I remember the hour vividly. I was given four spinal injections but could not be put to sleep. It was 12:45 a.m. when at last the inhalation of ether put an end to my wakefulness. The next morning I felt exceedingly miserable. I was completely and utterly weak and I had passed the hours since the operation beset by hallucinations of great power, which had exhausted me—these I recalled as pictures on small squares like a movie reel which had passed in lightning-like movement before my eyes, some depicting beautiful scenes, accompanied by thrilling performances of my own compositions; others ugly and frightening, full of devilish, grimacing figures—a sammelsurium (hodgepodge) of alternating exalting and horrible tableaux. I felt this to be the finale of the symphony of my life.

When my wife came to see me a little later, I told her about my graphic experience, adding that I felt my days were coming to an end. I said goodbye to her and asked her to take good care of our children. She took it all very calmly and, before she left, I fell into a deep, deep sleep. Upon awakening, I was astonished to find myself still among the living. My old habit of quick recovery again came to my rescue. After four days I left the hospital; the two orderlies who had to carry me down to the ambulance had, by their carelessness in lifting me from the bed to the stretcher, bent me almost double so that I cried aloud. "You hurt me," I felt compelled to tell them. This bending must have loosened the suture on the inside of my incision for a large hernia formed and a piece of my flesh was torn off inside my abdomen. I can still feel it now and then in this place or that and call it a floating island. More of this later. Some visits from friends shortened the days of the forced bed confinement which followed and, after a few weeks of further recuperation, I took up my work again.

An Alabama State Senator who had written the scenario for a movie, "The Bishop of the Ozarks", was anxious to produce it and, to this end, he engaged Finis Fox, a well-liked and capable director and producer. I was recommended by a young couple who were acquaintances of the Senator to be composer and musical director for the picture in which the Senator played the main role himself. Finis, thoroughly at home in movie matters, formed the exciting story into a well-rounded ensemble, and I helped him in his endeavor by underlining certain dialogue with suitable musical background. The preview took place in the Hollywood Theater and the picture was sold to Mr. Paul, then President of R.K.O. Finis Fox and I liked working together and both planned to continue it, but that much good fortune just could not be mine—Fox died soon afterward.

A short period of work at Paramount Pictures followed, which brought me in touch with Mr. Leipold, the music librarian for the corporation, who was also a composer and arranger. He studied composition with me and was a serious, talented musician, ending his studies by composing a fine string quartet. I acquired another pupil, Howard Jackson, also a composer at Paramount, who later left the studio and went to New York.

Lillian, Mark, and then Constance finished high school, Mark graduating at 16, after which he entered college to study forestry. He made fine progress and completed his studies at 18. One year after his graduation he was engaged by the Forestry Department to work on the Arroyo Seco project in surveying and planting trees; and later he was assigned to the Angeles National Forest. In the forestry club to which he belonged, he met a young lady in whom he showed a deep interest and soon thereafter married her, with his parents' blessing. He was restless as World War II progressed and expressed his desire to volunteer for service. His employers tried to discourage him, saying that the Department needed him, uttering the belief (or likely just the hope) that he would not be drafted. Nevertheless, he volunteered for the Navy, only to be put in the Seabees! He was a boatswain (petty officer) when he returned three years later.

No matter how heavily and severely life's whims and tasks have often laid cruel hands upon me, none was equal to my sorrow over the demise of my famous elder son after many painful years of suffering—the first death in my family. He died of liver cirrhosis December 23, 1937 at the age of 44 years—the very disease on which he wrote his doctoral thesis and was a specialist. A cum laude "In Memorium Dr. Ernst Hammer" was given at his interment by Dr. M. Straub. This memorial was printed in the journal of the Hollands Medical Association, January 1, 1938. Later it was reprinted as a small booklet, a copy of which was sent me by Marie. In his oration, Dr. Straub gave a complete resume of my son's career—how, at 22, he wrote a treatise on microscopic anatomy, published by the "Histologies Laboratorium te Amsterdam;" being made assistant to Dr. Shoo at the pathological-anatomic laboratory at the age of 25; his promotion to the directorship of the same laboratory; how he was honored by the French government, being made an Officier de Legion d'Honneur; how successfully he led his clinical demonstrations to assistants and doctors; how his counsel was asked by outstanding clinics, and how adept he was in solving anatomical intricacies. The speaker included mention of Ernst's education in Holland, Germany, and Switzerland, his mastery of three languages and the fact that he was an accomplished pianist and amateur watercolor painter. Dr. Straub ended his "In Memorium" with: "His clinical demonstrations were gripping lectures in the first place, useful for those who knew the subjects well upon which he built his premises. Then his listeners were always surprised by the conclusions he drew from his lectures."

"His gift of utmost care and thoroughness in all his research paired with the clear gathering of details into an imposing ensemble will live forth in the minds of those who were his assistants. To those who later came to the clinics, he gave demonstrations on how scientific thoroughness in judging a special case of sickness leads to results. To those in the narrower field of pathological anatomy, he showed the measurements to be used by the practitioner in that field. All of those who understood his extraordinary spirit will retain the memory of a gifted human being and an inspiring personality. Every circle where he dwelled is poorer through his death."

Chapter 25   Changes Afoot

Around 1939, Warner Brothers' accomplished the difficult feat of synchronization. Having waited 20 years, I went to their studio, then situated on Sunset Boulevard, to show Mr. Silvers, the Director of their Music Department, my piano score of "Faustina." He glanced through it and said enthusiastically, "We want an option on this!"

"No!" I answered firmly. "I have waited two decades for synchronization and I want a performance, not a pigeonhole."

But that was seemingly not to their liking. Off and on for several years I tried in vain to bring about the production of this dramatic and original work in its entirety. I had performed the music repeatedly with great success—but the score still rests unpublished in my library. I ceased my fruitless attempts, not ashamed to confess that life was worth too much to waste it in such useless and distressing pursuits.

Note from Melinda...

Probably another unfortunate decision on Fahta's part not to take the option. It must've been endlessly frustrating to be unable to bring about the culmination of your life's passion, but I wonder why he didn't seem to consider that producing a movie is a somewhat more complicated process than a symphony performance.

The tremendous upheaval resulting from the war was intensely felt in our household. I lost nearly all my pupils at the advent of World War II. It was impossible for me to find any employment in the field of music and I finally became determined to return to the country where I could be out of the labyrinth I now felt myself ensnared in so as to once again be master of a substantial realm. When I discovered an opportunity to exchange our house for a well-situated and productive farm near Ontario (about 40 miles east of Los Angeles) I gladly made the deal.

In spite of a house comprising three bedrooms, large living and dining rooms, kitchen, bath, washroom and exceptionally large screened front porch, Lilian was not very enthusiastic. Again, a new kind of life. The farm contained 20 acres of which five were planted in apricots, 13 were clear, and two were planted in alfalfa. Twenty-one large walnut trees lined my south and west boundaries and 32 peach trees flanked the east side. There was a good sized barn and corral, garage, 3,000 trays for the drying of apricots, chicken house and yard, many other kinds of fruit trees, and a mammoth concord grapevine spreading from house to garage. An enormous yellow blossoming acacia was a landmark for the southwest corner of Walnut and Bon View streets and two old, imposing jumbo olive trees created an impressive main entrance to the property.

Note from Melinda...

Out of all the houses Fahta bought during her childhood, I think this was my mom's favorite. I heard lots of stories about their lives here, the house itself, and, when she was descending into dementia I remember her telling me, "you know, when I look out my bedroom window I don't see this driveway, I see the driveway and the front yard of our house in Ontario." I always hoped that it was a comfort to her, that she would return, in her mind, to those family days she loved.

When we moved to our farm, I was happily optimistic about the future. I was confident that my 79 years were no stumbling block to the fulfillment of my farmer's chores. The winter season's less strenuous tasks even provided me some leisure time and the outdoor life exerted an enlivening influence upon both my physical and mental state. Every morning the school bus stopped at our gate to take the three younger children, Patricia, Elizabeth, and Randy to the reputable Chaffee Junior High School and high school, three and a half miles from the farm. Both Lillian and Constance had each married the only boys with whom they ever associated soon after graduating from high school, and these marriages produced my first two grandchildren, both fine boys.

I took a great liking to an animal very low in the estimation of humans, the pig. You will laugh when I state that I admire him for his cleanliness, cleverness, and friendly disposition. Pigs have never been treated right: left to wallow in mud, kicked around, altogether ill-treated, though his meat is a delight to almost everyone. Give a pig a clean bed in a small hut, clean water for drink as well as bathing and treat him kindly, like you treat a dog, and you will have acquired a true and gentle friend.

I now owned 12 thoroughbred breed sows, giving each a name. When I called one, it would immediately come to me to be petted, the rest of them following, also expecting to receive a friendly pat or two. I bought the oldest of the animals from a piggery where maltreating them was the order of the day. As a result, when I first went near her she would grunt angrily, but by and by her behavior changed. When she farrowed and I sat next to her in her hut to help her in her birth throes, she then grunted amiably and seemed to be satisfied with me handling her offspring.

Though the boar is generally considered to be a dangerous fellow, mine was a fine animal who acted like a well-bred dog; he was a thoroughbred Duroc of sturdy bone and muscle, with not much fat. He was excessively strong too and nothing could hold him in his corral when he wanted to take a little walk. The electric wire which enclosed the five-acre apricot orchard where I kept the sows was a sure "Keep Inside" warning for them; if they pushed their heads against it once they would never go near it again; but the roughneck boar would go right through it to pay a visit to his harem. If I saw him there, I would call, "Jerry!" his nickname—he had a more complicated name in the breeding register—and he would come straight to me, then follow me like a dog back to his corral.

Once I noticed his corral was empty and looked all around for him, but no Jerry was to be found anywhere. I saw my neighbor standing on his porch. "Have you seen Jerry?" I asked him.

"Yes," he said. "He went down the road."

Nearly a mile down, at the next crossroad, a bunch of cows had gathered at the corner of the fence of a neighbor's dairy farm—and there in their midst was Jerry, calmly lying in the meadow. "Jerry!" I called.

His ears went up. When I called a second time, he got up and came running toward me. Heading homeward, he wisely walked along inside the fence until he came to the opening where he had entered, then came out and followed me, like a dog heeling, bound for home. I opened the corral door and in he went. I hope this long discourse on the pig will convert many a reader to my opinion that pigs are fine, sociable animals. However, I will admit that my Jerry was somewhat exceptional.

A very serious incident taught me an important lesson. Though I knew Riverside County was subject to sandstorms every year, I had not associated them with our new farm. When the first one occurred, I had only 1.5 acres of alfalfa and 13 acres which lay fallow for the winter. The sandstorms were not overly-severe that first winter, but even so, the damage they did was eye-opening; sand-hills covered the land in their wake and all, including the alfalfa, had to be pegged down. Some of the newer farmers' vineyards were buried in the sand, the plants entirely submerged and made useless for several years. The following years, I always kept the ground planted throughout the four seasons. Only slight damage ever resulted again.

The second year, I planted three acres in sweet corn and the rest in black-eyed beans. At that time, the government controlled farm products and granted us $6.50 for a hundred pounds of black-eyed beans, the most profitable produce.

My nearest neighbor and I each owned half of a gas-pumping plant which gave us the necessary supply of water for irrigation; this engine was a dangerous one though. You needed an iron pole—four feet long and an inch in diameter—to stick into one hole after the other in the flywheel as you turned the wheel around to create enough momentum for the engine to start. But the holes in the flywheel were so worn that often the pole kicked back, as would sometimes happen when you cranked an old Ford, and if you did not grip it with all your might it could hurt you badly. We finally took the old gas engine out and put an electric one in its place.

Irrigating was a dour proposition on our sandy soil. The irrigating furrows had to be watched very closely—an enervating task if you have to watch many at once. One time I had to stay on the job 14 consecutive hours, living on sandwiches and coffee while overseeing this precarious situation. Another time, Randy, our youngest, was helping with the irrigating when I was called to the house; he was a big strong fellow who was then in junior high school. I asked him to watch the furrows in the cornfield carefully. When I came back from the house, there stood Randy, leaning on his shovel handle, talking to one of his school friends. One half acre of the corn had been converted into a lake.

The piggery grew and a fair income was received from it. My six week old weanlings, thoroughbred stock, brought $12.50. Prices, however, were always in flux and went downward from year to year…such is the farmer's lot. Depending on the size of his acreage, assuring he will always have a good income will not be easy, especially as prices fluctuate with the economy.

Our apricots were sold while still on the trees. People came in their cars, picked as many boxes of fruit as they needed and paid $1.50 per box. People used to come from many miles away for our apricots and peaches, and buyers would come to purchase our walnuts wholesale. When war-related gas rationing began, no purchasers for my apricots arrived and I had to quickly engage some cutters, dry my fruit, and take it to Hemet, but I received nothing for my apricots that year.

In the United States, the farmer is not as well off as his colleagues in Holland. There, the farmer brings his goods to town and sells them from house to house to willing buyers, an assured clientele. Here, the farmer is dependent upon the middleman who, after selling the produce, keeps a large commission. What is left, often very little, goes to the farmer. Will Truman's equalization theory ever have the wished-for success? If the farmer could only receive 75% of the prices paid for his products in the stores he would be secure.

Randy, an economical soul, saved his money and bought a beautiful year-old 3/4 Kentucky mare, a very gentle, strong animal who had been bred in the stable of one of my neighbors, a former Los Angeles police captain. From years of being around horses I had acquired a good deal of horse sense and knew that these clear, brown eyes and upstanding ears of our new four-hoofer were no signs of viciousness; nevertheless Randy seemed to be nervous about mounting her.

So I put the first saddle on her gleaming coat and she only shivered slightly, and then stood absolutely still. I asked Randy to mount her but he said he was afraid. I held the bridle and urged him again to step into the stirrup. After much coaxing, he swung up into the saddle. The mare, like a well-trained oldster, stood still until I gave Randy the reins, then she stepped in a fine gait around the corral and obeyed well after a few trotting rounds. Randy gained full confidence as he and the yearling got acquainted. All the time he owned her she never bucked or behaved badly and, by and by, the boy developed into a good horseman.

My wife, being a city-bred and city-loving person, did not like country life, although ours could hardly have been called such in the general sense of the term. We only lived three and a half miles from the friendly city of Ontario, and two hours' drive from Los Angeles. Also she complained that the farm did not net a large enough income. She seemed oblivious of the fact that the health-giving benefits of country life were excellent for the well-being of our children. Over these and other issues we gradually began to drift apart, and eventually I moved my sleeping quarters to a corner of the large screened porch.

I was nearing my 82nd year at this point but was still in splendid physical condition and not only took care of all the necessary field work, but also took care of pigs, chickens, and bees. The price of pigs continued to go down and down though: from $12.50 for weanlings it went to $10, $8, then to $5, $3, $2, and finally $1.50. For that last price I simply could not afford to raise them as I fed them only grain and alfalfa, never any garbage. I was glad to sell them all to one man for a near-reasonable price.

Pigs gone, a little leisure time was left me to carry out a long-nurtured dream: composing another symphony. But though I was able to complete most of the work, troublesome times came along and I found no more occasion to finish the remainder while at the farm. My wife's continued dissatisfaction and her insistence on moving back to Pasadena was appalling. One day I talked with a man who was eager to buy the farm. Since he would give me a decent cash price for it, I was willing to sell. Lilian's response to this transaction was to promptly go to Pasadena and make a deposit on a house I had not even seen.

There we were back in town again. For this house we paid cash, installed new furniture (we sold all our other furniture with the farm), and commenced a very strained life, each looking after our individual interests.

Patricia, who graduated from Chaffey High School when she was 16, had started as a bookkeeper at the Bank of America in Upland right after her graduation. When she was 18, she married her only boyfriend, who was then an ensign on a minesweeper. When we came back to Pasadena, she came with us, transferring to the First Security Trust Savings Bank, which was also one of Bank of America's institutions at that time.

Note from Melinda...

My dad was born in Sweetwater, Texas. His parents and younger brother came out to Southern California with most of the rest of his dad's family during the Depression; his dad died when he was 14.

His uncles were all really good salesmen, selling 'chicken hooey' in those days (e.g. feed which encouraged chickens to produce more eggs, and several times during rough financial periods I've wished I had the recipe for it), followed by cars and then real estate. When my mom and dad got engaged, of course Dad's family wanted to know who Mom's "people" were, and Dad said her father was a conductor. They ooh'd and aah'd and were mightily impressed. When they finally met Fahta, this dignified old gentleman, they asked him which railroad he worked for. I would've loved to have seen the expression on his face.

Elizabeth had graduated a year after Patricia and, when we moved, she also found a good position in a Pasadena business concern. Randy now attended Pasadena City College.

I was without occupation not counting a few music lessons I was giving. My continued studying and thirst for knowledge displeased my wife whose interests in life were diametrically opposite to mine. I continued the composition of my symphony, which also displeased her—an astonishing fact as she was herself a capable violinist—and I finally finished it. A few songs I composed were also the fruit of my precarious existence at this point in time.

Note from Melinda...

I think Fahta's being a little harsh in his estimation of Munna here. I can't imagine her being displeased by his studying or composing, being a musician herself. And she was always very proud of Fahta's accomplishments and made sure we knew that. I think, at 55, she was simply tired of the constant uncertainty and financial foibles of Fahta's existence, and wished for a little security for her future. We spent a lot of time with her as children. I remember once she told my older brother and me that she lived in a house just down the street from the Ford Theater, where President Lincoln had been assassinated. She was totally offended when my brother asked her if she had seen it. I also remember a single time when I was about six and my Uncle Randy, her youngest son, coaxed her into playing her violin. She would've been about 68 by then, but when she started to play and got caught up in the music, she looked like a young girl again. I think that's why I've always loved the violin.

We sold our Studebaker Commander and our concert grand. The 80 acres near Victorville—bought for cash and kept through the Depression—were still unsold. I worked a little triangular garden plot in the small backyard and kept six Rhode Island layers in good condition, having erected a strong shelter for them.

Looking back over the years I had spent in the United States, which I had entered with such great hopes for a prosperous future, and seeing the distinct diagram of my accomplishments I felt deeply grieved that all my strife, energy, and efforts had brought me to such an impasse. The prevailing conditions were totally unacceptable to me.

Patricia's ensign husband, Constance's sergeant husband, a radar man who helped organize a radar station in Manila, and Mark, all returned safely from the South Pacific War. Elizabeth was an artistically talented girl (she once made a good pencil profile of me in five minutes), and she took a course at the Wolfe Institute of Dress Design. When she was still a first year student, she sent some dress designs to a big New York concern which, intending to enter the Los Angeles field, had advertised for new ideas. A few days later she was called to the company's office and informed that her designs had sales appeal. They gave her six different bolts of cloth and asked her to make six dresses from them. She did so and took the finished garments to the office where they inspected each closely. They told her that two of them might sell well but they wanted size fourteen dresses; hers were size sixteen. She was told to keep the dresses and they gave her a hundred-dollar check. After her course in designing, Elizabeth found a fine job in a smart dressmaking establishment in Hollywood.

Note from Melinda...

I was sorry to be denied the chance of knowing Aunt Libby as an adult. I thought she was so beautiful and glamorous, she was artistic, and I think I would've enjoyed her very much. She was divorced from her husband, Willard, when I was quite young (apparently his parents believed he had married beneath him), and left with two small boys to raise solo. My mom always held a grudge against his parents because they were wealthy, Willard was an only child, and yet they refused to give Aunt Libby any financial help whatsoever when she became ill and the tumor in her brain made it increasingly impossible for her to function. They took her boys when she died and, over the years, Mom lost touch with them.

I now became acquainted with a 90-year old lady whom I had known years ago when she, with her husband, came to the United States from Holland as a young, energetic school teacher. Her husband's numerous family relations had all remained in Holland and, now and then, he made short visits to see them. He had become my mouthpiece, bringing me regular reports from the Old Country. From him, I learned of the deaths of my former wife, the doctor, and our daughter, Sis, both of whom had suffered severe hardships in the ugly, devastating European War. Marie was never strong after Ernst's birth but knew how to take care of her health and was 82 when she died; hers was a long and useful life. Sis died shortly after she did. It was Sis, deeply moved, who, in a few well-chosen words thanked Dr. Straub and the assembled friends of my son after the beautiful oration at his interment. Pax vobiscum ("peace to you").

The only intervals during which I felt some remnants of pleasure were the occasions when Randy and I went on hunting trips. He is as fond of outdoor life as me and both of us enjoyed this stimulating sport immensely. Only once did I have reason to resent his behavior.

Many young people going hunting lose their patience easily if they spot no game right away. Wandering in the lovely countryside and admiring the trees and flowers does not interest them as much as it awakes and holds the always inquisitive mind of a true Naturfreunde ("friend of nature"). That day, we hunted in really beautiful desert country. A small but deep valley was inviting, promising hunting grounds richly grown with trees, sage, and wildflowers. We had walked for some time, keeping a sharp outlook, when Randy broke out impatiently, "Oh let's go home, there's no game here!"

He turned and headed back to the car on top of the hill and kept calling me. Probably scared by the calls, three jackrabbits at once took flight in his direction. I dared not shoot as I could not see the boy. Eagerly I climbed up the hillside toward the car where he was still pouting and asking to go home. I saw the racing rabbits and would surely have pocketed my game but was so annoyed by Randy's clamoring that I put my fine fox-gun—a present from my wife—on the running board of the car while I called the dog, then got behind the wheel and we drove off. After about 10 miles I calmed down. Then I remembered my gun. I stopped the car, opened the door and looked for it on the running board where I recalled leaving it in the excitement. It was gone. Only the barrel holder lay there. We went back to search, but never found it.

I was severely punished for my temerity in never wearing a hat during all my years in California. My long hunting expeditions in the desert under the sun's scorching rays had wreaked havoc with my sensitive facial skin. Most obvious was a red spot on my left cheek. Consulting a specialist, I was advised my ailment was skin cancer. The doctor told me that the price of a cure would be $25. I paid him that amount and the treatment began. No improvement took place and, after a few days, a second spot appeared below the first one, both of them rapidly growing larger. In several more days another third spot appeared and began growing larger also. "We need radium treatments," the doctor said. He put four expensive radium needles, a painful operation, in my cheek and left me sitting in the waiting room for an hour and a half. Then he called me in and took them out again. In the following days the spots grew larger and I received a bill of $25 for the radium treatments. I went to the doctor. "You told me a cure would cost $25," I said to him. "Now it has come to $50 and there has been no improvement; in fact, I have become worse. You cannot expect me to pay for what you have done to me."

He guided me to another doctor's office. Pointing to my cheek, he told him, "Cut these out," and left.

As soon as he was gone, the new doctor looked at the spots. "I will not cut them out," he informed me. Then he washed the area with warm water and told me to repeat this three times daily! At the height of my disgust with all this bungling, I read in the newspaper of a clinic to be held at the Huntington Memorial Hospital. I went there and was thoroughly examined. I was asked for the name of the doctor who had treated me. Ethical scruples held my answer back. One of the doctors took me to an adjoining empty room and told me that it was necessary to know the exact amount of radium used for my treatment. Without that knowledge nothing could be done for me. I then gave him the name he requested.

He instructed me to go to Dr. Sharp, a cancer specialist. What a happy solution! He is a taciturn, monosyllabic sort of fellow, but sincerely kind and understanding, steadied by broad scientific knowledge. To my relief, he took great interest in my case. There had been too few radium needles in my face to do any good, he said, and they were not left in long enough. After three X-ray treatments he charged my poor left cheek with eight radium. I stood the intense pain without a murmur, which, I remember, evoked a deep basso grunt from him in reply, "You're a toughy!"

For a whole week I had to keep those wonder-working, precious-as-diamonds needles imbedded in my flesh. After their removal I felt like a newborn child. My doctor son, himself a great specialist, would have been proud of his colleague Dr. Sharp. Two other well-known specialists, Dr. de Mare and Dr. Williams were with Dr. Sharp in his office. Dr. Williams did several delicate operations on the other affected parts of my face. Today you can see hardly a mark of the work he did. I owe a debt of many thanks to these worthy gentlemen and the whole staff of outstanding physicians of the Huntington Memorial Hospital.

Life at home became more and more unbearable for me. Finally, after an unfortunate climax in our already-tense marital relationship, I decided to leave. I gave Lilian everything we owned including the Victorville property. Until I could arrange something better, I intended to stay for a while with a young man whom I had recommended for a job as a bassoon player in a W.P.A. orchestra after the death of his mother, a dear friend of the family, thus remedying his precarious state. The young man, whom I had known since his childhood, had always shown a deep interest in electricity, radio, and mathematics and was now employed by one of the large airplane plants in Burbank.

When I arrived at his home he was absent, but the house was open. Well enough befriended, I had no qualms about entering to await his return. He did not come home that evening. Not knowing when he would arrive and fearing somewhat for the valuable articles in the house with all the doors open, I decided to remain.

During the next few days I cleaned the house thoroughly—a process it badly needed. I now assumed my friend must be on vacation. It was summertime and a gang of boys had taken possession of the garage and made a mess of things in general; among other mischievous actions they had even broken down the four steps at the front entrance to the house. I called the leader of the gang and asked him to gather his crowd for a meeting in the garage. I addressed them in Boy Scout fashion, reminding them of their duties as future citizens. I was bold enough—knowing my young absent friend would concur with my idea—to ask them to build rather than destroy and then made them a proposition. I told them if they would put the front steps in place again and clean the garage and yard thoroughly, I would, in the name of my friend (who I could see never used the garage), let them use it as their headquarters.

How a mischievous boy can be changed into a gentle, law-abiding one!

To see these boys go about their cleaning job with such industry was a joy. In two days' time, garage and yard were clean and the front steps repaired. Then each of the boys brought a used piece of furniture from his home and, a few more days hence, the garage acquired the aspect of a comfortable clubroom: settee, card tables, a deep easy chair, a bookrack filled with all kinds of books and magazines. School started again and, after school, a contented and proud group of boys came there to enjoy a get-together—along with ice cream, soft drinks, and candy.

I stayed and stayed in the little house waiting for my friend's return. After I had waited for five long weeks a young man came to the door asking if the owner of the house had come back. I told him no and asked him if he knew where he was. He said that our mutual friend's employers had told him to take as long a vacation as he wanted as he had been working hard and merited a lengthy relaxation period. The young man further told me that the last message he had received from the lucky fellow had been a postcard from Canada saying he would be home shortly.

And so it was as just a few days after this gentleman's visit, my friend drove up in a fine yellow convertible. When he entered his house and saw me and his neatly-arranged property, his countenance took on an indescribably comical expression. We discussed his trip over half the continent and I then explained my situation and why I had remained in his house, telling him I would leave the next day. I informed him of the covenant I had made with the boys. Knowing him to be rather an introvert, I was not too surprised when I saw him grimace slightly, so in a way, I regretted what I had done. After an hour or so he left again and I felt rather deflated following his departure. He did not even thank me for my work in his interest, cleaning the utterly neglected little home, an inheritance from his mother which I had sold to her when I was in real estate years before.

The next day I went back to the family home, gathered my remaining belongings and moved into a small trailer. It was a cozy little place on a big open lot. Some inconveniences went with it but as it only contained one room and a number of small comforts, I liked it. When I was not trying to find a means of earning money, I was free to study and compose, undisturbed by disagreeable interactions. A few successful hunting trips brought a pleasant change in my monotonous diet and also allowed me to present friends with gifts of my hunting rewards.

After six months of trailer life, I sold a few of my possessions and moved to solid quarters where I rented a piano and started to compose continuously, my aim being to compose nine symphonies. The second and third were completed and I now began the composition of the fourth. My new abode consisted of only one medium-sized room. Having for so many years been a real family man, I felt I must dive into continuous work in liberating myself from overarching loneliness. Therefore, I again prescribed a definite work schedule for the patient and kept it scrupulously.

My meals, eaten regularly—8:00, 12:00, 6:00—I prepared on a two-burner electric plate. "Economy" was written all over the room in capital letters. I cooked simple but nourishing food, no fancy stuff, and enjoyed it. I have always liked cooking since I had to do it back in my military days. Later, on hunting trips and with the Boy Scouts, I found my liking for it and my knowledge of this skill was very useful. Now I saw it was practically a necessity to know something of cooking, and was glad I did.

My evenings were filled with diligent study. Five of them I spent at Pasadena City College, studying five different subjects; astronomy, semantics, creative writing, Spanish, and typing. After approximately a year, my financial resources were exhausted and I found I was forced to apply for a pension, at that time $65 per month. It was not so humiliating for me as I had not only waited 20 years until I asked for it but was fully aware that throughout my stay in the United States I had seriously performed the duties of a citizen of this great country. I had never missed a vote, be it in city, state, or national matters, I had gathered, as a Colonel of the Community Chest, a far greater sum than all the pension money I would ever receive, and my son and two sons-in-law had served honorably in the war.

I kept up my schedule for two years until my move to the Nature Friends' clubhouse high up in the mountains in Sierra Madre Canyon, northeast of Pasadena. I had attended several of their meetings and then was elected to be a member of the organization. As such, I was privileged to live in the clubhouse for an exceptionally small fee per week. The environment was inspiring with its glorious view of the wide valley. But it was no easy task to gather provisions in the town below and then climb back up the steep hill loaded down with them.

I was the only person living in the clubhouse as the other members came only on weekends. There was a piano and peaceful silence, and my days were filled with composing. The winter's icy air cramped my fingers though, and it was hard to keep on writing. To counteract the cold in some way, I started each day with a cold rub-down. The college evening studies ceased because it was difficult to get to the bus stop in time after classes to catch the 10 p.m. bus back and I had to wait an hour and forty-five minutes for the next one if I was late.

I went back to the best friends a human can have: books. I was careful in my choices. Philosophy and foreign literature—French, German, Swedish, and Hollands—were my preferences. Thus engaged, I succeeded in writing the latter part of my fifth symphony, the entire sixth, and most of the seventh.

After two years of packing food up the mountainside every day, I moved further down to the north part of Sierra Madre. This time I was more comfortably housed in a two-room-plus-kitchen apartment adjoining a 100-year old house, the elderly owners of which were the happiest couple I have ever met. In these solitary years, away from home, this was the most satisfactory place my lonely soul had yet discovered.

A friend of mine, a naval commander, Larry McGinnis, had bought a beautiful lot nearby on which to erect his future home. A number of fine fruit trees covered the place and a little one-room house occupied the rear of the lot. Larry, who owned a nice home on Baldwin Avenue, was spending almost all his time building a barbecue on his rear porch with a little sleeping bunk adjoining it. He was doing a beautiful job of it, all by himself, as he was a civil engineer, having specialized in construction. I offered to take care of his lot for him, which occupation would provide the physical exercise I needed. He was glad to be relieved of the task, so every day, an hour before supper, I occupied myself on the lot, irrigating and taking care of the trees and plants.

Larry owned a large well-marked German-bred dachshund called Nick. Many people in the United States misname this breed "dash-hound" which he is when he is running a piece of game. But the German name translated means badger dog. I like and admire this species greatly —for which I have been judge at several dog shows (along with the Doberman pinscher)— thinking it the best house dog in existence. He is almost always short-haired, though among the seven dachshunds I have owned during my lifetime I did have one beautiful long-haired one who received two prizes at the Pasadena Dog Show; but she was the least intelligent one of all. This was, however, no hindrance for her to learn to "sit up" when she was 12 years old through the insistence of my youngest daughter.

Nick, or Nicky, was a different animal though. When Larry's only daughter was married, Nick took her place in a way, and he knew it. Every one of the family loved him, but teased him a good deal. He was the best of watchdogs, barking and grunting at a stranger as if he were ready to tear him to pieces. When Nicky and I got acquainted, there began a mutual, indestructible friendship. He knew my approach and, as I entered the yard, he would race all around, wanting to play catch. Once when he was in the house and saw me approaching, he jumped right through the screen of the front door. But whenever he was with his master in their Packard and I came near the door without entering, a real uproar started and he barked so wildly it seemed as if he would actually bite me if he could. Why, I could never figure out.

Once Larry and Nick and I went hunting. Larry took a juicy piece of steak along which he expertly prepared for our supper. The bones were naturally Nick's property. He guarded his food with jealous vigor, growling deep in his throat. We made our beds on the ground, with Nicky ensconced nearby. He growled the whole night, defying anyone to come near his precious steak bones.

The next morning one of those terrible desert sandstorms raged and made it nearly impossible to start and maintain a decent campfire for the preparation of breakfast. Both of us being experienced campers, we conquered the difficulties, but then it was also not an easy task to douse the fire once our meal was finished. Just then, a "suicide" crow flew over our camp. I downed her with my faithful double-barreled shotgun.

You will probably wonder why I call the bird a "suicide" crow and here's the explanation. A crow is a societal bird. He feeds, steals, and nests in company. In the Old Country, a large crow nesting place is called a crow burg. This bird applies tactics you rarely find in other varieties of the feathered tribes. If you see an agglomeration of them, you will always see several watchers posted at strategic points. A weaponless wanderer passes unnoticed, but as soon as a hunter bearing a gun appears, a lookout gives a noisy warning signal and off goes the company of crows en masse. In my whole life I have never seen a group of crows fly over a hunter with a gun, and never does a crow fly alone unless he has been ostracized from his flock. It is an established fact that crows hold court when any of their kind is badly disliked or has committed a misdeed which demands punishment. If he is condemned, he is usually murdered right away. But because it is always a very large, strong crow who flies alone (though rarely seen), I have concluded that, to avoid bloodshed, those kind are excommunicated and would probably be put to death if they disobeyed the mandate. It is also logical that such a bird would not wish to live; thus, this crow I shot had flown into the face of danger in a manner in which he wouldn't have at another time. This was the biggest crow I had ever seen. Its wing span extended at least four feet. With one thrust of his four-inch beak he could have easily killed a common crow. And it was probably the oldest bird I have ever seen too. If Nicky had not been eager to pull so many of the feathers out, it would have been a fine museum piece.

After several years of loneliness, and knowing the absolute impossibility on my part of renewing the now-meaningless association with my wife, I applied for divorce proceedings. The children were all independently settled and Lilian, who had a substantial income from her inheritance, would be able to live a freer life after a divorce, which was granted. This fact carried with it no change in my own life. I have never seen Lilian since then; but my daughters—much too rarely—invited me to picnics here and there in peaceful parks where they brought their children and we passed a few happy hours together.

Randy was drafted and spent his service here and in Germany, returning home as first sergeant. Soon after his honorable discharge he married a fine young lady and bought a home. When he paid me a visit recently, I asked him to take me hunting someday, but he replied, "Gas is too expensive." How many times did I take him hunting? But such is the spirit of the new generation. A certain bitterness takes hold of me now and then, but I can usually combat it after a few minutes.

In the company of friends I am a sociable companion; at home, by myself, I always tried to keep that same spirit alive, very often without success though. But neither ebb nor flow in financial matters would change my basic philosophical attitude—I have steadfastly striven to keep that sound and unalterable through the years. Unfortunately, a person on a small pension income is misunderstood, even by people claiming—though they have no right to—to belong to the intelligentsia. As a result, some senators and assemblymen do not understand that the money spent to keep old people decently alive is not "lost" or a misspent resource, but instead circulates and makes for better business, creates a more even distribution of society's wealth, and makes it possible for these deserving citizens to spend their last days in peace—after all, they've helped to do their part in building up this great country of ours. It would help manifoldly if everyone discerned the real needs of the elderly; there is one need that even those with the kindest intentions do not perceive, and paradoxically, it is because of them that it exists.

Many old people need to work. Since 65 was made the age of retirement long ago, the average lifespan has increased tremendously. But people are still forced to retire at 65 and many are compelled to pass the rest of their lives in soul-destroying idleness. The positive psychological value of a person being allowed to earn his own way as long as possible should be obvious, yet apparently it is not. I was fortunate to be able to wait until I was 85 before I asked for a pension. Nevertheless, even after applying, I continued to work, keeping my mind active. Many old people could help themselves immensely through thought-provoking study or other stimulating work at home. If large musical compositions were salable, I would not need a pension, for, since my 82nd year, I have written seven symphonies plus an overture. If I am happy enough to sell these sentences I am setting down on paper at 90 years of age, I will then again be an independent man.

For two years, I had served as president of the Current Events Club of Pasadena and have been a member longer still. An assemblage of interested people gathered on an afternoon once a week in the lecture room of the public library to discuss the current happenings on our globe. Mr. Risser, a teacher of sociology at Pasadena City College, was our fine moderator. He was a gifted speaker, lively and eloquent, and representatives of other countries came and spoke about events in their homelands. At one of our meetings, a Russian lady, beautiful and sharp-witted, was telling us of wonderful Russia, and I asked her questions about several things she mentioned which did not conform with our ideas of conditions in her country. Diplomatically she would reply, "I cannot give you an answer to that; I avoid discussions about politics."

As transportation was so inconvenient between Pasadena and Sierra Madre, to my regret I had to discontinue this club activity. The same difficulty finally prevented my attending the French lectures which were held once a month at Pasadena City College as I always missed my 10 o'clock bus to Sierra Madre and had to wait an hour and forty-five minutes for the next one.

On again, off again. To ease up somewhat on my climbing up and down hills, I moved from the big garden in the higher section of town down to even ground. I was now only about 200' from the bus stop and grocery store, situated in small but comfortable quarters. One refreshing, sweet-scented day, Patricia and her lively little boy came to visit me and we enjoyed a nice picnic in a small Sierra Madre park. At my new dwelling place I often had the pleasure of seeing my old friend, Ed Voorhees, a retired English professor whom I met at a meeting of the Sierra Madre Poetry Club. He never came empty-handed when he visited me, instead always arriving with some of the delicious fruit of his garden as well as some interesting literature—generously providing food for the body and the soul.

I had the pleasure of meeting a very extraordinary person. Her name is Yvonne Olson. She lives with her father, an oilman, in one of the old mansions on Orange Grove Avenue in Pasadena. When 19 months old she was attacked by that monster, polio, and badly crippled. She was over 30 when I was introduced to her by my one pupil, Mrs. Ann Black, who had known Yvonne for many years. When you saw Yvonne, shriveled knees drawn up helplessly, only her hands of normal shape, moving around vigorously in her wheelchair in the living room, or in the kitchen preparing a meal, or disappearing into the automatic elevator to the upper floors, you could not help but admire this small but energetic human being, so full of life and interest in everything worthwhile with a beautiful, expressive face which was always so quick to break out into a buoyant laugh. She graduated from high school, reads good literature, knits and sews, plays Mozart Sonatas, cooks her own meals, and is continuously occupied. She likes to see a movie once in a while or go to a concert. Naturally she has to be carried to the car and placed there comfortably, but she cannot weigh very much as Ann can and does carry her as though she were a baby.

At a French lecture, I became acquainted with another pair who honored me with their friendship: Mr. and Mrs. Horne, who live on a high elevation in Sierra Madre. Mrs. Horne is the daughter of a German Major General; as a child, she was a playmate of the children of the famous Quartermaster General Ludendorff. My friends' garden contained 17 avocados and a number of other fruit trees. By profession, he is a combustion engineer and has several inventions to his credit. Their property is located upon a hill between two roads and terraced from the lower to the higher one which is dominated by their house. The view from there defies description: the whole valley from Hollywood to Ontario lies sprawled at your feet. At night, it is a magic panorama with the illumination of street and car lights. Mrs. Horne's hobbies are painting, which she does very well, and raising flowers, and Mr. Horne has to be exceedingly watchful to keep her from crowding her cherished little plants too near his fruit trees. I am deeply thankful for the many hours I spent in their invigorating and good-natured company. My work and the forbidding, long climb up to their mountain fortress were eventually the reasons I had to decrease my number of visits.

I had started the composition of my ninth symphony, the one which I decided should be the last of the series. As I am not one of those who incessantly try to get their works performed, nor am financially able to pay for the copying of the orchestra parts (which run into several hundred dollars for each composition), most of my works are probably doomed to extinction. Tant de travail pour rien (so much work for nothing)! How many millions of notes I have placed on paper I do not know, but the number must be staggering. "Faustina" still waits for the prince charming to bring her to life. I have never been able to find another Paul Bern who was the only one who sensed its value fully and would have produced it if death had not taken him.

As a composer, I am not of the modern school. To me modern music in its extremes is not music, but ugly noise, nothing more. Concerning my own works, I cannot have a competent judgment about them before they are performed by a good orchestra under capable leadership. The performance of my second symphony under my direction, even with only one short rehearsal, was a successful venture. Last year when I finished my ninth, I copied every orchestra part myself. How I would like to conduct it and learn of its merit! The other six exist only in score form. (My first symphony, which I composed when I was a young man, displeased me and I tore it up.) All this tremendous effort is seemingly useless.

We poor composers!

Halfway in the composition of the ninth symphony I was taken suddenly and violently ill. Some months past, I had paid a visit to the recently erected "City of Hope," a hospital comprising a number of buildings on an extensive piece of ground near the San Gabriel River in Duarte. The head nurse was kind enough to guide me through the main building to give me an insight into this splendidly equipped institution. From the balcony of an upper story, she pointed to a large group of bungalows resembling a village, the inspiration for the name of the hospital. Therefore it made sense when I was attacked by an indescribable pain to take my poor body to the "City of Hope."

Unceasing, atrocious pain in my abdomen made walking to and from the bus torture, and I was greatly relieved when I finally arrived and sank down upon a soft chair in the entrance hall of the hospital. After a few moments of relaxing, I asked in the secretary's office for a doctor. I was informed that none was in this building at present but one was expected soon. Then when I told the lady of my illness she told me I could not be helped in the hospital before I went to Eighth Street in Los Angeles for an examination. To this I replied I would await the arrival of a doctor. After half an hour's wait, one arrived. I went to his office and told him of my condition. He said there was no first aid department in the hospital and I could not be helped there. I would have to go to Los Angeles, be examined there, and if my case warranted it, be returned to the hospital; I listened to his words, dumbfounded. The "City of Hope" quickly morphed into a "City of Despair." The hospital was not located on a main road and I had to walk a mile and a half from the bus. I explained my position of increasing helplessness to him and said I could not get home. He said, "take a taxi."

I answered, "If I had the money for a taxi I would not have come here."

"Well then," he said, "I will order our driver to take you home."

I waited another half hour. No car came. Again I went to the secretary's office to ask about the car. "Oh, the driver is across there," she told me, pointing to a red building about a half mile away. He would be found at the garage there. Slowly and feebly I managed to get to the garage where I found the driver who was the only amiable person I met at this place. Arriving back at Sierra Madre at last, I had the driver let me out at a doctor's office. After a short wait, the doctor made a superficial examination and gave me a prescription to take to a pharmacist. The medicine had no effect; the pain was still persistent.

My daughter, Constance, was quite concerned about my illness when I called her. She phoned to Dr. Brinkley's Institute for Colonic Treatment for me. He phoned back that one of his representatives, a Dr. Vesky, lived in Pasadena. I knew the doctor personally from a visit I had paid him when I asked if he was a relative of the Vesky family in whose pensione I lived such pleasant days during my studies in Paris. He might be, he thought, but he did not know. He was kind enough to invite me to lunch after our exchange of recollections. Now, with great care, he gave me one of the famous colonic treatments. These inundations were repeated at three sittings, causing varicose veins on my legs which stood out half an inch. I quit these treatments as soon as I found that my ailment was the consequence of prostate trouble. Dr. Vesky gave me a bottle of medicine for that disturbance, declaring it was "terrific." Medicines have always been an abhorrence to me. Usually I throw them away and that is what I did this time. Only the newer, well-recommended ones, penicillin, and the "mycins" have found favor with me.

Alas, my suffering remained constant. Knowing that a young man occupying a room in the house where I lived drove every morning at seven o'clock to Los Angeles where he was employed, I asked him if he would take me to the Huntington Memorial Hospital which was on his route and he was kind enough to do so. I went to the first aid station there where a very kind young man, Dr. Lorentzen, relieved me in a short time. I mentioned Ernst and his career and, lo and behold, this doctor knew him! He had studied in Amsterdam and had attended some of Ernst's clinics. I must enter the hospital for treatment he said, and then told me, "We'll take care of you."

I have never met a finer, more congenial group of doctors than these always–helpful and friendly men at the Huntington. During the first years of my marriage to the M.D. in Amsterdam, I often came in contact with Hollands doctors. But never did I see there that solid, cooperative camaraderie I found in this American hospital. When the chief of the hospital staff saw my swollen varicose veins he bandaged both my legs from heel to hip with broad adhesive tape so tightly that, after the painful removal of the bandages, the veins had disappeared under the skin.

When I told him of the "floating island" in my abdomen, he looked at me in obvious disbelief, but started an examination. After a bit he found the culprit which seemed to surprise him. He then labored to situate it where he wanted it and after a long interval, not free of pain for the patient, he declared elatedly, "I placed it right!" meaning under the stomach (where it did not stay very long). One very compassionate doctor, the urologist, Dr. Jacobson, urged me to have my prostate removed for otherwise I would have to use a catheter the rest of my life. I was not yet ready to follow his counsel. But that continuous inconvenient handling of the catheter by myself at home plagued me and one day it left its place, causing me great pain. I had to return hastily to the hospital where Dr. Lorentzen installed it again and checked my discomfort. What a nuisance!

I was willing to agree to an operation but I could not pay for it. I told Dr. Jacobson about my situation but he reassured me, "Do not worry about that. We'll take care of you."

After that generous promise (which I believe came from the profession's ethics which demand free care for a doctor's family), I felt better. After a few days' preparation, including three X-ray sessions, I entered the operating room, my dear daughters sitting in the hall anxiously awaiting the outcome. Dr. Gallup, a friendly and energetic surgeon, was the executor. Dr. Jacobson told me that Dr. Gallup had introduced a new method for removing this "malfaiseur" and he wished to watch the procedure. I admired him for so freely acknowledging an accomplishment of a younger doctor. I was first submitted to an excessive pricking all over the back. I did not lose consciousness during the operation so I was aware of the activities of the doctors and attending nurse, but not in pain. That came afterward.

On Christmas Eve, the nurses' chorus sang Christmas carols in the halls and decorated sickrooms festively. I spent Christmas in the hospital but Constance brought me an immense bouquet of flowers and each of the others offered something. Convalescence was not a short process though. After a few days I could propel myself in a wheelchair, but my strength was only recovered slowly.

1952 introduced itself and, on its second day, Patricia came and took me to her home in Pomona. It is not easy for a mother who has to take care of a lively little boy and do important office work in her home along with her other household duties to also to take care of a recuperating patient. Very soon you feel that, as such, you are one too many. After two days, Constance offered to take me into her home. But on the second day there, her oldest boy, who had a bad cold, was placed in his own room again which I was occupying, so I took flight to the sofa. The next day I asked Constance's husband to take me back to Sierra Madre, though I was still a weak old man. It was not easy to take care of myself at first, but soon I began to rapidly improve.

Chapter 26   Renewal

Believe it or not, the eccentric elderly owners of my apartment were convinced I had a contagious disease! And wanting to move back to Pasadena again so I could finish my ninth symphony in more congenial quarters, after some inquiries I found a cute little four-room house, ideally situated in a very calm residential area, the 1000 block on Sierra Bonita Avenue, near stores and transportation. The owners of this property are sympathetic and accommodating people, and do everything they can to make my life here as agreeable as possible.

For the month of October, a week of foundational meetings was planned for a World Music Olympiad to be held in Pasadena. In July, I had received an invitation to be one of the delegates to this gathering. Being eager to show the other delegates from all parts of the globe—a great number of them were expected—that we Pasadenans were not remiss in musical culture, I took for granted it would be easy to interest our good citizens in arranging a festival reception with an evening of symphonic music played by a fine orchestra. Energetically, I undertook the process of organizing such a concert, hoping to provide our guests with the most excellent musical fare possible as has always been the custom for the host cities of past meetings of this sort.

An appointment with our Mayor was fruitless as he would be absent during the week's sessions; so he instructed me to see Mr. Winder, the Assistant Mayor. We held a long discussion of my proposition and Mr. Winder showed great interest in the matter, promising an answer in a few days. I never received one but, undaunted, continued my efforts. A long interview with John te Groen, President of the 14,000-strong musicians' union in Los Angeles, Local 47, was very helpful. He offered an ensemble of the finest musicians available. I then approached the Pasadena Chamber of Commerce. The president and its manager were, for some reason, powerless to raise the necessary funds. I went to see the president of the Parent-Teacher Association. She was very sympathetic and listened attentively as I stated a plan, which was to have every member of the P.T.A. pay a $1 entrance fee to the reception concert and keep the surplus for the Association. She nodded and said yes, that would be easy to do and we would see. Again I received no answer. The secretary of the School Board, Mr. Munson, was rather evasive when I talked to him. Here I was, running all over Pasadena, begging for a paltry $3,200, even sacrificing $500 of my own fee as conductor, but absolutely powerless to raise this sum needed for a worthy civic cause. I made one last call on one of our prominent citizens, an old acquaintance of mine. When I explained the situation to him he looked thoroughly disgusted and broke out: "Quit it! Quit it! Quit it! It stinks!"

Here was one person who felt as I now did too. How easy it would have been to raise $3,200 for a sports event! I followed the counsel of the "quit it" gentleman and ceased my one-man crusade.

September brought the yearly Pasadena Art Fair, always held on the plaza in the civic center. In years past I had never missed any of these events which clearly demonstrate the progressive artistic abilities of local exhibitors. Visiting this well-planned, diversified art display as often as possible during the days of each year's exhibit, I always made a point of seeing the last evening's worthy celebration in the form of ballets and other musical numbers. What happened there this year gave my coming days an entirely unexpected direction.

I was standing before a meritorious painting while chatting with two ladies who were also admiring the canvas when my interest was aroused by a young lady standing a few feet away viewing the same painting. I had seen her before, but where? Later, inspecting the displays on the south side of the plaza, one exhibit drew my special attention. It was a large stand where several artists were occupied in manufacturing fine Swedish copper handicrafts, work well-known to me having lived in that music and art-loving country for several years. A large crowd was watching the creative work of these artists and, among them, I saw the young lady I had noticed before. Her apparent eagerness to know more about the making of the beautiful copper pieces showed an inquiring, alert mind. My curiosity and interest got the better of me and I decided to approach her. I told her my name and asked her where I could have seen her before.

"Why, you spoke to me one Sunday afternoon at the Art Institute after a chamber music concert. Don't you remember? It was a clarinet quintet. I was the second violinist," she said.

"Ha! That's it. I remember now. Your playing impressed me very much. You seemed to be so . . . 'into it' as you might say."

She was a little embarrassed at that observation of mine. We then spoke a bit about the copper craft and then I hazarded a rather daring request. "Come and have a cup of coffee with me, won't you?" I asked her.

She gave me a wary look and hesitated. Then she smiled. "Well, I do know who you are and a few things about you. I guess it will be alright."

So I took her arm and we walked to the drugstore in the next block. Over coffee and doughnuts we talked, asking one another questions, each telling about ourselves, and discussing music, art, literature, psychology and other topics briefly, all in which we discovered we were mutually interested.

Miss Boylan told me of her great desire to learn to play the violin well and also of her recent college registration for the study of psychology and history. Besides these things, she earned her living doing office work in a wholesale book company eight hours a day. She was from Long Beach and had come to Pasadena to study with a prominent violin teacher here. She certainly was a girl. The stamp of absolute value marked all her vividly expressed ideas and was evident in her way of life—this 21-year-old conscientiously worked full-time testing problems in the business world, and then using her free hours in the evenings for her violin practice, lessons, classes, and studying. I asked her, greatly surprised, how she accomplished all this. "I love it—and I also want to get somewhere," she said simply, determination in her voice.

We left the drugstore still talking nonstop. Then we sat on a bus bench and continued our conversation. I had not enjoyed anything so much for years. She also seemed to take pleasure in talking with someone who understood her aims and had the same interests. After some reflection, I made another bold suggestion. "The subjects you have chosen for your college work are those which I have always liked best in my own studying. In fact, I am a member of the Psychological Society of New York. Why don't you come to my home, say tomorrow evening if you are free? I will be happy to help you with your two subjects and, if you think I could be of some use to you, in your violin study as well."

"Oh, thank you, but I don't think I had better. I don't really know you…"

"No, you don't, that's true. And I understand why you feel as you do. But I know I could help you and would like to, and I also don't want to end our new acquaintance. Won't you consider coming?"

"Well," she said after a pause, "alright, I'll come."

I gave her my address and then she said she must leave.

On the bus going homeward, my thoughts lingered over the pleasant hour I had passed with this earnest, intelligent young woman. I was keenly aware of the fact that in my early twenties I had cherished the same ideal of infallible happiness, the same to-the-stars ambitions as Miss Boylan—for that matter I have never really lost them. How is it possible, I asked myself as I further considered our conversation, that two persons 70 years apart in age could think in common terms and have such similar interests and aspirations? Ah, what is age but a simple passage of time which cannot bear upon those invariable human hopes, ambitions, or desires? I was glad I should see Miss Boylan again.

Having completed the tremendous job of copying my ninth symphony, my next self-prescribed task was to write my biography. I was fully aware of the difficulties involved, the necessity of a systematic accumulation of material strewn along a road 90 years in length. But it made no difference. At 90 or 20, work must be done. Nothing but sickness can hold me back from constant useful activity, whatever it might be, whether physical or mental labor. My most often stated maxim is: "Keep working and studying and you will never grow old." I spent the days after my meeting with Miss Boylan scribbling remarks about past events in my notebook. That evening she arrived at my home as she had promised.

We found this study method very satisfactory, so much so that she came every night that week. We soon realized an unusual symmetry and balance in our companionship and a truly unique unity of thought. After the first evening, I cooked dinner for Arlene (she told me to call her that) each time, which she seemed to enjoy a great deal. It was good to be able to eat with someone; I had not realized how lonely my meals had been. I gave her a couple of violin lessons that week. She had great talent and, with her clear-thinking mind and industrious nature, she was easy to teach.

There was only one unfortunate aspect of these evenings. Instead of working at her studies constantly, we tended to wander into discussions of other sometimes related, sometimes unrelated subjects. There might be no end to the number of things we could talk about, and we asked hundreds of questions and seemed to attempt to tell each other everything about ourselves, and everything we knew that was of interest to the other. It was like we were old bosom friends who had been parted for years and must bring each other up to date on all that has since transpired.

Of all the unexpected turns in the path of a life, none could be more surprising than for a 90-year old man to fall in love, and especially when the object of that sentiment is a 21-year-old girl! But such was the case. Though it was certain that I was lonely all these past years and had seriously considered marrying again, this could not account for my present feelings. All my life, I had looked for someone to really love, someone who would share my every mood so to speak; give me complete understanding. I thought it was a far-fetched ideal. I had given a youthful love to Selma long, long ago, but her parents had prevented us from marrying. Then my two marriages had neither one been for love. Happily, however, the first was very successful, though the second was unfortunate. Now I wanted to marry this girl whom I loved with all my heart, the ideal I had not found until I was 90 years old. But would she have me? I felt that age made no difference—but would she?

By the end of that week, I had built up my inner resources enough to ask her. I knew I would need them now more than ever if she refused me. I do not remember what I said to her except I made certain to tell her I did not want to rush her, that she should take time to think the matter over carefully. At the end of my hastily uttered word-barrage, I saw that Arlene seemed uncomfortable and uncertain. "I... I don't know what to say," she stammered. "You are more like a father to me. I do love and respect you in that way, but to marry you...?"

I guess she noticed my fallen face because she added, "I have enjoyed your fine companionship and I do so appreciate your kindness in helping me with my work. I wish I could repay you by marrying you. I know you are very lonely, but I just don't think I can. It is true we are amazingly alike in many ways and have the same interests, but these things cannot take the place of love." She stopped for a second—to get her breath it seemed. "The difference in our ages is probably the reason I can't love you. It is terribly hard to overcome an emotional viewpoint which has been with you all your life, even if logic tells you it is wrong. I will try, but, though I might be able to forget about age, I still may find I don't love you."

"Yes, I realize that. But I am glad you will think it over. I also hope you will consider the few risks involved in marrying an elderly man. I want you to be sure of your decision."

"Yes, I do too," she agreed.

After this, Arlene departed, obviously troubled. I passed a restless night, and the next morning I could not concentrate on my work. I had the feeling she would come that evening, though I knew it probably would not be that soon. But all my doubt and restlessness were ended at about six o'clock when Arlene arrived and, after a smiling, "Good evening!" said joyfully, "I am going to marry you!"

To commemorate this happy occasion we decided to go the next day, Sunday, to the weekly chamber music concert at the Los Angeles County Museum. It was the first time we were seen together and it came perilously near to being the last. A splendidly gleaming sun ushered in the day, promising fine weather for our happy trip. Impatiently, I kept switching my eyes to the watch lying on my table all morning, counting, counting the minutes advancing so slowly.

I started preparations for the dinner I had promised Arlene for 12 o'clock. As I am a rather serious cook and seem to be able to concoct a decent meal since I like the occupation so well, I now did my best to make it worthy of this special occasion. In the midst of my preparations, Arlene arrived and the dinner was served at noon by yours truly, always a stickler for being on time. I was pleased when she valiantly dispatched what I had contrived and expressed her admiration of my culinary skills.

Cheerfully, we started for Los Angeles, expecting to pass an hour of sublime joy hearing the superior work of musicians of virtuosic caliber providing flawless performances of masterworks of music. Those who were never given the privilege of being introduced to well-performed chamber music cannot comprehend what a supreme pleasure it is to be one of the initiated. It always has been inexplicable to me why these regular Sunday afternoon chamber music concerts at the County Museum are so poorly patronized, especially as they are provided without an admission fee. Will the time ever come when we will reverse our habits and find movies and other cheap entertainment un-patronized and symphonies, chamber music, oratorios, and other first-class works presented to "standing room only" houses?

As we sat listening to the music, I happened to say something to Arlene and was astonished to see a rather absent-minded expression on her face. I noticed she seemed to be preoccupied throughout the concert. On our way home her buoyant spirit seemed to have left her. After a monosyllabic bus ride, during which my own mood dampened in response, we arrived at my little house. Inside, Arlene took hold of my arm and, tears slipping down her cheeks, said tonelessly, "I cannot marry you."

I was struck speechless. Weeping, she tried to explain that, though it was stupid, she had felt as though everyone were staring at us on the streets and at the concert and she just could not stand that scenario all the time. She would always think society was silently pitying or condemning her for having married an old man. I put a comforting hand on her shoulder. "I thought you would be a person strong enough to withstand those attitudes inevitably surrounding such a marriage," I said in a strained voice. "But you are young, and I cannot expect too much. I will not try to persuade you. I have had many disappointments in my lifetime and have built a sound philosophy with which to accept them without becoming embittered. This will hurt more than anything yet, because when, after 90 years, a man finds his first love only to lose her again, it is naturally hard to bear, but I shall bury my thoughts in diligent work as I have done before and it will pass."

"Oh, I am so awfully sorry," she cried. "But I am convinced it is for the best, though I know it's difficult for you to understand my feelings. I know you have lost all respect for me, but I can't help myself. I just cannot think of this whole thing in any other way."

I placed both my hands on her shoulders. "Alright, Arlene," I said. "But I want you to do me a favor. I want you to think everything out carefully once more in the next few days. You are upset now, but you may see things in a different light tomorrow, or the next day. I fervently hope so. All I want to say is that you are welcome to come back any time you change your mind about marrying me."

She turned to the door. "If I happen to reconsider I will come, but please, please do not count on it. I don't think I will. Thank you for…goodbye…" She opened the door and quickly stepped outside. "Goodbye."

"Goodbye," I called sadly as I watched her hurry away down the walk.

After the shock of Arlene's unexpected departure passed, I felt not so deeply grieved as I would have thought. Why? I had a premonition such as I have experienced many times in my life. In most cases they turned out to be correct. I felt so sure she would come back; I waited patiently all day Monday, industriously writing down preliminaries for this autobiography. Monday evening came and, with it, the glowing face of Arlene appeared. "It's me," she cried. She ran to me and threw her arms around my neck, this time weeping for joy.

After a few days, we got around to discussing when we would marry. The series of preliminary meetings for the World Music Olympiad was dated two weeks hence. We decided to marry before it began. Neither of us knew of any good reason for waiting and did not want to. On the following Saturday, the eleventh day of October, a big greyhound bus carried us to Yuma. The Judge of the Superior Court who spoke the binding words was exactly the way we had dared hope he would be—pleasantly matter-of-fact and sympathetic with the unusualness of the situation. So were the two elderly lady witnesses.

 Note from Melinda...

The things your parents never tell you when you're a kid! Shortly after Mia Farrow married Frank Sinatra I happened to mention during a conversation with my mom how weird it would be to have a stepmother younger than you were. She said, "I did." I nearly fell off my chair. All during my childhood I had just assumed that Munna was a widow, not a divorcée. Nobody ever mentioned that Fahta had divorced her. And then, some years later, when I first read this manuscript, I took great exception to his description of his marriage to Munna as "unfortunate." All my life I've heard family stories from Mom, aunts, and uncles, and Munna herself which paint a very different picture. My mom remembers how attentive and considerate Fahta was with Munna, presenting her with the first flowers every spring, and taking her to the movies every Wednesday evening, both of them strolling down the sidewalk hand-in-hand. When I told my mom how much it upset me, she smiled and asked what else could Fahta say when it was his third wife doing the typing as he dictated? Good point. And now after re-reading this, preparing it for my kids to share with their kids, approaching senior citizenship myself and a widow, I am grateful that he found such a love at the end of his life and was not alone when he left this world.

My whole being is so filled with thankfulness for this beautiful marriage! What wonderfully happy days have followed our union (though lessened somewhat by the two weeks Arlene had to remain at her job). I could hardly get through those hours until she came home each evening.

My suffering was partially assuaged when I attended the Olympiad meetings, however only insofar as keeping my mind occupied. There weren't even 20 delegates! The South American Republics were well-represented, there was one delegate from Germany, the lady Secretary and myself were the only two delegates from the United States, and the President of the Olympiad organization was from Austria. He was a sympathetic speaker of choicest German which naturally had to be translated into English, during which it lost much of its exquisite flavor. There were a colorful group of visitors from Japan. I do not know if any of them were delegates as none spoke English, but they did not attend many of the meetings. Altogether the procedure looked so hopeless to me while everyone else seemed to take it in stride. I felt sadly compelled to tell them how unsatisfactory it was to have a World Music Olympiad without the full participation of all nations. The last two meetings were enlivened by the awakening of interest the South American delegates displayed. One of them spoke English fluently and, speaking for the rest, said they all promised to propagate the germ of our endeavors in their respective countries. On this somewhat more encouraging note, the preparatory sessions for the World Music Olympiad to be held in Salzburg in two years ended. They were the poorest meetings I have ever attended in my life.

Arlene concluded her work at the book company (she had saved her money and had enough to live on). You might find it of interest to hear about our daily schedule. In the wintertime, we were up at 7:00, then breakfast; Arlene practicing violin from 8:00 to 10:00, I worked on my biography until 11:30; Arlene did all the typing. I then prepared our dinner, after which we always rest until 2:00; I write the rest of the afternoon while Arlene studies German, history, or psychology and practices drawing or painting. Just before supper at 6:00, we walk a few blocks for our daily exercise and, after supper, we read and listen to the radio's symphonic program and the latest news—we still keep the same schedule, with slight variations. I cannot emphasize enough the importance of having a schedule and sticking to it if you wish to really accomplish something.

The eleventh of each month we go out and eat a special dinner in celebration of our anniversary, a ritual which keeps our vows alive instead of affirming them only once a year and which, we hope, we can continue to follow till the day when the minute and fleeting spark of life pulsates no more for me.

Note from Melinda...

I have never been able to find out anything about the third Mrs. Hammer, but the first time Libby took Fahta's lion-head violin for her lesson, I took with me a brochure about Fahta that Mom had given me so I could show it to the aforementioned Mr. Rachoff. He had never heard of Fahta, but he said he had once bought a violin bow from a woman named Arlene Hammer.

A few little skirmishes have given ample proof of Arlene's sound philosophical attitude, for immediately after they were over, we were again in our old sublime companionship, never looking back at any unpleasant occurrences except silently, in order to learn from them and be on our guard the next time, thus minimizing the number of distasteful episodes in our marriage. I am also happy to see that my wife thinks things over carefully and does not easily jump to conclusions. She is a tireless, efficient soul, examining any problem thoroughly in demanding an intelligent solution. Her help with this sizable undertaking has been invaluable to me. The nearly 91-year-old groom and his loving, clever 22-year-old bride look forward to every blessed working day with new courage, clasping our right hands firmly, and energetically saying together, "Today!" Dear friends and readers, I would counsel you to do likewise and learn its power.

So we are going calmly along among the transitory phases of time. Now this story of my life comes to its end. It is possible there may be more of some interest, but I cannot transcribe it further here. I must search for new outlets for my mental and physical energies. I would love to make use of my conducting abilities—I still feel I have so much to give to the musical world. The gifts the Great Donor has so graciously bestowed on me are going to waste. I also would like to see all my works placed in the Music Library of Congress where some of them are already and some of my writings have found acceptance. And I would like to have some of my compositions recorded and broadcast. Though they are not modern, they are nevertheless emanations of a true apostle of our beloved art. Through them, I have tried to give expression to some of the beauty of today's world, not by imitating the sounds of industry, but by translating the meaning of the industrial age into harmonic poetry. The wise man's philosophy today is as pleasing to the ear as it was 7,000 years ago. Let music proclaim its truths in a language of simplicity and harmony—the language also heard throughout all of nature.

Everyone knows what a sketchy document of incompletion a biography must be—all facets of experience, all aspects of minor importance cannot be adequately relayed. The whole story of a lifetime must be condensed into a book you can call yours after a few leisurely hours of relaxing reading! An autobiography, of course, is even less complete because of the impossibility of its writer being entirely objective about himself. But I will feel that this book has been worthwhile, if, through the reading of it, even one person finds the way to a better philosophy than mine, one which will lead him or her to a successful life.

THE END

Heinrich Hammer
1862 - 1954

Postscript

Two feature articles were uncovered during the creation of this book which post-date the completion of Fahta's original manuscript. The first is from the

Los Angeles Times

and pictures him and Arlene with a caption which reads:

"Celebration: Heinrich Hammer, noted symphonic conductor, and his wife, Arlene, run over a musical score at their Pasadena home. He will be 91 on Tuesday."

The article goes on to recount his musical accomplishments, both in Europe and the U.S. Here's a brief excerpt from the beginning of the article:

"The once world-famous orchestra conductor has marked time more than Time has marked him. His hair and mustache are gray but his blue eyes are as bright as they were 50 years ago and a baton is rock-steady in his muscular grip."

After highlighting aspects of his entire career in its various locations and iterations, the article concludes with:

"At 91, he confidentaly foresees his wife's success and publication of his drama and his autobiography. Money? "From somewhere some day it will come," he says with assurance.
Wouldn't be surprising if he began conducting again too. He's got what it takes —in all the seven languages he speaks."

CELEBRATION—Heinrich Hammer, noted symphonic conductor, and his wife, Arlene, run over a musical score at their Pasadena home. He will be 91 Tuesday.

Lifetime of Triumphs Recalled by Conductor

And this feature article is dated June 20, 1954 from the *Arizona Republic* newspaper, with the headline:

Phoenix Pair Find Love Ageless As Music

"Maestro Heinrich Hammer remembers rubbing shoulders with Edvard Grieg and Victor Herbert. But the 92-year-old symphony conductor obviously is not content to dwell among the gas-lit memories of past triumphs.

Only 1 ½ years ago, he wooed and won his attractive wife in a jet-propelled, California courtship that lasted less than two weeks.

She is 22.

TOGETHER they teach piano, voice, and violin at 1531 E. Indian School.

Echoes of memorable music and the men who made it before the turn of the century resound through their little house and studio."

The lengthy article recounts his long career in music, and concludes with:

"The Hammers came to Phoenix six months ago to teach. Hence, they are happy to see pupils most anytime. But don't bother them during the dinner hour or on the 11th of the month.

Like lots of newlyweds, they celebrate their wedding anniversary every month instead of waiting for the annual observance to roll around. On the 11th you'll always find them out to dinner, together. "

A family photo album...

Their home when writing
this book:

1045 N. Sierra Bonita Avenue
Pasadena, California

Munna & Fahta

His second family

Questions? Comments...? Kindly get in touch! And SEE MORE of the vintage newspaper articles on Maestro Hammer online:

www.StillLifeEnterprises.com

In closing, thank you for permitting me to escort you back in time so as to share my grandfather's journey with you. It's been my privilege and goal to honor his remarkable life—and hopefully I've succeeded.

I love you, Fahta...

Made in the USA
San Bernardino, CA
10 December 2018